Reference

OXFORD SURVEYS IN SEMANTICS AND PRAGMATICS

GENERAL EDITORS: Chris Barker, *New York University*, and Chris Kennedy, *University of Chicago*

ADVISORY EDITORS: Kent Bach, *San Francisco State University*; Jack Hoeksema, *University of Groningen*; Laurence R. Horn, *Yale University*; William Ladusaw, *University of Southern California*; Beth Levin, *Stanford University*; Richard Larson, *Stony Brook University*; Anna Szabolsci, *New York University*; Mark Steedman, *University of Edinburgh*; Gregory Ward, *Northwestern University*

PUBLISHED
1 *Modality*
Paul Portner

2 *Reference*
Barbara Abbott

IN PREPARATION
Intonation and Meaning
Daniel Büring

Questions
Veneeta Dayal

Indefiniteness
Donka Farkas and Henriette de Swart

Aspect
Hana Filip

Lexical Pragmatics
Laurence R. Horn

Subjectivity and Perspective in Truth-Theoretic Semantics
Peter Lasersohn

Mood
Paul Portner

Dimensions of Meaning
Chris Potts

Reference

BARBARA ABBOTT

OXFORD
UNIVERSITY PRESS

Great Clarendon Street, Oxford OX2 6DP

Oxford University Press is a department of the University of Oxford.
It furthers the University's objective of excellence in research, scholarship,
and education by publishing worldwide in

Oxford New York

Auckland Cape Town Dar es Salaam Hong Kong Karachi
Kuala Lumpur Madrid Melbourne Mexico City Nairobi
New Delhi Shanghai Taipei Toronto

With offices in

Argentina Austria Brazil Chile Czech Republic France Greece
Guatemala Hungary Italy Japan Poland Portugal Singapore
South Korea Switzerland Thailand Turkey Ukraine Vietnam

Oxford is a registered trade mark of Oxford University Press
in the UK and in certain other countries

Published in the United States
by Oxford University Press Inc., New York

© Barbara Abbott 2010

The moral rights of the author have been asserted
Database right Oxford University Press (maker)

First published 2010 by Oxford University Press

British Library Cataloguing in Publication Data

Data available

Library of Congress Cataloging in Publication Data

Library of Congress Control Number: 2009941584

Typeset by SPI Publisher Services, Pondicherry, India
Printed in Great Britain
on acid-free paper by the
MPG Books Group, Bodmin and King's Lynn

ISBN 978–0–19–920257–7 (Hbk.)
      978–0–19–920345–1 (Pbk.)

1 3 5 7 9 10 8 6 4 2

Contents

Acknowledgements   xi
General Preface   xiii

1 Introduction   1
   1.1 Two conceptions of reference   2
   1.2 NPs   4
     1.2.1 NPs with determiners   5
     1.2.2 NPs in sentences   7
   1.3 The contents and structure of this book   8
   1.4 Punctuation   10

2 Foundations   12
   2.1 Mill   12
     2.1.1 Denotation and connotation   12
     2.1.2 Mill on proper names   14
     2.1.3 Mill on propositions   15
     2.1.4 Summary   15
   2.2 Frege   15
     2.2.1 Identity statements   16
     2.2.2 Sense and reference   17
     2.2.3 Compositionality and the sense and reference
         of sentences   18
     2.2.4 Frege on propositional attitudes   22
     2.2.5 Frege on proper names   24
     2.2.6 Summary and comments   25
   2.3 Russell   26
     2.3.1 Quantification   26
     2.3.2 Russell's analysis of definite descriptions   28
     2.3.3 Russell on propositional attitudes   30
     2.3.4 Russell on proper names   33
   2.4 Comparisons of Mill, Frege, and Russell   36
     2.4.1 Sense vs reference   36
     2.4.2 Definite descriptions   36

2.4.3 Empty NPs   37

2.4.4 Propositional attitude contexts   38

2.4.5 Proper names   39

2.5 Concluding remarks   39

3 **Subsequent developments**   41

3.1 Semantic scope   41

3.1.1 Quantificational NPs   42

3.1.2 Some other sentence operators   43

3.1.3 Scope ambiguities   44

3.1.4 Modal operators   47

3.1.5 Some complications   49

3.1.6 Summary   51

3.2 Possible worlds, extensions, and intensions   52

3.2.1 Possible worlds   52

3.2.2 Extensions   52

3.2.3 Intensions   53

3.2.4 A note about time   56

3.3 Extensionality and intensionality   57

3.3.1 Extensionality   57

3.3.2 Intensionality   58

3.4 Propositions   60

3.4.1 Propositions as sets of possible worlds   61

3.4.2 Propositions as sets of situations   63

3.4.3 Intensional structure   64

3.4.4 Russellian singular propositions   65

3.4.5 Summary   66

3.5 Existence independence   66

3.6 Summary   68

4 **The proper treatment of quantification**   69

4.1 Grice and conversational implicatures   70

4.2 Introduction to Montague's work   75

4.3 Two problems   76

4.3.1 Rampant intensionality?   76

4.3.2 Quantificational NPs and generalized quantifiers   78

4.4 Overview of the PTQ grammar   83
    4.4.1 The English fragment   84
    4.4.2 IL   85
    4.4.3 The translation rules   86

4.5 Some examples   88

4.6 Individuals vs individual concepts   89

4.7 Proper names   91

4.8 Summary and developments   92
    4.8.1 Barwise and Cooper (1981) on generalized
           quantifiers   93
    4.8.2 Partee (1986) on type-shifting   96

4.9 Concluding remarks   98

5 Proper names   99

5.1 Review: Mill, Frege, and Russell   100

5.2 The cluster view   102

5.3 The return to Mill's view   104
    5.3.1 Descriptions neither necessary nor sufficient   104
    5.3.2 Kripke's modal argument   105
    5.3.3 Natural kind terms   107

5.4 The new theory of reference   107
    5.4.1 What connects names with referents?   108
    5.4.2 What is the semantic contribution of a proper name? 109
    5.4.3 Direct reference, rigid designation, singular
           and object-dependent propositions   110

5.5 Problems!   112

5.6 Solutions? Part 1: metalinguistic approaches   114
    5.6.1 Quotational approaches   115
    5.6.2 Causal description theories   117
    5.6.3 "The bearer of N"   118

5.7 Kripke's puzzle   120
    5.7.1 London/Londres and Paderewski   120
    5.7.2 Metalinguistic responses   122

5.8 Solutions? Part 2: hidden indexical and bite-the-bullet
    approaches   123
    5.8.1 Hidden indexical theories   124
    5.8.2 Bite-the bullet-approaches   125

5.9 Summary and conclusions   127

6 Definite descriptions   130

  6.1 Review   131
    6.1.1 The views of Mill, Frege, and Russell   131
    6.1.2 Comparison of referential and quantificational views   132

  6.2 Strawson's objections to Russell   135
    6.2.1 Expressions vs uses of expressions   135
    6.2.2 Presupposition vs assertion   136
    6.2.3 Incomplete descriptions   137
    6.2.4 Summary   140

  6.3 Donnellan's referential-attributive distinction   140
    6.3.1 Introduction of the referential construal   141
    6.3.2 Semantic analyses   143
    6.3.3 Kripke's pragmatic analysis   147
    6.3.4 Defense of the semantic analyses   150

  6.4 Indefinite descriptions   153

  6.5 Concluding remarks   156

7 Plurals and generics   158

  7.1 Plurals and mass terms   158
    7.1.1 Link's analysis   159
    7.1.2 Plural and mass definite descriptions   161

  7.2 Distributive, collective, and cumulative readings   162

  7.3 Genericity   165
    7.3.1 Statement genericity   165
    7.3.2 Bare NPs—Carlson's analysis   167
    7.3.3 Generic uses of singular descriptions   169
    7.3.4 Bare NPs—an alternative analysis   172

  7.4 The average American   174

  7.5 Concluding remarks   179

8 Indexicality and pronouns   180

  8.1 Character and content   182

  8.2 Essential indexicals?   186
    8.2.1 Belief states   187
    8.2.2 Belief *de se*   188

  8.3 Index vs denotation   189

  8.4 Demonstrative NPs   191

8.5 The interpretation of (third-person) pronouns: reference, coreference, and binding   194
   8.5.1 The "free variable" interpretation   195
   8.5.2 Dynamic semantics   197
   8.5.3 Quantificationally bound pronouns   198
   8.5.4 Non-quantificational binding   200
   8.5.5 Plural pronouns   203

8.6 Pronouns and descriptions   204
   8.6.1 Bound descriptions   205
   8.6.2 Descriptive pronouns   206

8.7 Concluding remarks   208

9 Definiteness, strength, partitives, and referentiality   209

9.1 Existential sentences   210

9.2 Characterizations of "definite NP"   214
   9.2.1 Uniqueness   214
   9.2.2 Familiarity   218
   9.2.3 Non-null intersection   221
   9.2.4 Type *e*   223

9.3 Strong and weak   226

9.4 Partitive NPs   230

9.5 Concluding remarks   237

10 NPs in discourse   238

10.1 Pronouns in discourse   239
   10.1.1 Donkey pronouns   239
   10.1.2 Dynamic semantics and unselective binding   240
   10.1.3 E-type pronouns   242
   10.1.4 Some remaining issues   246

10.2 Choosing NPs in discourse   251
   10.2.1 Prince (1981b, 1992)   251
   10.2.2 Ariel (1988, 1990)   253
   10.2.3 Gundel, Hedberg, and Zacharski (1993, 2001) 254
   10.2.4 What is encoded?   257

10.3 Referents   261
   10.3.1 Discourse referents   261
   10.3.2 Nonexistent entities   264

10.4 Concluding remarks   267

11 Taking stock   268

    11.1 Individual concepts   269

    11.2 Which NPs can be used to refer?   270

    11.3 Which NPs (if any) have a (singular) referent?   274

    11.4 Concluding remarks   280

References   281
Index   299

Acknowledgements

I am immensely grateful to the series editors, Chris Barker and Chris Kennedy, for encouraging me to take part in this series, persisting in their confidence throughout the process, and providing helpful comments on the almost-completed manuscript. John Davey, our Oxford manager, has been an absolute peach to work with. Many conversations, electronic and otherwise, have been very useful in checking facts, providing examples, tracking down references, uncovering historical background, and generally providing vital pieces of information: in particular I would like to thank (in no significant order) Mandy Simons, Eduardo García-Ramírez, Hans Kamp, Jeff Pelletier, Larry Horn, Ora Matushansky, Östen Dahl, Barbara Partee, Paul Elbourne, Grover Hudson, Greg Carlson, Lyn Frazier, Ezra Keshet, Ray Jackendoff, Erin Eaker, Richard Larson, Polly Jacobson, and Bob Matson. The Michigan State University Library has also been essential. I would like to thank the Leelanau County Walkie Talkies, especially Lyn Motlow and Kathy Turner, for their interest and encouragement. Kent Bach, whose work on reference has had a substantial influence on me, read Chapter 11 and gave me many very useful comments on it. I hope that he is not too disappointed with the final outcome. Carol Slater and Rich Hall (members of the long-standing mid-Michigan Philosophy Discussion Group) read several chapters in their early stages and did a lot to help me get going in the right direction. Carol also read the completed manuscript, and I'm very grateful to her for her wonderfully apt and detailed suggestions for improvement, many of which have been incorporated verbatim without acknowledgement into the final text. My brother Porter Abbott gave me useful feedback on several chapters, and instantly identified a couple of obscure literary references. My in-house philosopher Larry Hauser has provided all kinds of help throughout the process—welcome words of encouragement, useful observations, and creative suggestions (some of which unfortunately could not be used—e.g. the suggestion that the book should be titled *The Sex Lives of Noun Phrases*). In addition, he read late-stage versions of all of the chapters and still managed to come up with many much-needed improvements. My biggest debt is owed to Jeanne Dapkus, who read each and every chapter in more than one version and was untiring in providing detailed comments every time. Her perspective as the sort of intelligent non-specialist I like to write for was invaluable, and her keen insight and enthusiasm have gone substantially above and beyond what any author has any business hoping for.

Barbara Abbott

Michigan
July 2009

General Preface

Oxford Surveys in Semantics and Pragmatics aims to convey to the reader the life and spirit of the study of meaning in natural language. Its volumes provide distillations of the central empirical questions driving research in contemporary semantics and pragmatics, and distinguish the most important lines of inquiry into these questions. Each volume offers the reader an overview of the topic at hand, a critical survey of the major approaches to it, and an assessment of what consensus (if any) exists. By putting empirical puzzles and theoretical debates into a comprehensible perspective, each author seeks to provide orientation and direction to the topic, thereby providing the context for a deeper understanding of both the complexity of the phenomena and the crucial features of the semantic and pragmatic theories designed to explain them. The books in the series offer researchers in linguistics and related areas—including syntax, cognitive science, computer science, and philosophy—both a valuable resource for instruction and reference and a state-of-the-art perspective on contemporary semantic and pragmatic theory from the experts shaping the field.

In this book, Barbara Abbott explains the major lines of thought about reference, confronting what is arguably the most basic question of all for semantic and pragmatic theory: what is the link between words and the world? We routinely use language to convey information about the world to each other; however, the exact mechanisms by which words and phrases come to be "about" things in the world remain mysterious. Over the course of the past century, many significant advances in our overall understanding of natural language meaning have followed from advances in our understanding and conception of the reference relation. In this book, Professor Abbott provides us with an accessible, comprehensive, and enjoyable guide to the intellectual and empirical landscape of reference, which we expect to stimulate new lines of inquiry on this central question of meaning, even as it explains and elucidates old ones.

Chris Barker
New York University

Christopher Kennedy
University of Chicago

To Larry—my partner, friend, and kitchen man

1

Introduction

The first Project was to shorten Discourse by cutting Polysyllables into one, and leaving out Verbs and Participles, because in reality all things imaginable are but Nouns.

The other, was a Scheme for entirely abolishing all Words whatsoever; and this was urged as a great Advantage in Point of Health as well as Brevity. For it is plain, that every Word we speak is in some Degree a Diminution of our Lungs by Corrosion, and consequently contributes to the shortning of our Lives. An Expedient was therefore offered, that since Words are only Names for *Things*, it would be more convenient for all Men to carry about them, such *Things* as were necessary to express the particular Business they are to discourse on.

Jonathan Swift, *Gulliver's Travels*

If you use your finger to try to point something out to a cat, it will sniff your finger—it won't get the point, so to speak. But human babies point at things before they walk or talk, and apparently with the intention of getting another to focus on the same item (see, e.g., Hurford (2007)). This little piece of human behavior could be seen as the essence and beginning of reference. In the context of language, reference has something to do with the way linguistic expressions are related to whatever it is that we use them to talk and write about. As such, it lies at the very heart and soul of human language. However, saying more than that requires that we agree on what we are using the word "reference" (and its relatives "refer," "referent," etc.) to refer to! So trying to get a bit clearer on why that is a problem will be our first task in this chapter; hopefully by the time we have reached the end of the book we'll have an even clearer picture of what it is we've been talking about.

The subject matter of this book lies within the intersection of linguistics and philosophy of language so I have tried not to presuppose any technical apparatus from either discipline, hopefully making the book accessible to all. Hence in this introductory chapter we will need to cover some basic background, mainly concerning noun phrases (NPs), since they are an integral part of the book's content. We'll go over what I'll be assuming about their basic structure, what different kinds there are, and a tiny bit about how they fit into sentences. Following that is a summary of the rest of the book, and then a few words about punctuation.

1.1 Two conceptions of reference

As words like "reference" and "refer" are used in ordinary English, they apply to a relation involving people, linguistic expressions and things in the world. For example,[1] someone might say something like:

(1)   When you said "that jerk from the Dean's office," who were you referring to?

It is clear that people use linguistic expressions to identify entities they are talking about. When we speak of reference in this case, it is the three-place relation that holds when speaker x uses expression y to identify entity z. Since we are talking about the **use** of language here, we are talking about reference as a PRAGMATIC phenomenon. Under this pragmatic conception, to speak of an expression itself as referring would be a derivative way of speaking, like describing a knife as cutting well. Just as we do not think that knives can cut on their own, we shouldn't think that words can refer on their own.

The problem is that there is another possible way of viewing reference (or using terms like "reference") which has arisen as a consequence of the modern development of philosophy of language. The developers in question were often logicians: Mill, Frege, the early Wittgenstein,[2] Russell, Carnap. The investigation of logic—a family of unspoken languages developed for the study of mathematics—makes

---

[1] Perhaps this is the time to say that our language of exemplification will be almost exclusively English. However, the issues which we will be addressing are so fundamental that they would almost certainly arise in any natural language.

[2] It is customary in philosophy of language to speak as if there were two philosophers called "Wittgenstein," an early one and a later one. The fact is that when Ludwig Wittgenstein was young he wrote an important work called *Tractatus Logico-Philosophicus* (1922), which looked at language from the perspective of the formal languages of logic. Later on, in middle age, he changed his mind about everything and his other major work, *Philosophical Investigations* (1953), was largely devoted to arguing against his former self.

it convenient and natural to abstract away from language users. As a result there arose a tradition of speaking of linguistic expressions by themselves as referring or having a reference. When we think of reference in this way we are thinking of it as a SEMANTIC phenomenon, relating linguistic expressions directly to things out in the world. And the fact is that these early developers were the first to uncover and explore a number of crucial problems and issues surrounding the way we use words to refer to things. So quite a bit of the first part of this book will be looking at reference from that perspective—as a semantic relation between linguistic expressions and things, abstracting away from speakers and addressees. Starting in Chapter 6, pragmatic issues will begin to enter the picture and become more prominent (as will contributions from linguists). Possibly as a result of the coexistence of these two, quite different, uses of technical terms like "refer" and "reference" (i.e. the pragmatic use and the semantic use), it is difficult to isolate a single, unambiguous question about the nature of reference.[3]

I have been speaking generally about linguistic expressions, but these come in many categories. The pragmatic and semantic conceptions of "reference" differ also in which kinds of linguistic expressions can be involved in instances of referring. On the pragmatic conception it would only be NPs that could be involved (and a subset of NPs at that, as we will see in the next section), since these are the only kinds of linguistic expressions that we use to pick out particular entities which we wish to speak about. However on the semantic conception most kinds of linguistic expressions might be considered to have reference—not only NPs but verbs and verb phrases (VPs), adjectives and adverbs, etc. (When we come to consider Frege's work in Chapter 2, we'll see why.[4]) Nevertheless we will confine ourselves almost completely to NPs in this book, so let us look at this category of expression more closely.

---

[3] As we'll see in Chapter 2, the term "denote" has come into frequent use roughly replacing "refer" in the semantic sense.

[4] In classical Montague Grammar (Montague 1973), as we shall see in Chapter 4, expressions of every category except for determiners and conjunctions are assigned an extension, which is the formal counterpart of a referent; and in some developments of Montague Grammar determiners and conjunctions are assigned an extension too.

1.2 NPs

NPs have to have a noun in them—that's why they've traditionally been called "NPs."[5] Beyond that there are a number of subcategories (these are listed, with examples, below in Table 1.1). In some cases the noun in question exhausts the NP—it's a proper name (e.g. *Hilary Clinton*) or a pronoun (e.g. *it*). These two subcategories have in common that they cannot occur (in English anyway) with determiners or restrictive modifiers. (If one remarks *He's a real Einstein!*, they are using *Einstein* as a common noun.) Proper names will be our main concern in Chapter 5. However, they will pop up before then, and it will be useful to know that some nouns that are not spelled with a capital letter nevertheless behave syntactically and semantically like proper names: words for numbers—like *eight* or *ninety*—are prominent examples. The subcategory consisting of pronouns is also complex; we'll put off detailed consideration of them until Chapter 8. Both proper names and pronouns (in at least some of their uses) would be considered to be SINGULAR TERMS—NPs which can be used to identify particular entities, and thus to participate in reference under the pragmatic conception.

In the remaining kinds of NP, the potentially multi-word types, the obligatory noun is a common noun (the HEAD of the NP) and there may be one or more modifiers—adjectives, prepositional phrases, and/ or relative clauses—in addition to a determiner (frequently abbreviated "Det"). Whether any of these kinds of NPs can function as singular terms is a matter of debate, as we shall see. Determiners turn out to be crucial in subcategorizing the NPs that have determiners, and we'll look at some of these subcategories in a moment. However we should mention that some NPs with a head noun and possibly one or more modifiers, lack any determiner. These are sometimes called BARE NPs, and the head noun in this case must be either a plural count noun (as in, e.g., *noodles with cream sauce*), or a mass (noncount) noun (as in *overcooked spaghetti*). We won't get to bare NPs until the chapter on plurals and generics.[6]

---

[5] Many linguists currently prefer "determiner phrase," or "DP," for NPs, reflecting increased attention to grammatical morphemes. I have decided to stick with the traditional label, in part because many NPs do not have determiners, while they all share important syntactic behaviors.

[6] One final group, which we will ignore almost completely, is a group of NPs with no phonological form. Observe the examples in (i):

To summarize thus far: we have two types of one-word NPs—proper names (including number words), and pronouns. Potentially multi-word NPs either lack a determiner (these are the bare NPs), or have a determiner. In the latter case there are a number of subtypes, which we are about to look at.

1.2.1 NPs with determiners

I'm going to divide NPs with determiners into five subcategories. But before doing that it will be useful to have some idea of the structure of these NPs. (We will be avoiding issues of syntax as much as possible in this book, but we won't be able to avoid them completely.) (2) shows the structure of a typical example—*that jerk from the Dean's office*, from the sentence in (1) above.

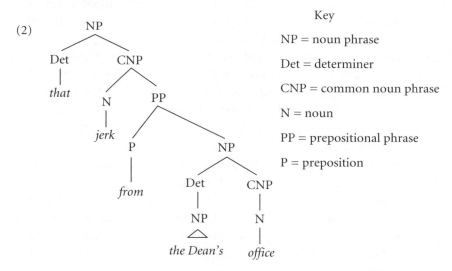

(2)

Key

NP = noun phrase

Det = determiner

CNP = common noun phrase

N = noun

PP = prepositional phrase

P = preposition

Most of the labels in (2) should be fairly self-explanatory, with one possible exception—the label "CNP," which stands for "common noun phrase," meaning 'phrase of the same category as a common noun.' The CNP constituent includes the head noun of the NP plus any of its

(i) a. Mary wants Ø to behave herself
     b. Ø están contentas   (Spanish)
         be pres. + 3pl. happy+fem.pl.
         "They are happy"

Many linguists would postulate null NPs for the places marked with Ø in the sentences in (i).

modifiers—adjectives, PP complements, relative clauses, etc. In other words the CNP is everything in the NP except the determiner.[7]

The five subcategories of NPs with determiners are:

(i) DEFINITE DESCRIPTIONS: those NPs whose determiner is the definite article *the*—e.g. *the king of France, the reason Sue jilted Harry, the book*. We'll look at definite descriptions in detail in Chapter 6.

(ii) POSSESSIVE NPs: NPs whose determiner is in the genitive case—e.g. *my book, the Dean's office, a book's cover*. Possessive NPs, especially those whose determiner NP is definite, are sometimes grouped with definite descriptions.

(iii) INDEFINITE DESCRIPTIONS: NPs whose determiner is the indefinite article *a/an*—e.g. *a way to cure cancer, an apple*. Although I will not be discussing the semantics of indefinite descriptions in much detail, they will provide a useful contrast to definite NPs at several points in this book.[8]

(iv) DEMONSTRATIVE DESCRIPTIONS: NPs whose determiner is *this, that, these,* or *those*—e.g. *these roses, that jerk from the Dean's office*. These are now often called "complex demonstratives," but I will stick with the older term. Demonstrative descriptions will be addressed in Chapter 8, which treats indexicality.

(v) QUANTIFICATIONAL NPs: NPs with a quantificational determiner like *all, most, few, many,* etc.,[9] e.g. *no trees with rough bark, few yellow-bellied sapsuckers, every present that my grandmother gave me*. Traditionally quantificational NPs have been seen as nonreferential; nevertheless this important subcategory will show up in several of the chapters of this book.

---

[7] The label "CNP" is derived from Montague (1973). In a truly pernicious piece of labeling, some linguists who now prefer "DP" for NPs, use "NP" as I am using "CNP," to denote the constituent consisting of the head noun and its modifiers, but minus the determiner.

[8] Another book in this series is devoted to indefinite NPs—*Indefiniteness*, by Donka Farkas and Henriette de Swart.

[9] My list here is based on pre-theoretic intuitions. We'll see in subsequent chapters that there is actually quite a bit of disagreement about which determiners are in fact quantificational. There are arguments for including both *a* and *the* in the quantificational group, and arguments for not including, e.g., *several* and *many*.

TABLE 1.1. Types of NPs, with examples

NP Type	Examples
Proper names	*Abraham Lincoln, Madonna, two*
Pronouns	*you, them, this*
Bare NPs	*yellow smoke, phones with ring tones*
Definite descriptions	*the ants that we ate, the old computer*
Possessive NPs	*Alex's game, most people's birthday*
Indefinite descriptions	*an old computer, a glass of wine*
Demonstrative descriptions	*this little piggy, those boxes*
Quantificational NPs	*most lost souls, several senators from the Midwest*

1.2.2 NPs in sentences

A typical philosopher's example sentence is given in (3).

(3)   Socrates was curious.

In this sentence the singular term *Socrates* identifies the entity under discussion, and the VP *was curious* identifies a property (being curious) which Socrates is being claimed to have had. (We're glossing over issues of tense and time here, as we will pretty much throughout the book, in the interests of simplicity.) Adjectives like *curious* are GENERAL TERMS—so called because they apply to lots of things. Most ordinary words, be they nouns, verbs, or adjectives, are general terms. In order to function grammatically as predicates, adjectives need to be supported by the verb *to be* in English, as in our example (3), and nouns need not only the verb *to be* but the indefinite article, as shown in (4) below. (The asterisk (*) in (4a) marks the example as ungrammatical.)

(4)   a.   *Socrates was philosopher.
       b.   Socrates was a philosopher.

Intransitive verbs can function as predicates on their own, as in (5).

(5)   Socrates talked.

Transitive verbs require an object NP to make a predicate.

(6)   Socrates liked fresh tomatoes.

That's probably enough grammar for now—we'll be introducing more as needed in the course of the book.

Before we leave sentences we need to introduce a very important term in semantics. The term PROPOSITION is frequently used for what a sentence expresses. In a declarative sentence, like those in (3)–(6) above, the proposition expressed is a claim made about the world; in an interrogative sentence, like (1), it is what is being questioned. This is pretty rough, but unfortunately giving a more explicit characterization of what propositions are is difficult, as we will see especially in Chapter 3. We can make one other observation here though: most sentences may be used to express different propositions on different occasions. This is because of INDEXICALITY—the fact that features of the context of utterance may play a role in determining what a sentence says. For a simple example, look at (7).

(7)   I'm going to Chicago tomorrow.

It's clear that (7) can be used to make many different claims depending on who the speaker is and when they utter (7). Indexicality is widespread in language, so it's almost never correct to talk about **the** proposition expressed by a sentence, or to describe a sentence as being true or false. One should instead speak of the proposition expressed by a sentence as uttered on such-and-such an occasion.[10] Nevertheless we will many times ignore indexicality, when it isn't relevant.

1.3 The contents and structure of this book

As noted above, the first part of this book looks at reference from a semantic point of view, focusing for the most part on the relation between NPs and what they stand for in the world, and putting to one side the use of NPs by speakers in conversational contexts. In Chapter 2 we will look at contributions from three major founding figures in philosophy of language, in their chronological order: John Stuart Mill, Gottlob Frege, and Bertrand Russell. This will introduce us to crucial questions which will concern us for the remainder of the book, as well as to some competing answers to those questions. Many of these questions are of the following form: What does an NP of such-and-such kind contribute to the propositions expressed by sentences in which it occurs? These are obviously semantic questions; occasionally

---

[10] Actually it's even inaccurate to speak of **the** proposition expressed in an utterance on such-and-such an occasion, since typically there is more than one. In an utterance of (7), for instance, we could separate the claim about going to Chicago from the claim about when that event is to take place. We'll ignore this too, for the most part.

(most notably in Chapter 5, on proper names) we will look at a related metaphysical question—How is it that an NP of this kind comes to make that kind of contribution?

In Chapter 3 we will be looking at developments subsequent to the work of the three founding figures, trying to get a more systematic picture of the situation in semantics which will hopefully provide a good background for the chapters that follow. In Chapter 4 we look at contributions from two other important figures—Paul Grice and Richard Montague. Grice's work won't be a central focus of this book, but will pop up from time to time in subsequent chapters. The semantics portion of Chapter 3 will have been especially useful preparation for our review of the work of Montague, which comprises the bulk of Chapter 4. Montague devised an explicit grammar (syntax and semantics) for a portion or fragment of English. NPs were of particular interest to Montague, and since he was able to solve some difficult problems involving them, his analysis will be of interest to us— especially the introduction of generalized quantifiers, Montague's use of individual concepts, and the notion of semantic type.

In Chapters 5 and 6 we look specifically at the two categories of NP that have probably received the most attention from philosophers— proper names and definite descriptions. Chapter 6 will also introduce a pragmatic perspective, where we consider the relation between what is semantically encoded in an NP and the ways that NP may be used. Following that, we'll broaden our perspective, and turn increasingly to contributions from linguists. In Chapter 7 we look at NPs with plural and mass head nouns, and NPs which are used generically, to make general statements. In Chapter 8 we turn more explicitly to language in context, to indexicality and pronouns. Chapter 9 investigates various cross-cutting properties of NPs such as definiteness, which have historically been linked with referentiality. Thus far we will have confined ourselves pretty much to sentence-level concerns; in Chapter 10 we open our perspective to issues involving NPs in discourse.

In the final chapter I will draw some conclusions from all this heavy lifting. Let me sketch now what these will be. Probably the most important conclusions will be that philosophical and linguistic research has yielded no clear-cut, obviously correct criterion for identifying either those NPs which encode the possibility for referential use, or those NPs which can be said to have a referent (in such-and-such an utterance). I do not think that renders the concept useless, however. Rather, I believe that it reflects the unfinished state of our knowledge of language and how it functions. On the positive side, I hope I will have convinced the reader that there are some advantages to thinking of reference in terms of individual concepts—explaining what those are requires more background and so will have to wait until Chapter 3. My foremost hope is that this book will provide a clear and accurate explanation of problems, issues, and analyses, as well as some insights into the complexity of noun phrase interpretation. But a word of warning: as the reader perhaps has already noticed, there are many currently unsolved problems in this area. If we can get a clear picture of what they are and why they are difficult to solve, that will be something. Then too, they say that tolerance of doubt and ambiguity is the sign of a mature mind.

It would be a good idea to state here some of the things we won't do (in addition to solving all these difficult, unsolved problems). We will not give quantificational NPs nearly the attention they deserve. Since (as noted above) quantificational NPs are typically viewed as not referential, I have limited their treatment to what seems necessary to contrast them with referential NPs.[11] The section on generic NPs is way too brief, and probably many others are too, and beyond that there is much more to say about **any** of the issues that we attack. Reference is a huge area, with a literature that just doesn't quit. Even in those areas that are dealt with here in some depth, many important authors and their ideas will not even be mentioned. There's just too much. I hope that the references provided along the way will give the reader sufficient indication of where to begin looking. And finally, I will not have anything at all to say about figurative uses of language—metaphor, metonymy, synecdoche, and so forth.

1.4 Punctuation

Here are my conventions: when citing OBJECT LANGUAGE expressions, that is, examples that we are investigating like *that jerk from the Dean's office*, I use italics, unless the example is displayed with a number. I also use italics for terms borrowed from Latin, like *de dicto* and *de re*. Double quotation marks are used for technical terms like "reference"—expressions of the METALANGUAGE (here, English, when

---

[11] Interested readers who want to know more about quantification are directed to the very thorough treatment in Peters and Westerståhl (2006).

it is used as a language for doing linguistics or philosophy in). However when technical terms are being defined (hopefully close to their first use) I'll use small capitals, as I just have with "object language" and "metalanguage." I'll also use double quotes for quoting what people say. There is no widespread convention for citing the meaning of an expression (as opposed to the expression itself, as in the preceding examples). Kaplan (1969: 120) suggested little raised *m*'s as "meaning marks," but that hasn't caught on. On those occasions when it's useful to cite meanings I'll use single quotes: e.g. *bald* in German means 'soon'. Single quotes will also be used for quotes within quotes. And boldface is for **emphasis!**, plus it has an additional use in Chapter 4, since Montague used boldface (instead of italics) for object-language expressions. We've already noted that an asterisk is used to mark an ungrammatical example—something that is ill-formed syntactically. A related convention is the use of the crosshatch (#) to mark anomaly or infelicity—a semantic and/or pragmatic problem. Maybe (8) is a good example.

(8)   #Colorless green ideas sleep furiously.

As you might guess, there are times when it's not clear whether an asterisk or a crosshatch is appropriate.

2

Foundations

> In the proposition "Mont Blanc is over 1,000 metres high," it is, according to [Frege], the *meaning* of "Mont Blanc," not the actual mountain, that is a constituent of the *meaning* of the proposition.
>
> Bertrand Russell, "On denoting"

In this chapter we review some of the most important contributions made by three figures of central importance in philosophy of language, focusing in particular on issues relevant to our quest for clarity on the nature of reference. As mentioned in Chapter 1, these were logician types, who tended to look at language abstracting away from use. Moving chronologically, we will start with John Stuart Mill and what he said in some early portions of his 1843 work *A System of Logic*. We turn then to what are probably the two most important papers in philosophy of language: Gottlob Frege's classic 1892 paper "On sense and reference" and Bertrand Russell's "On denoting", from 1905. In §2.4 we will compare and contrast the views of these three figures; §2.5 contains some concluding remarks.

2.1 Mill

Three main contributions by Mill will be of interest to us as we proceed: his distinction between denotation and connotation, what he had to say about proper names, and his view of propositions.

2.1.1 Denotation and connotation

What an expression DENOTES, according to Mill, is what it applies to in the world—the denotation of a word like *sausage* is all the sausages there are or ever have been, everything that may properly be called "a sausage." Denotation is, thus, very like reference, viewed semantically.

(Indeed, as (foot)noted in Chapter 1, people today often use "denote" and "denotation" when speaking of words-world relations, instead of "refer" and "reference," since the latter are more problematic.) Importantly, though, Mill asserted that many terms also CONNOTE—they imply the possession of certain attributes or properties on the part of the entities they denote, and **the entities in question are denoted in virtue of their possession of these properties**. Thus we have the introduction of a mechanism for achieving reference—namely connotation.

Mill introduced the distinction between denotation and connotation in discussing the meanings of general terms—ordinary nouns, verbs, and adjectives. Here is a quote from Chapter 2 of *A System of Logic*, in which Mill clarifies not only the difference between denotation and connotation, but also the relation between them.

The word *man*, for example, denotes Peter, Jane, John, and an indefinite number of other individuals, of whom, taken as a class, it is the name. But it is applied to them, because they possess, and to signify that they possess, certain attributes. These seem to be, corporeity, animal life, rationality, and a certain external form, which for distinction we call the human. Every existing thing, which possessed all these attributes, would be called a man; and anything which possessed none of them, or only one, or two, or even three of them without the fourth, would not be so called.   (Mill 1843: 38)

One might quibble with this example on a variety of grounds (and Mill himself discussed several complexities in the attributes suggested), but I hope the idea is clear—a term connotes a set of necessary and sufficient conditions which together determine what it denotes.

It is important to be clear that the word "connotation" is used somewhat differently today, in a way which should not be confused with Mill's use. Today it means attributes or attitudes which are stereotypically associated with the referents of words, but which are neither necessary nor sufficient for membership in the denotation; today we may speak of a word having good or bad connotations. A good example to bring out the difference between our current sense of "connotation" and "connotation" in Mill's sense is the pair *bachelor* and *spinster*. These are very similar in connotation using Mill's sense of "connote," differing only in the feature of gender. Thus all and only bachelors and spinsters have the properties of being adult unmarried humans; the two groups differ only in whether they are male (bachelors) or female (spinsters). However, owing to social and political factors that we need not go into here, the two words have very different connotations in the more modern sense of "connotation," and in fact *spinster* has such bad ones that it has virtually been drummed out of the language.

As noted, Mill's example of *man* above is a common noun—a general term. However Mill also considered definite descriptions to be connotative. Thus, to use one of his examples, *the father of Socrates* denotes Sophroniscus in virtue of the fact that Socrates was Sophroniscus's son (Mill 1843: 45). Thus *the father of Socrates* has both denotation (Sophroniscus) and connotation (the property of having been the father of Socrates). In this respect definite descriptions differ from proper names, according to Mill.

2.1.2 Mill on proper names

Mill thought that proper names were different from ordinary words and phrases, and in particular from definite descriptions, in lacking a connotation.

> Proper names are not connotative: they denote the individuals who are called by them; but they do not indicate or imply any attributes as belonging to those individuals. When we name a child by the name Mary, or a dog by the name Caesar, these names are simply marks used to enable those individuals to be made subjects of discourse.   (Mill 1843: 40)

Mill acknowledged that there may have been some motivation in choosing a name for somebody or something in the first place, but held that once the name was given it denoted its denotation independently of that motivation. So Mary need not be a saintly lass to be called *Mary*, nor Caesar a warlike puppy. One well-known example Mill used to argue for this view is the name *Dartmouth*—the city in England, which was originally named that because it lay at the mouth of the Dart river.

> If sand should choke up the mouth of the river, or an earthquake change its course, and remove it to a distance from the town, there is no reason to think that the name of the town would be changed. That fact, therefore, can form no part of the signification of the word; for otherwise, when the fact confessedly ceased to be true, the name would cease to be applied. Proper names are attached to the objects themselves, and are not dependent on the continuance of any attribute of the object.   (Mill 1843: 40)

One could add that Dartmouth College, in New Hampshire, does not lie at the mouth of any river named Dart, or any river at all for that matter, though the Connecticut river does run near it.

This view of proper names is sometimes termed a "*Fido*-Fido" view, the idea being that you have the name (*Fido*) and you have the dog itself (Fido), and that's all there is.

2.1.3 Mill on propositions

Like many others, Mill thought that propositions play three important roles: they are what sentences express, they are the objects of belief, and they are what can be true or false.

> The answer to every question which it is possible to frame, must be contained in a Proposition, or Assertion. Whatever can be an object of belief, or even of disbelief, must, when put into words, assume the form of a proposition. All truth and all error lie in propositions.   (Mill 1843: 21)

This passage suggests that a proposition is a linguistic or quasi-linguistic item, something with a form, and often Mill does speak of propositions in those terms (cf. Mill 1843: ch. 4). However, we cannot associate propositions too closely with a **particular** natural language if we want to say (as most people do) that sentences in different languages may be used to express the same proposition, or that speakers of different languages share beliefs. In any case the main thing to note here is the identification of the content of what we say with the content of what we believe or doubt. Given that what people assert can be true or false, and that what people believe can be true or false, if what they assert and what they believe are propositions then we unify the bearers of truth and falsity.

2.1.4 Summary

To summarize: Mill distinguished denotation from connotation—attributes implied by an expression, and which determine its denotation. However, proper names he held to lack connotation—they are just like marks or labels of the things which they denote, and do not imply the possession of any characteristics by those things. Finally propositions are the objects of belief, as well as what is expressed by sentences.

2.2 Frege

We turn now to Frege, and as promised, we will focus in particular on "Über Sinn und Bedeutung" (Frege 1892b), or "On sense and reference" (as it is commonly translated). We will review five main points from this paper: what Frege had to say about the problem of identity statements, his distinction between sense and reference, his ideas about the sense and reference of whole sentences which rest on the important principle of compositionality, his comments on sentences about propositional attitudes, and finally his famous footnote on proper names.

2.2.1 Identity statements

Frege begins this paper expressing a concern about identity statements—statements like (1a), whose logical form is given in (1b).

(1)   a.   My next door neighbor is our district representative.
      b.   a = b

The problem is, what are such statements about? If they are about the referents of the NPs represented by *a* and *b* in (1b), then such statements should be trivial, if true. After all, as Bishop Butler said, every thing is what it is and not another thing (1729: xxix). Why, if identity statements are simply about their referents, are statements like (1a) not as obvious as statements like (2a), which has the form in (2b)?

(2)   a.   My next door neighbor is my next door neighbor.
      b.   a = a

Statements of the form in (2) are ANALYTIC—true in virtue of just the meanings of the expressions used.[1] What they express is also knowable A PRIORI—that is, just on the basis of reflection and in advance of any experience in the world. But statements of the form in (1) do not seem analytic, and they are definitely not knowable *a priori.*

Another possibility is that the essence of such statements is linguistic, that identity is a relation between linguistic expressions. That would explain the difference between (1) and (2), since different linguistic expressions are involved. But, to use one of Frege's examples, a sentence like (3)[2]

(3)   The morning star is the evening star.

represents a significant astronomical discovery, not some piddling accomplishment of grammarians or lexicographers.

---

[1] Quine (1953b) contains an attack on the concept of analyticity, stemming from his semantic holism. See Fodor and Lepore (1992) for discussion.

[2] Here and below, following Frege, I use *the morning star* to mean 'the brightest nonlunar heavenly body seen just before dawn,' and *the evening star* to mean 'the brightest nonlunar heavenly body seen in the early evening.'

Frege's solution to the problem presented by identity statements[3] is to be found in his theory of sense and reference.

2.2.2 Sense and reference

Frege's distinction between sense and reference is quite similar to Mill's distinction between connotation and denotation. (I do not know why Frege did not refer to Mill on this, since elsewhere (e.g. Frege 1884) he cited Mill.) In his most famous characterization Frege described the sense of a phrase as giving a MODE OF PRESENTATION of its referent.

> It is natural, now, to think of there being connected with a sign..., besides that to which the sign refers, which may be called the reference of the sign, also what I should like to call the *sense* of the sign, wherein the mode of presentation is contained.   (Frege 1892b: 57; italics in original)

Frege included a nice example to clarify what he had in mind. Picture a triangle with three lines drawn, one from each corner to the mid-point of the opposite side. Label these lines *a*, *b*, and *c*. Figure 2.1 contains a drawing to help you out with this.

Then think about the definite descriptions *the point of intersection of a and b* and *the point of intersection of b and c*. These two definite descriptions have the same reference—each refers to, or denotes, the point in the middle of the triangle where the three lines *a*, *b*, and *c* meet. But the two NPs signify or direct your attention to that point in different ways—they differ in their mode of presentation of that referent.

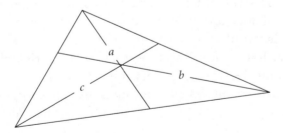

FIGURE 2.1. Modes of presentation

---

[3] As pointed out by Salmon (1986: 12) this problem is not confined to identity statements, but arises in many sentence types, e.g.

(i)   If the morning star is a planet, then the evening star is too.

Beyond this, Frege did not say a lot in positive terms about what senses are. He was careful to distinguish them from any kind of idiosyncratic ideas, attitudes, or impressions that a person might associate with a word or phrase or its referent. This is similar to the distinction we made above between Mill's concept of "connoting" (corresponding to Frege's sense) and "connotation" as we use that word today (which corresponds to the incidental associations we have with words). Instead, senses belong to the language and are shared by all its speakers.[4]

We can now see how Frege used the concept of sense to solve his problem with identity statements. If sentences of the form $a = b$ are true then the expressions represented by a and b must have the same reference. However if they are not synonymous expressions then they will differ in sense—they will present their shared referent in different ways. Thus sentences of the form $a = b$ can be expected to have a different cognitive impact from sentences of the form $a = a$. This constitutes an important argument in favor of recognizing senses.

2.2.3 Compositionality and the sense and reference of sentences

Frege introduced the sense-reference distinction with singular terms, most clearly with definite descriptions; however, he was also concerned with the sense and reference of whole sentences, and what he said about this raises issues that will be important to us in what follows.

In the background of Frege's discussion was his assumption of a principle which is of crucial importance in the study of meaning—the principle of COMPOSITIONALITY. According to this principle, the meanings of sentences (or other syntactically complex expressions) are a function of—that is, are determined by—the meanings of their parts (ultimately the words that go to make them up), plus the syntactic structure that holds those parts together. Such a principle may seem bland and uninteresting; to see its importance it helps to note the existence of expressions whose meanings are not compositional, not predictable from their parts. These are idioms, like *hole in the wall*,

[4] "The sense of a proper name is grasped by everybody who is sufficiently familiar with the language" (Frege 1892b: 57). It may be noted that for Frege, unlike us, "proper name" serves as a term for definite NPs generally: "I call anything a proper name if it is a sign for an object" (Frege 1892a: 47n.). For the most part in "On sense and reference" when Frege uses the term "proper name," he is focusing on definite descriptions. What he says about actual proper names is something we will get to shortly.

meaning a small shop, or *trip the light fantastic*, meaning to dance. Idioms have to be learned as wholes, like words. Since it is apparently the case that the meanings of ordinary nonidiomatic sentences do not have to be learned one by one in this way but are rather comprehensible on first use, we must assume that sentence meanings are compositional—predictable from their parts plus their syntactic structure. There is no feature more crucial to the functioning of human language.

Since Frege was arguing for two levels of meaning—sense and reference—for him compositionality is a two-level principle. The sense of a sentence is determined by the senses of its parts (plus syntax), and the reference is determined by the referents of the parts (plus syntax).

So, what is the reference of a sentence? Frege first considered whether the proposition—Frege used the term "Gedanke," or thought—associated with a sentence should be considered to be the referent of that sentence. He concluded that it should not, for a reason which relies on his assumption of the compositionality of reference. If the proposition expressed by a sentence were the referent of the sentence, then it would be determined by the referents of the parts of the sentence, so exchanging one part for something with the same reference should not change the proposition expressed. However, in actual fact, we can exchange a part of a sentence for another one with the same reference, and **change** the proposition expressed.

> . . . the thought in the sentence 'The morning star is a body illuminated by the Sun' differs from that in the sentence 'The evening star is a body illuminated by the Sun.' Anybody who did not know that the evening star is the morning star might hold the one thought to be true, the other false. The thought, accordingly, cannot be the reference of the sentence, but must rather be considered as the sense.   (Frege 1892b: 62)

Since exchanging coreferential constituents can change the proposition expressed by a sentence, propositions cannot be what sentences refer to. Frege concluded that the proposition expressed by a sentence is instead its sense. Notice, incidentally, Frege's implicit assumption in this passage that propositions, in addition to being what sentences express, are what people believe (hold to be true). In this respect Frege's view of propositions is similar to Mill's.

So what is the reference of a sentence—i.e. what is it that remains constant when a part of a sentence is exchanged for a coreferential expression? The truth value. To use Frege's same example: if it is true that the morning star is actually a planet, and the morning star is the same as the evening star, then it must also be true that the evening star is a planet. The principle Frege is using here has been codified as the LAW OF SUBSTITUTIVITY, which says that coreferential expressions may be substituted for each other in any statement without changing the truth value.[5] As Shakespeare put it (in *Romeo and Juliet*): "That which we call a rose by any other name would smell as sweet." If we regard the truth value of a sentence as its referent, then this principle is just an instance of compositionality at the level of reference.

The idea that sentences refer at all might seem strange, and even if we accept that, to conclude that the referent is a truth value (of which there are only two—true and false) might seem even more of a struggle. However, Frege argued, that just means that getting the import from a sentence involves more than its reference; the sense is essential too. And Frege had another argument to show that the reference of a sentence is its truth value. This argument involved NPs that do not refer to anything—so-called EMPTY NPs like *the city of gold* or *the fountain of youth*. Such NPs often show up in literature where, Frege pointed out, we are more concerned with sense than with truth value. And as long as we are interested only in the artistic qualities of the text we don't care whether the NPs in it refer or not. However, "[t]he question of truth would cause us to abandon aesthetic delight for an attitude of scientific investigation" (Frege 1892b: 63), and in that case we would have to determine whether the NP in question really had a referent or not. And if indeed it were an empty NP, then sentences in which it occurs would lack a truth value.

We have been speaking in general terms, but there are exceptional cases which need to be taken account of. For example, not every sentence with an empty NP would be considered by Frege (or by us) to lack a truth value. Consider (4).

(4)   *The fountain of youth* is an example of a definite description.

---

[5] In the course of his argument that the reference of a sentence is its truth value, Frege quoted Leibniz: "*Eadem sunt, quae sibi mutuo substitui possunt, salva veritate*" (Frege 1892b: 64, italics in original). This means, roughly, 'those which can be substituted for each other, preserving truth, are the same,' which (ignoring the obvious use-mention problems) is the principle of identity of indiscernibles. However, this is **not** the principle Frege was actually using, but is instead its converse! The principle Frege was actually using, the law of substitutivity, has also been called "indiscernibility of identicals" by Quine (1953a: 139). Despite the foregoing, the law of substitutivity is also sometimes referred to as "Leibniz' Law."

(4) is a true sentence, certainly not one that lacks a truth value. The reason is that when expressions are being quoted or discussed—mentioned instead of used, as philosophers put it—they do not have their customary reference. Instead, they stand for or refer to themselves. And we cannot necessarily substitute terms which are ordinarily coreferential when they occur in quotation contexts either. Take the example in (5)

(5) Bob Dylan gave himself the name *Bob Dylan*, presumably because it sounded more poetic than his original name.

The first occurrence of the name *Bob Dylan* in (5) is used in the normal way, to refer to the person it refers to. However in the second occurrence the name itself is being talked about—it is being mentioned rather than used. We can exchange the first occurrence with a coreferential term *salva veritate*, but not the second. (6a) is true, like (5), but (6b) is not.

(6) a. Robert Zimmerman gave himself the name *Bob Dylan*, presumably because it sounded more poetic than his original name.

   b. Bob Dylan gave himself the name *Robert Zimmerman*, presumably because it sounded more poetic than his original name.

Actually I made a little slip when I said we could not replace the second occurrence of *Bob Dylan* in (5) with a coreferential term. Once we remind ourselves that expressions which are being quoted refer to themselves, then we realize that in this context we can only substitute an expression which will refer to the same **name**, in this case perhaps something like: *the name spelled B-o-b D-y-l-a-n*. Although *Bob Dylan* and *Robert Zimmerman* are coreferential, "*Bob Dylan*" is not coreferential with "*Robert Zimmerman*." There is no problem with substitutivity as long as we are careful to note that expressions may refer to different things in different contexts.

   To summarize Frege's ideas up to now: we have a distinction between the reference of an expression and its sense—the way in which the reference is presented. Sentences also have sense and reference: the sense of a sentence is the thought or proposition it expresses, and its reference is its truth value. However, in some contexts expressions undergo a shift in reference; for example, in quotational contexts expressions denote themselves rather than their customary reference.

2.2.4 *Frege on propositional attitudes*

There is another class of potentially troublesome examples, and those are sentences about PROPOSITIONAL ATTITUDES. Propositional attitudes are mental attitudes like belief, hope, fear, desire, and so forth, when these attitudes are directed towards possible or actual situations or states of affairs. The term "propositional attitudes" reflects the common traditional assumption that we have already seen with Mill and Frege—that attitudes like belief are directed towards propositions; whether that is ultimately correct will depend at least in part on what propositions turn out to be. We will return to this issue below and in the next chapter.

When describing a propositional attitude, a propositional attitude verb like *believe, want,* or *deny* will occur with a sentential complement, as in the examples in (7) below; the complements are underlined.

(7) a. Sue believes that <u>French people are all healthy</u>.

b. Fred hopes that <u>his grandmother will not forget his birthday</u>.

c. Lee wants <u>to have a big party</u>.[6]

d. Mary knows that <u>the morning star is the planet Venus</u>.

e. Mary is unaware that <u>the evening star is the planet Venus</u>.

Thus propositional attitude verbs denote relations between the sentient beings (people and higher-level animals) denoted by their subjects, and the propositions expressed by their sentential complements. Frege referred to the complements of propositional attitude verbs as "reported speech" or "indirect discourse," although in most cases (like those in (7)) there may be no actual speech involved.

Note that the law of substitutivity appears to fail in the complements of propositional attitude verbs, as it appeared to fail in the context of quotation. We can well imagine a Mary for whom both (7d) and (7e) seem true. As Frege pointed out in the quotation cited above, someone who does not know that the morning star is the evening star might hold one but not the other to be a planet. But that means that substituting *the evening star* for *the morning star* in example (7d) would turn that truth into the falsehood in (8):

---

[6] It is actually not clear that the complement of *want* here **is** sentential. Within Chomskyan linguistics it would be analyzed as a sentence with a null subject (PRO). However Montague (1973) analyzed such complements as VPs rather than full sentences.

(8)   Mary knows that the evening star is the planet Venus.

This phenomenon is sometimes known as REFERENTIAL OPACITY, the idea being that NPs in these contexts (like *the morning star* and *the evening star* in the examples above) are not able to shine clearly through to their referents. Thus the contexts created in the complements of propositional attitude verbs are sometimes called OPAQUE CONTEXTS.[7]

Frege argued that apparent failures of substitutivity such as the one we have just seen should not be regarded as casting doubt on his analysis. Rather, they indicate a situation similar to what we saw with quotational contexts. In the complements of propositional attitude verbs, expressions also show a shift in reference, but in this case they refer not to themselves, but to their customary sense. In this way the law of substitutivity is not challenged by examples like (7d) and (7e). If Frege is right about the shift of reference in propositional attitude contexts we should not have expected to be able to substitute *the evening star* for *the morning star* in sentence (7d), since in that context, following *Mary knows that*, these NPs are no longer coreferential. Since they have different senses, they refer to different things in propositional attitude contexts.

It is not only NPs in the complements of propositional attitude verbs which undergo a shift of reference, according to Frege. Indeed, the entire sentential complement undergoes the same kind of shift. It is clear that we could not substitute clauses following a propositional attitude verb based only on their truth value, and expect to preserve the truth value of the whole. Here is a (slightly modified) pair of examples which Frege gave to demonstrate this point (Frege 1892b: 66):

(9)   a.   Copernicus believed that the earth revolves around the sun.
       b.   Copernicus believed that the planetary orbits are ellipses.

In (9) one true sentence (*the earth revolves around the sun*) is replaced with another true sentence (*the planetary orbits are ellipses*). However (9a) is true but (9b) is false—Copernicus thought that the planets moved in circles rather than ellipses. Frege concluded: "In this case, then, the subordinate clause has for its reference a thought, not a truth

---

[7]   The term "referential opacity" was coined by Quine (1953a: 142). As we will see in the next chapter, the phenomenon of the apparent failure of the law of substitutivity is somewhat more widespread than just the context of propositional attitude verbs.

value.... This happens after 'say,' 'hear,' 'be of the opinion,' 'be convinced,' 'conclude,' and similar words" (Frege 1892b: 66). Another way of looking at this is to say that the relations expressed by propositional attitude verbs are relations between people (or other sentient beings) and propositions, not truth values.

2.2.5 Frege on proper names

We saw that Mill claimed that proper names have no connotation but only denotation. But if Frege were to hold that view he would be in a difficult position. For one thing, compositionality of sense requires that the constituents of a meaningful sentence have a sense to contribute to the whole. If proper names did not have a sense, Frege's views would predict that sentences containing proper names should be defective or unable to express a complete proposition. But this does not seem to be the case.

In "On sense and reference" Frege addressed the issue of the sense of proper names in a famous footnote, quoted here in its entirety.

In the case of an actual proper name such as 'Aristotle' opinions as to the sense may differ. It might, for instance, be taken to be the following: the pupil of Plato and teacher of Alexander the Great. Anybody who does this will attach another sense to the sentence 'Aristotle was born in Stagira' than will a man who takes as the sense of the name: the teacher of Alexander the Great who was born in Stagira. So long as the reference remains the same, such variations of sense may be tolerated, although they are to be avoided in the theoretical structure of a demonstrative science and ought not to occur in a perfect language.   (Frege 1892b: 58n.)

Taking this footnote at face value, it seems to say that proper names do have a sense, and a sense which is furthermore similar to the sense which a definite description has. This is a DESCRIPTIONAL view of proper names—a view that proper names express properties that determine their reference. In contrast, we can say that Mill's view of proper names is a NONDESCRIPTIONAL one since, as we saw, he believed that proper names do not have a sense/connotation, but only denotation.[8]

Frege's discussion of his example hints at a troublesome consequence of this doctrine: it seems to predict that there are people for whom the sentence *Aristotle was born in Stagira* is analytic, and knowable *a priori*. Those would be people for whom the sense of the name

---

[8] The useful terms "descriptional" and "nondescriptional" in this sense were introduced by Salmon (1981).

Aristotle includes the information that Aristotle was born in Stagira. For those people (10a) and (10b) should be synonymous.

(10) a.   Aristotle was born in Stagira.
      b.   The teacher of Alexander the Great who was born in Stagira was born in Stagira.

However, while (10b) does seem to be analytic and knowable *a priori*, (10a) does not. Hence we may have our doubts about Frege's view of proper names. We will return to this issue at length in Chapter 5.

2.2.6 Summary and comments

As we have seen, Frege, like Mill, recognized two levels of significance for linguistic expressions—sense/connotation and reference/denotation. However, in Frege's view sentences as well as NPs have both reference and sense. The reference of a sentence is its truth value, and the sense of a sentence is the proposition (or thought) it expresses. Also Frege postulated a shift in reference for propositional attitude contexts, where expressions refer to their customary sense instead of their customary reference. And Frege and Mill explicitly disagreed on proper names—Mill holding that they have no connotation while Frege held that they have a sense similar to the sense of a definite description (although with the possibility of variation among speakers).

Note that Frege's assumption of compositionality on both levels (sense and reference) means that **all** of the constituents of a sentence should be expected to have reference as well as sense, at least if that sentence is expected to have a truth value (be either true or false). This puts Frege's notion of reference at odds with the pragmatic notion of reference, where it is only definite NPs (and only in some of their uses, as we shall see) that can be said to be used by speakers to refer to things. As a consequence philosophers often focus in particular on SINGULAR REFERENCE—a semantic relation corresponding more closely to the pragmatic one in that it only involves NPs that apply to a unique individual. We will return to this issue at the end of the book, but for now it should be noted that people will often use the terms "denote" and "denotation" for the relation between expressions and what they apply to when it is not clear whether any conception of reference is appropriate. This kind of looser usage for "denote" and "denotation" has undoubtedly been encouraged by the paper of Russell's that we are about to examine.

2.3 Russell

Russell's "On denoting" (Russell 1905) was, in part, a reply to Frege's "On sense and reference." However to understand Russell's paper it helps to know also that his underlying concern was to account for our acquisition of knowledge. Russell was a philosophical empiricist, and as such believed that all, or almost all, knowledge comes to us through direct perception. This is what Russell called "knowledge by acquaintance": "I say that I am *acquainted* with an object when I have a direct cognitive relation to that object, i.e. when I am directly aware of the object itself" (Russell 1917: 165). How, then, are we able to know about things that are removed from us and with which we have never been in perceptual contact? How can we know, to use one of Russell's examples, that the center of mass of the solar system is a point? How can we know anything about the center of mass of the solar system given that we have no perceptual contact with that entity? This latter kind of knowledge Russell called "knowledge by description," and in "On denoting" he showed how it could be reduced to knowledge by acquaintance. The trick was to analyze denoting phrases, NPs, away. We will look first at the analysis of (overtly) quantificational NPs and then we will turn to Russell's analysis of definite descriptions. Following that we will see what Russell had to say about propositional attitude contexts and what he thought about proper names.

2.3.1 Quantification

The model for Russell's analysis was predicate logic, which had only recently been developed (by Frege among others) in the latter half of the nineteenth century. In traditional predicate logic, overtly quantificational NPs like *every opportunity, no envelope* do not have an analysis *per se*, but only in the context of a complete sentence. Consider the example in (10a), whose ordinary translation into predicate logic is given in (11b).

(11) a. Every good boy deserves fudge.
      b. $\forall x[\text{good-boy}(x) \rightarrow \text{deserves-fudge}(x)]$

(11b) says roughly (when translated back into English morpheme-by-morpheme) "For every x, if x is a good boy, then x deserves fudge." The upside-down A is the UNIVERSAL QUANTIFIER of logic, and the arrow ($\rightarrow$) stands for the if-then relation; together, these two symbols represent the meaning of *every*. We can see that under this analysis, the quantificational determiner *every* has taken center stage, as the main predication combining with two open sentences—*good-boy(x)* and *deserves-fudge(x)*. Since these are open sentences (i.e. sentences with a free variable in them) they can be looked at as expressing properties—in this case the property of being a good boy, and the property of deserving fudge, respectively. So at bottom, *every* is expressing a relation between these two properties—the relation such that everything that has the first one also has the second one.[9] Crucially, for Russell's concern with knowledge, as long as we understand what good boys are and what deserving fudge is, as well as the relevant logical elements, we can understand all of (11). We don't have to have acquaintance with any particular good boys—just the defining property.

Another example is given in (12).

(12)   a.   No person is an island.
       b. $\sim\exists x[\text{person}(x) \& \text{island}(x)]$

The tilde in (12b) represents negation, and the backwards *E* is the EXISTENTIAL QUANTIFIER. (12b) reads, roughly, "It is not the case that there is an *x* such that *x* is a person and *x* is an island." We can see that this has the same truth conditions as *No person is an island*, and once again the quantificational element (*no* in this case) has been analyzed as expressing a relation between two properties, in this case the properties of being a person and being an island.

Under this type of analysis there is no constituent left corresponding to the quantificational NPs in these sentences at all. If we remove the translations of the predicates of (11a) and (12a) (*deserves fudge*, and *is an island* respectively) from the logical forms in (11b) and (12b), what remains is the translation of the subject NPs *every good boy* and *no person*. These are, respectively, the nonconstituents given in (13) below:

(13)   a. $\forall x[\text{good-boy}(x) \rightarrow \ldots(x)]$
       b. $\sim\exists x[\text{person}(x) \& \ldots(x)]$

The denoting phrases have been analyzed away. As noted above, we cannot give a translation for quantificational NPs like *every good boy* and *no person* on their own, but only in the context of a whole sentence.

---

[9]   We'll see some different ways to think about the semantic structure of quantificational NPs in the next two chapters.

As we saw in Chapter 1, indefinite descriptions in English are NPs beginning with the indefinite article *a/an*. That article is derived historically from the word *one*, and so it should not be surprising that indefinite descriptions are often regarded as quantificational expressions when they occur in argument positions in a sentence (as opposed to being used predicatively). Thus a sentence like (14a) would be translated into logic as (14b).

(14) a. A dog is barking.
      b. ∃x[dog(x) & is-barking(x)]

Once again the determiner takes center stage, expressing the main predication in the sentence—a relation between two properties. The two properties involved in (14) are the properties of being a dog and barking, and the relation is that of sharing at least one instance.

When an indefinite description is used predicatively, as in *Rover is a good hunter*, then it just shows up as a predicate in the corresponding logical form.

(15) a. Rover is a good hunter.
      b. good-hunter(Rover)

The fact that we require an article for this kind of predicative use should be regarded as a grammatical peculiarity of English.

2.3.2 Russell's analysis of definite descriptions

We are now ready for the *pièce de résistance* of Russell's theory— his analysis of definite descriptions, which the early twentieth century British logician Frank Ramsey famously called "the paradigm of philosophy." What Russell did was to treat the definite article *the* as though it were a quantificational determiner like *every* and *no*, and thus to analyze it as expressing a relation between properties.

One of Russell's examples is (16a), and the analysis is in (16b).

(16) a. The king of France is bald.
      b. ∃x[rule(x, France) & ∀y[rule(y, France) → y = x] & bald(x)]

There are three clauses in (16). The first says that there is an entity which rules France—it requires the existence of such an entity. The second (beginning with the universal quantifier) says that there is at most one such entity—i.e. it imposes a uniqueness requirement.

Thus on Russell's view, definite descriptions specify that there is an entity that uniquely satisfies the descriptive content of the NP. The third clause in (16b) says that that (unique) entity is bald.[10] As with the overtly quantificational NPs, we have no constituent in the logical form which corresponds to the NP *the king of France.* And *voilà*—Russell has explained why we do not have to be personally acquainted with his majesty in order to learn interesting new things about him.

A notational note: there is a way to abbreviate the first two clauses of (16b) into a logically equivalent expression which is somewhat more compressed. Here it is:

(17) $\exists x \forall y \, [[rule(y, France) \leftrightarrow y = x] \,\&\, bald(x)]$

The double-headed arrow ($\leftrightarrow$) reads in English "if and only if." The format in (17) is a bit easier to read in addition to saving ink.

As if it were not enough to have shown how knowledge by description can be reduced to knowledge by acquaintance, Russell also applied his theory to the solution of several other puzzles. One involved propositional attitudes, and we will come to it shortly, but another one involved empty NPs like *the king of France,* and here is how Russell described the problem.

> By the law of excluded middle, either "A is B" or "A is not B" must be true. Hence either "the present King of France is bald" or "the present King of France is not bald" must be true. Yet if we enumerated the things that are bald, and then the things that are not bald, we should not find the present King of France in either list. Hegelians, who love a synthesis, will probably conclude that he wears a wig. (Russell 1905: 485)

As we have seen above in (16b) and (17), under Russell's analysis *The king of France is bald* does not have the logical form *A is B.* Instead, it is a complex existential statement and is simply false. Its negation, whose logical form is in (18), is true.

(18) $\sim\exists x \forall y \, [[rule(y, France) \leftrightarrow y = x] \,\&\, bald(x)]$

I am skipping over a few complications here; see below in §2.4.3. However, we can see that the law of the excluded middle has been preserved.

---

[10] If you read "On denoting," which I highly recommend, you will find a very cumbersome English paraphrase instead of a symbolic version such as that in (16b), but this is essentially what it says.

2.3.3 Russell on propositional attitudes

George IV wished to know whether Scott was the author of *Waverley*, so (19) is true:

(19) George IV wished to know whether Scott was the author of *Waverley*.

Now Scott **was** the author of *Waverley*, so the NPs *Scott* and *the author of Waverley* are coreferential. But of course we can't substitute *Scott* for *the author of Waverley* in (19) or we would derive the false (20).

(20) George IV wished to know whether Scott was Scott.

As Russell assures us, "an interest in the law of identity can hardly be attributed to the first gentleman of Europe" (Russell 1905: 485).

We know Frege's solution to this problem: we can only substitute phrases with the same sense in propositional attitude contexts, and *the author of Waverley* does not mean the same thing as *Scott*. However Russell did not care much for Frege's solution.[11] As an empiricist Russell could not be happy with the invocation of senses for NPs and in fact his approach did not invoke them. (However we should note that Russell's empiricism did not stop him from accepting properties or universals as the denotations of predicate expressions.)

Russell's solution to the problem involving George IV is remarkably simple (although there are some attendant complications). We cannot substitute *Scott* for *the author of Waverley* in (19) because, on Russell's analysis, there is no constituent corresponding to *the author of Waverley* to substitute something else for. Q.E.D.

But how exactly does Russell's analysis apply to (19)? The very observant reader will have noticed that there are two ways to apply it. (Here come the complications.) That is because the NP *the author of Waverley* occurs in an embedded sentence in (19). Recall that Russell's analysis applies to NPs only in the context of a sentence. That means that in the case of (19) we could apply it to the embedded sentence *Scott was the author of Waverley* or to the whole sentence *George IV wished to know whether Scott was the author of Waverley*. Ignoring details about the analysis of the matrix clause (*George IV wished to know whether*), the two logical forms are given in (21a) and (21b) respectively.

---

[11] Unfortunately the direct criticism of Frege's solution which Russell gave in "On denoting" is famously bollixed up—see the critique in Searle (1958b) and the comments in Kaplan (1977: 496, n. 23).

(21) a. George IV wished to know whether $\exists x \forall y$ [[wrote(y, *Waverley*) $\leftrightarrow$ y = x] & x = Scott]

    b. $\exists x \forall y$ [[wrote(y, *Waverley*) $\leftrightarrow$ y = x] & George IV wished to know whether x = Scott]

Russell described *the author of Waverley* as having SECONDARY OCCURRENCE when analyzed with respect to the embedded sentence as in (21a), and PRIMARY OCCURRENCE when analyzed with respect to the sentence as a whole as in (21b). In terminology more commonly used today, *the author of Waverley* would be described as having NARROW SCOPE in (21a) and WIDE SCOPE in (21b). (We will have more terms for this distinction shortly.)

Since we have two nonequivalent analyses for (19), we predict an ambiguity in that sentence, and Russell claimed that indeed it **is** ambiguous.

> [W]hen we say, "George IV wished to know whether Scott was the author of *Waverley*," we normally mean "George IV wished to know whether one and only one man wrote *Waverley* and Scott was that man"; but we *may* also mean: "One and only one man wrote *Waverley*, and George IV wished to know whether Scott was that man."... The latter might be expressed by "George IV wished to know, concerning the man who in fact wrote *Waverley*, whether he was Scott." This would be true, for example, if George IV had seen Scott at a distance, and had asked "Is that Scott?"
>
> (Russell 1905: 33; italics in original.)

It must be admitted that it is very difficult to hear (19) as a report of the situation described here by Russell. Probably this has something to do with the fact that *the author of Waverley* is functioning as a predicate in (19), which makes it more difficult for it to have the wide-scope reading. Fortunately, Russell had a better example of the ambiguity at hand:

> I have heard of a touchy owner of a yacht to whom a guest, on first seeing it, remarked, "I thought your yacht was larger than it is"; and the owner replied, "No, my yacht is not larger than it is." What the guest meant was, "The size that I thought your yacht was is greater than the size your yacht is"; the meaning attributed to him is, "I thought the size of your yacht was greater than the size of your yacht."
>
> (Russell 1905: 33)

Of course Russell is using a comparative term here instead of a definite description, but there are abundant examples of the ambiguity of using definite descriptions. A classic comes from Linsky (1967: 74) and is given in (22).

(22)   Oedipus wanted to marry his mother.

This example has the two interpretations indicated in (23).

(23)   a.   Oedipus wanted it to be the case that his mother was his
             wife.
       b.   Oedipus wanted to marry a certain woman, who happened
             to be his mother.

And sure enough, Russell's analysis provides us with two logical forms
for (22), as shown in (24).

(24)   a.   Oedipus wanted [∃x∀y [[Oed's mother(y) ↔ y = x] &
             marry(Oed, x)]]
       b.   ∃x∀y [[Oed's mother(y) ↔ y = x] & Oedipus wanted
             [marry(Oed, x)]]

(We are assuming here, following common practice, that possessive
NPs with pronominal determiners, like *his mother*, are semantically
equivalent to definite descriptions.) (24a) gives the narrow-scope version, which attributes to Oedipus a desire to commit incest. This
reading is false of course—Oedipus was horrified when he found out
that he had married his own mother. (24b) gives the wide-scope
version, which is true; Oedipus wanted to marry Jocasta, and it happened that Jocasta was his mother.

Apparently Frege never noticed this ambiguity. At least he never said
anything about it as far as I know. However, this kind of ambiguity has
been noticed for a long time. One of the many pairs of terms labeling
the two readings is the pair "*de dicto*" and "*de re*," which date from
medieval times when Latin was the language of scholarship in Europe.
The (false) narrow-scope reading of (22) is the DE DICTO one, so called
because the actual words used are crucial to the content of the propositional attitude reported. The DE RE reading is the (true) wide-scope
one, on which the attributed propositional attitude concerns some
particular thing, or *res* in Latin. (See Kneale (1962: 212–13) for discussion of the origins of these terms.) Two more terms in common use are
Quine's term "opaque" and its opposite "transparent"—"opaque" for
the narrow-scope reading which was apparently the only one that Frege
noticed, and "transparent" for the wide-scope one.[12]

---

[12] Quine (1953a: 142, n. 2) attributes the term "transparent" to Russell, and coined
"opaque" in contrast to it.

As noted above, technically on Russell's analysis the law of substitutivity does not apply to examples like the one about George IV, because once Russell's analysis has been applied there is no constituent left corresponding to the NP to substitute another NP for. However that would mean that, technically, we could **never** substitute an NP for a coreferential definite description, since Russell meant his analysis to apply to all definite descriptions and not just ones in propositional attitude contexts. But we know that many times the law of substitutivity works. Russell acknowledged that actually "verbal" substitution **is** possible, but only on the wide-scope reading—the one where the denoting term gets primary, or wide-scope, occurrence. For (22) that is the reading given in (23b/24b). Thus if we substitute *Jocasta* for *his mother* in (22) we get (25).

(25)   Oedipus wanted to marry Jocasta.

Like the wide-scope reading of (22), (25) seems true.

2.3.4 Russell on proper names

We have seen that while Mill ascribed to proper names denotation only, and not connotation, Frege held the descriptional view that proper names have a sense which is similar to the kind of thing that is expressed by a definite description. The translation of *Scott* as simply *Scott* in the logical forms given above for the sentences about George IV suggests that Russell might have agreed with Mill on proper names, but in fact his view turns out to be close to Frege's.

As noted in passing above, Russell did not approve of Fregean senses. Russell was one of those who believed that reference is all there is to meaning. (That is why he needed a different solution to the apparent failures of the law of substitutivity.) If proper names lacked connotation, as Mill thought, then their semantic significance would be exhausted by their reference. Russell had a particularly vivid view of the propositions expressed using purely referential expressions. If the name *Socrates* were such an expression, then its referent would form a part of propositions expressed with it. For example, our simple model sentence from Chapter 1, repeated here in (26a), would have the content represented in (26b).[13]

---

[13] Angle brackets (<,>), as in (26b), indicate an ordered sequence of items—in this case an ordered pair.

(26)   a.   Socrates was curious
       b.   <Socrates, the property of being curious>

Note that the first element of the proposition represented in (26b) is
not the name *Socrates* but rather the person Socrates himself. I will call
such propositions—i.e. propositions containing one or more actual
entities—RUSSELLIAN SINGULAR PROPOSITIONS.[14] These are quite
different from the propositions expressed using definite descriptions
and (other) quantificational NPs, on Russell's theory, whatever the
form of quantificational propositions ultimately turns out to be. (We
will look at various theories of propositions in the next chapter.)

Incidentally, the existence of Russellian singular propositions was an
explicit source of disagreement between Russell and Frege. In a letter in
November 1904, Frege commented to Russell "... Mont Blanc with its
snowfields is not itself a component part of the thought that Mont
Blanc is more than 4000 metres high" (Gabriel et al.: 1980: 163). The
following month Russell responded: "I believe that in spite of all its
snowfields Mont Blanc itself is a component part of what is actually
asserted in the proposition 'Mont Blanc is more than 4000 metres
high' " (Gabriel et al. 1980: 169).[15] However the existence of Russellian
singular propositions is one thing; being able to express them is quite
another.

Recall that Russell was concerned with knowledge, and specifically
how we can gain knowledge about entities with which we have had no
direct acquaintance. Since we do not have any direct acquaintance with
Socrates (unlike Mont Blanc), Russell thought that we could not grasp

---

[14] Many people just use "singular proposition" to mean Russellian singular proposition. However I want to recognize a different kind of singular proposition, which will be
introduced in the following chapters.

[15] The idea of having actual entities as parts of propositions always makes me think of
Whorf's description of the (Russellian!) Hopi in contrast to Standard Average European
ways of thinking about things:

Now, when WE think of a certain actual rosebush, we do not suppose that our thought goes
to that actual bush, and engages with it, like a searchlight turned upon it. What then do we
suppose our consciousness *is* dealing with when we are thinking of that rosebush? Probably
we think it is dealing with a "mental image" which is not the rosebush but a mental
surrogate of it. But why should it be NATURAL to think that our thought deals with a
surrogate and not with the real rosebush?... A Hopi would naturally suppose that his
thought... traffics with the actual rosebush—or more likely, corn plant—that he is
thinking about. The thought then should leave some trace of itself with the plant in the
field.   (Whorf 1941: 149f.; italics and small caps in original)

the proposition represented in (26b). "*Every proposition which we can understand must be composed wholly of constituents with which we are acquainted*" (Russell 1917: 173, italics in original). The only way to grasp such a proposition would be to be presented with direct, perceptual evidence of Socrates, which is not possible in today's world. But we seem to be able to understand sentences like (26a), so (26b) must not be the correct type of analysis for them.

Toward the end of "On denoting" Russell briefly considered proper names for mythical or imaginary entities.

A proposition about Apollo means what we get by substituting what the classical dictionary tells us is meant by Apollo, say "the sun-god." All propositions in which Apollo occurs are to be interpreted by the above rules for denoting phrases. If "Apollo" has a primary occurrence, then the proposition containing the occurrence is false; if the occurrence is secondary the proposition may be true.

(Russell 1905: 491)

This kind of analysis was also Russell's way of solving the problem of the informativeness of ordinary sentences containing proper names; he extended the descriptive paraphrase approach to proper names in general, and not just names for mythical entities. A sentence like *Socrates was curious*, on this view, might be regarded as shorthand for something like (27).

(27)   The famous Greek philosopher who drank hemlock was curious.

And then the definite description *the famous Greek philosopher who drank hemlock* would be unpacked according to his analysis.

Russell eventually concluded that the only true proper names—that is, the only NPs which can be used in the expression of these special Russellian singular propositions—are those which guarantee a referent with which interlocutors have perceptual acquaintance. Ultimately he declared that the demonstrative pronoun *this* was the only such expression in English (Russell 1917: 177 & n. 5). Furthermore he eventually came to the view that the only things with which one could be acquainted were sense data, and not physical objects like people or chairs. "It will be seen that among the objects with which we are acquainted are not included physical objects (as opposed to sense-data)...." (Russell 1917: 169). This view is in conflict with the earlier one as expressed in Russell's letter to Frege about Mont Blanc which was quoted above—Mont Blanc is definitely a physical object rather than a sense datum, yet what Russell said in his letter about its belonging to a proposition implies that it can be an object of acquaintance. I will continue to refer to propositions containing physical objects as "Russellian singular propositions" for the remainder of the book, even though this label is not completely consonant with Russell's ultimate views.

2.4 Comparisons of Mill, Frege, and Russell

Let us try to compare the various views we have been looking at, to see their similarities and differences.

2.4.1 Sense vs reference

Here we see that the views of Mill and Frege are quite similar: for both, expressions in general have both a sense/connotation and reference/denotation. Russell is opposed to this view; as a direct reference theorist, he rejects the postulation of senses for expressions. However we need to be careful here not to overstate the differences. As noted in passing above, Russell did accept the idea of properties or universals as denotations for predicative expressions: "When we examine common words, we find that, broadly speaking... substantives, adjectives, prepositions, and verbs stand for universals" (Russell 1912: 93). But most people today would consider a property or universal to be the **sense** of a predicative expression, and the corresponding set its denotation or reference. We will return to this in Chapter 3.

2.4.2 Definite descriptions

Here again Mill and Frege seem opposed to Russell. For both Mill and Frege, definite descriptions are referential expressions, where their reference is mediated or determined by their sense/connotation. Now we might see Russell's famous analysis of definite descriptions as spelling out the sense of such expressions; the properties associated with the head noun and any other content words in a definite description are present in the Russellian analysis, as well as the meanings of the logical expressions involved which spell out Russell's interpretation of *the*. However this "sense" of a definite description is not one that mediates a connection with a referent, since, as we have seen, under Russell's analysis definite descriptions do not **have** a referent. Rather definite descriptions do not exist as constituents at all but instead are to be seen as quantificational NPs, like *every bird* and *no bath*. This is a major difference between Russell's view and those of Mill and Frege.

Note that Russell called definite descriptions "denoting expressions" (recall that his paper was "On denoting"). This might seem strange, since according to his analysis, technically, they don't denote anything— at least not in the sense that Mill, say, would speak of denoting (or Frege would speak of referring). But in fact Russell also considered obviously quantificational NPs, like *every woman* and even *no apple* as denoting expressions. As noted above, this strange usage of Russell's has undoubtedly encouraged the more liberal use of "denote" and "denotation" (as opposed to "refer" and "reference") that we now see.

2.4.3 Empty NPs

Another important difference between Frege and Russell is found in how they treated empty NPs like *the golden mountain* or *the present king of France*. Frege believed that the lack of a referent for such NPs meant that sentences containing them lack a truth value—this follows from the principle of compositionality. That would be true both for Russell's example (16a), repeated here as (28a), and for its negation in (28b).

(28) a.   The king of France is bald.
      b.   The king of France is not bald.

Instead, according to Frege, both positive and negative sentences containing definite descriptions PRESUPPOSE the existence of a referent (Frege 1892b: 68ff.). (We return to this idea below in Chapter 6.)

Russell was apparently not keen on the idea that sentences can lack a truth value—recall his defense of the law of the excluded middle: *p or not p*. On the other hand for Russell, all NPs (except for *this*) lack a referent, since all must disappear under analysis. As we have seen, on Russell's analysis (28a) is simply false. (28b) is actually a little more complicated. Negation is a SENTENCE OPERATOR—an expression which combines with a sentence to form a new sentence. Thus Russell's analysis predicts an ambiguity in (28b), depending on whether the analysis of the definite description has wide or narrow scope with respect to the negation. The two versions are given in (29).

(29) a. $\sim\exists x \forall y$ [[rule(y, France) $\leftrightarrow$ y $=$ x] & bald(x)]
      b. $\exists x \forall y$ [[rule(y, France) $\leftrightarrow$ y $=$ x] & $\sim$bald(x)]

As we saw earlier, (29a), which is the logical negation of Russell's analysis of (28a), is true, thus preserving the law of the excluded middle. On the other hand (29b) says that there is one and only one ruler of France and he is not bald, and that is false.

At this point one might decide that either view has a certain amount of plausibility, but there is one decided advantage to Russell's view, and that is what he has to say about existence statements—and more particularly true negative ones, like (30).

(30)   The king of France does not exist

A Russellian logical form for (30) is given in (31).

(31) $\sim\exists x\forall y\ [\text{rule}(y, \text{France}) \leftrightarrow y = x]$

(31) says that it is not the case that there is one and only one entity which rules France, and this is true, like (30). On the other hand, for Frege sentences like (30) present a real problem; he has to explain why they not only do not lack a truth value, but are in fact true. We will be returning to this problem more than once in the following chapters.

2.4.4 Propositional attitude contexts

Here is yet another major difference between Frege and Russell, and one where Russell again seems to have the advantage. Frege, apparently only recognizing the *de dicto* or opaque readings of propositional attitude sentences, asserted that expressions in these contexts undergo a shift of reference whereby they refer to their customary sense. However, as we have seen, Russell's analysis of definite descriptions predicts an ambiguity in these contexts, since as quantificational NPs they may be unpacked with either wide or narrow scope. The fact that propositional attitude sentences are indeed ambiguous in the way Russell's analysis predicts is an argument in favor of his analysis. Recall Linsky's example, repeated below in (32).

(32)   Oedipus wanted to marry his mother.

Now Frege might claim that he can account for the ambiguity in question by replying simply that the shift in reference is optional for NPs—*his mother*, in (32), might refer either to its customary sense or to its customary reference. However as it turns out, the number of readings available increases if we add more propositional attitude verbs. So consider (33).

(33)   The oracle predicted that Oedipus would want to marry his
         mother.
   a.   Jocasta was such that the oracle predicted that Oedipus
         would want to marry her.
   b.   The oracle declared "Oedipus's mother is one whom Oedi-
         pus will want to marry, though he won't know that she is
         his mother."
   c.   The oracle predicted that Oedipus would want to commit
         incest.

(33) has the three readings indicated above in (a)–(c). Since we have
two layers of embedding, this is exactly what Russell's analysis predicts.
Frege, on the other hand, does not seem to have a way of accounting
for these facts.

2.4.5 Proper names

Finally we come to a point of agreement between Frege and Russell.
And here Mill is on the other side of the fence. As we saw, Mill held the
nondescriptional view that proper names are not connotative—they
have only denotation. On the other hand Russell and Frege agree on a
descriptional view of proper names, holding that they are semantically
equivalent to definite descriptions. For Frege this means that they
express that kind of a sense, and for Russell it means that they are
viewed as going proxy for a definite description, and when in the
context of a sentence must be so unpacked.

2.5 Concluding remarks

The work of Frege and Russell has brought to light a couple of problem
areas for any theory of reference. One lies in the fact that, despite what
Shakespeare or the law of substitutivity says, coreferential expressions
(in particular coreferential definite descriptions) fail to be semantically
equivalent. We have seen two different kinds of solution to this problem. Frege postulates senses in addition to referents, and a shift of
reference in propositional attitude contexts. Russell analyzes definite
descriptions as quantificational NPs, causing them to disappear as
constituents. Of these two solutions, Frege's may seem to be the
more intuitively appealing. At least it seems obvious that, e.g., *the
star of Evita* has a meaning in addition to its referent, Madonna.

Of course Russell's analysis retains the meaningful parts of that definite description, but his allowing "verbal" substitution only when an NP has primary occurrence, or wide scope, could be considered ad hoc. And furthermore definite descriptions do not **seem** like quantificational expressions: they seem referential. (This point is stressed in Kaplan 1972.) On the other hand, as we have seen, Russell's approach has some definite advantages in its treatment of propositional attitude sentences and its treatment of empty NPs, especially as they occur in true negative existence sentences.

We have noted that despite their apparent opposition, there is much in common between the views of Russell and Frege. It is also true that at least some of their views are not inconsistent with each other. One could believe both that expressions have a sense as well as a reference, and that denoting phrases are inherently quantificational and produce scope ambiguities when contained in the complement of a propositional attitude predicate. In fact both of these views were sustained and formalized during what Kaplan has called "The Golden Age of Pure Semantics" (Kaplan 1978: 223). We will look at some of the background developments leading up to the Golden Age in the next chapter, and then in the following chapter take a look at Montague grammar—if not the pinnacle achievement of the Golden Age then something close to it.

3

Subsequent developments

> The intension of an individual expression is a concept of a new kind; it is called an *individual concept*.
>
> Rudolf Carnap, *Meaning and Necessity*

In Chapter 2 we reviewed some of the important contributions of Mill, Frege, and Russell. Key ideas reviewed there have been incorporated into current theories of semantics, and in the next chapter we will see one important example of that incorporation in the work of Montague. Before we do that, however, we need to take care of some background work. In reviewing Russell's work, we were introduced to the phenomenon of expressions with scopal properties, so first off in this chapter we will look more closely at semantic scope and scope ambiguity. Following that we will review some of the important developments in semantics which followed on the heels of our three early figures, focusing on what is called "possible worlds semantics," and some notions which have been defined in terms of possible worlds. We will also take a closer look at propositions, and try to get clearer on the various conceptions of this all-important concept. The penultimate section looks at "existence independence"—another characteristic of (some) propositional attitude sentences (in addition to the failure of substitutivity which we have already seen); and the final section summarizes.

3.1 Semantic scope

In the first subsection below we look more closely at quantificational NPs and how best to think about them. Following that we turn to some (other) sentence operators—expressions which combine with sentences to make sentences. We turn next to scope ambiguity in §3.1.3. §3.1.4 looks at modal operators, and in §3.1.5 we consider some complicating factors. We finish the section with a brief summary.

3.1.1 Quantificational NPs

In the last chapter we saw the standard analysis of quantificational NPs—i.e. how quantificational NPs would standardly be translated into logic. One of our examples from that chapter is reproduced here as (1).

(1) a.   Every good boy deserves fudge.
     b. $\forall x[\text{good-boy}(x) \rightarrow \text{deserves-fudge}(x)]$

(1b) is the traditional logical analysis of (1a), and makes clear that the quantificational determiner *every* expresses a relation between two properties—in this case the property of being a good boy, and the property of deserving fudge. One problem with this representation, however, is that it does not reflect the different status of these two properties as they are expressed in the English sentence. The property of being a good boy combines with the universal quantifier *every* to form the semantic content of the NP; the property of deserving fudge is then what is being predicated of every good boy.

Following Irene Heim (1982), let us distinguish these two properties. We'll call the property expressed by the CNP ("Common Noun Phrase"—*good boy* in this example) the RESTRICTION on the quantifier, and that expressed by the rest of the sentence (*deserves fudge*, in this case) the SCOPE. In the English sentence it looks like the scope of the quantificational NP is just the predicate *deserves fudge*, which expresses a property. However we could also see this scope as being a sentence, more specifically an open sentence—a sentence with one or more variables corresponding to missing arguments. This is reflected in the logical form: *deserves-fudge(x)*. Looked at in this way, the quantificational NP is a sentence operator, albeit a complex one.

We introduced the concept of sentence operators in the last chapter, in connection with negation. Negation is a simple sentence operator—it just takes a (closed) sentence, and that sentence is its scope. A negative sentence like (2a) below is formed simply by combining negation with another sentence, (2b) in this case.

(2) a.   Mary didn't leave.
     b.   Mary left.

In this case the traditional logical notation, as in (3), shows the relationship clearly.

(3)   ~(left (Mary))

Quantificational NPs are more complicated in several ways: the quantifier itself (expressed by the determiner of the NP) actually combines with two open sentences (the restriction and the scope), and it binds a variable in both of them. However, as we have seen, the two open sentences have a different status from each other. The surface syntax of English does not make all these logical relationships clear, and neither does the traditional logical form. The format in (4) is intended to reflect these relationships a bit better.

(4)   every$_x$ [good-boy(x)](deserves-fudge(x))

The subscript on *every* indicates which variable this quantifier binds. The square brackets enclose the restriction on the quantifier, and the parentheses surround the scope. This notation, which also has the advantage of suppressing the logical connective, is sometimes referred to as RESTRICTED QUANTIFIER notation. The difference is that the individuals considered for satisfaction of the main predication in the scope—deserving fudge, in this example—are only those which satisfy the restriction. We will use this notation from time to time in what follows, although we will also revert to traditional logical notation too at times.

3.1.2 Some other sentence operators

Let us look at some other sentence operators. Conjunction and disjunction in English, expressed with *and* and *or* respectively, are sentence operators that are midway between simple and complex. They combine with two sentences, but they don't bind any variables and the sentences are parallel, and can be reversed without changing truth conditions.[1] The translations for (5a) and (6a) below are shown in (5b) and (6b). As before, we are using the ampersand (&) for conjunction; ∨ (from Latin *vel*) is the common symbol for disjunction.

(5)   a.   Sue is at home and Bill is in town.
      b.   at-home(Sue) & in-town(Bill)

(6)   a.   Fred'll be here at six or he'll call you.
      b.   here-at-six(Fred) ∨ call(Fred, you)

[1] Of course there may be stylistic reasons why one order may be preferred to another, especially in sentences describing sequences of actions.

Here (as with negation) traditional logic does a good job of showing the relationships expressed (and English is pretty good in this case too).

In logical languages the three connectives &, ∨, and → are treated pretty similarly, but there are big differences in English between *and* and *or*, on the one hand, and *if*, on the other. While grammatically *and* and *or* are coordinating conjunctions, *if* is a subordinating conjunction which introduces an adverbial modifier. The semantics of sentences with an *if* clause—CONDITIONAL sentences—is also more complicated than it is for sentences with the other connectives. There are (at least) three kinds of conditionals: indicative conditionals, as in (7a) below; subjunctive conditionals, as in (7b); and generic conditionals, as in (7c).

(7)   a.   If Mary was in Paris last year, she spoke French.
       b.   If Mary had been in Paris last year, she would have spoken French.
       c.   If someone is in Paris, they usually speak French.

The semantics of all three types of conditionals is the subject of ongoing research. In addition, many other constructions seem to have an implicit conditional element, making the correct analysis of conditionals even more important. Unfortunately we will not be able to spend much time at all with conditionals in this book, although subjunctive conditionals like (7b), which concern hypothetical states of affairs in other possible worlds, will come up below as an example of an intensional construction.

3.1.3 Scope ambiguities

We now have a number of expressions with scope: the sentence operators we have just been looking at (quantificational NPs, negation, the binary sentence connectives), together with the propositional attitude verbs we saw in the last chapter, which take sentential complements. One thing that makes the existence of such expressions interesting is that when you have more than one of them in a sentence, there is the possibility of SCOPE AMBIGUITY—different interpretations depending on which expression takes the other in its scope. Perhaps the simplest sort of case is where we have two quantificational NPs in the same sentence, like the famous example in (8) (adapted from Chomsky 1957: 100f.).

(8)   Everyone in the room knows two languages.

Using our new notation, we can represent the two readings as in (9).

(9)   a. $every_x$ [in-the-room(x)] (two_y [language(y)] (knows(x, y)))
       b. two_y [language(y)] ($every_x$ [in-the-room(x)] (knows(x, y)))

The reading in (9a) says that for each person in the room there are two languages that they know—i.e. everybody is bilingual. The (9b) reading says that there are two languages, say Urdu and Dogrib, that everybody in the room knows.

   We can get another common type of scope ambiguity by combining a quantificational NP with negation as in (10) below.

(10)   All that glitters is not gold.
       a.   Not everything that glitters is gold.
       b.   Nothing that glitters is gold.

We can use the restricted quantifier notation again to show the scope ambiguity more clearly as in (11).

(11)   a. $\sim all_x$ [glitters(x)] (gold(x))
       b. all_x [glitters(x)] ($\sim$ gold(x))

In the (10a) interpretation shown in (11a), the negation has the wider scope and includes the quantificational element within it, while in the (10b) interpretation shown in (11b) it is the quantifier that has the wider scope, which includes the negation. (12) below gives another example—recall from the last chapter that indefinite descriptions like *a huge mistake* are often regarded as quantificational.[2]

(12)   I didn't notice a huge mistake.
       a. $\sim a_x$ [huge mistake(x)] (notice (I, x))
       b. a_x [huge mistake(x)] ($\sim$ notice (I, x))

According to the reading in (12a), I didn't notice any big mistakes so I'm probably in the clear. However the reading in (12b) says there's a huge mistake that I overlooked—bad news!

   The examples above have involved either two quantificational NPs or a quantificational NP combined with negation. We can also construct examples involving a quantificational NP and a propositional attitude verb, as shown in (13).

---

[2] Indefinite descriptions are not always regarded as quantificational by everyone—this is an issue that will concern us in the chapters to come.

(13) Mary thought she had read every book on the list.
      a. every$_x$ [book on the list(x)](Mary thought (read (Mary, x)))
      b. Mary thought (every$_x$ [book on the list(x)] (read (Mary, x)))

The (13a) reading, where *think* is within the scope of the quantified NP *every book on the list* means that each of those books is such that Mary thought she had read it, though she might not be acquainted with the list itself. (Think of an interviewer asking Mary about this book and that, without revealing the list.) On the other hand the (13b) interpretation, with the reverse scope dependence, conveys that Mary thought she had completed the reading list. Here she may have even forgotten what the individual books on the list were.

One of the generalizations to emerge in the last chapter, in the section on Russell, was that definite descriptions in propositional attitude contexts may be construed in two ways, either with narrow scope with respect to the propositional attitude verb (*de dicto*), or with wide scope (*de re*). Thus our example about Oedipus, which is repeated here in (14),

(14) Oedipus wanted to marry his mother.

has the two interpretations indicated below in (15a) (the *de dicto* interpretation) and (15b) (*de re*).

(15) a. Oedipus wanted it to be the case that his mother was his wife.
      b. Oedipus wanted to marry a certain woman, who happened to be his mother.

We can represent this ambiguity using our new notation as in (16).

(16) a. Oed wanted (the$_x$ [mother-of-Oed(x)] (marry(Oed, x)))
      b. the$_x$ [mother-of-Oed(x)](Oed wanted (marry(Oed, x)))

We can see now that this ambiguity is of a piece with those we have been considering.

As we should now expect, there is a similar phenomenon with indefinite descriptions, and here the ambiguity is somewhat more salient than with definite descriptions. Continuing with the wedding theme, examples like (17) are common in the literature.

(17) Bill hopes to marry a Norwegian.

(17) has the two interpretations paraphrased in (18); the corresponding logical forms are given in (19).

(18)   a.   Bill hopes to have a Norwegian spouse.
       b.   There is a particular individual, who happens to be
            Norwegian, whom Bill hopes to marry.

(19)   a.   hopes (Bill, a_x [Norwegian(x)] (marry(Bill, x))
       b. a_x [Norwegian(x)] (hopes(Bill, (marry(Bill, x)))

The narrow-scope reading represented in (18a)/(19a) is often called NONSPECIFIC, and the wide-scope one in (18b)/(19b) SPECIFIC, although the exact application of this pair of terms is subject to some variation and controversy, and we will be using them somewhat differently in the chapters to come.

   Incidentally, it should be clear that having **pairs** of terms like "*de dicto*"-"*de re*," "opaque"-"transparent," or "nonspecific"-"specific," is misleading in suggesting that the ambiguity in question is, in general, a simple binary one. That is only true if there are just two scope-taking expressions involved; readings have the potential to multiply with every added layer of embedding, although subject to constraints. We saw this toward the end of Chapter 2; recall our example *The oracle predicted that Oedipus would want to marry his mother*, which has three readings. The same thing occurs with indefinites: the naturally occurring example below in (20) was reported by Kripke (1977: 259).

(20)   Hoover charged that the Berrigans plotted to capture a high American official.

The intended reading gives *a high American official* widest scope (apparently it was Kissinger that Hoover had in mind), but (20) could also convey that Hoover just thought the Berrigans were plotting about someone but he didn't know who (with intermediate scope for *a high American official*), or that Hoover charged that the Berrigans were trying to come up with a potential victim (with narrowest scope for the NP).

3.1.4 Modal operators

Modal operators are expressions having to do with what is possible or necessary whether it be according to logical laws, natural laws, what is desirable, or another parameter. Here we will confine ourselves to the logical interpretation, for simplicity's sake (though see note 3 below). Modals can take a variety of grammatical forms: in addition to predicates like *it is necessary/possible that*, which take a sentential complement overtly, the modal element may be realized by an adverb like *possibly*, or *necessarily*, or by a modal auxiliary verb such as *can*, or *must*. Nevertheless the semantic structure of such sentences reveals that in each case the modal element is applying to a sentence (more properly, to the proposition it expresses) and consequently we get the expected scope ambiguities. (Indeed, the terms "*de dicto*" and "*de re*" originated in connection with modal sentences: see Kneale (1962) for discussion.)

Below are some examples, with logical forms showing the scope interactions between the modal element and a quantified NP; $\Box$ is the logical symbol for necessity, and $\Diamond$ is the symbol for possibility.

(21)   The number of planets is necessarily greater than 7. [= Quine 1953a: ex. 18.]
    a. $\Box$ the$_x$ [number-of-planets(x)] (x > 7)
    b.   the$_x$ [number-of-planets(x)] ($\Box$ x > 7)

(22)   Every student might fail the course.
    a. $\Diamond$ every$_x$ [student(x)] (fail(x))
    b.   every$_x$ [student(x)] ($\Diamond$ fail(x))

(21a) gives the false reading of (21) according to which there could not possibly have been fewer than 8 planets. Intuitively this is not right, and it even seems possible in the future for our solar system to lose another planet (we have already lost Pluto through demotion, and if we blow up the earth that would do the trick). (21b) gives the true reading; there are currently 8 planets, and 8 is necessarily greater than 7. Turning to (22), (22a) gives the reading which says that there might be a total wipe-out of students in the course. On the more plausible reading in (22b) the only claim is that each student runs the risk of possible failure. This could be true when (22a) is not true (say, because grading is done on a curve which defines the median grade as a passing one).[3]

---

[3] From all that we have said up to now it seems that modals are simple sentence operators, like negation, and that does seem to be true of modals on the logical interpretation. However, as noted at the outset of this subsection, modals can have other interpretations. Consider example (i), for instance.

(i)   Mary must be at the meeting.

The modal *must* in (i) can be read in at least two ways. Read deontically, (i) constitutes a directive concerning Mary's future behavior, issued by the speaker. Read epistemically, (i) represents a conclusion of the speaker based on some kind of evidence, and the meeting is now. Kratzer (1977) has argued that in these kinds of cases modals have a tacit restriction which varies depending on the kind of interpretation.

Modal contexts share another property with propositional attitude contexts, in addition to providing an environment for scope ambiguities, and that is the fact that the law of substitutivity also appears to fail in modal contexts, on readings where NPs have narrow scope. For example as we saw above, (21) on the narrow-scope reading represented in (21a) is false. However if we substitute *8* for *the number of planets* we get (23),

(23)   8 is necessarily greater than 7

and (23) seems to be unambiguously true. (As noted in Chapter 1, number words like *8* behave like proper names, and as such they do not seem to vary scope.) Despite the broad similarity between modal and propositional attitude contexts in apparent failures of substitutivity, later on when we look more closely we will see that there are differences between modal and propositional attitude contexts in this respect, and that the propositional attitude contexts present a more serious problem.

3.1.5 Some complications

Above we alluded to the fact that there are constraints on scope ambiguities. One constraint is that the relative scopes of two propositional attitude verbs is fixed by their syntactic construction in English. In (20) above, for example, it is not possible for the verb *plot* to take the verb *charge* within its scope. The fact that *plot* is syntactically part of the complement of *charge* prevents it from having wider semantic scope than *charge*.

Various other syntactic constructions impose constraints too. Relative clauses (clausal noun modifiers) are one kind of syntactic ISLAND; the idea is that relations with the rest of the sentence are cut off. Thus questioning an item within a relative clause isn't possible, as illustrated below in (24).

(24)   *Which mouse did the cat [who caught _] choke?

The relative clause is bracketed in (24), and the underline indicates the place where *which mouse* logically occurs. Relative clauses are also islands for quantificational NPs, which cannot take scope outside them. The pair of examples in (25) (from Rodman (1976)) illustrates this fact.

(25)   a.   Guinevere has a bone in <u>every corner of the house</u>.
        b.   #Guinevere has a bone [which is in <u>every corner of the house</u>].

In (25a) the NP *every corner of the house* can take scope over *a bone*, giving a sensible reading according to which every corner of the house has one of Guinevere's bones in it. But this reading is not possible for (25b), since *every corner of the house* is within the relative clause, and cannot escape to take wide scope. The only reading is the nonsensical one which requires one bone to be in many corners.

Other constraints on scope ambiguities are the result of semantic and/or pragmatic factors. Sebastian Löbner (1985) and Daniel Rothschild (2007) have noted a distinction in definite descriptions. One kind has a CNP which by itself determines a unique individual. Examples are in (26) below.

(26)   *the king of France, the president of the club, the tallest person in Rhode Island*

Such definite descriptions are called "semantic" by Löbner, and "role-type" by Rothschild. The other kind have a CNP which does not, by itself, determine a unique individual. Instead, use of the definite article signals a unique satisfier of the CNP in context. Examples are in (27).

(27)   *the woman I had lunch with, the man with a limp, the book on the table*

These are called "pragmatic" by Löbner, and "particularized" by Rothschild. As Rothschild points out, only the former get a natural narrow scope interpretation with respect to a logical modal.[4] Compare (28a) with (28b).

(28)   a.   Jeanne might have been <u>the president of the club</u>.
       b.   #Jeanne might have been <u>the woman I had lunch with</u>.

An interpretation in which the underlined definite description has wide scope is odd for either of these examples, since it implies that Jeanne could have been a different person. The narrow-scope reading for (28a) is natural—it says that had things turned out differently, Jeanne could have been chosen for the role of president of the club. The narrow-scope reading for (28b) is somewhat strained because it

---

[4] In reviewing your intuitions on the following pair of examples it is important to read *might* as giving a logical possibility, not an epistemic one (i.e. what might be the case for all the speaker knows), since the epistemic modals behave somewhat differently.

requires an assumption that I regularly have lunch with some woman or other.

There are other examples which are more problematic, and which have in fact led some scholars to treat scope very differently from what has been suggested hitherto. (29) is one such example (from Bäuerle (1983), cited in Elbourne (2005: 104); see also Abusch (1994), Percus (2000), Schwarzschild (2002)).

(29)   George believes that a Mancunian woman loves all the Manchester United players.

The intended interpretation of (29) is one according to which George sees a bunch of men on a bus who, unbeknownst to him, constitute the Manchester United team. He forms the belief that there must be some Mancunian woman who loves all these men—thus *a Mancunian woman* has narrow scope with respect to *believes* since George has no particular woman in mind. If we try to represent this reading as in (30) below, there is a problem.

(30)   all$_x$ [Manchester-United-player(x)]   (believes   (George,   a$_y$ [Mancunian-woman(y)] (loves(y, x))))

(30) represents George as believing that for each Manchester United player there is some Mancunian woman who loves him, which is not the intended reading. Rather, we would need to treat the Manchester United players as a group, while still giving them wide scope. The exact determination of the constraints on scope-taking and its proper analysis are very complex and still a subject of active research.

3.1.6 Summary

In this section we have looked at a number of scope-taking expressions. We have seen that ambiguities of scope may arise whenever we have two or more of these in a single sentence, although exactly how many readings result may depend not only on the number of scope-taking expressions but also on syntactic, semantic, and pragmatic factors. We have not, so far, said anything very specific about the interpretation of NPs within the scope of other expressions. The readings involving propositional attitude verbs and modals are especially problematic, and so we turn now to a device which has figured extensively in the modern analysis of those readings.

3.2 Possible worlds, extensions, and intensions

3.2.1 Possible worlds

Possible worlds semantics gives us a way to incorporate something like Fregean senses into a formal semantics. The idea of possible worlds goes back at least to Leibniz, who thought that all of the possible worlds were part of God's conception, and that He chose this one to be actual because it was the most perfect. (Leibniz was the model for Professor Pangloss, in Voltaire's *Candide.*) The appearance of possible worlds in modern semantics owes a lot to Rudolf Carnap (1947), who introduced the notion of a state description as a concrete version of Leibniz's possible worlds. A state description is a maximal consistent set of sentences, and can thus be seen as a description of a possible world. The definitions below of "extension" and "intension" are directly derived from those given by Carnap.

As conceived of in modern semantics, possible worlds are simply alternative ways things might have been, with "things" construed very broadly so as to include everything. (So "possible universe" might have been a better term than "possible world".) The universe and everything in it is a certain way, and that is one possible world—the actual world. However we can easily imagine things that could have been different: Genghis Khan might have been thrown from his horse as a child and spent the rest of his life as a woodcutter, the US Supreme Court might have called for a recount of Florida ballots in the 2000 Presidential election, the Milky Way might not have existed, one of the banana slices on my cereal this morning might have been a millimeter thicker. For each difference in the way things might have been (and all that that difference entails) we have a difference in possible worlds.

3.2.2 Extensions

The EXTENSION of a term or a predicate is what it applies to or is true of—what it refers to (in the semantic sense) or denotes. The extension of a singular term is its referent. The extension of a predicate expression is generally taken to be the set of entities that the predicate applies to. Note that this is different from Russell's view of the reference of a predicate expression. As we saw in Chapter 2, Russell held that general terms referred to properties, or universals. As we will see below, in possible worlds semantics properties correspond to **senses** of predicates rather than their reference or extension.

Turning finally to sentences, following Frege, the extension of a sentence would be its truth value.

Before moving on, let us look at this picture of extensions in a slightly mathematical way which will bring out its compositional elegance. First, note that corresponding to any set we have an equivalent functional concept—the CHARACTERISTIC FUNCTION of that set. Characteristic functions always map to one of two values—typically 1 and 0, which can also be thought of as truth and falsity. For example the characteristic function of the set of students maps any student to the value 1, and everything else to 0. This equivalence between a set and its characteristic function gives us permission to regard the extension of a predicate expression either as the characteristic function of a set, or as the set itself—whichever is more convenient for the task at hand. If we take the characteristic function view of a predicate expression, then it will be able to take the extension of a singular term as its argument and yield a truth value—the extension of a sentence. Suppose we have a simple sentence like (31).

(31)   Mary is a student.

If the extension of *Mary* is a person (Mary), and the extension of the predicate *is a student* is the characteristic function of the set of students, then combining the subject with the predicate in (31) will automatically give us a truth value—1 (or true) if Mary belongs to the set of students, and 0 (or false) if Mary does not.

Seeing things this way makes the semantic behavior of combining these types of expressions very elegant, as well as perhaps making it seem not so strange to regard truth values as the extensions of sentences, and it will be important to keep it in mind in what follows in this chapter and the next. We will also make use of the set/characteristic function equivalence once again below in a slightly different context.

3.2.3 Intensions

We turn now to intensions.[5] The value of incorporating possible worlds into one's semantics is that we can recognize a reference or

---

[5] Note the funny spelling of "intension" with an "s." According to Geach (1962: 157n.) it originated in a spelling error by the noted nineteenth-century Irish mathematician Sir William Hamilton.

extension for expressions not only in the actual world but also in other possible worlds. The possible worlds formalization of the notion of the INTENSION of an expression brings these extensions together, and gives us something like a Fregean sense. In the most straightforward system, intensions are uniformly functions from possible worlds to extensions. Consider first singular terms: the extension of the definite description *the inventor of bifocals* in the actual world is Benjamin Franklin. The intension of that NP is a function which picks out of each possible world whoever it is who invented bifocals in that world (if there is any such person—eventually we will get to the problem of what happens if there is no such person). The intensions of singular terms are called INDIVIDUAL CONCEPTS.

I want to make a distinction between two kinds of individual concepts, variable and constant, which will be useful in subsequent chapters. As just noted, the definite description *the inventor of bifocals* denotes different people in different possible worlds, depending on the facts—who it is in each world who invented bifocals in that world. The individual concept expressed by that NP, then, will be a function that will give different results at different worlds—a VARIABLE INDIVIDUAL CONCEPT. On the other hand intuitively the individual concept expressed by the name *Benjamin Franklin* is different—in this case there is no basis for changing the reference of the name in different possible worlds.[6] It is true, there are possible worlds in which Benjamin Franklin is not **called** *Benjamin Franklin*, but those are not relevant here, just as the existence of possible worlds in which the name for four is *five* doesn't mean that two plus two might be five. Since we want to use possible worlds to provide a semantics for English, we need to keep our English constant. Thus the individual concept expressed by *Benjamin Franklin* is a CONSTANT INDIVIDUAL CONCEPT—a function which picks the same individual, Benjamin Franklin, out of every possible world. (In general, functions which give the same value for every argument are called "constant functions.") Constant individual concepts are useful because they correspond one-to-one to individuals.

We turn now to VPs or predicates—e.g. *is blue*, *talks like Rambo*, or *is a dog with spots*. The extension of a predicate expression can, as we have seen, be taken as the set of all the things which have the property

---

[6] In distinguishing proper names from definite descriptions in this way, I am tacitly assuming that Mill's nondescriptional view of proper names is correct, and thus that Frege and Russell were wrong. We look in detail at this issue below in Chapter 5.

TABLE 3.1. A tidy picture from the Golden Age of Pure Semantics

Type of phrase	Extension	Intension
definite NP e.g. proper name (*Marie Curie,...*), definite description (*the capital of France,...*)	an entity	an individual concept: a function from possible worlds to entities
VP e.g. *sing, be blue, write a letter*	a set of entities (alternatively, a function from entities to truth values)	a property: a function from possible worlds to sets of entities
S e.g. *Marie Curie wrote a letter*	a truth value	a proposition: a function from possible worlds to truth values (alternatively, a set of possible worlds)

in question. The intension of a predicate would thus be a function which yields, for each possible world, the set of things in that world which have the relevant characteristics.[7] This kind of intension is often considered to be the formal analysis of what a PROPERTY is.

Finally, as we have seen, the extension of a sentence is generally taken to be its truth value; its intension, then, is a function from possible worlds to the truth value the sentence has in each world. But, as we have also recently seen, the notion of a function with just two possible values is equivalent to a set. So, a function from possible worlds to truth values is equivalent to a set of possible worlds—the set in which the sentence has the value true. And this formal notion of sentence intension is a common analysis of what propositions are (though as we know, there are others—we return to this issue in §3.4 below). These notions we have just reviewed are summarized in Table 3.1.

It was suggested above that the characterization of intensions in terms of possible worlds is a formalization of the Fregean notion of sense. As we shall see below, it is not clear that this is entirely legitimate, but there are some arguments in its favor. As we saw in Chapter 2, Frege described sense as the mode of presentation of a referent. One could understand this as being something which, in conjunction with facts about the world, allows us to determine what the referent of the

---

[7] For the purposes of defining intensions, it is easier think of the extension of a predicate as a set rather than the corresponding characteristic function.

expression is. And that is what the intension of an expression models. A function from possible worlds to extensions says, in effect "Give me the facts about how things are and I will give you the extension." Given the close correspondence between referents and extensions, the parallel between senses and intensions should be clear. We return to this issue below in §3.4.

3.2.4 A note about time

The tidy picture given above and summarized in Table 3.1 is an oversimplification in one respect. We have noted that expressions may have different extensions in different possible worlds, depending on how the facts are arranged. However, facts can change over time as well, and thus expressions can experience corresponding changes. This is true not only for predicates like *is red* and *walks to school* but for also NPs like *the sixth grade teacher at New Paltz Elementary* and *Mary's boyfriend* which could naturally have different referents at different points of time within a single world, because of changes in what the facts are over time.[8] Thus to provide a satisfactory semantics, our intensions ought to take into account not only possible worlds but moments of time; those functions should be seen as functions from pairs of worlds and times, or world-time points, where each point is understood as a possible world at one time during its history.

One might ask whether this change in reference or extension that can occur with changes in time is not just an instance of indexicality (variation in reference which correlates with variation in features of the context of utterance of expressions). Thus the reference of *I* depends on who the speaker is, the reference of (demonstrative) *that* depends on what the speaker is pointing at, and so forth. Do we not need to consider a whole complex of indices in defining intensions—including not just possible world and time, but also

---

[8] There is another temporal aspect to NPs—one which concerns the time at which the CNP content holds of a denoted entity. Compare the examples in (i).

(i)   a.   The three fugitives are now in jail.
       b.   #There are three fugitives now in jail.

In (ia) we can use the term *fugitive* to describe people who are no longer fugitives, but not in (ib). We will not have space here to consider this kind of thing. See Musan (1999) for discussion.

speaker, addressee, location, indicated objects, etc.?[9] Although it is true that there are indexical temporal expressions—like *now, tomorrow*, and tense-markers—there is a difference between time and possible world, on the one hand, and the other proposed indices on the other, and that is that the other proposed indices do not change what the facts are. When we consider changes in reference that depend on possible world and time, we are considering changes that occur because of strictly extralinguistic facts; these changes occur for all kinds of expressions (e.g. *red, bachelor*), and not just indexical ones. On the other hand the variation that occurs for indexical expressions arises specifically because those expressions are defined in terms of features of the context of utterance in which they occur. We will return to the topic of indexicality, and how best to treat it, below in Chapter 8. Meanwhile, in the discussions of intensionality to follow, though I may sometimes neglect to mention moments of time in addition to possible worlds, they should always be assumed to be there unless explicitly excluded.

3.3 Extensionality and intensionality

Now that we have definitions of extensions and intensions, we can develop a few more useful concepts which apply to contexts.

3.3.1 Extensionality

A context is EXTENSIONAL if only the extensions of any of the constituent expressions are involved. In extensional contexts it is always possible to substitute a coreferential expression without changing the truth value. (We are following Frege's principle of compositionality of extensions here.) Ordinary predicates like *run, bump into, be bald*, express properties of, or relations among, ordinary entities—the referents of their NP arguments. As a consequence, given familiar identities, the (a) sentences below entail the (b) sentences.

(32)   a.   The inventor of bifocals was bald.
       b.   Benjamin Franklin was bald.

---

[9] In fact initially it was proposed that intensions should be functions from complexes including various indexical features such as speaker and place of utterance. (See, e.g., Lewis (1972: 175) and the works cited there.) However Kaplan (1977) argued for separating indexicality from intensional factors. We return to this issue below in Chapter 8.

(33) a. Socrates was curious.
      b. The ancient Greek philosopher who drank the hemlock was curious.

(34) a. Suzanne bumped into Ronald Reagan.
      b. Suzanne bumped into the 40th president of the US.

Although most predicates taking just NP arguments create extensional contexts, most embedded sentence contexts are **not** extensional. However there are a few. A prominent group of extensional sentence operators are the TRUTH FUNCTIONAL operators like *and, or,* and *not.* The truth value of a sentence in which one of these truth-functional operators is the main connective depends only on (is a function of) the truth values of its sentential argument(s). Consider the examples in (35).

(35) a. Mary didn't leave.
      b. Either the tree has a parasite or it needs water.

(35a) (our example (2a) from above) combines negation with the sentence *Mary left,* and (35a) is true if that sentence is false and false if it is true. (35b) is true if at least one of the two embedded sentences (*the tree has a parasite, it needs water*) is true, and false if they are both false. We could substitute any other sentence with the same truth value for any of these sentential arguments, and the truth value of the whole sentence would remain the same. The result might sound strange in the case of (35b)—we usually expect clauses combined with *or* to have something to do with each other—but the truth value would not be affected. Thus, suppose in this case that the tree does not have a parasite but that it does need water. Then we could substitute any other true sentence for *it needs water*—say *the world is round*—and preserve the truth value; the resulting sentence *Either the tree has a parasite or the world is round* sounds funny, but it is true.

3.3.2 Intensionality

A context is INTENSIONAL if what is expressed involves the intension of at least one of its constituents.[10] If a context is intensional, then

---

[10] There is a pernicious terminological situation that must be pointed out. The terms "intensional" and "intensionality" should not be confused with "intentional" and "intentionality." The latter pair have a use in semantics related to the fact that words refer to

substituting a coreferential expression within it may indeed change truth value. As noted above, most expressions which take sentential complements create intensional contexts. Modal operators are one kind of example. They take sentences as complements, and we cannot substitute a sentential complement of a modal operator on the basis of extension, i.e. truth value, alone and expect to preserve truth of the whole. In a sentence like (36)

(36)   It could have been the case that Boston was now the US capital.

the property of being possibly true (true in some possible world) is being predicated of the proposition that Boston is now the capital of the US.[11] (36) itself is true—although the US capital happens to be Washington DC, it is easy to imagine alternative possible worlds in which the founding fathers made a different decision about where to put the capital. The embedded sentence, *Boston is now the US capital*, is of course false given the way things have turned out in the actual world. However if we substitute another false sentence for that one in (36), we may go from truth of the whole, to falsehood. Thus in (37) below,

(37)   It could have been the case that $2 + 2 = 5$.

we have substituted $2 + 2 = 5$ for *Boston is now the US capital*. Unlike (36) though, (37) is false. Mathematical facts are necessarily the way they are.

Given that modal operators create intensional contexts, we expect the parts of those arguments to be intensions as well, and thus that we cannot substitute coreferential NPs within the complements of modals. And in fact that is the case: (38a) below is intuitively true, but not (38b).

(38)   a.   Al Gore might have been the 43rd president of the US.
       b.   Al Gore might have been George W. Bush.

Although George W. Bush was the 43rd president of the US in the actual world, that identity does not hold in all possible worlds, and in particular not in possible worlds in which Al Gore was the 43rd president.

---

things—the intentionality of language (and thought) is the fact that we can speak about (and think about) things external to the language (and our thoughts). Thus intentionality is more closely related to reference than sense.

[11]   I have used the present tense here because example (36) speaks of an alternative to the current US capital. The past tense in the complement sentence as it occurs in (36) is a result of sequence-of-tense rules plus the (morphological) past tense of *could*.

A subset of modal sentences consists of subjunctive conditionals, as in (39).

(39)   If the Supreme Court had insisted on a ballot recount, Al Gore would have been the 43rd president of the US.

Intuitively, in a true subjunctive conditional the *if* clause spells out conditions on possible worlds that will make the consequent (i.e. the modalized main clause) true. (Compare the analyses in Stalnaker (1968); Lewis (1973).) Like the other modal sentences, subjunctive conditionals are intensional.

Sentences about propositional attitudes are also (at least) intensional. As we noted in Chapter 2, in a propositional attitude sentence we cannot substitute complement clauses which merely have the same extension—i.e. the same truth value. Recall the examples about Copernicus, repeated below in (40).

(40)   a.   Copernicus believed that the earth revolves around the sun.
        b.   Copernicus believed that the planetary orbits are ellipses.

Although both complement clauses are true, (40a) is true while (40b) is false. So we cannot be guaranteed of a truth-preserving substitution based merely on the truth value of the embedded complement sentence. And again, given compositionality, this means that we also cannot substitute NPs within a propositional attitude complement sentence on the basis of reference alone, at least not on their narrow scope, *de dicto*, readings, as we have seen many times (recall the examples about Mary and the morning star, George IV and the author of *Waverley*, and Oedipus and his mother). However propositional attitude sentences are different from modal sentences: although sameness of intension is necessary for substitutivity in both cases, it is sufficient only in the case of the modals, as we will soon see.

3.4 Propositions

It is time to take a closer look at propositions. Several different conceptions of what propositions are have been lurking around, and it's time to bring them into the light to see what the problems are. We can be guided in this task by the claim, which we found to be implicit or explicit in comments of Mill and Frege, that propositions are simultaneously the objects of propositional attitudes and what are expressed by sentences. Of course this raises a potential terminological problem (which in fact is realized in some cases), namely, if you have a conception of propositions which turns out not to be adequate for capturing sentence meanings or the objects of propositional attitudes, do you keep on calling those things "propositions" and get another name for, e.g., the objects of the attitudes, or do you insist that whatever propositions are they are the objects of the attitudes? Unfortunately different people make different choices, so the buyer must beware.

We'll look first at the possible worlds conception of propositions which we saw just a few pages back. There are some problems with that view, so we'll follow that with some other possible analyses.

3.4.1 Propositions as sets of possible worlds

Propositions, on the possible worlds conception, are sets of possible worlds or, equivalently, functions from possible worlds to truth values. This conception fits naturally with the view that intensions in general, formalized as functions from possible worlds to extensions, can be taken as a formal analysis of Fregean senses. So let us see what can be said in favor of this view before we turn to the problems for it. Let us measure it against the two roles propositions have been assumed to fill—sentence meanings and objects of propositional attitudes.

Identifying sentence meanings with sentence intensions reflects the idea that to give the meaning of a sentence is to give its truth conditions—to specify what the world would have to be like for the sentence to be true. "Specify what the world would have to be like for a sentence to be true" is just another way of saying "specify what possible worlds a sentence would be true in." There is a great deal of appeal in this approach. First, it captures the idea that when we know what a sentence means, then all we need are the relevant facts about the world to know whether that sentence is true or not. And conversely, if we are in control of the relevant facts but are unsure whether a given sentence is true, that indicates that we do not have a full grasp of its meaning. Secondly, this view of sentence meanings accords well with what seems to be a primary function of language, and that is to allow us to convey information to each other about the way the world is. If someone tells us something true that we did not know before, and we believe that person, then we have learned something about the world. These very basic facts support the popular view that the proposition a sentence expresses, seen as its meaning, is appropriately analyzed as a function from possible worlds to truth values, or a set of possible worlds.

Turning to the idea that propositions defined as sets of possible worlds are the objects of propositional attitudes, we can find arguments in its favor too. To have a belief, on this approach, is to believe the actual world to be a member of a given set of possible worlds—those where the believed proposition holds. To have a desire is to have a preference among alternative sets. It is not surprising that the attractiveness of this picture has caused it to be embraced and defended even in the face of the grave difficulty which we are about to examine.[12]

The problem is that sets of possible worlds are apparently not fine-grained enough to allow us to adequately distinguish either all the different sentence meanings from each other, or all the different objects of propositional attitudes. One kind of problematic case is presented by sentences about mathematical facts. (We'll look at some other problematic cases below in Chapter 5.) As noted above, mathematical facts are generally assumed to hold necessarily—that is, in all possible worlds. But on the possible worlds view of propositions, being true at the same set of worlds counts as being the same proposition. This means that there can only be one necessary proposition on the possible worlds view—the proposition that is true in all possible worlds. However (a) there seem to be differences in meaning among statements of mathematical truths, and (b) it seems possible for people to, say, believe to be true some of those statements and not others. Consider the examples in (41) and (42).

(41) a. Two plus two equals four.
      b. Any map can be successfully colored in four colors.

(42) a. Mary knows that two plus two equals four.
      b. Mary knows that any map can be successfully colored in four colors.

By "successfully colored", we mean that no border has the same color on both sides. (41b) states the four-color theorem, which was long thought to be true and which has now been proved (with the help of computers). So (41a) and (41b) are both necessarily true, and hence they express the same proposition on the possible worlds conception of

---

[12] Stalnaker has been one of the most consistent defenders of sets of possible worlds as objects of propositional attitudes. See, e.g., Stalnaker (1976, 1984, 1999).

propositions. However these two sentences certainly do not seem to have the same meaning—so this is one way in which sets of possible worlds do not adequately capture the Fregean concept of sentence sense—the thought a sentence expresses.

Similarly we cannot distinguish the pieces of knowledge ascribed to Mary in (42a) and (42b) on the possible worlds view, yet it seems obvious that one of these sentences could be true and the other false—e.g. that Mary knows that two plus two is four, but does not know that she only needs four colors to color all her maps. Thus sets of possible worlds do not seem adequate for the analysis of propositional attitude sentences either.[13] Propositional attitude sentences are therefore sometimes described as being not only intensional, but HYPERINTENSIONAL. (This problem does not arise for modal sentences, whose complements are adequately seen as being sets of possible worlds.)

This problem has been known about for a long time; indeed Carnap (1947) had pointed it out, and proposed an alternative account of the objects of propositional attitudes. We'll get to that shortly, but first we should look at one possible modification of the possible worlds view.

3.4.2 Propositions as sets of situations

Barwise and Perry (1981, 1983) introduced the idea of using sets of situations, rather than possible worlds, in the analysis of propositional attitude sentences. A SITUATION, on their account, consists of entities bearing relations at a particular place and time. Thus a situation is like a little scenario which is typically much smaller than a possible world

---

[13] One might wonder whether or not sentence meanings and the objects of propositional attitudes always coincide, in the sense that adequacy or inadequacy of a definition of one is always mirrored by adequacy or inadequacy in the definition of the other. Benson Mates (1950) offered an interesting example that seems to show that they do **not** always coincide. Assume that we have a pair of terms that are generally agreed to be totally synonymous—say *oculist* and *eye doctor*. Still, the two will not be intersubstitutable in the propositional attitude sentence in (ia) below; (ia) seems true, but (ib) could possibly be false.

(i)   a.   Nobody doubts that whoever believes that oculists are oculists believes that oculists are oculists.

       b.   Nobody doubts that whoever believes that oculists are oculists believes that oculists are eye doctors.

In pointing out this kind of example Mates was presenting a problem for Carnap's intensional isomorphism idea, which we meet below in §3.4.3.

(although maximal COURSES OF EVENTS (sequences of situations) did correspond to possible worlds in some formulations). Crucially, if an entity is not a part of a certain situation, nothing is implied about that entity, unlike the case of possible worlds, which are informationally complete. If we consider the pair of sentences in (41) above, we can now distinguish them. (41a) denotes[14] all those situations containing the number two and in which two added to itself yields four, while (41b) denotes a different set of situations involving maps. Thus the two are distinguished semantically. Similarly we have two different objects of belief for Mary in the examples in (42).

The original Barwise and Perry program suffered to some extent from some shifts in assumptions and the lack of a complete formalization.[15] However a modified version of situation semantics received a major boost in an article by Angelika Kratzer (1989). An important aspect of Kratzer's version is the part of ($\leq$) relation, specifying when a situation can be part of a larger situation. On this version, then, possible worlds are simply maximal situations that are not a part of any larger situation. Kratzer argued that by adding constraints to capture what may legitimately be regarded as parts of a situation, several problems in the analysis of subjunctive conditionals (such as (7b) and (39) above) could be solved.[16] Since then a number of others have adopted approaches based on situations (cf. e.g., Elbourne (2008) and the works cited there). In the coming chapters we will see occasions where it is useful to have something like situations at hand and we will make use of them.

3.4.3 Intensional structure

As noted above, Carnap was well aware of the problem that logically equivalent sentences present for the analysis of meaning and the objects of propositional attitudes as sentence intensions. Carnap's solution was to introduce INTENSIONAL STRUCTURE into the

---

[14] The use of "denote" here is correct. Barwise and Perry follow Davidson (1969) in rejecting both Frege's sense–reference distinction and his claim of a shift in reference in propositional attitude contexts. On the Barwise and Perry view, sentences (or more properly utterances) never denote truth values, and always denote sets of situations.

[15] See the articles in *Linguistics and Philosophy* Volume 8:1, especially those by Partee and Soames; and see also Barwise (1989).

[16] But see the discussion of Kratzer's paper in Kanazawa et al. (2005), which casts doubt on Kratzer's analysis.

picture: two sentences are intensionally isomorphic (i.e. they have the same intensional structure) if they have the same syntactic structure, and all of the parts of that structure (each of the corresponding words and phrases) have the same intension. It might be thought that this would tie the objects of belief too closely to a particular language, but by having the same "structure," Carnap intended something more abstract than the details of one language. To use his example, the two sentences in (43) below would be considered to be intensionally isomorphic (cf. Carnap 1947: 56f.).

(43)   a. $5 > 3$
       b. $Gr(V, III)$

The exact order of constituents isn't important; what is important is the fact that, in both cases, we have a predicate expressing the same two-place relation (that of being greater than), plus two names for the same numbers (five and three).

In order to make Carnap's idea workable we might envision the objects of propositional attitudes to be sentences of some ideal formal language, or perhaps a mental language of some kind, where the "words" and "phrases" that make the sentences up are senses (meanings) or intensional entities—functions from possible worlds (or situations) to extensions. See Lewis (1972) for an approach developed along Carnapian lines.

We should note that Carnap did not call these structured intensional entities "propositions," reserving that term for sentence intensions (sets of possible worlds). (This is one of those terminological pitfalls associated with the word "proposition" which we alluded to above.) However currently many scholars do use the term "proposition" for such structured entities, seen as the objects of propositional attitudes as well as sentence meanings. It is an interesting question as to whether propositions seen as sets of situations would be individuated on exactly the same lines as if they were analyzed as intensional structures of the type Carnap proposed.

3.4.4 Russellian singular propositions

Recall from the preceding chapter that Russell thought that on those rare occasions when one is using the demonstrative pronoun *this* to refer to something in the immediate surroundings, one could express a particular kind of proposition—one that has an actual entity in it.

Standing in front of a red barn, for instance, one might utter (44a), and express the proposition represented in (44b).

(44) a.   This [pointing at the barn] is red.
      b.   <the barn, the property of being red>

The proposition represented in (44b) is a structured entity (in this case an ordered pair) which contains the barn plus the property of being red. This idea is somewhat similar to Carnap's except that in place of an individual concept we have an ordinary individual. We will see in subsequent chapters that many philosophers of language currently like the idea of Russellian singular propositions; however I will try to argue against them.

3.4.5 Summary

In this section we have reviewed several possible analyses of propositions. We began with the possible worlds view, and saw a serious problem for it—the fact that it does not individuate propositions finely enough. Following that we looked at some alternatives—the use of situations instead of possible worlds, and then a view of propositions as structured combinations of intensions, or intensions in combination with actual entities. Although the problem for possible worlds semantics looks serious, we're nevertheless going to stick with it for one more chapter since it was an integral part of the Golden Age of Pure Semantics, and thus of Montague Grammar. But first we need to look at one other feature of intensional (including hyperintensional) contexts.

3.5 Existence independence

The reader will recall that a context is extensional if just the extensions of any of the constituent expressions are involved. Thus, as we have seen, the contexts created by modal operators and propositional attitude predicates are not extensional: they do not allow substitution *salva veritate* of complement clauses with the same truth value or, within those complement clauses, substitution of coreferential NPs on their narrow-scope, *de dicto*, interpretation. There is another characteristic shared by some of these intensional predicates, and that is their ability to occur with empty or nondenoting NPs in their complements. So, for example, something like (45)

(45)   Mary wants to meet <u>a Martian</u>.

could be true on the narrow-scope reading. The (old-fashioned style) logical form for (45) on the narrow-scope reading,

(46)   Mary wants $\exists x[\text{Martian}(x) \ \& \ \text{meet}(\text{Mary}, x)]$

shows an existential quantifier within the scope of *wants*, which does not imply real world existence. Similarly nondenoting definite descriptions can occur *de dicto* in the intensional contexts of true sentences, as illustrated in (47).

(47)   Dreamers think that <u>the philosopher's stone</u> will solve all their problems.

Following Graeme Forbes (2006), let us call this property EXISTENCE INDEPENDENCE. Ordinary extensional contexts do not have this property. Examples like those in (48)

(48)   a.   Mary met <u>a Martian</u>.
        b.   <u>The philosopher's stone</u> is on display in Philadelphia.

must be literally false (or without any truth value) because of the emptiness of the relevant NPs.

Although existence independence overlaps to a large extent with intensionality, the two are not completely coextensive. For example, some propositional attitude predicates are FACTIVE, meaning that the truth of their complement clause is implied. Examples are *know, be happy (that), regret*. Such verbs will give rise to the *de dicto-de re* ambiguity, and failures of substitution on the *de dicto* readings. Thus, as we have seen, (49a) and (49b) can differ in truth value.

(49)   a.   Mary knows that the morning star is a planet.
        b.   Mary knows that the evening star is a planet.

However given the nonexistence of the philosopher's stone, (50) cannot be literally true.

(50)   Mary knows that the philosopher's stone is on display in Philadelphia.

Since a sentence with *know* implies that the complement of *know* is true, the falsity of the complement in (50) means that the whole sentence cannot be true. Thus the existence independence property does not occur with factive predicates. Nevertheless this property has traditionally been taken to be a hallmark of intensionality. Thus, according to Chisholm, the important late nineteenth- to early twentieth-century German philosopher and psychologist Franz Brentano believed that

what is common to mental phenomena and what distinguishes them from the physical is "intentional inexistence", which he also described as "reference to a content" and "direction upon an object". Mental phenomena, he said, may be defined as phenomena that "include an object intentionally within themselves".... The essential point, as he later emphasized, is that a person could think of a horse even if there were no horse.   (Chisholm 1967: 365)

This property was also important to Montague, as we shall see.

3.6 Summary

In this chapter we have looked more closely at some of the concepts and phenomena that were introduced in Chapter 2. We looked more closely at the semantics of quantificational NPs, seeing that they could be viewed as complex sentence operators. We developed a simple notation that was intended to reveal the structure of such NPs better than either natural language or traditional logical notation. (But don't worry—we'll have lots more formal notation in the next chapter.) We looked at the scope ambiguities that arise when two or more scope-taking expressions interact, as well as some complications for these sentences. We turned then to some of the basics of possible worlds semantics, focusing on the formal characterization of intensions, which represent to some degree the Fregean notion of sense. We saw one problem for possible worlds semantics, and looked at some alternative ways to think about the important concept of propositions, using situations instead of possible worlds, or viewing propositions as structured objects. However, we are going to put those alternatives aside for the time being, while we look at Montague's work, since he used possible worlds semantics to construct the most explicit grammar of an interesting fragment of English that the world has ever seen.

4

The proper treatment of quantification

"Contrariwise," continued Tweedledee, "if it was so, it might be; and if it were so, it would be; but as it isn't, it ain't. That's logic."

Lewis Carroll, *Alice Through the Looking-Glass*

At the beginning of the twentieth century predicate logic with quantification had only recently been formalized. In fact only the syntax was formalized at that time; it remained until the work of Tarski and others during the 1930s to formalize the semantics for quantificational languages. Much of the original motivation for developing formal languages was for the investigation of mathematics, but the relation between these formal languages and natural languages (English, Swahili, Ojibwa, etc.) was always of interest. The philosophical community was of two minds about this relation. Formalists like Frege, Russell, the early Wittgenstein, and Carnap tended to think that, because of their explicitness and lack of ambiguity, formal languages were superior to natural languages for philosophical investigation. On the other hand so-called "ordinary language" philosophers like the later Wittgenstein, Austin, and Strawson were of the opinion that natural languages, with all the richness of the distilled insight of generations of speakers, were excellent tools when used with care and that formal languages had perils of their own.

In the late 1960s two philosophers of strikingly different backgrounds, a young American logician and an established and highly respected British ordinary language philosopher, each challenged a crucial background assumption in the formalist vs ordinary language debate—the assumption that natural languages and formal languages are quite different from each other. Richard Montague began his paper "Universal grammar" with characteristic boldness:

There is in my opinion no important theoretical difference between natural languages and the artificial languages of logicians; indeed, I consider it possible to comprehend the syntax and semantics of both kinds of languages within a single natural and mathematically precise theory. On this point I differ from a number of philosophers.... (Montague 1970: 222)

Only a few years earlier, in his William James Lectures delivered at Harvard University in 1967, H. Paul Grice had remarked:

I wish... to maintain that the common assumption... that the divergences [between natural and formal languages] do in fact exist is (broadly speaking) a common mistake, and that the mistake arises from an inadequate attention to the nature and importance of the conditions governing conversation. (Grice 1975: 24)

Besides indicating something of the difference in personalities between the forbidding Montague and the gentler-sounding Grice, the two quotations above also give a hint as to the different approaches the two took in addressing this "common mistake" of overestimating the divergences between formal and natural languages. Montague applied the methods of formal languages to natural language, while Grice sought an explanation for the apparent divergences in the conversational use of natural language. The two carried out their respective programs with remarkable success, and as a consequence subsequent generations of linguists have had at their command a much more sophisticated arsenal of formal devices, while at the same time having access to the groundwork for a systematic program for separating semantic from pragmatic facts and accounting for the latter. It would be very difficult to overestimate the impact either Montague or Grice has had on semantic theory in contemporary linguistics.

In this chapter we look at the contributions of each of these important figures. We'll have space for just one brief section on Grice's work, which will hopefully supply us with what we need for the purposes of this book. Montague's work, besides being much more difficult than Grice's, is also more central to our concerns. Thus the remainder of the chapter will be devoted to it, plus some developments which arose out of it.

4.1 Grice and conversational implicatures

As we have just seen, Grice believed that apparent troublesome differences between natural and formal languages could be explained by attention to the fact that natural languages are used for conversation.

His William James lectures, titled "Logic and conversation," were never published as such, although eventually the second lecture, which contained the essentials of his approach, was published under the title "Logic and conversation" (Grice (1975); that lecture together with revised versions of some of the remaining lectures appeared posthumously as part of Grice (1989)). Grice's main concern in this work was to give a systematic explanation for apparent divergences between the semantics of logical operators ($\sim$, $\rightarrow$, $\forall$ and so forth) and their natural language counterparts (*not*, *if*, *every*, etc.). However, as we shall see, the concepts he developed have proved even more fruitful and far-reaching.

First, Grice distinguished WHAT IS SAID in an utterance from two other contributions to the total that a speaker may convey: CONVENTIONAL IMPLICATURES and CONVERSATIONAL IMPLICATURES. What is said, according to Grice, corresponds essentially to the truth conditions of the utterance. This includes the primary proposition expressed under the possible worlds conception of propositions, plus anything else that is entailed by that proposition.[1] (One proposition is ENTAILED by another if its truth is required for the other's truth.)

Conventional implicatures are propositions semantically encoded in an utterance but secondary to that which makes an utterance true or false. (1) is one of Grice's examples (note the wry sense of humor).

(1)   He is an Englishman; he is, therefore, brave.

According to Grice (1) would be true if and only if the person referred to with *he* is both English and brave. So what is said in an utterance of (1) would remain the same if *therefore* were replaced with *and*. The element of meaning conveyed by *therefore*—the implied connection between being English and being brave—is one example of a conventional implicature. Another example is to be found in (2):

(2)   Even George could solve this problem.

According to Grice's way of thinking, (2) is true if George could solve the indicated problem. The idea conveyed by *even*—that others could solve the problem more readily than George—is another example of a conventional implicature.

Conversational implicatures, the centerpiece of Grice's work, are rather different (and thus the similarity of the term to "conventional

---

[1] As noted above in Chapter 1, it is really a mistake to speak of **the** proposition expressed by (a use of) a sentence, since typically more than one proposition is expressed.

implicatures" has proved somewhat problematic). Conversational implicatures are propositions which a speaker assumes a hearer will gather as a result of their (the hearer's) assumption that the speaker is being cooperative in the conversation—is trying their best to tell the truth, to give an appropriate amount of information, to be relevant, and so forth. (I'm making a long story very short here—Grice developed a whole theory of conversation in order to give an account of conversational implicatures.) Here are a couple of Grice's examples: (i) You have run out of gas. I say:

(3)   There's a gas station around the corner.

I conversationally implicate that for all I know, the gas station is open and has gas to sell. (ii) I am writing a letter of recommendation for a student of mine. I write:

(4)   This student has excellent handwriting and usually was in class
       on time.

I conversationally implicate that this student is not very good at the subject matter.

Conversational implicatures are a pragmatic phenomenon; as such they can be cancelled, denied, or otherwise gotten rid of. In this they are unlike semantically encoded elements of meaning (entailments and conventional implicatures). Thus if I try to get rid of an entailment, or a conventional implicature of my utterance, anomaly is the result, as shown in (5).

(5)   a.   #He is English and he's brave—although he's a coward.
       b.   #Even Einstein could solve this problem.

In (5a) an entailment of the first part of the utterance (that he is brave) is contradicted in the second part with the assertion that he's a coward, and the result is anomaly. Similarly in (5b) our real world knowledge that Einstein was a very smart person conflicts with the conventional implicature associated with *even* in this sentence, and again the result is anomaly. Conversational implicatures, on the other hand, can be contradicted or denied without anomaly. The utterer of (3), for example, could have continued their utterance as in (6), getting rid of the conversational implicatures without any anomaly.

(6)   There's a gas station around the corner, but it may well not be
       open. And given how scarce gas is these days, it probably doesn't
       have any gas.

The fact that these additions are felicitous means that what they deny cannot be encoded in the first part of the utterance.

One of the apparent divergences which Grice was concerned with was the difference between the logical quantifier $\exists$, on the one hand, and its English counterpart *some*, on the other. In English if I assert (7), for instance,

(7)   Some students passed the test.

my addressee will naturally conclude that some of the students failed— that not all of them passed. That is, my addressee will conclude that (8) is **not** true.

(8)   Every student passed the test.

This kind of inference is so ready and natural as to suggest that *some* might actually **mean** "not all"—it might have that encoded as a part of its semantics. But that would make *some* definitely distinct from its counterpart in logic. The sentences in logic which correspond to (7) and (8), which are given below in (9) (in traditional notation), are perfectly consistent with each other.

(9)   a. $\exists x[\text{student}(x) \ \& \ \text{passed-the-test}(x)]$
      b. $\forall x[\text{student}(x) \rightarrow \text{passed-the-test}(x)]$

In fact, given the existence of students, (9b) **entails** (9a).

What Grice proposed is that *some* semantically encodes the same meaning as the logical particle $\exists$, and that the "not all" proposition which typically gets conveyed in an utterance like (7) is a conversational implicature. If the speaker in this case knew that all of the students had passed, it would have been more informative to say that. If we assume that the speaker was being cooperative, and thus giving all the relevant information, we would conclude that the speaker was not in a position to say that all of the students passed. Hence they conversationally implicate that not all of the students passed.

As it turns out this is just one example from a large and significant category of conversational implicatures, called SCALAR IMPLICATURES.[2] Natural languages have many sets of vocabulary items which group themselves on a scale of force. Some examples from English are given in (10):

---

[2] Scalar implicatures received their name as well as their original investigation from Horn (1972). See Horn (2004) for a survey of implicature and further references.

(10)   a.   *all/every > most > some > a few*
       b.   *certain > likely > probable > possible*
       c.   *freezing > cold > chilly*

Use of any other than the strongest of one of these sets will typically convey that, as far as the speaker knows, any stronger items do not apply. So if I assert (11), for example:

(11)   It's possible that this sample contains gold.

I convey that it's not probable, much less likely or certain, that it does. This is another example of a scalar implicature. Scalar implicatures, like the other conversational implicatures we have seen, are cancelable, as shown by the naturalness of the examples in (12).

(12)   a.   Some students passed the test—indeed all of them did.
       b.   It's possible that this sample contains gold—and in fact I'm quite certain that it does.

The speaker of either sentence in (12) contradicts with the second part of their utterance what would have been conversationally implicated by the first part, and no anomaly results.

Scalar implicatures deny a more informative proposition. There is another, opposite, kind of conversational implicature which **is** a more informative proposition. Someone who asserts (13), for instance,

(13)   Alexander was able to complete the project.

would normally convey something stronger—that Alexander actually did complete the project. We could call implicatures like this "informativeness" implicatures (following Levinson (2000)). Another example is given in (14):

(14)   Jalen doesn't like spinach.

Normally utterance of (14) would convey something stronger than just that Jalen lacks a positive attitude toward spinach—namely, it would convey that she actually dislikes spinach. Informativeness implicatures, like other kinds of implicatures, may be cancelled without anomaly, as illustrated in (15).

(15)   a.   Alexander was able to complete the project, but chose not to.
       b.   Jalen doesn't like spinach, but she doesn't dislike it either—she's pretty neutral on it.

Obviously there is much more to be said here—why are there these different competing kinds of implicature, and what determines which kind is drawn? Unfortunately pursuing these issues would take us too far afield; for a more substantial introduction to the topic of conversational implicature, see Horn (2004) and the works cited there. I hope that from these brief remarks the reader can get some sense of the potential significance of Grice's contributions, as well as an idea of what is meant by "implicature." And now that we have seen a little bit of how we might view natural language semantics as closer to the semantics of formal languages, it is time to see how natural languages might in fact be treated just like formal languages.

4.2 Introduction to Montague's work

Montague's work was the culmination of a whole series of developments in the application of symbolic logic to the semantics of natural language, accomplished during the twentieth century through contributions of a number of important figures: Tarski, Carnap, Church, Prior, Hintikka, Kripke, Kaplan, and others, in addition to Frege and Russell. We reviewed some of those developments in the last two chapters. In this chapter we will concentrate on Montague's most well-known accomplishment—the grammar which he presented in his 1973 paper "The proper treatment of quantification in ordinary English," otherwise known as PTQ.

Before getting started I must warn readers, especially those new to formal semantics, that Montague's work, while extremely complex and elegant, is correspondingly difficult, and his compact presentations make no concessions to the uninitiated reader. Indeed, practicing logicians were known to find his work challenging when it first appeared. In fact Montague's work almost certainly would not have had the influence it has had in linguistics without the assistance of Barbara Partee, who promoted it in the early 1970s (after Montague's untimely death) and provided clear explanations of its workings to linguists in a number of lectures and papers—most notably her class at the 1974 Linguistic Society of America Summer Institute, and her lengthy 1975 paper "Montague Grammar and Transformational Grammar." I am taking the trouble to present the PTQ grammar here for several reasons, among them its inherent value as a complete and explicit grammar which solves important problems in semantics, its historical importance for linguists, and its elegance and beauty. There are also concrete contributions which can be traced back to the PTQ grammar—the introduction of generalized quantifiers, the systematic use of (and notation for) semantic types, and the use of individual concepts.

Below we will look first at a couple of problems in the description of natural language which particularly concerned Montague. Following that, we turn to a somewhat detailed overview of the PTQ grammar itself. This is followed in §4.5 by some illustrative examples, a discussion of individuals vs individual concepts in §4.6, and some remarks about Montague's treatment of proper names in §4.7. In §4.8 we look at a couple of important papers which appeared subsequent to PTQ and which developed aspects of this work. There is a brief concluding section at the end of the chapter.

4.3 Two problems

In this section we look at two particular problems which Montague wanted to solve with his PTQ grammar. The first was allowing for intensional constructions, and the second concerned quantificational NPs. Let us look at each of these in turn.

4.3.1 Rampant intensionality?

As we saw in the quote from Montague at the beginning of this chapter, Montague believed that natural languages could be described with the same kind of rigor and explicitness which is routine in the description of "the artificial languages of logicians." Intensionality is one big difference between natural language and traditional formal languages. Since mathematical facts do not involve hopes and dreams, and are all necessarily the way they are, there is no need for propositional attitude or modal notions in a language geared to talk only of mathematical facts. But as noted above, logicians have always been interested in the semantics of natural language, and as we saw in the last chapter, intensional logics involving possible worlds had been developed beginning with Carnap's work in the 1940s. However Montague found a way to adapt intensional logic more directly to natural language than had been done before, and in a way that was more sensitive to natural language structure.

To accomplish the task of treating a natural language like a formal language Montague had to provide for the full panoply of intensional constructions. This includes not only modal sentences and sentences about propositional attitudes like the ones we have looked at in earlier chapters, but also some other troublesome constructions which we have not yet seen. For example, the propositional attitude sentences we have seen up to now all had complements which were either obviously clausal (as in (16a)) or could plausibly be seen as clausal, as in (16b).[3]

(16) a. The students are forgetting <u>that the morning star is Venus.</u>
      b. Oedipus wanted <u>to marry his mother.</u>

However, simple transitive verbs like *look for* and *seek* also seem to create intensional contexts, as shown by the characteristics of failure of substitutivity and existence independence. For example, it seems that (17a) could be true without (17b) being true, and (17c) has a reading which does not require the existence of unicorns for its truth.

(17) a. Oedipus is looking for his mother.
      b. Oedipus is looking for Jocasta.
      c. Oedipus is looking for a unicorn.

Oedipus could be looking for his mother while sitting in the same room with Jocasta, not realizing that she was his mother, which would make (17a) true and (17b) false. And (17c) could be true even though there aren't any unicorns. This presents a problem for Russell's analysis: because there is only one clause in (17a), there is only one way to apply his analysis to the denoting phrase *his mother*. That means that *his mother* can only have wide scope (primary occurrence, in Russell's terms), so the (apparent) failure of substitutivity and lack of existence entailment are not accounted for, nor is the nonspecific reading of (17c).

Quine (1956: 101f.) had noticed this problem, and suggested a paraphrase like the one in (18) (this was not exactly Quine's example):

(18) Oedipus is endeavoring that he find his mother.

In (18) we have an embedded clause, and thus we can represent both narrow-scope and wide-scope interpretations as in (19).

(19) a. the$_x$ [mother-of-Oed(x)](endeavor(Oed, find(Oed, x)))
      b. endeavor(Oed, the$_x$ [mother-of-Oed(x)](find(Oed, x)))

---

[3] As we noted in Chapter 2, although it is common to regard infinitival VP complements as in (16b) as containing an empty PRO subject, Montague himself did not do so.

However Montague was worried about some other verbs which seem to create intensional contexts, but which resist paraphrase with a sentential complement, like *worship* and *conceive*.[4] Thus, for example, when I worship my idol (Elvis Presley), there doesn't seem to be any proposition involved—I simply worship **him**, and there's no way to paraphrase it with an embedded sentence. Montague also thought there were **intransitive** verbs, e.g. *rise*, whose **subject** position was intensional—if the temperature is equal to 90° and is rising, still we cannot conclude that 90° is rising, which suggests a failure of substitutivity. (Montague credited this example to his colleague "Professor Partee.") He also thought that some prepositions, e.g. *about*, created intensional contexts; *Mary is talking about a unicorn* does not imply that there are any unicorns.

Montague's conclusion was that intensionality could be found throughout English, that any category of expressions that take arguments contains at least one or two expressions that create opaque or intensional contexts. As a result he analyzed **every** argument position as potentially intensional.

4.3.2 Quantificational NPs and generalized quantifiers

The other big problem for Montague involved the analysis of NPs. Recall that Montague wanted to treat natural languages like the formal languages of logic. For the latter sort of language, the syntax is constructed in such a way as to make the semantic interpretation as transparent as possible. The tight compositionality of these languages is embodied in the fact that, corresponding to each syntactic rule allowing constituents to be combined to form a phrase there is a semantic rule saying how the meaning of that phrase is determined by the meanings of the constituents that make it up. This is sometimes referred to as RULE-TO-RULE CORRESPONDENCE. As a consequence, constituents of a given syntactic category must all make the same

---

[4] Here Montague was using existence independence, rather than failure of substitutivity, as his criterion for intensionality. In retrospect it appears that by the substitutivity criterion *worship*, at any rate, is not actually intensional. On the other hand it has been argued that the Quinean paraphrases for verbs like *seek* are not adequate, and Partee (1974) pointed out a number of other simple transitive verbs (*owe*, *advertise for*) which show the characteristics of *de dicto-de re* ambiguity and/or existence independence but which do not have adequate paraphrases with sentential complements. On the basis of this and other evidence, she argued convincingly that on balance the Montagovian solution of allowing intensionality in direct object position was necessary. See Forbes (2006) for a recent treatment.

type of contribution to phrases containing them, although the particulars will differ. For example, if an expression of some syntactic category (say verb phrase, or VP) denotes a set, then all the other expressions of that category will also denote sets, although which particular set each denotes will naturally vary.

In natural languages it does not appear to be the case that expressions that behave alike syntactically necessarily behave alike semantically, and the category of NPs appears to be a case where there is a major mismatch. Let us assume, for the time being, that Mill was right about proper names—that they simply denote whatever they denote without implying any properties. This assumption is reflected in the fact that in a typical logical language proper names would correspond to individual constants, symbols that belong to the same category as individual variables but that stand for particular entities. Thus the usual translation for a sentence like (20a) would be something like (20b).

(20)   a.   Kim talks.
       b.   talk(k)

As we have seen, *talk* is naturally construed as a function from entities to truth values: applied to the denotation of *k* (the person Kim) it yields the value true if Kim talks, and false if she does not. Similarly pronouns are often assimilated to individual variables of logic, in at least some of their uses. So, ignoring gender, a sentence like (21a) might receive the translation in (21b).

(21)   a.   She talks.
       b.   talk(x)

Of course neither (21a) nor (21b) expresses a complete thought as is; we would need to link the pronoun or the variable to something else for that.

Turning now to quantificational NPs, we have seen that they receive quite a different translation. The sentences in (22) would receive the corresponding translations in (23) in traditional logic.

(22)   a.   No canary talks.
       b.   Every canary talks.
       c.   The canary talks.
(23)   a. $\sim\exists x[canary(x) \ \& \ talk(x)]$
       b. $\forall x[canary(x) \rightarrow talk(x)]$
       c. $\exists x[\forall y[canary(y) \leftrightarrow y = x] \ \& \ talk(x)]$

The translations of the NPs in (22) are very different from the translations *Kim* and *she* received in (20b) and (21b). In (23a), for example, *no canary* receives the discontinuous translation $\sim\exists x[canary(x) \&\dots(x)]$. Note that the same holds true if we use the restricted quantifier notation introduced in the last chapter, according to which the representations for the sentences in (22) would appear as (24).

(24) a. $no_x\,[canary(x)](talk(x))$
      b. $every_x\,[canary(x)](talk(x))$
      c. $the_x\,[canary(x)](talk(x))$

Here again *no canary* receives a discontinuous translation (*no_x [canary (x)](... (x))*).

However, in a natural language proper names and pronouns have exactly the same privileges of occurrence as quantificational NPs; in any position in a sentence where a proper name or a pronoun could occur, there could instead be a quantified NP, and vice versa.[5] However, if the logical forms in (20b), (21b), (23)/(24) are the correct analysis for the corresponding English sentences, quantificational NPs have a very different type of meaning from pronouns and proper names: while *Kim* and *she* get an analysis as a constituent, the quantificational NPs are analyzed only in the context of the sentence in which they occur and there is no constituent which corresponds exactly to them. This is an obstacle to a compositional analysis of English: we need a semantics which can assign an interpretation to every syntactic constituent type—an interpretation which can then combine with the interpretations of constituents which that type combines with, to yield the interpretation for the whole expression.

There seems to be no way to analyze quantificational expressions in general as being of the same type as individual constants;[6] there is no ordinary type of entity that we could assign as a referent to quantificational NPs like *no canary* or *every canary* that would allow the truth conditions of sentences like (22a) (*No canary talks*) and (22b) (*Every canary talks*) to come out correctly. (The case of *the canary* might turn out to be different; for the time being though, like Montague, we are

---

[5] There is actually at least one possible exception to this claim: a vocative NP (e.g. as in *Kylie—we're ready to leave now!*) must be a proper name or *you* (with or without an epithet like *bastard*). On the other hand maybe the location of a vocative NP doesn't count as being a "position in a sentence." I.e. maybe they are extra-syntactic.

[6] Below in Chapter 9 we will see that this, like almost every other statement in philosophical and linguistic semantics, has not gone unchallenged.

going with Russell on definite descriptions.) What Montague did was invent a new kind of interpretation that would work for both proper names and quantificational NPs: in the PTQ grammar all NPs denote sets of properties. To say that Kim talks is equivalent to saying that the property of talking is one of Kim's properties, and to say that every canary talks is to say that the property of talking is one that every canary has.

Let us introduce a new operator—the LAMBDA operator—which will help us to express this symbolically. The Greek letter λ (lambda) symbolizes a set-forming operation. For example, where x is a variable over individuals, the expression in (25) represents the (characteristic function of the) set of individuals that talk.

(25) $\lambda x[talk(x)]$

This has the same denotation as the predicate *talk* by itself. Assuming that k stands for Kim, (26) below says that Kim is a member of the set of individuals who talk (i.e., that applying the characteristic function of the set of talkers to Kim will yield the value true).

(26) $\lambda x[talk(x)](k)$

This is equivalent to saying that Kim talks; thus the formula in (26) is equivalent to the simpler formula in (27).

(27) $talk(k)$

We will return to this kind of equivalence shortly.

Up to now we have looked only at logical representations in what is called "first-order logic." First-order logic only has variables which range over ordinary individuals like people and chairs. But Montague used a higher-order logic—with variables ranging over sets of individuals, sets of sets of individuals, and so forth, as well as intensional entities of all types, such as individual concepts, properties, and properties of properties. Let us ignore properties and other intensional entities now, though, to have a slightly simpler introduction of the main idea behind Montague's analysis of NPs. I will use a capital S as a variable over sets of individuals. Then (28) represents the set of sets that Kim belongs to.

(28) $\lambda S[S(k)]$

If we combine the expression in (28) with a predicate like *talk*, we will get the formula in (29).

(29) $\lambda S[S(k)](talk)$

(29) says that the set of talkers is one of the sets that Kim belongs to. This formula, like the one in (26) above, is equivalent to (27).

In general, where X stands for a variable of any type, and $[\ldots X \ldots]$ is a sentence containing that variable, then $\lambda X[\ldots X \ldots]$ represents the set of things of the kind that the variable X stands for which satisfy the formula $[\ldots X \ldots]$. And when the lambda expression is combined with an expression of the same type as the variable, then the equivalence in (30) holds:[7]

(30) $\lambda X[\ldots X \ldots](A) \equiv [\ldots A \ldots]$

This equivalence allows us to move back and forth between expressions with lambdas and those without—a process called "lambda conversion." We have already talked about the two instances given explicitly below in (31).

(31)   a. $\lambda x[talk(x)](k) \equiv talk(k)$
        b. $\lambda S[S(k)](talk) \equiv talk(k)$

It can be seen that both of the equivalences in (31) are instances of the schema in (30).

Now we can use the device of lambda notation to represent the appropriate set of sets to interpret *no canary, every canary,* and *the canary*. These are shown in (32).

(32)   a. $\lambda S[\sim\exists x[canary(x) \mathbin{\&} S(x)]]$
        b. $\lambda S[\forall x[canary(x) \to S(x)]]$
        c. $\lambda S[\exists x[\forall y[canary(y) \leftrightarrow y = x] \mathbin{\&} S(x)]]$

The expressions in (28) and (32) are all of the same form ($\lambda S[\ldots S \ldots]$), and they all denote the same type of thing—a (characteristic function of a) set of sets. In each case we can combine these expressions with set-denoting expressions. Thus (33a) below says that the set of talkers is one that no canary belongs to. Using the lambda conversion equivalence in (30), we can convert this to (33b), which was our original traditional logic translation for *no canary talks*.

(33)   a. $\lambda S[\sim\exists x[canary(x) \mathbin{\&} S(x)]](talk)$
        b. $\sim\exists x[canary(x) \mathbin{\&} talk(x)]$

---

[7]   In some instances the equivalence in (30) does not hold. None of those occur here.

Using this type of analysis, we achieve the desired effect of assigning all kinds of NPs in English the same type of interpretation—all (even pronouns) are interpreted as sets of sets.

In the analysis just reviewed, NPs are analyzed as GENERALIZED QUANTIFIERS.[8] A generalized quantifier is simply a set of sets of entities. Actually, as we will see below, Montague used sets of properties in his analysis because of his concern with intensional constructions. However, the upshot is the same—that proper names and quantified NPs are able to have the same type of interpretation, and to combine with predicate expressions in the same way. It is important to be clear that a generalized quantifier serves as the interpretation for a complete NP, not just its determiner. Often, when we speak of "quantifiers," we are talking about quantificational determiners like *every* and *most*. We could think of quantificational determiners as expressing a two-place relation (between the CNP content and the rest of the sentence), while the generalized quantifier interpreting a whole NP expresses a one-place relation (aka a property) of what the rest of the sentence expresses. Toward the end of this chapter, and later on in Chapter 9, we will see other important applications of this concept which were developed initially by Jon Barwise and Robin Cooper in their seminal paper "Generalized quantifiers and natural language" (Barwise and Cooper 1981).

4.4 Overview of the PTQ grammar

We are now ready to put all of this together. As noted above, what has become known as "Montague Grammar" (or "Montague Semantics" by those who are interested only in the interpretive part) is based on the style of grammar Montague laid out in his (1973) paper "The proper treatment of quantification in ordinary English," or PTQ. The PTQ grammar does not analyze the whole English language, but instead a manageable (but recursive, and hence infinitely large) fragment. Montague designed the fragment to contain samples of the most interesting and challenging constructions, including the various kinds of intensional constructions he was worried about, as well as quantified NPs (including indefinite and definite descriptions) and proper names.

---

[8] Logicians prior to Montague had talked about generalized quantifiers (cf. the references in Barwise and Cooper (1981: 159)), but apparently Montague was unaware of this work. In any case he did not use the term "generalized quantifier" himself to describe his analysis of NPs in English.

The PTQ grammar has a three-part structure. The first part is a logician-style syntax for the fragment of English mentioned above. The second part consists of a complete grammar—syntax and semantics—for a rich intensional logic which Montague called "IL." This formal language was created to be fully as expressive as the English fragment. The third part of the PTQ grammar contains a set of completely explicit rules for translating each of the infinite number of expressions in the English fragment into IL. Thus the semantics for the English rides piggyback on the semantics for the formal language. (The auxiliary language IL was included in PTQ for "perspicuity" (Montague 1973: 256); in other work (Montague 1970) Montague gave a grammar for a fragment with direct interpretation of English, not via an auxiliary formal language. See Jacobson (2000), Barker and Jacobson (2007), and the works cited there for recent developments in the latter kind of approach.)

Let us look more closely at each of these parts of the PTQ grammar, beginning with the syntax of the English fragment, and moving on to the IL grammar and finally the translation rules.

4.4.1 The English fragment

Above I described Montague's syntax for the English fragment as "logician-style." In so doing, I meant a syntax that starts with basic expressions (i.e. words) in their various categories, and then specifies how these may be combined to form phrases and sentences. Because of the strict compositionality of this type of grammar and the requirement of rule-to-rule correspondence, the categories are particularly important. The syntactic categories used by Montague did not correspond exactly to those in use by linguists at the time, because of another feature of Montague's approach—the use of a CATEGORIAL GRAMMAR. In a categorial grammar, the category labels incorporate information about argument structure: for example, the category of intransitive verb phrases (that is, phrases which are the same category as intransitive verbs—this corresponds to VP in linguists' grammars) is labeled t/e, which means it is the category of expressions which combine with an entity-denoting expression to make a truth-value-denoting expression (i.e. a sentence). Montague introduced the handy mnemonic abbreviation "IV" for this category. The categories t and e are the only simple, non-argument-taking categories, and there are no expressions of category e in the fragment. We might have expected proper

names or pronouns to be of category e; however, as we have seen, all
NPs will receive the generalized quantifier type of interpretation, and
this is reflected in the syntax. So NPs are t/(t/e), or t/IV—they require
an IV to make a sentence. Montague abbreviated this category T (for
"term phrase"). Transitive verbs need an object NP to form something
which is of the same category as an intransitive verb; thus they are IV/
T, which is shorthand for (t/e)/(t/(t/e)).[9]

4.4.2 IL

Turning to the logic IL, an important aspect of Montague Grammar is
his use of semantic TYPES. In Montague Grammar, types identify
categories of expressions in IL, and there is a close match between
half of these types and the syntactic categories of the English fragment.
Thus, like the two elementary categories of the English syntax, the two
elementary types of IL are t and e. And for every syntactic category A/B
of expressions which take a B argument to make an expression of
category A, there is a corresponding type of the intensional logic.
Montague used a different notation for the compound types than he
had used for the compound categories of the English fragment. Also,
somewhat confusingly, he chose to write the parts of his IL types in
reverse order from the parts of the English syntax categories. In the
English fragment, the argument category is given **second**—A/B's take
B arguments. However in IL, the type of the argument is given **first**:
$<b,a>$ is the symbol for the type of expressions which take a b type
argument to make an a type.[10]

The IL types differ in another, more important, way from the
English categories, and that is the existence of a special set of types
for expressions denoting intensions. (Recall Frege's claim of a shift in
reference whereby expressions may come to denote their customary
senses; as we will see, Montague follows Frege in this idea.) These
intensional types are all of the form $<s,a>$, where a is some type. The

[9] The reader might wonder about Montague's category CN (for "expression of the
category of common nouns"), which was the source of our CNP. The story here is a little
complicated. In the PTQ grammar, CN is an abbreviation of t//e. The double slash was
needed to distinguish this category from IV (the category of verb phrases in PTQ), which
abbreviates t/e. CN and IV are alike semantically—members of both categories are general
terms, and thus denote sets of entities (or functions from entities to truth values). However
syntactically, in English, the two categories behave differently.

[10] Montague also italicized the type names in IL, but not the category names in the
syntax fragment. I do not know the explanation for this difference.

"*s*" here does not stand for a type of expression, unlike the situation with the other compound types. Instead it can be thought of as standing for the set containing possible worlds at moments in time, since IL expressions of type $<s,a>$ denote functions from possible worlds and times to denotations of type a. Montague introduced the raised caret prefix, $^\wedge$, to notate this shift from having a regular denotation to denoting the corresponding intension. Thus if a is an IL expression of type a, then $^\wedge a$ is of type $<s,a>$.

There is another piece of notation which will be useful in what follows—one which does the opposite of the raised caret. This symbol is a raised inverted caret prefix, $^\vee$, and it converts an expression denoting an intension to one denoting the corresponding extension at a particular world and time. Thus if a is an IL expression of type $<s,a>$, then $^\vee a$ is an IL expression of type a. We will have examples below.

4.4.3 *The translation rules*

Turning to the translation part of the PTQ grammar, in translating English sentences into IL, Montague assumed IL contained constant expressions corresponding to most of the words in the lexicon of the English fragment. (Some English words got special treatment; we will see examples shortly.) For convenience those IL constants were spelled the same as the English words—they were distinguished by occurring with a prime. Another peculiarity of Montague Grammar is that he used boldface to cite both English words and the corresponding IL constants, rather than the more customary italics or quotation marks. Thus **love** from the English fragment translates into the IL constant **love**′. Ignoring intensionality, and given that **love** is a transitive verb and thus of category IV/T, or (t/e)/(t/(t/e)), we would expect **love**′ to be of type $\ll <e,t>,t>,<e,t\gg$. However, we cannot ignore intensionality here. Recall Montague's belief that intensionality could be found in any category of argument-taking expression. That means that each argument-taking expression must take expressions from an intensional category. This is reflected in the mapping Montague created between the categories of the English fragment and the types of IL, which guides the translation from the English into IL. The mapping (the function f) is given in slightly modified form in (34) (cf. Montague 1973: 260).

(34)   a. $f(e) = e$
       b. $f(t) = t$
       c. $f(A/B) = \ll s, f(B) >, f(A)>$

So the actual type of **love'** (and the IL translation of any other transitive verb) is: $\ll s, \ll s, \ll s,e>,t\gg,t\gg, \ll s,e>,t\gg$. In ordinary words (sort of), **love'** takes as its object argument a property of properties of individual concepts $(<s, \ll s, \ll s,e>,t\gg,t\gg$—this is the type of Montague's intensionalized generalized quantifiers), and yields a set of individual concepts $(\ll s,e>,t>)$.

One exceptional group of words consists of proper names like **Mary**, and the word **ninety**.[11] IL contains individual constants corresponding to these names: m and n denote the person Mary and the number ninety, respectively. However these expressions are of type e. Since the English words are NPs (category T, a.k.a. t/(t/e)), they receive translations as Montague's fancy kind of generalized quantifier—that is, as expressions denoting sets of properties, similar to what we saw above in (28) for the name *Kim* but now fully intensionalized. For **Mary**, the translation is in (35).

$$(35) \quad \lambda P[^{\vee}P(^{\wedge}m)]$$

In (35) P is a variable over properties (functions from world-time points to sets). The caret preceding m shows that the properties we are talking about are actually properties not of individuals, but rather of individual concepts—those functions from world-time points to individuals that are the intensional counterpart of individuals. $^{\wedge}m$ is of type $<s,e>$. On the other hand the inverted caret is required to convert P, which is of type $<s, \ll s,e>,t\gg$, to an expression of type $\ll s,e>,t>$ so that it can combine with $^{\wedge}m$. (Without the inverted caret, P would only have been able to combine with an expression denoting a possible world-time point, but there are no such expressions in IL.) To summarize: Mary's individual concept is the one that picks Mary out of each possible world and moment of time, and (35) denotes the set of properties that that individual concept has.

The translation rules for complex phrases (formed by putting expressions together) mirror the rules of the English syntax, thus reflecting the tight rule-to-rule compositionality of Montague's system. Corresponding to each syntactic rule which combines categories of expressions to form expressions of another category, there is a translation rule which tells how to translate expressions of the resulting category based on the translations of the inputs. Most of these rules are rules of functional application—where an argument-taking expression

[11] Recall from Chapter 1 that number words behave like proper names.

is combined with its argument. By way of example, Montague's translation rule for transitive verbs is given (in slightly modified form) below in (36) (cf. Montague (1973: 261)). Recall that IV/T is the category for transitive verbs, and T is the category of term phrases, or NPs.

(36)   If δ is a phrase of category IV/T, and β is of category T, and δ, β translate into δ', β' respectively, then $F_5(\delta, \beta)$ translates into $\delta'(^\wedge \beta')$.

F_5 is the rule of the English syntax which combined the two input expressions (a transitive verb and its direct object) syntactically to form an IV phrase (a VP). The main thing to notice is that the rule in (36) causes the translation of the transitive verb to take an IL expression which denotes the **intension** of the denotation of the translation of the argument expression (the direct object). Thus the IV phrase **loves Mary**, for example, will translate into **loves**$'(^\wedge \lambda P[^\vee P (^\wedge m)])$.

4.5 Some examples

Let us look now at some examples of the interpretations assigned by Montague's PTQ grammar. First of all, a sentence like (37) would receive the two translations shown in (38) (using *o* as a constant denoting Oedipus).

(37)   Oedipus wants to marry his mother.

(38)   a.   **want-to**$'(^\wedge o, {}^\wedge \lambda y[\exists x \forall z[[\textbf{mother-of}'(z, {}^\wedge o) \leftrightarrow z = x] \& \textbf{marry}' (y, x)]])$

       b. $\exists x \forall z[[\textbf{mother-of}'(z, {}^\wedge o) \leftrightarrow z = x] \& \textbf{want-to}'(^\wedge o, {}^\wedge \lambda y [\textbf{marry}' (y, x))]]$

The opaque, narrow-scope, *de dicto* interpretation (the one that is false) is represented in (38a), which says roughly that Oedipus (or more properly his individual concept) is in the wanting relation to the property of being married to Oedipus's mother. The transparent, wide-scope, *de re* interpretation (the one that is true), is represented in (38b), which says that Oedipus's mother is such that Oedipus is in the wanting relation to the property of being married to her. Essentially we have a combination of Russell's scope analysis, plus Frege's intensionality.

   Recall that a major motivation for Montague was being able to account for the *de dicto-de re* ambiguity, and the opacity on the *de dicto* interpretation, which occurs with transitive verbs like *seek* which do not take a sentential complement. (40) below gives two interpretations for example (39). (This is not Montague's ultimate analysis of this sentence, for reasons we will get to in the next subsection.)

(39) **John seeks a unicorn**

(40) a. **seek′**($^\wedge j$, $^\wedge \lambda P \exists x$[**unicorn′**(x) & P(x)])

    b. $\exists x$[**unicorn′**(x) & **seek′**($^\wedge j$, x)]

According to (40a) John's individual concept is in the seek relation to the property of being a property that some unicorn has. This is appropriately nonspecific and does not imply the existence of unicorns. Thus we can see that Montague's generalized quantifier analysis of NPs has another beneficial result (in addition to allowing a uniform type of meaning for all NPs), which is that it allows a *de dicto* reading of *John seeks a unicorn* without postulating a sentential complement for *seek*.[12] (40b) gives the initial translation for the *de re* reading for (39)— the one that says that there is some particular unicorn that John is looking for.

4.6 Individuals vs individual concepts

I mentioned above that (40) was not Montague's ultimate analysis for (39). To explain why requires going a little deeper into his analysis, and his use of individual concepts. Recall that Montague thought that intransitive verbs like *rise* and *change* were intensional in their subject position. The crucial example concerned the invalid instance of substitution in (41).

(41) a. The temperature is rising.

    b. The temperature = 90°.

∴c. 90° is rising.

Montague's translations for (41a,b) are given in (42a, b) respectively— note that (41a) is not ambiguous, unlike the case with other intensional predicates, so it receives only the one translation in (42a).

(42) a. $\exists x[\forall y[$**temperature′**$(y) \leftrightarrow y = x]$ & **rise′**$(x)]$

    b. $\exists x[\forall y[$**temperature′**$(y) \leftrightarrow y = x]$ & $[^\vee x] = n]$

---

[12] See Forbes (2006) for a recent critique of Montague's and other approaches to the *seek* problem, and an alternative analysis.

Now look at the last clause of (42b), and recall that the superscript inverted caret prefix $^\vee$ indicates the extension (at some world-time point) of whatever it is prefixed to. This would only be well-formed if it is prefixed to something that denotes an intension. The fact is that the lower case x's and y's in the representations from the PTQ grammar which we have been looking at are in fact variables over individual concepts (functions from possible worlds to individuals), not individuals. That being the case, we can see how the substitution is blocked: rising, in (42a), is being predicated of an individual concept which varies with time, while what is identical to $90°$ according to (42b) is not an individual concept but rather the extension of that concept at a particular time.

Although *seek* seems to be intensional as far as its object position goes, it does not seem to be intensional for the subject position. If John is seeking a unicorn, and John is the manager of the Detroit Zoo, then the manager of the Detroit Zoo is seeking a unicorn. (Similar remarks go for the subjects of complement-taking propositional attitude verbs like *believe* and *want*.[13]) Furthermore, as we noted before, **most** simple intransitive and transitive verbs (as well as common nouns) are completely extensional. To get what he viewed as the correct interpretation for all of these predicates, Montague introduced another set of constants, symbolized by adding a "downstar" suffix, $_*$, to an existing constant of IL. These were to be interpreted as extensional counterparts for the original intensional translations. Thus although the direct translation of *Mary loves John* into IL would result in (43a), the formula in (43b) was defined so as to be logically equivalent.

(43)   a. $\textbf{love}'(^\wedge m, {}^\wedge j)$
       b. $\textbf{love}'_*(m, j)$

While (43a) says that the **love**′ relationship holds between Mary's individual concept and John's individual concept, (43b) says that a corresponding relation, **love**′$_*$, holds between the simple individuals Mary and John.

Montague also introduced different variables—u and v—to range over ordinary individuals. Using these, we can give the ultimate analyses for *John seeks a unicorn* (example (39) above), in (44) below.

(44)   a. $\textbf{seek}'(^\wedge j, {}^\wedge \lambda P \exists u[\textbf{unicorn}'_*(u) \ \& \ {}^\vee P(^\wedge u)])$
       b. $\exists u[\textbf{unicorn}'_*(u) \ \& \ \textbf{seek}'_*(j, u)]$

---

[13] Although see Crimmins and Perry (1989) for a different view.

(44a) differs from the initial translation into IL given in (40a) above only in quantifying over unicorn individuals rather than individual concepts of unicorns. This formula does not require the actual existence of unicorns: the object of John's seeking here is a property of properties—a function from possible worlds (and times) to sets of properties. On the other hand (44b) is thoroughly extensional—the **seek**$'_*$ relation is said to hold between John (not his individual concept) and some existing unicorn (also not an individual concept). Given the nonexistence of unicorns, this must be false.

As we have just seen, in the initial translations from the English fragment into IL, all predicates were treated as intensional and all NPs involved property sets of individual concepts rather than individuals. The primary reason for this was the perceived intensionality of *rise* and *change*. However soon after the publication of PTQ, several papers appeared challenging Montague's analysis of these verbs. We noted above that *rise* and *change* do not give rise to a *de dicto-de re* ambiguity, unlike other intensional predicates. Also, Rich Thomason (1974) and Ray Jackendoff (1979) gave evidence that the *be* in *The temperature is ninety* is not the *be* of identity—note that *The temperature is identical to ninety* sounds odd. Michael Bennett (1974) proposed a revision of the PTQ grammar which did away with the intensionality of IV and common noun expressions. Instead of denoting sets of individual concepts, these were taken to denote sets of ordinary individuals. This revised version of PTQ has been almost universally accepted in place of Montague's original and is the one presented in the standard introduction to Montague Grammar in Dowty, Wall, and Peters (1981). However, as I have said, I intend to argue in several places in the coming chapters that the idea that we are speaking customarily of individual concepts rather than individuals has much to recommend it, and for this reason I've sketched the PTQ grammar in its original form.[14]

4.7 Proper names

Before concluding this presentation, I would like to make a few comments about Montague's treatment of proper names (and number words). Despite Montague's incorporation of elements from both

---

[14] The use of individual concepts has received some recent support in the work of Aloni (2005a, b) and Elbourne (2008).

Frege and Russell in the PTQ grammar, his analysis of proper names actually has more in common with Mill than with Frege and Russell. Although proper names were made to denote generalized quantifiers (sets of properties) in order to make them semantically unitary with quantificational NPs, nevertheless at the base of the property sets in question there is a single individual in the case of proper names, unlike the quantificational NPs. It is true that the property sets associated with each proper name may vary from world to world (since individuals have different properties in different worlds); however these property sets are in no way equivalent to descriptions like those suggested by Frege and Russell. Thus Montague, like Mill, had a nondescriptional view of proper names. These property sets contained properties of individual concepts instead of individuals, but a meaning postulate which Montague included required that the individual concepts in question be **constant** individual concepts, requiring them to pick out the same individual from each world-time point.

Montague's meaning postulate is given in (45) (cf. Montague (1973: 263)).

(45) $\exists u \, \Box \, [u = \alpha]$, where α is j, m, b, or n.

The individual constants j, m, and b formed the basis for the property sets interpreting the names *John*, *Mary*, and *Bill*, respectively (these were the three proper names in the PTQ English fragment), and the constant n formed the basis for the interpretation of *ninety*. The meaning postulate in (45) says that for each of these individual constants, there must be some one individual which is denoted by that constant in every possible world and time. (The box, $\Box$, as it occurs in Montague Grammar should be read "necessarily always," as it requires that the formula to which it is prefixed be true at all world-time points.) As we will see in the following chapter, Montague was not alone in supporting a return to Mill's view of proper names.

4.8 Summary and developments

Montague's PTQ grammar is an extremely elegant piece of work but it is also extremely difficult technically, and this has been a very condensed presentation. Thus the reader (especially a novice) may feel their head spinning a bit at this point. If not every detail of the foregoing sections is crystal-clear on first reading, that is OK; here are the most important points which I hope the reader has come away with:

(i) An outline of what a completely explicit syntax and (compositional) semantics for an interesting fragment of a natural language might involve.

(ii) The generalized quantifier analysis of NPs, and how that allows a consistent semantics for proper names as well as quantified NPs, and also allows an analysis of *de dicto* interpretations which does not depend on an embedded sentence.

(iii) Montague's semantic types, and what they correspond to.

(iv) The possibility of having a semantics built on individual concepts.

The reader may also be cheered by the fact that the preceding sections on Montague's work are by far the most difficult portions of this book—from here on everything should seem quite easy.

We turn now to a couple of important papers developing aspects of Montague's work. The titles of the papers make clear which aspects those are: the first is Barwise and Cooper's "Generalized quantifiers and natural language" (1981), and the second is Partee's "Noun phrase interpretation and type shifting principles" (1986). I should note that neither of these papers is particularly concerned with issues of intensionality, and so both work with extensionalized systems, leaving intensions out of the picture for simplicity's sake. The same is true of many other contributions within this tradition.

4.8.1 Barwise and Cooper (1981) on generalized quantifiers

As we have seen, Montague's use of generalized quantifiers allowed him to solve the problem of assigning an interpretation to quantificational NPs, and furthermore a type of interpretation which could also be used for proper names and pronouns. This important step really opened the door to an investigation of the semantic properties of NPs—a door which Barwise and Cooper walked through in impressive fashion. We will put off consideration of some of the properties which they explored until Chapter 9. At this point I just want to note a few aspects of this classic work.

Like Montague, Barwise and Cooper defined a formal language[15] which could be used to interpret a fragment of English. However as

---

[15] Actually a whole family of languages.

noted above, their fragment and the corresponding formal language were purely extensional, which helped to keep the complexity down substantially. Another move which simplified things in a helpful way was to incorporate much of the set-theoretic apparatus needed to provide the semantics for quantificational expressions into the meta-language. That allowed them to take advantage of another aspect of the generalized quantifier analysis—the fact that it allows us to include quantificational determiners like *most,* which cannot be given an analysis in an ordinary first-order language.[16]

Let us look first at the Barwise and Cooper interpretation for the determiner *every.* In the rule in (46) below, the double vertical lines signify a semantic value, and A in these formulas stands for the set denoted by the CNP with which the determiner combines (the restriction). E stands for the universe of discourse—the universal set of everything that is assumed to exist. X is a variable over sets. There is also some set-theory notation in this formula: the curly brackets surround the specification of a set, the text before the colon introduces the variable which will range over potential members of the set and what follows the colon is a specification of the criteria for membership. $\subseteq$ is the symbol for the subset relation.

(46) $\|\mathbf{every}\|\ (A) = \{X \subseteq E : A \subseteq X\}$

So, (46) says that when the meaning of *every* combines with a set A, the result is the set containing all the subsets of the universe of discourse of which A is a subset—i.e. all the supersets of A. The net effect is the same as in the PTQ grammar, minus the intensionality. The corresponding rule of the PTQ grammar would be something like (47) (using the notation of Barwise and Cooper rather than Montague's, leaving out intensionality, and using $=>$ to symbolize translation).

(47) $\mathbf{every}\ A => \lambda X \forall x [A(x) \rightarrow X(x)]$

This says that *every A* translates into a logical formula which denotes that set of sets X such that everything that belongs to A belongs to X,

---

[16] See Appendix C of Barwise and Cooper (1981) for a formal proof of this impossibility. To get a sense for it in a relatively informal way, note that there is no formula of the form in (ib) which would satisfactorily serve as the translation of a sentence like (ia).

(i)   a.   Most apples are tasty.
       b. $Most_x[apple(x) \otimes tasty(x)]$

The problem is finding a connective to fill in for $\otimes$; the reader can verify that none of $\rightarrow$, &, nor $\vee$ will do the trick, either by themselves or combined with each other and/or $\sim$.

which is another way of saying that A is a subset of X, i.e. that X is a superset of A. The net effect is the same (which is good, because the truth conditions were right before), but in Barwise and Cooper's approach the meaning of *every* has been expressed directly as a relation between sets, and the relationship in question is spelled out in the metalanguage.

Now, using the Barwise and Cooper approach, we can spell out the meaning of *most* in formal terms. Let us first assume, for the sake of simplicity, that *most* means something like "more than half". (It is true that oftentimes *most* conveys something stronger; we'll just assume that that's a conversational implicature, perhaps of the informativeness kind.) Then we'll need a couple more notations: ∩ stands for the intersection operation, and single vertical lines around the specification of a set stand for the CARDINALITY of the set—how big it is or how many members it has. Now we can give the definition in (48).

(48) $\|\mathbf{most}\|(A) = \{X \subseteq E: |A \cap X| > 1/2\, |A|\}$

(48) says that when the meaning of *most* combines with a set A, the result is all those sets which contain more than half of the members of A.

There is one other way in which the Barwise and Cooper grammar diverges from the PTQ grammar, and that has to do with the treatment of definite descriptions. Aside from the intensionality and the generalized quantification, Montague's analysis of definite descriptions was essentially the same as Russell's. Thus (49a) below would wind up with an interpretation equivalent to (49b).

(49)   a.   The apple is tasty.
       b. $\exists x \forall y[[\mathbf{apple}'(x) \leftrightarrow x = y]\ \&\ \mathbf{tasty}'(x)]$

(49b) says, of course, that there is one and only one apple and it is tasty. Recall from Chapter 2 that Frege had a different view of definite descriptions, regarding them as referential expressions. For him that meant that a sentence containing a definite description without a referent, such as Russell's example (50) (as uttered in 1905, or today for that matter)

(50)   The king of France is bald.

would fail to have a truth value. In this latter respect, Barwise and Cooper sided with Frege rather than Russell on the analysis of definite descriptions. Their rule for *the* is given in (51).

(51) $\|\mathbf{the}\|(A) = \|\mathbf{every}\|(A)$, if $|A| = 1$, and is undefined otherwise.

This rule requires there to be a unique entity belonging to any set A if the value of *the A* is to be defined, and in this their analysis is similar to Frege's. Of course Barwise and Cooper (following Montague) do see definite descriptions as quantificational rather than referential in that they express generalized quantifiers, but they also see all other NPs—even proper names and pronouns—as quantificational as well, in that sense. Definite descriptions are the subject of Chapter 6, and the issue of referentiality vs quantification will return there and in subsequent chapters.

The main point of the Barwise and Cooper article was to define formally, and attempt to account for, many interesting semantic properties of different kinds of NPs. We will look at some of these properties, and what Barwise and Cooper had to say about them, in Chapter 9.

4.8.2 Partee (1986) on type-shifting

As we have just seen in this chapter, one of Montague's accomplishments was to allow all sorts of NPs—proper names and pronouns in addition to (overtly) quantified NPs—to have the same kind of interpretation, as generalized quantifiers. However there is some evidence that, in at least some contexts, some NPs may have a different kind of interpretation—correspond to a different type, in Montague's sense of "type." Partee (1986) argued that NPs in an extensional version of English would actually correspond to three different semantic types: e, which is the type of expressions denoting simple entities; $<e,t>$, which is the type of expressions denoting sets of entities; and $\ll e,t>,t>$, the type of generalized quantifiers. Ordinary proper names of individuals would most naturally be interpreted as of type e—the individual constants Montague used (j for John, m for Mary, b for Bill, and n for ninety) were of this type. Partee suggested that proper names may be "coerced" into the generalized quantifier interpretation on occasion, such as when they are conjoined with an overtly quantified NP, as in (52) (the assumption being that only like categories may be conjoined).

(52)   Fido and all the cats were running around the house.

Montague's work already suggests a way of deriving a generalized quantifier from an individual constant. If we have a type e individual constant standing for Fido, say f, then using S as a variable over sets we can construct a generalized quantifier expression denoting Fido's property set: $\lambda S[S(f)]$. As desired, this is of type $\ll e,t>,t>$.

To see the naturalness of the third type, $<e,t>$, note the interpretation of indefinite descriptions when they occur in predicate position, as in (53).

(53)   Morgan is a flutist.

As we saw in Chapter 1, when indefinite NPs like *a flutist* are used predicatively, as in (53), they seem to function as general terms—that is, as expressions denoting sets. And note that many (perhaps most) languages would express (53) without any article or other determiner in the predicate. Montague did not treat predicate NPs as any different from NPs in argument position; on his analysis (53) was equivalent to *There is a flutist who is (identical to) Morgan*. However this is not the most natural approach since intuitively *a flutist*, in (53), is functioning just like an adjective like *tall* or *skillful*.

In order to get the predicative interpretation we would like for (53), something of type $<e,t>$, we need to be able to take the generalized quantifier interpretation of *a flutist* and derive a predicate, equivalent to the CNP *flutist* with which the article *a* combined. Let's look first at that generalized quantifier, given in (54).

(54) $\lambda S[\exists x[\text{flutist}(x) \; \& \; S(x)]]$

This is the set of sets which contain at least one flutist. To derive a suitable predicate from such a generalized quantifier, Partee proposed the type-shifting rule in (55), where $\wp$ is a variable over generalized quantifiers (sets of sets).

(55) $\lambda\wp[\lambda x[\{x\} \in \wp]]$

(55) applies to a generalized quantifier and, as Partee put it, "finds all the singletons therein, and collects their elements into a set" (Partee 1986: 127). (A SINGLETON is a set with only one member.) It is clear that, combined with (54), this rule is going to get us the set of flutists, exactly what we want. (56a) below shows (55) being applied to (54) (with the individual variable in the latter changed to avoid any clash with the variable in the former). (56b) shows the result of λ conversion.

(56)   a. $\lambda\wp[\lambda x[\{x\} \in \wp]] \, (\lambda S[\exists y[\text{flutist}(y) \; \& \; S(y)]])$
       b. $\lambda x[\{x\} \in \lambda S[\exists y[\text{flutist}(y) \; \& \; S(y)]]]$

(56b) denotes the set of entities x such that the singleton (i.e. set with just one member) containing x belongs to the set of all those sets that contain at least one flutist. A bit of reflection shows that this set of entities will contain all and only flutists.

In addition to functioning as generalized quantifiers and as predicates, indefinite descriptions may seem to be able to be of type *e*. This is on some occasions when they occur as arguments (that is, nonpredicatively), and especially when they initiate a series of references, as in (57).

(57)   <u>A woman</u> came to our house yesterday. <u>She</u> wanted us to support <u>her</u> campaign for the senate.

However this is an issue of some controversy, and furthermore it is not obvious how to get an *e* type meaning from the generalized quantifier treatment of indefinite descriptions. We will return to this issue below, in Chapter 9.

4.9 Concluding remarks

We have covered a lot of ground in this chapter, and most of it quite rough and difficult at that. I hope the rather condensed presentation of the PTQ grammar in this chapter has given you at least some idea of the brilliance of Montague's work, as well as an understanding of some of its essential features. Readers who would like to know more are urged to take a look at the excellent introduction in Dowty, Wall, and Peters (1981), and the works cited there. Grice's work too has been tremendously influential—the references given above in §4.2 should provide a good starting place.

5

Proper names

> *Esmeralda*: What is your name?
> *Butch*: "Butch."
> *Esmeralda*: What does it mean?
> *Butch*: I'm American, honey. Our names don't mean shit.
>
> *Pulp Fiction*

From a semantic point of view proper names turn out to be interesting expressions (to use a polite term). Some of their peculiar nature is reflected in their ambivalent status as words of a language. Historically they must have seemed like prototypical words: Latin *nomen* "name" gives us the word "nominal" which often means (merely) verbal as opposed to real, as well as the word "noun" for the most salient part of speech. To name somebody or something can mean to identify them or it via a linguistic expression (typically an NP). (And Frege used the phrase "proper name" for all kinds of singular terms.) On the other hand when we look closer, proper names may also strike us as strange kinds of words after all. They are unusually arbitrary—so arbitrary that nonstandard pronunciation conventions may be maintained that would not be allowed for just one ordinary word (one thinks of athletes' names like *Bret Favre* ([farv]), or *Malavai* ([malaviya]) *Washington*)—and most names are not listed in the dictionary. Proper names may call to mind the quip about whales—that from a distance they seem to loom large in the category of fish, but on closer look they turn out not to be fish at all.[1] However I should make clear that I do not agree with the corresponding conclusion in the case of proper names. (See Abbott (2005) for arguments that proper names are indeed part of natural language.)

As we will see, proper names cause a lot of problems for semantic analysis, to the extent that David Kaplan once remarked "if it weren't

---

[1] I had thought this quip was Quine's, but I have not been able to locate an exact source.

for the problem of how to get the kids to come in for dinner, I'd be inclined to just junk them" (Kaplan 1978: 224). In this chapter we will look at some of those problems. We will start with a review of what Mill, Frege, and Russell had to say about proper names, and then in §5.2 we will introduce another possible descriptional analysis of proper names, the "cluster" view. Following that, in §5.3, we take a look at some arguments against descriptional views, and in favor of a return to something like Mill's nondescriptional position; §5.4 summarizes the result of these arguments. The success of these arguments has left us in a difficult position, as we will see in §5.5, and we look into one kind of possible solution in §5.6—these are the metalinguistic approaches. In §5.7 we will look at a puzzle, devised by Saul Kripke, which leads us to a new way of looking at the problem of proper names and suggests that the metalinguistic approach is not going to do. Then in §5.8 we will look at two other types of analysis which claim better results. §5.9 gives some conclusions.

5.1 Review: Mill, Frege, and Russell

We saw in Chapter 2 that in his discussion of connotation and denotation, Mill set proper names aside as expressions which do not imply any properties of their referents, but have only denotation—recall his example of Dartmouth, whose name would probably remain the same should the river Dart change its course. Despite the fact that this nondescriptional view accords well with our ordinary intuitions, both Frege and Russell held the contrary view that proper names are **not** devoid of sense or connotation, but instead express something similar to what is expressed by a definite description. Thus in his famous footnote 2 of "On sense and reference" Frege remarked that the name *Aristotle* might mean something like 'the student of Plato who taught Alexander the Great.' Similarly by way of illustration Russell used the description *the first Chancellor of the German Empire* as what we might associate with the name *Bismarck* (although he also suggested that in actual fact "the description in our minds will probably be some more or less vague mass of historical knowledge" (Russell 1917: 171)).

It is worthwhile reminding ourselves why such brilliant philosophers would adopt such a counterintuitive view of proper names. Russell was concerned with knowledge and believed that all knowledge was ultimately reducible to knowledge attainable via our senses, and thus that all of semantic content must at bottom be defined in sensory terms. Since we appear to use many proper names with understanding, but without first-hand, perceptual knowledge of their denotations, it cannot be the case that those denotations constitute the semantic significance of the names. Rather, as with the *Bismarck* example, it must be that we associate with the name a collection of concepts ultimately definable in terms of perceptual categories, and sufficient to determine Bismarck uniquely.

Even without that type of motivation, there are technical reasons for postulating a descriptional theory of proper names. These reasons are of the same type that led Frege to propose senses in the first place. First of all there is the fact that coreferential names do not seem semantically equivalent: when we substitute one for another in an identity sentence, for example, we can observe a marked change in cognitive impact, as seen in (1a, b).

(1)   a.   Tracy Marrow is the same person as Tracy Marrow.
      b.   Tracy Marrow is the same person as Ice-T.

While (1a) is analytic (true in virtue of its meaning), (1b) seems synthetic—or at least definitely not knowable *a priori* (i.e. purely by reflection). And when we turn to the opaque contexts created by propositional attitude predicates, as noted by both Frege and Russell, we seem to be able to go from truths to falsehoods (and vice versa) by substituting coreferential names.

(2)   a.   Lois Lane knew that Superman could leap tall buildings in a
           single bound.
      b.   Lois Lane knew that Clark Kent could leap tall buildings in a
           single bound.

Assuming for the sake of the example that the Superman comics are accurate historical records, (2a) is true while (2b) seems false. If proper names are associated with descriptive content, then coreferential names may nevertheless be associated with different descriptive contents.

And then there is the problem of names without referents (empty names). People may argue over the status of (3).

(3)   Santa Claus is a jolly fat guy.

But regardless of whether it is seen as true, false, or none of the above, it is definitely meaningful, which should imply that all of its constituents are meaningful too. And nobody would deny that (4) is both meaningful and true.[2]

(4)   Santa Claus doesn't really exist.

All of these examples pose serious problems for Mill's view of proper names. He does not seem to have a way of accounting for the non-equivalence of coreferential names or for the significance of nonreferring names. On the other hand if proper names are really like definite descriptions, then most of these problems disappear. And if in addition we adopt Russell's view of definite descriptions then they all seem to disappear.

5.2 The cluster view

Before turning to the arguments for returning to Mill's position, we need to consider one other possible view of the semantics of proper names. We saw in Chapter 2 that Frege had hinted at a problem for the description theory of proper names. Someone who holds that *Aristotle* means "the pupil of Plato who taught Alexander the Great" will have a different attitude toward (5) than someone who holds that it means "the teacher of Alexander the Great who was born in Stagira".

(5)   Aristotle was born in Stagira.

For the latter sort of person, of course, (5) would be synonymous with (6)

(6)   The teacher of Alexander the Great who was born in Stagira was born in Stagira.

and thus should seem analytic. However, the fact is that probably there is no one for whom (5) sounds analytic, and the same would hold true if a different CONTINGENT (i.e. non-necessary) property of Aristotle were substituted for the property of being born in Stagira.

---

[2] Actually there are those who would deny this, as we will see in Chapter 10. (One should never say "nobody would deny" when one is tromping around in philosophical territory.)

The cluster view of proper names is a kind of looser description theory that seems as though it might avoid this problem. On the cluster view, we associate a lot of different descriptive content with a proper name, and no one single description is taken to give **the** sense of the name. The later Wittgenstein was one person who held this view.

> We may say, following Russell: the name 'Moses' can be defined by means of various descriptions. For example, as 'the man who led the Israelites through the wilderness', 'the man who lived at that time and place and was then called "Moses" ', 'the man who as a child was taken out of the Nile by Pharaoh's daughter', and so on. . . .
>
> But when I make a statement about Moses,—am I always ready to substitute some *one* of these descriptions for 'Moses'? . . . Is it not the case that I have, so to speak, a whole series of props in readiness, and am ready to lean on one if another should be taken from under me, and vice versa?   (Wittgenstein 1953: §79)

Wittgenstein's conclusion, hinted at in this passage, was that proper names like *Moses* are used without any one associated description. Rather, there is a cluster of descriptions associated with the name that support its use.

John Searle holds a view of proper names which is very similar to Wittgenstein's.

> Suppose we ask the users of the name 'Aristotle' to state what they regard as certain essential and established facts about him. Their answers would be a set of uniquely referring descriptive statements. Now what I am arguing is that the descriptive force of 'This is Aristotle' is to assert that a sufficient but so far unspecified number of these statements are true of this object.   (Searle 1958a: 171)

Once again we have the idea that there is a collection of descriptions associated with a name, no single one of which serves as its meaning. As Searle notes, this seems to solve the problem that Frege anticipated:

> . . . suppose we agree to drop 'Aristotle' and use, say, 'the teacher of Alexander', then it is a necessary truth that the man referred to is Alexander's teacher—but it is a contingent fact that Aristotle ever went into pedagogy (though I am suggesting that it is a necessary fact that Aristotle has the logical sum, inclusive disjunction, of properties commonly attributed to him . . .).   (Searle 1958a: 172)

(Here "the logical sum," or "inclusive disjunction," means 'at least one.') Thus on this type of view proper names do have a sense of sorts, but it is a different, and looser, sort of sense than definite descriptions have.

5.3 The return to Mill's view

Keith Donnellan's 1970 paper "Proper names and identifying descriptions", and Saul Kripke's series of lectures titled "Naming and necessity" (Kripke 1972/1980), argued strongly against both of the descriptional theories of proper names just reviewed: the Frege-Russell idea that a proper name may be associated with a single description[3] and the cluster of descriptions view of proper names put forward by Wittgenstein and Searle. Kripke explicitly argued for a return to Mill's nondescriptional[4] view. Others had come to much the same conclusion (e.g. Marcus 1961; Kaplan 1969; Montague 1973), but Kripke's defense of the nondescriptional view was the most extensive and has turned out to be the most influential. We will look at some of the arguments here; later, in §5.6.3, we will look at a couple of other arguments Kripke used.

5.3.1 Descriptions neither necessary nor sufficient

Both Donnellan and Kripke pointed out that, contrary to the description theories, knowledge of identifying descriptions is neither necessary nor sufficient for referential use of a proper name. First of all, people simply may not know any properties which uniquely identify the referent of a name they use. They may have only recently heard of Cicero, say, and not know anything more about him than that he was an ancient Roman. Second, someone may associate a name with a uniquely identifying description which does not correctly identify the bearer. A student, for example, falling asleep during a lecture may get the impression that Socrates was the author of *The Republic*. Even a whole community of speakers, we may imagine, might have been fooled about the unique properties of somebody they use a name for; if the people who say that Bacon wrote the Shakespearean plays are correct, we who think of Shakespeare as the author of "Hamlet," etc., may even turn out to be such a community. Yet if it turned out to be the case that Bacon in fact did write everything we attribute to

---

[3] Describing the single description view as "Frege-Russell" may not be completely accurate. For one thing, as we saw in Chapter 2, Frege held that the description associated with a name could vary from person to person. And the quote from Russell cited above indicates that Russell's view was actually not that a single description could necessarily be associated with a proper name, but in fact something more like a cluster of descriptions.

[4] As noted above in Chapter 2, the terms "descriptional" and "nondescriptional" were introduced by Salmon (1981); they did not appear in "Naming and necessity."

Shakespeare, leaving us with no uniquely identifying description of Shakespeare, we would **not** conclude that the name "Shakespeare" has no referent—that Shakespeare did not exist. These examples show that knowledge of identifying descriptions is not required for the use of a proper name.

Conversely, associated identifying descriptions are not sufficient to determine the reference of a name. Consider the Shakespeare example again: if identifying descriptions **were** sufficient to determine reference, then when it is determined that Bacon did indeed write all of Shakespeare's plays we should conclude that we, or anyway those of us who have no other way of identifying Shakespeare, have been using the name *Shakespeare* to talk about Bacon all this time—and hence were wrong when we said, for example, that Shakespeare was an actor at the Globe Theater (since Bacon was not an actor there). But obviously we would not so conclude. This example comes from Donnellan (1970: 376); Kripke constructs a more fanciful one according to which Gödel, known to many only as the person who proved the incompleteness of arithmetic, actually stole the proof from somebody named *Schmidt*. In that situation the headline declaring *Gödel stole proof!* clearly refers to Gödel, and not to Schmidt. (Cf. Kripke 1972/1980: 82ff.)

5.3.2 Kripke's modal argument

One of Kripke's main arguments against description theories was based on intuitions about the reference of expressions in alternative possible worlds or states of affairs. Consider first a definite description like *the student of Plato who taught Alexander the Great*. This phrase denotes Aristotle in the actual world, because he is the one who has the property expressed in the description. However, had circumstances been different—had, for example, Xenocrates rather than Aristotle taught Alexander the Great—then *the student of Plato who taught Alexander the Great* would refer to Xenocrates, and not to Aristotle. Any definite description which expresses a contingent property of an individual (and this includes all of the sample definite descriptions cited from Frege, Russell, Wittgenstein, and Searle) will be liable to denote different individuals at different possible worlds—they express variable individual concepts.

Proper names seem to be different from definite descriptions: they do not seem to be able to vary their reference from possible world to possible world. Kripke coined the term RIGID DESIGNATOR for expressions which have this property of invariant reference (Kripke 1972/1980: 48). To put the property in more Carnapian/Montagovian terms, on this view proper names express constant individual concepts—functions which pick the same entity out of each possible world.[5] Some definite descriptions are rigid designators, e.g. *the sum of two and five*, which denotes seven in any possible world. And conversely perhaps something like *Miss America* is a proper name which **does** vary its reference, not only from world to world but also time to time.[6] However, unlike *Miss America*, most proper names **are** rigid designators; and unlike *the sum of two and five*, most definite descriptions are **not** rigid designators.

These differing intuitions about definite descriptions versus proper names show up in modal sentences. Thus we regard (7) as true.

(7)   Aristotle might not have been the student of Plato who taught Alexander the Great.

Furthermore it does not matter what kind of contingent property we are predicating of Aristotle—we could substitute any other non-necessary property in the predicate of (7), like having been the author of the *Nicomachean Ethics*, or having been the student of Plato's who was born in Stagira, and (7) would still be true. On the other hand (8) strikes us as false.

(8)   Aristotle might not have been Aristotle.

Roughly speaking, this is the inverse of the analyticity problem Frege seemed to be anticipating in his footnote, and which the cluster theory of proper names seemed designed to solve. However, Kripke pointed out that (9) is also true:

(9)   Aristotle might have had none of the properties commonly attributed to him.

But the truth of (9) appears to be inconsistent with not only the single definite description view of proper names but also the Wittgenstein-Searle cluster view. The difference between (7) and (9), on the one

---

[5] What happens in worlds where the entity does not exist has been an issue of some contention. We will return to it below, in §5.4.3.

[6] The example of *Miss America* is attributed to David Lewis by Dowty, Wall, and Peters (1981: 134). Ellen Prince (personal communication) has also suggested *George/Georgette Spelvin*, the name given in play programs for an actor playing a second role in the same play.

hand, and (8), on the other, again indicates a crucial difference between proper names and identifying descriptions and provides support for Kripke's claim of rigid designation for proper names: since the name *Aristotle* must designate the same individual in any possible world, there is no possible world in which that individual is not Aristotle.

Thus on Kripke's view proper names have two distinctive semantic properties—unlike all definite descriptions they are nondescriptional, and unlike most definite descriptions they are rigid designators.

5.3.3 Natural kind terms

Although this takes us outside the scope of this book, it is worth noting that Kripke made some other claims in "Naming and necessity" which extended the Millian view in ways that Mill himself might not have approved of. Kripke argued that certain common nouns associated with naturally occurring categories are similar to proper names in being nondescriptional. These words are sometimes referred to as NATURAL KIND TERMS: examples are the names of species of plants or animals, like *elm* and *tiger*; words for well-defined substances like *gold* and *water*; and words for natural phenomena like *heat* and *light*. The arguments in this case are a little more complex (see Abbott (1989) for discussion), but basically the point is that the extension of these natural kind terms is not determined by any properties semantically associated with the words—like proper names, they do not have a Fregean type of sense. In so arguing, Kripke was very much in tune with the views and arguments of Hilary Putnam (1975), as he acknowledged.

5.4 The new theory of reference

The widespread (though not total) acceptance of the arguments of Donnellan, Kripke, Putnam and others concerning proper names (and natural kind terms), as well as other work by David Kaplan on indexical expressions which we will get to below in Chapter 8, resulted in what has come to be known as "the new theory of reference." There is some temptation to put scare quotes around both "new" and "theory" in citing that label—the former because the approach has antecedents in Mill and Russell, and the latter because Kripke, at any rate, made clear that he did not claim to be presenting a **theory** of proper names: "I may not have presented a theory, but I do think that I have presented a better picture than that given by description theorists" (Kripke 1972/1980: 97). Nevertheless, if we accept these arguments, and conclude that a return to a Millian, nondescriptional view of proper names is in order, we are left with a couple of questions. One is the metaphysical question of what it is that associates names with their referents—in virtue of what does a name refer to an entity? The other is the semantic question of the contribution of proper names to the meanings of the phrases and sentences in which they occur. Let us start with a brief look at the former before turning to the latter.

5.4.1 What connects names with referents?

Both Donnellan and Kripke suggested what has come to be called the "historical chain" or "causal chain" answer to the question of what associates names with their referents. (Hence the new theory of reference is sometimes also called "the causal theory.") The idea is that there is an original naming or dubbing of a referent, ideally by someone in direct perceptual contact with that individual. (Causation comes in here: the requirement of direct perceptual contact means that the entity being named causes the perceptual inputs of the namer.) Subsequently the name is passed down through the speech community, and, in the case of famous individuals, possibly borrowed into other speech communities, as a name of that individual. It is this causal/historical chain that legitimizes our use of names to refer to their bearers.

There are several questions one might raise about this picture. For one thing, it seems to hold of many other kinds of words—not just proper names and natural kind terms but words for artifacts like *basket* and *viola*. For another, one might wonder about the importance of the initial perceptual contact. This would not be possible in the case of abstract things like numbers, but as we have seen the names of numbers (*one*, *two*, *eight*, *ninety*, etc.) seem to behave like proper names in many respects. But without the requirement of perceptual contact the historical chain picture seems to hold of **any** expression—not just words for observables but words like *nefarious* and *hypothesize*. Despite these questions we will see below that, in the wake of the new theory, the causal/historical chain picture has assumed special significance for proper names in the eyes of at least some philosophers.

5.4.2 What is the semantic contribution of a proper name?

When we turn to the semantic issue, things get a bit more complicated. There are two possibilities that seem pretty clearly within the spirit of the new theory. (There are, of course, many other possibilities; we will get to some of them later.) One possibility, following Carnap, is to regard proper names as expressing constant individual concepts. (We assumed this above in Chapter 3.) Using a bit of Montagovian notation, we might represent (10a) below as (10b) on this view.

(10)   a.   Bill Gates is wealthy.
       b. $<^\wedge b$, being wealthy$>$

Recall that the $^\wedge$ prefix represents an intension—a function from possible worlds and times to extensions. In (10b) we let b be an individual constant assigned to Bill Gates, and $^\wedge b$ denotes the function that picks out Bill Gates at every world-time point. Thus this option incorporates the rigid designation idea. It also seems consistent with the nondescriptionality idea: since any contingent identifying properties of an entity (like, in this case for example, being the founder of Microsoft) would **not** be held by that entity in all the possible worlds in which the entity existed, such a constant individual concept would not be equivalent to the individual concept expressed by a definite description expressing one or more of those properties (e.g. *the founder of Microsoft*). I've resisted the introduction of acronyms, but it will be useful to have a shorthand to refer to this view of what is expressed by sentences with proper names, so let us call it "the CIC view" (for "Constant Individual Concept").

The other possible semantic analysis that seems clearly within the spirit of the new theory would include a return to Russell's early concept of singular propositions. Recall from Chapter 2 that Russell believed that the propositions expressed by sentences with true proper names must contain the actual entity referred to by the name. While Russell thought that only the proximal demonstrative *this* was capable of being used to express such propositions (and thus that *this* was the only genuine proper name), some papers of Kaplan's (1977, 1978) have been instrumental in promoting the extension of this view to many other types of expressions, including ordinary proper names.[7] On this view (10a), for example, would express the

---

[7] It should be noted that, initially at least, Kaplan himself supported this view of proper names only weakly. Compare §XXII of Kaplan (1977).

proposition indicated in (11)—the one containing just the person Bill Gates and the property of being wealthy.

(11)   <Bill Gates, being wealthy>

This idea has now gained a number of adherents (e.g. Salmon (1986); Richard (1990); Soames (2002); Forbes (2006), among others), and is currently one of the dominant philosophical views of the semantics of proper names. Let us call this view "the RSP view" (for "Russellian Singular Proposition"). We will see below (and also later in Chapters 10 and 11), that the CIC view has advantages over the RSP view, which supports the position that NPs in general express individual concepts.

5.4.3 Direct reference, rigid designation, singular and object-dependent propositions

Before continuing, we need to clarify some terminology. Kaplan (1977) introduced the terms "direct reference" and "directly referential" in connection with the new theory, and they have caught hold. However Kaplan's move in the direction of RSPs was not something which Kripke was specifically promoting in "Naming and necessity"; indeed, it seems that Kripke had in mind something like the CIC view. His characterization of rigid designators as having the same reference in all possible worlds is certainly more like a constant individual concept than it is like introducing an actual entity into a proposition.

One difference between the two approaches comes into play when we consider what happens at worlds in which an entity, which is named at the actual world, does not exist. With the CIC approach we have (at least) two options—we could assume that the function in question is a partial function, which simply has no value at such a world, or we could instead let the function represented by $^\wedge b$, for example, pick out Bill Gates even in worlds in which he does not exist. At times Kripke has seemed to incline toward the former view: "a designator rigidly designates a certain object if it designates that object wherever the object exists; if, in addition, the object is a necessary existent [i.e., it exists at all possible worlds], the designator can be called *strongly rigid*" (Kripke 1972/1980: 48–9). In distinguishing rigid from strongly rigid designation, Kripke seems to suggest that a name like *Bill Gates* would express only a partial function, since Bill Gates is presumably not a necessary existent. However, this is not the only possible interpretation of that comment, and in the introduction to the 1980 edition of *Naming and Necessity* Kripke remarks "...I say that a proper name rigidly designates its referent even when we speak of counterfactual situations where that referent would not have existed" (Kripke 1980: 21, n. 21), suggesting the total function view. But the point is that on the CIC approach, the question arises of what to do in worlds in which the entity does not exist, however we resolve it. On the other hand, if we take the RSP approach we would seem to have the individual there in the proposition regardless.[8]

In his paper "Afterthoughts" (Kaplan 1989), Kaplan clarifies what his motivation was in introducing the terms "direct reference" and "directly refer." Apparently his intention was to distinguish these terms from Kripke's "rigid designation" and "rigidly designate," and to have his terms incorporate the idea of expressing an RSP—where an actual entity is a constituent of what is expressed. Rigid designation is then a **consequence** of direct reference. Using his distinctive metaphorical style, Kaplan characterizes the relationship in this way:

If the individual is loaded into the proposition...before the proposition begins its round-the-worlds journey, it is hardly surprising that the proposition manages to find that same individual at all of its stops....In this way we achieve rigid designation. Indeed, we achieve the characteristic, direct reference, form of rigid designation, in which it is irrelevant whether the individual exists in the world at which the proposition is evaluated.   (Kaplan 1989: 569)

If a proper name expresses a constant individual concept (whether or not it fails to have a reference in worlds in which the named entity does not exist), it would be a rigid designator, but would not be considered to be directly referential by Kaplan. "The 'direct' of 'direct reference' means unmediated by any propositional component..." (Kaplan 1989: 569), and of course an individual concept **is** a propositional component.

Not everyone uses the terms "direct reference" and "directly referential" in Kaplan's restricted way. Some use them instead to mean merely the absence of a Fregean sense. Nathan Salmon has characterized the term as follows: "We may say that a nondescriptional singular

---

[8] We are assuming here that the individuals we are speaking of do exist in the actual world. If they don't, then, as we shall see in the following section, and especially in Chapter 10, things are not so straightforward.

term is *directly referential*, and that it *directly denotes* its referent, since its denotation is not mediated by a descriptive sense" (Salmon 1981: 16, italics in original). And Alan Berger refers to the " 'new theory of direct reference'... according to which the reference of [proper names and natural kind terms] are determined directly without the mediation of a Fregean sense" (Berger 2002: xi; later in the book (p. 53) Berger acknowledges Kaplan's more restricted notion). In this book I have tried to stick to Kaplan's intended usage.

While we are in the business of clarifying terminology, there are a couple of other terms worth noting. One is "singular proposition": many people use this to mean RSP, but once we have CIC propositions as an option they should also be considered to be singular propositions. And the other term is OBJECT-DEPENDENT, as applied to this kind of proposition. The issue is similar—those who assume the RSP approach take object-dependent propositions just to be RSPs. However propositions containing CICs could also be considered to be object-dependent. Nevertheless I will not use the term "object-dependent" any more in this book, because of its strong suggestion of the RSP view.

5.5 Problems!

At the beginning of this chapter we had reminded ourselves of why one might want to endorse a description theory of the reference of proper names. It was because then we had a hope of solving the problems of (a) the apparent nonequivalence of coreferential names like *Tracy Marrow* and *Ice-T*, or *Clark Kent* and *Superman*, and (b) what to do about empty names like *Santa Claus*. If we have been persuaded to give up description theories, we seem to run the risk of being left with these problems, so let us take a closer look to see if that is the case.

We'll start with the problem of empty names, and here we'll see a difference depending on which of the two nondescriptional views—the RSP view or the CIC view—we adopt. Recall our examples: (3) is repeated here as (12).

(12)   Santa Claus is a jolly fat guy.

If the name *Santa Claus* lacks a referent, then on the RSP view, there is nothing to serve as the subject of the proposition expressed in (12). However on the CIC view it seems that we **would** have something to serve as subject—the constant individual concept expressed by the name *Santa Claus*.[9] Similar remarks go for existence statements. Our example (4) is repeated here as (13).

(13)   Santa Claus doesn't really exist.

Once again, on the RSP view there is nothing to serve as the subject of the proposition expressed. On the CIC view, we have the constant individual concept expressed by *Santa Claus* to serve as subject. And if this individual concept is a partial function which lacks a value at the actual world, then that explains the truth of (13).

Although briefly stated here, I believe that this difference between the CIC view and the RSP view of proper names is quite significant.[10] We will return to the issue of empty names in Chapter 10 below, when we consider more generally what it is we're talking about, and there we will see somewhat more fully the advantages of the CIC approach.

In the case of coreferential names, there were two notable subcases of apparent nonequivalence. Recall first the identity sentence situation;[11] our first example is repeated here as (14).

(14)   a.   Tracy Marrow is the same person as Tracy Marrow.
        b.   Tracy Marrow is the same person as Ice-T.

These are indeed a problem on the new theory, whichever version we adopt. On the CIC approach, both proper names will express the same constant individual concept—the one which picks Tracy Marrow/Ice-T out of each possible world. As a consequence (14a) and (14b) will both express the same proposition. And on the RSP version both sentences of (14) express the same proposition as well—in this case

---

[9] Things are not as simple as this, unfortunately. There is the problem of determining which entity that constant individual concept is to pick out of any possible world. We will return to this issue below, in Chapter 10.

[10] Interestingly, Brock (2004) points out that descriptional theories of proper names that attempt to incorporate rigidity by claiming either (a) that proper names always have wide scope, or (b) that they contain a tacit *actually*, are subject to similar problems.

[11] As we noted above in Chapter 2, Salmon (1986: 12) pointed out that identity sentences aren't the only ones with this kind of problem. We can see a similar kind of nonequivalence in the pair in (i).

(i)   a.   If Ice-T lives in Hollywood, then Ice-T lives in Hollywood.
       b.   If Ice-T lives in Hollywood, then Tracy Marrow lives in Hollywood.

If people consistently refer to this problem as one of identity sentences, it is because Frege chose to focus on that particular type.

the proposition will be the one consisting of two instances of Tracy
Marrow/Ice-T together with the identity relation. Thus we have not
accounted for the difference in cognitive impact between these two
sentences.

The other difficult subcase was presented by sentences about propositional attitudes. Our example (2) is repeated here as (15).

(15)   a.   Lois Lane knew that Superman could leap tall buildings in a
            single bound.
       b.   Lois Lane knew that Clark Kent could leap tall buildings in
            a single bound.

The problem here is that it seems that (15a) is true while (15b) is false;
we need to be able to account for this difference. And once again this
old problem crops up on either version of the new theory. Since
Superman **is** Clark Kent, both names express the same constant individual concept, and so we cannot distinguish the two different attitudes which seem to be attributed to Lois. Similarly on the RSP view
we have a single proposition—one containing Superman (aka Clark
Kent)—to serve as object of Lois Lane's knowledge and we have not
distinguished (15a) from (15b).

As we've seen, these problems arising from the apparent lack of
semantic equivalence of coreferential proper names return on the new
theory of reference, no matter which of the two versions we adopt. Of
these problems, the one involving propositional attitude sentences has
been seen as the more serious since it involves possible changes in truth
values, and hence truth conditions, and that is the one we will focus on
for the remainder of this chapter.

5.6 Solutions? Part 1: metalinguistic approaches

The problem of proper names in propositional attitude sentences is a
very difficult one, and thus it should probably not be surprising that
there have been many different attempts to solve it. Broadly speaking,
these attempts can be grouped into three categories: metalinguistic
approaches, hidden indexical approaches, and bite-the-bullet approaches.
In this section we'll take a look at metalinguistic approaches, which
involve crucial use of the names themselves in one way or another,
holding off on the other two types until §5.8 below. Within the
metalinguistic group there are a number of different approaches,

each with its own variations. We'll look at three of these: an early one, prominently associated with Quine and involving quotation, and then two others which involve modifications of the Frege/Russell descriptional approach.

5.6.1 Quotational approaches

One early metalinguistic approach to propositional attitudes in general, in response to the problem of referential opacity as discussed in Chapter 2, was suggested by W.V. Quine (though ultimately he rejected it). Quine (an empiricist, like Russell) was very suspicious of intensional concepts, including the notion of a proposition, and suggested that the objects of propositional attitudes might be taken instead to be sentences. "Instead of '*w* believes that . . .' we may say: '*w* believes-true '. . .''" (Quine 1956: 109). Along these lines we might reformulate (15a, b) above as in (16) (still maintaining our assumption that the Superman comics are an accurate historical record).

(16)   a.   Lois Lane knew-to-be-true "Superman can leap tall buildings in a single bound."
         b.   Lois Lane knew-to-be-true "Clark Kent can leap tall buildings in a single bound."

Of course if asked, Lois would accept the complement in (16a) but not that in (16b), and thus we seem to be able to account for the apparent difference in truth value.[12]

Despite its apparent solution to the problem of coreferential proper names in propositional attitude sentences, Quine's approach has not found favor in general. One problem is that presented by languageless creatures to whom we would want to attribute propositional attitudes. It seems perfectly reasonable to attribute to a dog a desire to be taken for a walk, or to conclude that a cat knows that its food bowl is empty. Quine himself anticipated this objection with the following comment:

This semantical reformulation is not, of course, intended to suggest that the subject of the propositional attitude speaks the language of the quotation, or any language. We may treat a mouse's fear of a cat as his fearing true a certain English sentence. This is unnatural without being therefore wrong. It is a little like describing a prehistoric ocean current as clockwise.   (Quine 1956: 109)

---

[12]   However see below, in §5.7, where we see a parallel problem involving only one name.

Somehow Quine's analogy is not satisfactory. Technically he may be right, but still we would like our analysis of sentences about propositional attitudes to tell us something about what propositional attitudes are attitudes toward, and his solution does not seem to offer us this possibility in general.

Donald Davidson (1969) presents a revised version of Quine's approach. Although the paper is called "On saying that", Davidson views his approach as not only a "a correct analysis of indirect discourse" but also "an analysis that opens a lead to an analysis of psychological sentences generally (sentences about propositional attitudes, so-called)" (Davidson 1969: 93). In this paper Davidson proposes construing the *that* which may precede complements of verbs of saying as a demonstrative which indicates the sentence in question. Thus (17a) is analyzed as (17b):

(17) a. Galileo said that the earth moves.
      b. Galileo said that. The earth moves.

Davidson supports this cute analysis with citation to remarks in the Oxford English Dictionary suggesting that, historically, the source of the complementizer *that* is something quite like this. However for Davidson, the *that* plus the *said* that precedes it are much more than they appear. On his view they incorporate an appeal to a "samesaying" relation; the idea is that the speaker's utterance of *the earth moves* is put forward as saying the same thing as an utterance of Galileo's. One of Davidson's aims is to account for the failure of substitutivity, and he says "... if the second utterance [i.e. the embedded sentence] is different in any way at all, the first utterance *might* have had a different truth value, for the reference of the 'that' would have changed" (Davidson 1969: 108; italics in original). Fair enough, but this does not tell us why exchanging proper names for the same entity matters to saying the same thing while, for example, exchanging an active sentence for a passive one does not.

It was in this paper that Davidson launched his famous barb against Frege:

If we could recover our pre-Fregean innocence, I think it would seem to us plainly incredible that the words "the earth moves", uttered after the words "Galileo said that", mean anything different, or refer to anything else, than is their wont when they come in other environments.   (Davidson 1969: 108)

But a more sympathetic view might see Frege as trying (among other things) to determine what our propositional attitudes relate us to—his dubbing of those entities as "thoughts" (*Gedanken*) reinforces this view. And for reasons already stated, this makes the Fregean approach, despite its problems, more appealing than the quotational one.

5.6.2 Causal description theories

Following the appearance and absorption of Kripke's and Donnellan's arguments against the traditional descriptional theories of proper names, a number of philosophers have offered modified versions of those theories. The modified versions incorporate something like a causal-historical chain into the descriptive content expressed by the name, where the causal-historical chain provides the mechanism by which a name is linked to its referent. Searle (1983) is a partial example. Recall the "cluster" view from Searle (1958a), which was sketched above in §5.2. The newer paper suggests that among the cluster of identifying descriptions associated with a name can be ones which recapitulate the causal chain. "The descriptivist says that one sort of identifying description that one can attach to a name 'N' is 'the person referred to by others in my linguistic community as 'N''" (Searle 1983: 244). However Searle is only a partial example, because, in this work anyway, he holds that descriptions of this kind are not always semantically associated with a name, but only sometimes.

> In general, the contribution that a name makes to the truth conditions of statements is simply that it is used to refer to an object. But there are some statements where the contribution of the name is not, or is not solely, that it is used to refer to an object: in identity statements, in existential statements, and in statements about Intentional states [i.e. statements about propositional attitudes].   (Searle 1983: 258)

What Searle is saying here is that in some occurrences, names are nondescriptional but in others—in statements of identity, existence, or propositional attitudes—they are descriptional and incorporate information about the relevant speech community. This sort of view would seem to present a problem for a compositional semantics in which the meanings of phrases are determined by the meanings of their parts. The meaning of a phrase containing a proper name, on Searle's view, would not be determined by its parts but instead would require information from the larger context—whether the phrase occurred as part of a propositional attitude sentence, for example.

Many others have held the more straightforward view that proper names simply do express this type of metalinguistic content. Thus David Lewis remarks:

Did not Kripke and his allies refute the description theory of reference, at least for names of people and places? . . .

I disagree. What was well and truly refuted was a version of descriptivism in which the descriptive senses were supposed to be a matter of famous deeds and other distinctive peculiarities. A better version survives the attack: *causal descriptivism*. The descriptive sense associated with a name might for instance be 'the place I have heard of under the name "Taromeo" ' or maybe 'the causal source of this token: Taromeo', and for an account of the relation being invoked here, just consult the writings of the causal theorists of reference.

(Lewis 1997: 353, n. 22; italics in original)

Michael Devitt has proposed a somewhat similar theory on which the causal chain linking a use of a name to the original dubbing serves in lieu of a sense for the name (cf. Devitt 1981; Devitt and Sterelny 1999).

This type of approach to the meaning of a name suffers from a number of problems. For one thing, most ordinary speakers have no knowledge of the causal theory of how names get their meaning, so the descriptive sense associated with names they use confidently would contain elements which are totally opaque to them. In the case of Devitt's version of this type of approach the situation would be even worse, since the chain itself is intended to function as a Fregean sense; even those of us who are familiar with the causal chain theory typically don't know anything about where we picked up a name in the first place. Then too, the causal chains in question are constantly changing as new links are added, in ways that are completely unknown to us. But it would not seem correct to say that the meaning of a name is constantly changing.

5.6.3 "The bearer of N"

A third type of metalinguistic approach, and probably the one most people have in mind today when they use the term "metalinguistic" to describe a theory of proper names, is perhaps the simplest; it holds that the meaning of a name N is something like "the entity named *N*" or "the bearer of *N*". Kent Bach is a prominent and long-standing proponent of this approach (see e.g. Bach 1987, 2002), but others who have put forward similar ideas are Katz (1977, 2001),

Recanati (1993), Geurts (1997), and Justice (2001). This approach would seem to have a good chance of solving the problem of coreferential names in propositional attitude contexts: since, for example, the names *Superman* and *Clark Kent* would now differ in meaning (one meaning 'the bearer of *Superman*' and the other meaning 'the bearer of *Clark Kent*'), we would not expect them to be substitutable in propositional attitude contexts.

In "Naming and necessity" Kripke responded to an early proponent of this type of metalinguistic theory, William Kneale, who had made the following suggestion:

> ...ordinary proper names of people are not, as John Stuart Mill supposed, signs without sense[.] While it may be informative to tell a man that the most famous Greek philosopher was called Socrates, it is obviously trifling to tell him that Socrates was called Socrates; and the reason is simply that he cannot understand your use of the word 'Socrates' at the beginning of your statement unless he already knows that it means "the individual called Socrates".   (Kneale 1962: 629–30)

Kripke was not impressed with this argument, and responded with a touch of sarcasm:

> In the same sense, I suppose, you could get a good theory of the meaning of any expression in English and construct a dictionary. For example, though it may be informative to tell someone that horses are used in races, it is trifling to tell him that horses are called 'horses'. Therefore this could only be the case because the term 'horse', means in English 'the things called "horses"'.   (Kripke 1972/1980: 69)

This response of Kripke's to Kneale's theory is sometimes called the "generality" argument, because holders of the metalinguistic theory need to explain why their theory should not apply generally. Kripke also thought that Kneale's approach was circular:

> We ask, 'To whom does he refer by "Socrates"?' And then the answer is given, 'Well, he refers to the man to whom he refers.' If this were all there was to the meaning of a proper name, then no reference would get off the ground at all.
>
> (Kripke 1972/1980: 70)

Kripke's modal argument, given above in §5.3.2, would also seem to apply against metalinguistic theories of the meaning of proper names. Thus (18a) seems false while (18b) seems true.

(18)   a.   Aristotle might not have been Aristotle.
       b.   Aristotle might not have been the person called *Aristotle*.

The recent proponents of this type of metalinguistic theory who were listed above have responded to Kripke's arguments.[13] Thus Bach (1987, 2002) argues that (18a) does have a reading under which it is true and means the same as (18b). He also has responses to Kripke's circularity and generality arguments which the reader may want to consider. (See also Recanati (1993: ch. 9).) However there is an additional problem to be faced, to which we now turn.

5.7 Kripke's puzzle

Kripke was not unaware of the problems presented by a return to Mill's nondescriptional theory of proper names, especially for our understanding of sentences about propositional attitudes, and he addressed them from an interesting direction in a follow-up paper titled "A puzzle about belief" (Kripke 1979). Recall that we have framed this problem, as is traditional, as a problem of failure of substitutivity— when we substitute one proper name for a coreferential one in a propositional attitude context, as we did in the sentences about Lois Lane and her beliefs about Superman/Clark Kent, we run the risk of going from a truth to a falsehood (or vice versa). In "A puzzle about belief" Kripke argued that substitution of one name for another was not the source of the problem. He did this by showing that the same problem could arise without substitution.

5.7.1 London/Londres and Paderewski

Kripke's first example involved a French lad, Pierre, who, while growing up in France, has learned many things about a foreign city called *Londres*. On the basis of postcards and picture books, Pierre forms the belief that this city is a beautiful one, and indeed willingly asserts (19).

(19)   Londres est jolie.

---

[13] A recent article by Daniel Rothschild (2007), while not defending the metalinguistic theory, argues that Kripke's modal argument does not have force against it. Rothschild's argument depends on the distinction between role-type descriptions and particularized descriptions which was mentioned above in Chapter 3. Briefly, he argues that descriptions like *the individual named N* are particularized, and thus do not take narrow scope with respect to logical modals. Thus he holds that (18b) (which is from Abbott (2001)) is not felicitous on the intended reading.

But then poor Pierre is kidnapped, forced into the slave trade, and finds himself in the very worst part of London. He acquires English by the direct method (that is, with no explicit instruction), and asserts vehemently (20).

(20)   London is not pretty.

The simple question Kripke poses for us is the following: Does Pierre, or does he not, believe that London is pretty?

It is important to be clear that what needs answering is Kripke's simple question. Describing the situation in other terms is not difficult at all—indeed, that is exactly what Kripke has done (and I have summarized here). And it is quite clear **why** the puzzle arises. What is not so clear is how to resolve it—how to answer the simple question. Note too that Kripke intended this question to be taken *de dicto*. Taken *de re* the answer is straightforward: Pierre believes, of London, that it is pretty. Of course he also believes, of London, that it is not pretty. But having contradictory *de re* beliefs about a single entity is not so puzzling—it seems relatively easy to fail to recognize something one has encountered before. On the other hand taking Kripke's question *de dicto* does pose us with a real problem, since on the *de dicto* interpretation, sentences about beliefs are supposed to represent those beliefs from the point of view of the believer.

Kripke gave another instance of this puzzle, even more pressing than the one about Pierre. This one involves Peter, a monolingual English speaker. Peter knows of Paderewski the great pianist and composer. He has also heard several times of the Polish statesman Paderewski, but does not know that this is the same person, and he also believes quite strongly that politicians never have musical talent. So the simple question this time is: Does Peter, or does he not, believe that Paderewski had musical talent?

Kripke himself seems to have believed that these questions are unanswerable. He wrote:

When we enter into the area exemplified by... Pierre, we enter into an area where our normal practices of interpretation and attribution of belief are subjected to the greatest possible strain, perhaps to the point of breakdown. So is the notion of the *content* of someone's assertion, the *proposition* it expresses.

(Kripke 1979: 269, italics in original)

Although Kripke could not answer his own question, others have tried, and indeed, we can find all four possible answers scattered about in this literature: yes, no, yes and no, neither yes nor no. Plus some others. Some of these will emerge in the following sections, when we consider what the metalinguistic theoreticians have offered in response, and what the hidden indexical and bite-the-bullet theories of belief attribution have to say. For the remainder of this discussion we will focus on the Paderewski version of the problem, since it has the crucial features of the London/*Londres* case, plus the added challenge of involving just a single name in a single language.

5.7.2 Metalinguistic responses

As we saw in the preceding section, there are (at least) three types of metalinguistic approach to the problem of proper names in propositional attitude contexts. Those in the first, Quinean, category, which involves attributions of a relation to a sentence or utterance, do not seem capable of dealing with the Paderewski case. Since these approaches are more or less purely linguistic, and there is no difference in either the name (*Paderewski*) nor the referent (Paderewski), there seems to be no way to deal with Peter.

The second type of metalinguistic theory involved incorporating information about a causal chain into a descriptive bundle for a proper name. While Peter himself would be the terminus of two distinct causal chains going back to Paderewski, in our vocabulary we can have only one, and thus we are left with the problem of answering Kripke's simple question about Peter. Devitt himself, a prominent holder of the metalinguistic causal chain approach, has leaned at different times toward different answers. In Devitt (1984) he inclined toward denying both that Peter believes that Paderewski had musical talent, and that Peter believes that Paderewski did not have musical talent. But Devitt (1990), while showing sympathy for the opposite view—that both versions of the question get "yes" answers—seems to side ultimately with Kripke's view that our linguistic resources do not make it possible to answer it.

Bach, a prominent holder of the "bearer of *N*" metalinguistic approach, has the following to say about the Paderewski problem:

Peter's two beliefs are that the bearer of 'Paderewski' who was a pianist had musical talent and that the bearer of 'Paderewski' who was a statesman had no musical talent. In short, Peter believes that Paderewski the pianist had musical talent and that Paderewski the statesman did not. And, of course, he did not believe that they were one and the same. In this way NDT [Nominal Description Theory—Bach's term for his version of this type of theory] can treat only 'the bearer of "N"' as semantically equivalent to 'N' while construing other descriptions under which one has beliefs . . . about a certain bearer of 'N' merely as cognitively (or contextually) associated with particular uses of 'N'. This is how NDT can distinguish Peter's two beliefs without assuming anything about how many bearers "Paderewski" has.   (Bach 1987: 167)

Bach's idea (one that he discusses at length in the rest of the book and elsewhere (e.g. Bach 2004, 2006)), is that how we describe people's propositional attitudes does not make the contents of those attitudes fully explicit. Presumably, then, Bach would also side with Kripke—that his simple question is unanswerable; but unfortunately he does not say this in so many words.

5.8 Solutions? Part 2: hidden indexical and bite-the-bullet approaches

The two remaining approaches to the problem of proper names in sentences about propositional attitudes that we will consider arose in conjunction with acceptance of both the Kripke-Donnellan view that names do not express a Fregean sense, and the Kaplan direct-reference view that names contribute their referents to the propositions expressed using them, resulting in RSPs which contain the actual entity named by the name. As we saw above in §5.5, this lands us in a serious problem with the sentences about Lois Lane, repeated here in (21).

(21) a.   Lois Lane knew that Superman could leap tall buildings in a single bound.
      b.   Lois Lane knew that Clark Kent could leap tall buildings in a single bound.

The complement clauses of both (21a) and (21b) would be the same proposition—the one consisting of Superman/Clark Kent and the property of being able to leap tall buildings in a single bound. Thus we cannot account for our intuitions that (21a) is true while (21b) is not.

   The two approaches we are about to look at introduce additional elements referencing the state of mind—the mental content—of the subject, but introduce these elements in different ways and at different levels. Hidden indexical theories introduce the mental content elements as part of the truth-conditional semantics of belief sentences, but varying with respect to context of utterance. In bite-the-bullet approaches, the mental content is a purely pragmatic inference.

5.8.1 Hidden indexical theories

Prominent hidden indexical theories (e.g. those of Schiffer (1977, 1992); Perry (1979); Crimmins and Perry (1989)), regard propositional attitude verbs like *believe* as having more arguments than are made explicit in actual utterances.[14] Crucially, they contain an argument which is intended to convey the mode of presentation of elements in the proposition, belief in which is being asserted. You will recall the term "mode of presentation" from our discussion of Frege's work in Chapter 2. It is (a translation of) the term Frege used to characterize senses. Recall Frege's triangle example from Chapter 2, in which the central point of the triangle was presented in two different ways. Modern theorists use the term "mode of presentation" with a strong psychological tinge that it's not clear Frege would have agreed with. In current work the term is intended to capture the perspective of the subject of the propositional attitude toward the parts of the proposition they are being said to believe, or to hold another propositional attitude toward. This perspective need not be linguistically encoded or even encodable, and it may be completely idiosyncratic. Another term for this way of grasping a proposition is NARROW CONTENT, which is distinguished from the proposition itself, or the BROAD CONTENT of a belief. (See e.g. Putnam (1975); Fodor (1980). For something more recent, see Segal (2000) and the works cited there.)

These theories are called "hidden indexical" theories because the additional element of mode of presentation (the narrow content) is hidden—i.e. not represented explicitly in the sentence; and because this additional element is indexical—it can vary from utterance to utterance, depending on the context.

Let us apply this type of approach to the examples about Lois Lane. The sentences in (21a, b) above would receive a logical form something like that in (22).

---

[14] There are several other sorts of hidden indexical theory worth mentioning. Mark Richard (1990) regards the complement of a belief sentence as expressing a translation of a sentence which is couched in the mental language of the believer and resides in that believer's "belief box." A part of the truth conditions on belief sentences requires that the translation be an acceptable one, and this can vary from context to context. And Graeme Forbes (1990, 2006) proposes the addition of a tacit "as such" modifier to the logical form of propositional attitude sentences.

(22)   Knew(Lois, <Clark Kent, leaping-tall-buildings-hood>, m))

According to (22), the proposition known by Lois is the RSP containing Clark Kent (aka "Superman") and the property of being able to
leap tall buildings in a single bound. The m in (22) is intended to stand
for a mode of presentation (in the current sense) by which Lois grasps
this proposition. That will include the way she understands the leaping
property involved (which is not in question here) as well as, crucially,
the way she conceives of the entity Clark Kent. Utterance of (21a), with
the name *Superman*, will naturally be taken to express an instance of
(22) in which the mode of presentation of Clark Kent would involve a
cape, a big S on the shirtfront, and some super properties. Thus (21a) is
used to express a truth. On the other hand utterances of (21b), with the
name *Clark Kent*, would express a version of (22) with a mode of
presentation involving a nerdy appearance and working at *The Daily
Planet*, among other things. Since under the latter mode of presentation Lois would not attribute flying capability to the guy, (21b) used in
this way expresses something false.

   Does Peter believe that Paderewski had musical talent? Well, according to hidden indexical theorists, he does and he doesn't. In a context
in which (23)

(23)   Peter believes that Paderewski had musical talent.

expresses a mode of presentation involving Paderewski's being a pianist and composer, (23) would be true. However in a context in which
(23) expresses a different mode, one involving Paderewski being the
Polish statesman, (23) would be false. One problem with this solution
to the puzzle of Peter and his beliefs about Paderewski is that it does
not tell us how to evaluate Kripke's question—Does Peter, or does he
not, believe that Paderewski had musical talent? Presumably that
question must be taken as inevitably ambiguous or indeterminate,
and yet Kripke himself, the utterer, would probably deny that.

5.8.2 Bite-the-bullet approaches

I term this last category of theories we will consider "bite-the-bullet"
approaches because they accept the consequences of the Kripke/
Donnellan analysis of proper names, combined with the direct reference
theory of Kaplan, without adding anything to the semantics of propositional attitude sentences to make up for the loss of Fregean senses.

Nathan Salmon (e.g. (1989, 1990)) and Scott Soames (e.g. (2002)) are and the most prominent adherents of this kind of approach.

Salmon and Soames agree with the hidden indexical theorists that belief itself involves a mode of presentation of a proposition to the believer. However they do not hold that English sentences about belief semantically encode any indication of that mode of presentation, although they do believe that it may be conveyed in an utterance of such a sentence. More specifically, the way in which we describe the contents of a belief would, in most contexts, convey pragmatically, perhaps as a kind of Gricean conversational implicature, the thought that the believer would accept the names or descriptions used. Thus on this approach (21a) and (21b) are both true, because Lois does have the belief that Clark Kent is able to leap tall buildings in a single bound. Of course she wouldn't put it that way, because the name *Clark Kent* is associated in her mind with the Clark Kentish mode of presentation of Superman. When we assert (21b), semantically we express the proposition that Lois knowingly attributes leaping ability to the individual Clark Kent, but we also convey pragmatically the idea that the term we use, in this case *Clark Kent*, is one that accurately reflects Lois's perspective. It is the falsity of this pragmatically conveyed proposition which leads us to mistakenly regard (21b) itself as false.[15] On this view, Peter **does** believe that Paderewski had musical talent (because there is at least one mode of presentation on which he has this belief). The answer to Kripke's simple question is "Yes."

The pragmatic approach of Salmon and Soames has received support from Jennifer Saul (1997, 1998), who points out that we have a similar problem in substituting coreferential proper names in ordinary simple sentences! Compare (24a) and (24b) (from Saul (1997)).

(24)   a.   Clark Kent went into a phone booth, and Superman came out.
       b.   Clark Kent went into a phone booth, and Clark Kent came out.

---

[15] I should note that Soames (2002) separates out "partially descriptive" names, such as *Professor Ruth Marcus*, whose semantic value includes some descriptive content in addition to their referent—in this case being a professor. If *Superman* is a partially descriptive name which includes something about super powers, then the account in the preceding paragraph would have to be revised to use different examples. Soames himself expresses indecision as to whether or not *Superman* is partially descriptive (Soames 2002: 121–2).

Assuming a typical scene from the comic book, it may seem that we go from a truth to a falsehood here, by substituting *Clark Kent* for *Superman*. The problem is that we have no propositional attitude verb to offer us an extra argument position, and no believing subject to whom to attribute a mode of presentation. We do have the pragmatic alternative however. Although (24b) may **seem** to be false, it is only what it conveys pragmatically—that Clark was still in his nerdish mode when he emerged from the phone booth—that is false. In support of this suggestion Saul pointed out the apparent cancellability of this implicature in (25):

(25)   Clark Kent went into the phone booth, and Clark Kent came out, but nobody recognized him. [= Saul 1997: ex. 1**]

Any analysis which makes (24b) false, instead of just misleading, will have a problem with the apparent truth of (25).

5.9 Summary and conclusions

It is time to try to sum up the contents of this chapter, and then evaluate the situation. As we have seen, the arguments of Kripke, Donnellan, and others for the nondescriptionality of proper names have proved convincing to many, although not to everyone. A major group of exceptions are the holders of metalinguistic views according to which a name *N* expresses something like "the bearer of *N*." Kripke's arguments against this view—that it is circular and would apply as well (or ill) to all words in a language—as well as Kripke's modal argument have been replied to at length by Bach and others, in the works cited above, but it must be said that, at this point in time anyway, not everyone has been convinced.

If we do not adopt one of the metalinguistic views, we are left with the issue of what the contribution of a proper name is to propositions expressed by sentences (or utterances) containing it. As we have seen, a vocal contingent opts for the Kaplanian view that names contribute their referents to such propositions, those propositions thus being RSPs. This leaves us with the pressing problems of (a) names of nonexistent individuals, and (b) propositional attitude contexts. The latter problem has received the most attention, and two main approaches have been put forward. In the hidden indexical approach, propositional attitudes are seen as three-place relations, with the third relatum intended to capture a way the subject of the propositional attitude conceptualizes the propositional components. In the bite-the-bullet approach, this conceptual information is held to be conveyed only pragmatically.

Speaking as a linguist and as a speaker of English, I must say that I find the arguments of Mill and Kripke for the nondescriptionality of proper names completely convincing. Indeed, despite the dominance of Frege and (especially) Russell in twentieth-century philosophy of language, logicians seem to have consistently regarded proper names as the natural-language counterparts of individual constants in logic, which are simply assigned values. (Compare, for example, the treatment in Copi (1953: 281).) This was true well before Donnellan's and Kripke's works on the subject, when philosophers of language in other contexts seemed to accept either the Frege-Russell descriptional view, or the modified Wittgenstein-Searle cluster view.

I do not, however, think it is wise to take the further step suggested by Kaplan and adopted by so many others, and conclude that the entity denoted by a proper name is its meaning, or what it contributes to the semantic content of sentences containing it. And note that to call this view Millian, as many do (e.g. Salmon (1989, 1990)), seems wrong as well—Mill said the proper names **lacked** connotation; he did not say that they connoted their denotation.

I am going to go against both Mill and Kaplan here, and advocate the Montagovian line of viewing proper names as expressing a constant individual concept.[16] There are several advantages in so doing, some of which were mentioned above. One is that we don't have a problem with our ability to grasp propositions expressed with proper names, despite not having first-hand acquaintance with the individuals denoted by those names. On this I agree with Russell: if the proposition in question were one containing an actual entity, then lack of acquaintance with that entity should interfere with my grasping the proposition. (See also (Matthew) Davidson (2000).) Another advantage is that we don't have the problems with names of fictional beings that the RSP view has.

---

[16] Actually this only counts as going against Mill if individual concepts are viewed as connotations. However, for other kinds of NPs this identification does indeed make sense.

We will have a semantic constituent for sentences about Santa Claus, despite his nonexistence. (As I hinted above, this advantage is more far-reaching than it may appear at first, and we will return to it in Chapter 10.) And finally, on the CIC approach we can still adopt the pragmatic explanation suggested by Salmon, Soames, and Saul for the failure of coreferential names to be completely equivalent despite their semantic equivalence.

6

Definite descriptions

...I would give the doctrine of this word [*the*] if I were "dead from the waist down" and not merely in a prison.

Bertrand Russell, "Descriptions"

Much has been written about definite descriptions. This may seem reasonable in light of the fact that *the* is the most commonly used word of English. On the other hand, English is apparently in the minority of languages in having a definite article to worry about.[1] In any case, in this chapter we will attempt to get clear on what all the fuss is about. We'll begin by reviewing what Mill, Frege, and Russell had to say about definite descriptions. At that point it seems that a major issue is whether definite descriptions are referential expressions, or are instead quantificational expressions. However we will see that this issue is more complicated than it first appears. In §6.2 we'll review some important challenges to Russell's theory given by P. F. Strawson. Following that, we examine Keith Donnellan's claim that definite descriptions have two interpretations—referential and attributive. Interest here has generally focused on the claim of a referential interpretation, and whether it is semantically encoded or (merely) conveyed pragmatically. In §6.4 we look at a distinction in indefinite descriptions similar to the one Donnellan claimed for definite descriptions. The concluding section summarizes the chapter.[2]

---

[1] In his valuable cross-linguistic investigation of definiteness, Christopher Lyons remarks that "the encoding of simple (in)definiteness is far from universal; indeed, languages marking it are in a distinct minority" (1999: 48).

[2] We will confine our attention here to definite descriptions as they occur in syntactic argument positions—as subjects or objects. See Graff (2001) for an examination of definite descriptions which function as predicates (including an interesting suggestion that this function is fundamental to their other occurrences).

6.1 Review

6.1.1 The views of Mill, Frege, and Russell

For both Mill and Frege, definite descriptions were referential expressions. In Mill's terms, they have a denotation in addition to their connotation; in Frege's terms, they have *Bedeutung* (reference), as well as *Sinn* (sense). A definite description such as *the star of Evita*, for example, refers to (denotes) the singer Madonna. That is because she possesses the property expressed by the NP (its sense or connotation), namely the property of having been the star of the movie *Evita*.

On the other hand in Russell's view *the star of Evita* is of the same semantic type as obviously quantificational NPs like *every actress, some surprises,* and *no child of mine.* They are all quantificational expressions, and thus received an analysis only in the context of a complete sentence, as shown in (1)–(4); here I've given the logical forms in the restricted quantification format.

(1) a. Every actress exercises.
    b. $\text{every}_x[\text{actress}(x)]\ (\text{exercises}(x))$

(2) a. Some surprises are unwelcome.
    b. $\text{some}_x\ [\text{surprise}(x)]\ (\text{unwelcome}(x))$

(3) a. No child of mine is umbrageous.
    b. $\text{no}_x\ [\text{child-of-mine}(x)]\ (\text{umbrageous}(x))$

(4) a. The star of *Evita* was born in Michigan.
    b. $\text{the}_x\ [\text{star-of-}Evita(x)]\ (\text{born-in-Michigan}(x))$

In each case the quantifier (*every, some, no, the*) expresses a relation between two properties—the one expressed by the CNP (common noun phrase) with which they combine (*actress, surprises, child of mine, star of Evita*), and the one expressed by the predicate (VP) that the NP combines with to make a sentence (*exercises, are unwelcome, is umbrageous, was born in Michigan*).[3]

---

[3] The restricted quantification forms are a bit easier to read, and are in common use these days, but they do obscure a couple of interesting features of Russell's analysis of *the*. If we look at the old fashioned logical form in (i), these are revealed.

(i) $\exists x \forall y [[\text{star-of-}Evita(y) \leftrightarrow y = x]\ \&\ \text{born-in-Michigan}(x)]$

First, this logical form is more complex than the ones for the other determiners, e.g. *every* and *some*, shown below in (ii).

(ii) a. $\forall x[\text{actress}(x) \rightarrow \text{exercises}(x)]$
     b. $\exists x[\text{surprise}(x)\ \&\ \text{unwelcome}(x)]$

6.1.2 Comparison of referential and quantificational views

We need to try to get clearer on the essential differences between a referential view of definite descriptions and a quantificational analysis. Note first that one could incorporate aspects of Russell's quantificational analysis into a referential one. On Russell's analysis definite descriptions assert the existence of a unique entity meeting the descriptive content of the CNP. The core of this meaning ("unique entity meeting the descriptive content of the CNP") could be viewed instead as part of the sense or connotation of a definite description, by one who wanted to maintain a referential view.[4] So this does not distinguish between the two theories.

According to the logical forms in (1)–(4), quantificational NPs are not logical constituents. As we saw in Chapter 2, this feature of Russell's analysis was important in his solution to the problem of the apparent failures of substitutivity in opaque contexts. On the other hand in Chapter 4 we saw that Montague was able to devise a formal semantics in which definite descriptions and (other) quantificational expressions do indeed receive an interpretation by themselves. They are interpreted as generalized quantifiers—sets of sets; so (ignoring intensionality) *the star of Evita* would denote the set of sets of which Madonna is a member. On yet another hand, as we know

While the forms in (ii) specify only a relation between the CNP set and the VP set, (i) imposes a particular condition on the CNP set (stars of *Evita*), namely that it be a singleton, in addition to specifying the relation between this set and that denoted by the predicate (the set of entities born in Michigan). And secondly, the relation in question could be looked at either as the same as that expressed in (iia), with the universal quantifier, or as expressed in (iib), with the existential quantifier. That is, given a unique star of *Evita*, we could say that the stars of *Evita* are a subset of the Michiganders (like the universal), or we could say that there is a non-null overlap between stars of *Evita* and Michiganders (like the existential). Of course the logical form in (i) uses conjunction (&) as its main connective, like (iib), but there is a logically equivalent form with the *if-then* connective (→), as shown in (iii).

(iii) $\exists x \forall y [\text{star-of-}Evita(y) \leftrightarrow y = x] \& \forall z [\text{star-of-}Evita(z) \rightarrow \text{born-in-Michigan}(z)]$

Indeed, philosophers of language will often offer a paraphrase of Russell's analysis that sounds more like (iii) than (i). And recall the Barwise and Cooper definition of *the* from Chapter 4, according to which *the* means *every* (with the additional condition that the restriction set be a singleton).

Incidentally, this raises the question of what to do about plural definite descriptions, like *the stars of Evita*. We will get to that in the next chapter, but I can say now that there is a relatively straightforward extension of Russell's analysis to cover these.

[4] Below in Chapter 9 we will consider a number of alternatives to uniqueness as the essence of definiteness.

from Chapter 3, sets are really equivalent to functions of a certain type—characteristic functions. In this sense sets are "unsaturated" kinds of things—they are searching for an argument, in combination with which they can yield a truth value. So really *the star of Evita* would denote a function from sets to truth values—the value true for sets to which Madonna belongs and false for those to which she doesn't. Thus even though Montague solved the problem of providing definite descriptions (and (other) quantificational NPs) with a denotation, it was still a very different kind of denotation from the kind envisioned by Mill and Frege—essentially a function rather than an ordinary entity like a person or a chair. This is reflected in the type difference discussed by Partee (1986) which we looked at the end of Chapter 4—the difference between being of (extensional) type $\ll e,t>,t>$ and being of type e.

There are a couple of important points to bear in mind here. The first is that the **truth conditions** assigned to sentences containing definite descriptions under a Montagovian generalized quantifier semantics are the same as those assigned according to an old fashioned Russellian logical form. In general there may be many ways to analyze a given NP which will give similar results, and it is not always easy to tell when one is correct and another is not. The second important point is that Montague analyzed **all** kinds of NPs as generalized quantifiers— overtly quantificational NPs and definite descriptions as well as proper names and pronouns. That was the whole point—to have a unified semantic type for all NPs. However as we saw at the end of Chapter 4, Partee (1986) has suggested that not all kinds of NPs are most naturally interpreted as generalized quantifiers—of type $\ll e,t>,t>$. Proper names and pronouns, in at least some of their uses, seem more naturally to be of type e.

There is another property which seems to distinguish quantificational NPs and that is participation in scope ambiguities. As we saw above in Chapter 3, overtly quantificational NPs do participate in such ambiguities; thus (5) below can mean either that there is one particular book that every child read, or that every child read some book or other, with possibly as many different books as there were children involved.

(5)   Every child read a book.

Although (6) below seems to be unambiguous, that is probably because the definite description *the book* is best understood anaphorically, as denoting a particular book which has been introduced into the context.

(6)   Every child read the book.

On the other hand an example like (7) clearly shows the expected ambiguity.

(7)   Every child read the book that had been assigned to them.

(7) can mean either that there is a particular assigned book which every child read, or that every child had been assigned a possibly different book which they read.[5] This suggests a quantificational analysis, but may not insist on it. As we noted in Chapter 3, the discovery of readings apparently not accounted for under a traditional scope analysis has led a number of researchers to pursue alternatives.[6]

The upshot is that deciding whether definite descriptions are referential or quantificational is not at all a straightforward task. We have seen that they **can** be analyzed quantificationally, but so can all NPs. As Peters and Westerståhl note: "one should resist the temptation to call something a quantifier expression simply on the grounds that its meaning *can* be analyzed in terms of quantification" (2006: 16; italics in original). We must leave this issue in its unresolved state for now.

---

[5] Contrast Peters and Westerståhl (2006), who suggest that definite descriptions do not participate in this type of scope ambiguity. By way of argument they offer example (i)

(i)   The novices chose a mentor.

which they say "unambiguously entails that all novices have the same mentor" (17, n. 12). However one could dispute this judgment. Note that (ii) does not imply that all students chose the same major.

(ii)   In their sophomore year the students chose a major.

Similarly (iii) has a sensible reading, involving different apples.

(iii)   The children ate an apple for lunch.

A complicating issue here is the fact that these definite descriptions are plurals, which brings issues of group vs distributive interpretations into the picture—something we will get to in the next chapter.

Ultimately Peters and Westerståhl themselves seem to hedge on whether definite descriptions are quantificational, noting on the one hand that they can be analyzed as quantifiers (121), but on the other (as we see in the main text below) that simply because an NP can be analyzed in quantificational terms doesn't mean that it is a quantifier (16).

[6] Elbourne (2005: 98–112) argues specifically against the Russellian quantificational analysis of definite descriptions, and in favor of a Fregean analysis.

6.2 Strawson's objections to Russell

P. F. Strawson's 1950 paper "On referring" was a critique of Russell's "On denoting,"[7] and it behooves us to spend a little time on this critique since it raises issues central to our problem of the referentiality of definite descriptions. We will look here at three different points Strawson argued for.

6.2.1 Expressions vs uses of expressions

One of Strawson's main points was to stress the distinction between expressions of a language and uses of those expressions on particular occasions. He argued at length that it is a mistake to think of definite descriptions themselves as referring; rather, people use definite descriptions to refer to things. " 'Mentioning', or 'referring', is not something an expression does; it is something that some one can use an expression to do" (Strawson 1950: 326). This is a statement of the pragmatic view of reference which we saw in Chapter 1, and Russell's famous example *The king of France is bald*, for which Strawson inexplicably substituted (8),

(8)   The king of France is wise

played directly into Strawson's hands. Strawson pointed out that it is silly to wonder who the referent of *the king of France* is without knowing when (8) was uttered. In 870, for example, (8) would naturally be used to make a claim about Charles II ("the Bald"), whereas five hundred years later one would have been making a different statement, about Charles V ("the Wise"). Thus we cannot, in general, associate a referent with a definite description, although we can associate a meaning with it. The meaning gives directions for the use of the expression to refer; the referent arises only on a particular occasion of use.

In part, this point of Strawson's can be summarized by saying that definite descriptions can be indexical, like more obvious indexicals such as *I* and *now*—that is, they depend in part on elements of the

---

[7] Note the date—45 years after "On denoting" first appeared. One might attribute this to the glacial pace of research in philosophy, but even within philosophy that's a long time to wait for critical objections to one's theory. Rather it's a tribute to the strength of Russell's paper. And it's a tribute to Russell's longevity that he was still around and able to compose a stinging rebuttal to Strawson's paper (Russell 1957).

context of utterance to determine a denotation.[8] We will have more
to say about indexicality in Chapter 8. However we should consider
whether this indexicality means that definite descriptions cannot be
said to refer. It is true that we cannot associate a single referent with
a definite description while abstracting away from occasions of use,
but it does not follow that we could not say that, e.g., *the king of
France*, as it is used on a particular occasion has a referent, just as we
might want to say that when I say *You should be paying attention* to
one of my students, the word *you* has that student as its referent on
that occasion.

6.2.2 Presupposition vs assertion

As part of his critique Strawson pointed out that when we use definite
descriptions we do not **assert** that there is one and only one entity
fitting the description used, as Russell's analysis suggests. Rather, he
said, the existence and uniqueness of a referent are only implied, in a
special sense of "imply." (Two years later Strawson introduced the term
"presuppose" for this special sense of "imply" (Strawson 1952: 175).)
Strawson argued that if the implication of existence fails, as it would
for utterances of (8) following 1848, these utterances would lack a truth
value. Strawson's conclusion on this issue is similar to that of Frege
(which we saw above in §2.4.3), although arrived at for different
reasons.[9] Frege associated referents, including truth values, with linguistic expressions themselves, and it is in virtue of compositionality
(on the level of reference) that a sentence containing a nonreferring
constituent would lack a truth value. For Strawson, as we saw in the
preceding subsection, referents belong to the users of expressions
rather than the expressions themselves, and he seemed to base his
argument for lack of truth value primarily on our intuitions.

Now suppose some one [*sic*] were in fact to say to you with a perfectly serious air:
'The king of France is wise'. Would you say, 'That's untrue'? I think it's quite certain
that you wouldn't. But suppose he went on to *ask* you whether you thought that
what he had just said was true, or was false;.... I think you would be inclined, with
some hesitation, to say that you didn't do either; that the question of whether his

---

[8] In his reply to Strawson (mentioned in the previous footnote), Russell remarked that if
he had replaced *the (present) king of France* with *the king of France in 1905*, "the whole of
[Mr. Strawson's] argument would have collapsed" (Russell 1957: 385).

[9] Strawson's failure to mention Frege's views in this connection is probably a result of
the general neglect of Frege's work during the first part of the twentieth century.

statement was true or false simply *didn't arise*, because there was no such person as the king of France.   (Strawson 1950: 330; italics in original, and footnote omitted)

Despite the sharp difference in their line of argumentation, Strawson and Frege agree that if there is nothing denoted by a definite description, the sentence containing it (or a statement made by a sentence containing it) lacks a truth value.

Since Strawson's paper a large body of work has accumulated on presuppositions, investigating many other constructions in addition to definite descriptions which seem to convey elements of meaning that are not asserted. A central issue has been whether or not presupposition failure does indeed result in a truth-value "gap," as asserted by Strawson and Frege—that is, whether or not presuppositions are a semantic phenomenon. There was a flurry of technical work on what are often called "three-valued logics" providing a formal apparatus for such an approach (cf. e.g. van Fraassen (1966, 1971)). The alternative to the semantic view is a pragmatic one, according to which presuppositions are constraints on assertability or appropriateness; Stalnaker (1973, 1974, 1978) has been an early and consistent supporter of this view. Possibly the dominant view held by linguists today (though not yours truly) is the semantic one involving truth-value gaps; von Fintel (2004) is a recent contribution.[10]

6.2.3 Incomplete descriptions

The previous point concerned the implication of existence that is associated with definite descriptions. Strawson's critique raised another point against Russell that has also received, and continues to receive, a lot of attention, and this point concerned the other clause of Russell's analysis—the implication of uniqueness. Here is what Strawson says about that.

Consider the sentence, 'The table is covered with books'. It is quite certain that in any normal use of this sentence, the expression 'the table' would be used to make a unique reference, *i.e.* to refer to some one table.... Russell says that a phrase of the form 'the so-and-so', used strictly, 'will only have an application in the event of there being one so-and-so and no more'. Now it is obviously quite false that the phrase 'the table' in the sentence 'the table is covered with books', used normally

---

[10] Briefly, my own view is that presuppositions arise as a consequence of the way information is packaged in an utterance. More details can be found in Abbott (2000, 2008b).

will 'only have an application in the event of there being one table and no more'. It is indeed tautologically true that, in such a use, the phrase will have an application only in the event of there being one table and no more *which is being referred to*, and that it will be understood to have an application only in the event of there being one table and no more which it is understood as being used to refer to. To use the sentence is not to assert, but it is (in the special sense discussed) to imply, that there is only one thing which is *both* of the kind specified (*i.e.* a table) *and is being referred to* by the speaker.   (Strawson 1950: 332; italics in original)

Definite descriptions like *the table* in Strawson's example, which are used successfully despite the multitude of entities fitting the description used in the world at large, have come to be called INCOMPLETE (sometimes also "indefinite") definite descriptions. And the problem for Russell is that, according to his analysis *the CNP* entails that there is at most one entity with the property expressed by CNP, but lots of times that isn't literally the case.[11]

Stephen Neale, in a lengthy and vigorous defense of Russell's analysis, points out that a similar problem occurs with obviously quantificational determiners. Thus (9), to use Neale's (1990: 98) example,

(9)   Everyone was sick.

uttered in response to a question about a dinner party, would convey, not that everyone in the whole wide world was sick but only that everyone at the party was sick. So it is not obvious that the existence of incomplete definite descriptions can be used to argue that definite descriptions are not quantificational. Nevertheless the problem is a serious one, inspiring two main lines of attack, which I will call "the expansion approach" and "the contraction approach."[12]

The expansion approach involves expanding an incomplete definite description in some way so that it is complete. Let us take Strawson's example in (10) to illustrate.

(10)   The table is covered with books.

---

[11] Note that Strawson does not deny the uniqueness aspect of definite descriptions, and his comments here are not really sufficient to determine an analysis which solves the problem. The issue of the **nature** of the uniqueness claim, which is the one we are concerned with, has somehow gotten confounded with the issue of its **status**—asserted or only implied in this special sense of "imply."

[12] These approaches have other labels: "explicit" vs "implicit," "semantic" vs "pragmatic." See Reimer and Bezuidenhout (2004: part I) and the works cited there, for extensive discussion.

We might propose that the NP *the table* is an abbreviation of, or is elliptical for, some longer NP with extra descriptive content, e.g. *the table in this room* or *the table over there*. The main problem with this idea is that the extra content is fundamentally underdetermined: if pressed, speakers could supply a variety of supplementary contents which would do the job of explicitly picking out the table in question equally well. We do not have a clear intuition that one as opposed to another is in fact the one that was intended, and even if we did there is no way that an addressee would be guaranteed to arrive at the very same one, and yet we have no sense of a failure to communicate anything in the normal use of an incomplete description.

The contraction approach begins with the idea that in a typical conversation the relevant universe of discourse does not contain everything in God's universe, but only that tiny subset of items relevant to the conversation at hand. That being the case, use of a definite description does not require that the description apply uniquely within the whole universe but only within that relevant small set. Similar remarks would go for other quantificational NPs. Various ways of formalizing this idea have been suggested—typically by proposing some kind of tacit index associated with either determiners or CNP expressions.[13] Such indices could specify a situation within which a denotation for the NP is to be found (recall the introduction of situations as mini possible worlds, which we reviewed above in Chapter 3). Thus a logical form for (10) might look like (11).

(11)   the$_x$[table-in-s(x)](covered-with-books(x))

The *s* in (11) is a variable over situations, the idea being that in an utterance of (10) the variable will get identified as the particular situation under discussion.[14]

---

[13] See, among others, Stanley and Szabó (2000a) and Elbourne (2005), but see also Bach's (2000) reply to Stanley and Szabó (and Stanley and Szabó's (2000b) reply to Bach). Bach himself takes the unusual position that Russell's analysis is literally correct as to what is said using a definite description; the more constrained proposition that is understood is conveyed pragmatically.

[14] The introduction of variables into our semantic representations, such as the *s* in (11), should not be treated casually. If we take such a variable merely as a shorthand for the fact that speakers intend their addressees to interpret their utterances relative to a salient context that is one thing. But if it is intended as an actual element of the logical form of an expression, the result must be seen as a weakening of the associated theory. We will see a number of other instances in subsequent chapters where people have postulated extra variables in their semantic representations, and these instances raise the same issue.

Despite the popularity of contraction approaches they are not without problems. James McCawley pointed out the following example:

(12)   Yesterday **the dog** got into a fight with **a dog**. **The dogs**
       were snarling and snapping at each other for half an hour. I'll
       have to see to it that **the dog** doesn't get near **that dog** again.
       (= McCawley 1979: ex. 21, boldface in original)

Even if we constrain the relevant universe to the situation being
described by the speaker of (12), there are still two dogs there.[15]
David Lewis, citing examples like this one of McCawley's, concluded
that "[t]he proper treatment of descriptions must be more like this:
'the *F*' denotes *x* if and only if *x* is **the most salient *F*** in the domain of
discourse" (Lewis 1979b: 241; boldface in original). Yet putting things
this way seems a bit arbitrary; surely the requirement of salience should
be derivable from the exigencies of conversation and not have to be
specified as part of the meaning of *the*. In other words, the speaker says
the F intending that the addressee be able to identify a unique item; if
that item is not the most salient one possessing the property F, the
addressee is liable to misunderstand the utterance. We will return to
this issue below, in Chapters 9 and 10.

6.2.4 Summary

As I have tried to indicate in the foregoing, each of these points raised
by Strawson—the indexicality of definite descriptions, the fact that the
existence (and uniqueness) of a denotation should be regarded as
presupposed rather than asserted, and the problem of incomplete
descriptions—has stimulated lively discussion and debate in the last
half century of philosophy of language. However it is time now to turn
to another challenge, directed at both Russell and Strawson.

6.3 Donnellan's referential-attributive distinction

In his classic 1966 paper "Reference and definite descriptions" Keith
Donnellan argued that neither Russell nor Strawson had the correct

---

[15] McCawley's example is frequently cited but I have to confess some wariness about it.
It seems to me that there is a common use of definite descriptions like *the dog, the baby, the
house* to refer to one's own dog, baby, or house which is somewhat specialized—such
definite descriptions become almost like proper names of those entities.

view, since both had missed a systematic ambiguity in the way definite descriptions can be used. In this section we look first at Donnellan's referential-attributive distinction, focusing in particular on the referential construal. Then we will take a look at some proposals for a semantic analysis. Kripke has argued against one of these proposals, and proposed instead a pragmatic analysis, so we'll look next at that. Finally, we turn to some responses to Kripke from those who think that the distinction is indeed a semantic one.

6.3.1 Introduction of the referential construal

Some people prefer to have the definition first and the examples afterwards, but occasionally it is easier to go in the reverse order. Consider one of Donnellan's examples, given in (13):

(13)   Who is the man who is drinking a martini?

Imagine, as one possible context for (13), that the speaker—a minister at a church picnic where alcoholic beverages are strictly forbidden— has just heard that someone has smuggled in a cocktail. In this case the speaker does not have a particular individual in mind. The content of the description forms an integral part of the question, and the speaker desires identifying information about whoever fits that description. This is an example of the ATTRIBUTIVE use, and it is generally held to comport well with Russell's analysis. Indeed, we might give a para-phrase of the minister's inquiry in Russellian terms as follows: *There is a man drinking a martini here, and I want to know who it is.* But now imagine quite a different context—a bar scene, for instance, where two people are chatting and one of them becomes interested in the identity of the handsome individual on the other side of the room. The speaker of (13) in this case is simply interested in getting their addressee to know who it is they are asking about, and any other description that served that purpose (*the guy in the blue shirt, the hunk sitting at the end of the bar*) would have done as well. This is an example of Donnellan's REFERENTIAL use of definite descriptions.[16]

---

[16] Note that the referential-attributive distinction cross-cuts the distinction noted in Chapter 3 above between "role-type" or "semantic" definite descriptions and "particular-ized" or "pragmatic" definite descriptions. *The man drinking a martini* is a particularized definite description, and as we have seen it can be used either attributively or referentially. Similarly a role-type description like *the tallest student in the class* could be used either way as well.

Donnellan gave several features distinguishing referential from attributive uses of definite descriptions. Crucially, for an attributive use the content of the description used is central to the utterance, whereas for the referential use it is not. For the attributive use, the speaker is concerned with whoever or whatever should happen to satisfy the description used, whereas for the referential use they are concerned instead with that entity her-, him-, or itself, and not as description satisfier. It follows that while a speaker using a description attributively merely assumes that there is someone or something fitting the description used, in the referential use the speaker makes a stronger assumption concerning a particular person or thing, that they are the one fitting the description.

Donnellan also argued for an additional characteristic of the referential use, but this one has turned out to be more problematic. Consider another of his examples, given in (14).

(14)   The murderer of Smith is insane.

Let us put aside the attributive reading (where, say, the police have just come upon the body of the brutally murdered Smith). Let's instead jump to a later time, when it is widely assumed that Jones is the one who murdered Smith. We are now in the courtroom, and Jones is behaving extremely crazily—ranting at the judge, taking off his clothes, and so forth. Someone in attendance might utter (14), intending to refer to Jones and perhaps even nodding at Jones during the utterance. But suppose it turns out that Jones, although insane, is actually innocent—he didn't murder Smith. (Instead, Smith died of natural causes.) Donnellan held that nevertheless the person who asserted (14), using the description *the murderer of Smith* referentially, made a true statement. In general, then, Donnellan held that a speaker, using a definite description referentially, could say something true about an entity even though the intended referent failed to satisfy the description. For convenience, let us call this THE MISDESCRIPTION CHARACTERISTIC. We'll see below that many supporters of Donnellan have rejected this characteristic—it just does not seem to be correct to say that under the circumstances envisaged, the utterer of (14) has said something true.

In the years since Donnellan's paper appeared there has been general agreement that he is on to something, but widespread disagreement as to its nature. The crucial question is: Is the referential-attributive distinction something that is semantically encoded, or is it purely pragmatic? Donnellan himself was a bit ambivalent on this question.

> The grammatical structure of the sentence seems to me to be the same whether the description is used referentially or attributively: that is, it is not syntactically ambiguous. Nor does it seem at all attractive to suppose an ambiguity in the meaning of the words; it does not appear to be semantically ambiguous. (Perhaps we could say that the sentence is pragmatically ambiguous: the distinction between the roles that the description plays is a function of the speaker's intentions.)   (Donnellan 1966: 297)

Note that the pragmatic contribution envisaged here is in the choice, by the speaker, of how the description is used. But that would be no different from the case with any ambiguous expression. In general it is the speaker's intentions which determine which reading of an ambiguous expression is being used, for example whether their utterance of *I'll meet you by the bank* concerns a river or a financial institution. As we'll see below in §6.3.3, the most popular pragmatic view of the referential construal sees its pragmatic aspect somewhat differently. But first let us look at a couple of proposals for a semantic analysis.

6.3.2 Semantic analyses

Four years after Donnellan's paper appeared, in 1970, David Kaplan gave a talk in which he proposed a semantic analysis for Donnellan's referential reading of definite descriptions. (Unfortunately the paper, "Dthat," was only published somewhat later, in 1978.) Kaplan (following Hintikka (1967)) pointed out the similarity between Donnellan's referential-attributive distinction and the *de re-de dicto* ambiguity of NPs in propositional attitude contexts. The latter ambiguity would show up in an example like (15).

(15)   Marie believes that the murderer of Smith is insane.

For the *de re* interpretation, imagine a situation in which Marie has observed strange behavior in a neighbor of hers, someone who, unbeknownst to her, happens to have murdered Smith. For the *de dicto* reading imagine instead that Marie's beliefs are a result of what she has read in the paper about sweet lovable Smith and the violence with which he was murdered by some unknown person.

(16) below gives the logical forms for the two readings of (15).

(16)   a. $\text{the}_x[\text{murderer-of-Smith}(x)](\text{believe}(\text{Marie}, \underline{\text{insane}(x)}))$
       b. $\text{believe}(\text{Marie}, \underline{\text{the}_x\,[\text{murderer-of-Smith}(x)](\text{insane}(x))}$

The contents of Marie's belief in the two cases are underlined. (16a) gives the *de re* reading, according to which Marie's belief involves a particular individual, the one who murdered Smith although Marie might not be aware of that. Suppose that Jones murdered Smith. Then the object of Marie's belief, according to (16a) is a proposition which is true in all those worlds in which Jones is insane. (16b) gives the *de dicto* reading, according to which Marie has a general belief concerning whoever it is that murdered Smith. Here the object of her belief is a proposition which is true at any world in which whoever murdered Smith in that world is insane. The two beliefs attributed to Marie in (15) seem entirely parallel, respectively, to the referential and attributive interpretations of the complement clause (i.e. (14)) which Donnellan had put forward.

There is another parallel between the *de re* reading of a propositional attitude complement and the referential reading of an ordinary simple sentence. As we saw above in Chapter 2, *de re* readings permit substitution of coreferential NPs (while *de dicto* readings may not). Now see what Donnellan says about the referential use:

> ...when a definite description is used referentially, a speaker can be reported as having said something *of* something. And in reporting what it was of which he said something we are not restricted to the description he used, or synonyms of it; we may ourselves refer to it using any descriptions, names, and so forth, that will do the job.
>
> (Donnellan 1966: 303; italics in original)

This characteristic, exactly parallel to substitutivity on the *de re* reading of NPs in propositional attitude contexts, is a natural consequence of the fact that referential uses of definite descriptions involve assertions concerning the referents themselves, abstracting away from the content of the description.

The ambiguity of (15) was easily represented as in (16), since we have an embedded sentence, and so two possible scopes for the embedded definite description. But in the case of the referential-attributive distinction we do not have any complement-taking predicate to vary scope around. However Kaplan figured out a way to achieve the same effect without any layer of embedding. First, let us assume that the standard Russellian analysis of definite descriptions gives us the attributive reading. For (14), repeated here as (17), that reading would be as in (18).

(17)   The murderer of Smith is insane.

(18)   the$_x$ [murderer-of-Smith(x)](insane(x))

(18) represents a proposition which is true at any world in which whoever murdered Smith in that world is insane. This is exactly the same as the object of Marie's belief reported above in (15) on the *de dicto* interpretation and represented in (16b). So the problem is to find an appropriate proposition for the referential understanding of (17).

Recall from Chapter 2 the idea of Russellian singular propositions—propositions with actual entities in them.[17] In the last chapter we saw that many people believe that sentences with proper names express such propositions. Kaplan believes that this analysis is also appropriate for demonstrative NPs (e.g. *that chipmunk*), as we'll see in Chapter 8. In "Dthat," he proposed that definite descriptions used referentially were similar to demonstratives and deserved the same type of analysis. It is a way of construing them as rigid designators. Thus (17) on its referential reading would receive the analysis in (19).

(19)   <Smith's murderer, the property of being insane>

(19) represents a proposition consisting of whoever it is that murdered Smith plus the property of being insane. This proposition would have the value true at any world in which the person who actually murdered Smith was insane, whether or not that individual murdered Smith in that world, exactly as with Marie's *de re* belief represented in (16a) above. This seems to capture the sense of the referential use that Donnellan was arguing for: the description itself does not play a role in the proposition expressed, which instead has a *de re* quality to it. Of course we have had to use that description to represent the proposition, but the first element of the proposition itself is a person, independent of any properties they might have.

As we saw in the last chapter, there is an alternative sort of analysis to Russellian singular propositions like that in (19), one which employs constant individual concepts in place of actual entities.[18] On this view the proposition expressed by (17) on the referential reading would contain, not the actual person who murdered Smith, but instead that person's individual concept—the function that picks them out of every world and time. This is a different way to interpret a definite description used rigidly. In order to represent this analysis of definite descriptions in a way parallel to (19), we need to devise a bit of notation. Let us

---

[17] Donnellan himself had alluded to these ideas of Russell's in this connection (cf. Donnellan 1966: 302f.).

[18] Something like this was suggested by Stalnaker (1972: 389ff.). See also the comments from Kripke (1977) quoted in the following subsection.

first use $[A]_a$ to stand for the denotation of A at the actual world. And then we can borrow Montague's up arrow ($^{\wedge}$) to form an expression denoting the intension of whatever it combines with. So $^{\wedge}[\textit{Smith's murderer}]_a$ is to represent a function that picks out of every world and time whoever it is that actually murdered Smith. If we replace the first constituent of (19) with this, we get (20).

(20) $<^{\wedge}[\textit{Smith's murderer}]_a$, the property of being insane$>$

The notation (which I have kind of cobbled together) is not so essential here. What is essential is the idea that we have an analysis of Donnellan's referential interpretation which involves a constant individual concept instead of an actual entity. We achieve the same effect as with the Russellian singular proposition represented in (19), in that the description used to pick out an entity does not figure in the proposition expressed.

We saw in Chapter 5 that the individual concept alternative seemed to avoid some problems that arose with the Russellian singular propositions in the case of nondenoting proper names, and we can expect a similar advantage in the present application. Thus suppose I say something like (21).

(21)   My mother was energetic.

Since I knew my mother well and intend to predicate a property of her independent of the fact that she was my mother, mostly likely I am using *my mother* referentially. On Kaplan's view the proposition I express should contain my mother, Bobbie Abbott. However she is no longer with us, raising questions about the status of that proposition. If, however, we suppose that referential uses express constant individual concepts, this problem does not arise. We'll be returning to this issue below, in Chapter 10.

I would like to make another point in connection with the constant individual concept analysis of Donnellan's referential interpretation, and that is what it suggests about the attributive interpretation. If (20) is a suitable logical form for (17) on its referential reading, then (22) might be a suitable logical form for (17) on its attributive reading.

(22) $<^{\wedge}[\textit{Smith's murderer}]$, the property of being insane$>$

(22) is just like (20) with the exception that the subscript a has been omitted. The idea is that (22) represents a proposition whose first constituent is the **variable** individual concept associated with the

definite description *the murderer of Smith*—the individual concept that picks out of any world whoever it was that murdered Smith in that world. It is often assumed that Donnellan's attributive reading is to be analyzed in Russellian terms, that is quantificationally. This is a natural assumption given the historical contrast between quantificational expressions and referential ones, plus the fact that Donnellan called his referential interpretation "referential." However, we see now that the attributive interpretation need not be seen as necessarily quantificational.

Finally, returning to the referential interpretation, note that neither Kaplan's analysis as in (19), nor the constant individual concept version in (20), incorporates the misdescription characteristic assumed by Donnellan. (A number of other scholars have also rejected this aspect of Donnellan's story, e.g. Wettstein (1981, 1983); Reimer (1998); Devitt (2004).) That is, on either analysis, we find whoever it is that actually murdered Smith, and then form a proposition involving either that person or their individual concept. If the speaker intended to be speaking about someone else (e.g. in the courtroom situation where Jones is behaving crazily, but in fact was not guilty of murdering Smith), that intention is not represented.[19]

We turn now to the most popular pragmatic analysis of Donnellan's referential-attributive distinction, that proposed by Saul Kripke.

6.3.3 Kripke's pragmatic analysis

Kripke (1977) presented a critique of Donnellan's referential-attributive distinction and proposed a pragmatic analysis, one quite different, however, from that suggested by Donnellan's brief remark quoted above. The title of Kripke's paper, "Speaker's reference and semantic reference," gives a strong clue as to the position he was arguing for. Kripke invoked a distinction between, on the one hand, what a speaker may wish to convey, and succeed in conveying, by means of an utterance, and on the other hand what is actually linguistically encoded in the utterance itself. (We have already seen this distinction in the work of Grice summarized briefly in Chapter 4.) Kripke's goal was to establish that uses which Donnellan would describe as referential are

---

[19] Kaplan (1978: 239f.) explicitly addressed this issue with respect to demonstratives, arguing that although speaker intentions do play a role in fixing reference where there is some degree of indeterminacy, they are not enough to overcome a direct conflict with the content of the utterance itself. However, somewhat later he changed his mind on this point (cf. Kaplan (1989: 582–4)).

uses in which the speaker may convey a proposition concerning a particular entity but where that proposition nevertheless is not encoded in the utterance. I will argue that Kripke's critique and analysis are weakened by his excessive focus on the misdescription characteristic that we have seen reason to abandon.

Kripke did stress that he had no knock-down argument against Donnellan, and that the considerations he brought to bear are primarily methodological. "Any conclusions about Russell's views *per se*, or Donnellan's, must be tentative" (Kripke 1977: 255). His main argument was of an interesting form: suppose that we stipulate that a language has such-and-such a semantics. Then if a certain phenomenon would arise in such a language, the fact that that phenomenon arises in English cannot be used to argue that English does **not** have the semantics in question. In the specific case at hand, the semantics in question is a Russellian analysis of definite descriptions. Kripke argued that a Donnellan-type referential use of definite descriptions would arise in a language stipulated to have such a Russellian semantics, and thus the existence of such a use in English does not mean that English is not Russellian.

Kripke actually stipulates not one but three "Russell languages." All are like English with the possible exception of the nature of definite descriptions. In the weak Russell language, the truth conditions of sentences with definite descriptions are those put forward by Russell. However in this type of language, as described by Kripke, definite descriptions are semantic constituents and have semantic referents.

... 'The present King of France is bald' is to be true iff exactly one person is king of France, and that person is bald. On the weak Russell language, this effect can be achieved by assigning semantic reference to definite descriptions: the semantic referent of a definite description is the unique object that satisfies the description, if any...   (Kripke 1977: 265)

Such a language does not really represent the quantificational alternative. And since Kripke, in this part of the paper anyway, does not consider the propositions expressed and stipulate their truth conditions in other possible worlds, the weak Russell language is perfectly consistent with an ambiguity for definite descriptions resulting from the difference between variable and constant individual concepts.

The intermediate Russell language is indeed stipulated to have a quantificational analysis of definite descriptions, while the strong Russell language doesn't even have definite descriptions. Instead of saying *The man drinking champagne seems happy*, speakers of the strong Russell language must instead say something like *There is a unique man who is drinking champagne, and every man drinking champagne seems happy.*

Having defined his Russell languages, Kripke continues as follows:

> Would the phenomenon Donnellan adduces arise in communities that spoke these languages? Surely speakers of these languages are no more infallible than we. They too will find themselves at a party and mistakenly think someone is drinking champagne even though he is actually drinking sparkling water. If they are speakers of the weak or intermediate Russell languages, they will say, "The man in the corner drinking champagne is happy tonight." They will say this precisely because *they think, though erroneously, that the Russellian truth conditions are satisfied*. Wouldn't we say of these speakers that they are referring to the teetotaler, under the misimpression that he is drinking champagne? And, if he is happy, are they not saying of him, *truly*, that he is happy? Both answers seem obviously affirmative.
>
> (Kripke 1977: 265–6; italics in original)

Since what Kripke takes to be the defining phenomenon of Donnellan's referential usage, i.e. the misdescription characteristic, would arise in a language stipulated to be Russellian, he argues that the fact that it arises in English does not mean that English is not Russellian.

Furthermore, he argues, we need the concept of speaker reference anyway, for circumstances where Donnellan's distinction would not apply. In fact the concept of speaker reference is introduced with an example involving proper names. Two people see someone at a distance whom they take to be Jones, but who in fact is Smith. The following conversation ensues.

(23)   A: What is Jones doing?
        B: Raking the leaves.

About this example Kripke says the following:

> 'Jones,' in the common language of both, is a name of Jones; it *never* names Smith. Yet, in some sense, on this occasion, clearly both participants in the dialogue have referred to Smith, and the second participant has said something true about the man he referred to if and only if Smith was raking the leaves (whether or not Jones was).
>
> (Kripke 1977: 263; italics in original)

No one would propose an ambiguity of the Donnellan type for proper names. But Kripke views the Smith-Jones case as quite parallel to Donnellan's distinction for definite descriptions, remarking, for example, that "anyone who compares the Smith-Jones case ... with Donnellan's cases of definite descriptions, must surely be impressed by the similarity of the phenomena" (Kripke 1977: 267). That being the case, postulation of an ambiguity for definite descriptions is unwarranted and hence methodologically unsound.

It should be clear from the foregoing how central a role the misdescription characteristic plays in Kripke's critique of Donnellan's distinction. In fact Kripke does consider, briefly and in passing, the type of semantic analysis that we looked at above in the preceding subsection, specifically the constant individual concept version of that analysis. "Another type of definite description, $\iota x \phi x$, a 'rigid' definite description, could be introduced semantically by the following stipulation: let $\iota x \phi x$ denote, with respect to all possible worlds, the unique object that (actually) ϕ's..." (Kripke 1977: 259). As defined by Kripke, this iota expression, $\iota x \phi x$, is a formal equivalent of our expression in (20) using Montague's up arrow; thus it expresses a constant individual concept. However Kripke appears to dismiss this alternative as a possible analysis of Donnellan's referential reading, because it does not incorporate the misdescription characteristic.

> ...a rigid definite description, as defined above, still determines its referent via its unique satisfaction of the associated property—and this fact separates the notion of such a description from that of a referential description, as Donnellan defines it.
>
> (Kripke 1977: 260)

And in fact Kripke does not go on to consider this type of analysis further or offer any arguments against it.

6.3.4 Defense of the semantic analyses

I mentioned above that Kripke's paper has been extremely influential. However it has not won everyone over. In this section we will look at some responses to Kripke's arguments which have been put forward in defense of a semantic analysis of the referential use of definite descriptions. But first we need to clear away one potentially confounding issue.

Recall Strawson's point that incomplete descriptions (e.g. *the table*) present a problem for Russell's analysis. It might be thought that incomplete descriptions are always used referentially, and thus that accepting Donnellan's view of the referential use could solve this problem. The story would go something like this: on the referential use of definite descriptions, reference is determined by the speaker's intention, and thus the absence of sufficient descriptive content to narrow the application of the description to a unique entity does not matter. The problem is that incomplete descriptions are **not** always used referentially. Christopher Peacocke, for example, has suggested the example of a school inspector who is visiting a school for the first time and, noting the rampant lack of discipline, remarks as in (24).

(24)   The headmaster doesn't have much control over the pupils.

Despite its being incomplete, use of *the headmaster* in this case would be attributive (cf. Peacocke (1975: 209)). Thus the existence of incomplete descriptions cannot be used to support a semantic analysis of Donnellan's referential interpretation, so let us turn to some other considerations.[20]

In the preceding subsection I tried to suggest that Kripke's case is weakened by his reliance on the misdescription characteristic. As we have seen, a good part of Kripke's direct defense of Russell rests on this one feature of Donnellan's distinction—and yet this is a feature which is definitely not central to the distinction itself, and which can (and should) be abandoned. We must, of course, accept the idea of speaker meaning and speaker reference, distinct from the semantic content of our words, since it is clear that people can misspeak. The story of the two interlocutors who mistake Jones for Smith is an obvious example, as would be the kind of misdescription uses of definite descriptions envisaged by Donnellan and Kripke, where it is assumed that an innocent person murdered Smith, or is holding a glass of champagne instead of sparkling water.[21] But of course it is not inconsistent to hold that this distinction between speaker reference and semantic reference differs from Donnellan's distinction between referential and attributive use of definite descriptions.

Recently more direct rebuttals of Kripke's position have been put forward. Marga Reimer (1998) and Michael Devitt (2004) both make a case in favor of recognizing the referential use as semantically

---

[20] In the course of looking at suggested solutions to the problem of incomplete descriptions above in §6.2.3, we noted two possible approaches—the expansion approach, involving additional tacit descriptive content; and the contraction approach, involving a narrowed domain of discourse. Interestingly, Bach (2004) has suggested that the expansion approach is appropriate for incomplete descriptions used attributively, while the contraction approach is appropriate for incomplete descriptions used referentially.

[21] There are actually important differences between the two cases, as George Wilson (1991) points out. In the case of the definite descriptions the speaker makes a mistake in describing somebody, whereas in the proper name case s/he mistakes one person for a different one.

encoded.[22] The line of argument is this: given that a particular type of sentence is used systematically and regularly to express a certain kind of proposition (in this case a singular proposition—of either the Russellian or the constant individual concept type), and where the proposition in question is governed by the linguistic expressions occurring in the sentence, then that in itself is evidence that the sentence encodes that meaning.

In support of this line Reimer notes that one could use Kripke's style of argument involving the Russell languages to reach a false conclusion. Originally, for example, the verb *incense* in English meant "make fragrant with incense." However, it acquired its present meaning of "anger" via a natural metaphorical transition. One might try to adapt Kripke's line of argument to show that *incense* still has only its original meaning, since in a language in which that meaning is stipulated to be the only one, speakers would still use the verb metaphorically to mean "anger." Clearly arguing in this way would be a mistake—what began as a metaphorical use has become frozen, and is now an additional meaning of the verb. Interestingly, toward the very end of his paper Kripke alluded to exactly this type of mechanism. Concerning the utility of his distinction between speaker's reference and semantic reference he remarked ". . . I find it plausible that a diachronic account of the evolution of language is likely to suggest that what was originally a mere speaker's reference may, if it becomes habitual in a community, evolve into a semantic reference" (Kripke 1977: 271). Given that English has had definite descriptions for at least a thousand years, and that in all likelihood most uses of them during that time have been referential, we should not be surprised to find the referential use semantically encoded.[23]

At this point the weight of evidence appears to be in favor of considering the referential use of definite descriptions to be semantically encoded. Let us now look at some additional evidence for this conclusion. This additional evidence is to be found in parallels between the referential use of definite descriptions and the specific use of indefinite descriptions.

[22] See also Wilson (1991), who argues that the referential use is actually pronominal in nature. We will look at Wilson's views below in Chapter 8. Salmon (2004) has a nice extended discussion and evaluation of the referential-attributive issue.

[23] Actually, as any good dictionary will tell you, the definite article in English evolved out of a demonstrative, and thus the referential use was undoubtedly the original one and the attributive use the newcomer.

6.4 Indefinite descriptions

We noted above that the attributive-referential distinction for definite descriptions in unembedded contexts is quite parallel to the *de dicto-de re* ambiguity which these descriptions have when they occur embedded under a propositional attitude verb or a modal. Indeed, the semantic analyses we looked at in §6.3.2 were able to recapture that distinction despite the lack of any predicate to vary scope around. We know that indefinite descriptions have an ambiguity very similar to the one definite descriptions have when they occur in opaque contexts. (25) is an example from Chapter 3.

(25)   Bill wants to marry a Norwegian.

As we saw there, (25) has the two interpretations paraphrased in (26) and formalized in (27).

(26)   a.   Bill wants to have a Norwegian spouse.
       b.   There is a particular individual, who happens to be Norwegian, whom Bill would like to marry.

(27)   a.   Bill wants an$_x$[Norwegian(x)] (marry(Bill, x))
       b.   an$_x$[Norwegian(x)](Bill wants (marry(Bill, x))

The narrow-scope interpretation represented in (26a) and (27a) is very parallel to the *de dicto* interpretation of definite NPs in propositional attitude contexts, with the descriptive content of the NP forming a part of the object of the attitude in question. And the wide-scope reading of (26b)/(27b) is quite parallel to the *de re* interpretation of definites, where an individual is involved in the relevant desire, rather than their description. Thus we might ask whether indefinite descriptions also participate in anything like Donnellan's attributive-referential distinction. Indeed, it has been argued that they do.

   Lauri Karttunen (1969a) pointed out that a sentence like (28) can be used to make two different kinds of statement.

(28)   Mary had lunch with a logician.

Used nonspecifically, (28) simply reports what type of person Mary had lunch with, and could be used in answer to the question *What sort of person did Mary have lunch with?* But used specifically (28) is intended to introduce an entity into the discourse, and could be followed with, for example, *He told her about some fascinating proofs.* Other descriptions of the specific use characterize it as "referential," and mention the speaker's having a particular individual in mind (in this case, as the logician Mary had lunch with); see for example Partee (1972); Chastain (1975); Fodor and Sag (1982).

Notice that in some contexts, indefinite descriptions occur unambiguously. In directives such as (29),

(29)   Get me a logician!

for example, *a logician* can only be understood nonspecifically. The explanation for this lack of ambiguity is obviously pragmatic: the indefinite description by itself does not identify any particular individual. If the speaker of (29) intended it specifically, the directive would be anomalous since the addressee would not be given sufficient information to comply. On the other hand there are several methods for disambiguating in the opposite direction. One is to add *certain*, as in (30):

(30)   Mary had lunch with a certain logician.

In (30), *a certain logician* can only be understood specifically. And casual speech can disambiguate with the use of an alternative indefinite determiner, namely the nondemonstrative (and non-anaphoric) indefinite *this* determiner which occurs in examples like (31):

(31)   There was this dishy logician at Mary's party last night.

As pointed out by Prince (1981a), indefinite *this* NPs can only be understood specifically, so that (32)

(32)   Mary had lunch with this logician.

(with the non-demonstrative, non-anaphoric, indefinite *this*) does not have a nonspecific interpretation. And correspondingly, neither *certain* nor the indefinite *this* can occur felicitously in an imperative, as shown in (33).[24]

(33)   a.   #Get me a certain logician!
        b.   #Get me this dishy logician!

Thus the nonspecific-specific distinction with indefinite descriptions is quite parallel to the attributive-referential distinction with definite descriptions, but with the added feature of possible disambiguation and the potential for creation of anomalous utterances such as those in

---

[24] In testing your intuitions about (33b) be careful to hear *this dishy logician* as a specific indefinite, and not as a demonstrative. Assume that no dishy logician is present or has been mentioned.

(33). These facts argue in favor of the semantic encoding of both distinctions. However this conclusion leaves us with the problem of providing a suitable semantics for the indefinite cases.

At the end of Kaplan's paper "Dthat" (the paper which proposed Russellian singular propositions as a semantic analysis of Donnellan's referential interpretation), Kaplan appended a list titled "Exciting Future Episodes." Number 4 on this list was the following: "Extending the demonstrative notion to *in*definite descriptions to see if it is possible to so explicate the ± specific idea. (It isn't.)" (Kaplan 1978: 241, italics in original) To see what the problem is, consider (28) again.

(28)   Mary had lunch with a logician.

Let us assume that the quantificational analysis represented in (34) is an adequate rendition of the nonspecific interpretation for *a logician*.

(34) $an_x[logician(x)](had\text{-}lunch\text{-}with(Mary, x))$

This formula represents the proposition that is true at any possible world where Mary had lunch with a logician, where the logician can vary from world to world. Now the problem is to come up with a good analysis for the specific reading.

If we wanted to adapt Kaplan's analysis of the referential interpretation of definite descriptions to the analysis of the specific interpretation of indefinite descriptions, we would want to see the proposition expressed as being one of those Russellian singular propositions—something that looks like (35).

(35)   < __, the property of having had lunch with Mary>

The problem is, how to find an entity to fill in the (underlined) first slot in this proposition. Unlike a definite description, the indefinite *a logician* does not determine a unique denotation. One suggestion would be to have the first constituent of (35) be whatever logician the speaker had in mind in uttering (28). For example, if the speaker had had J. J. Smartypants in mind, then according to this suggestion the proposition expressed would be (36).

(36)   <J. J. Smartypants, the property of having had lunch with Mary>

But suppose that Mary actually had had lunch with a different logician, K. K. Keen, and not with Professor Smartypants. Then (36) would be false, but it would be very hard to consider (28) false under those circumstances—after all, she **did** have lunch with a logician. There does not seem to be any way to come up with an entity to fill that slot in the Russellian singular proposition.

We noted above in §6.3.2 that there is an alternative to Kaplan's analysis of the referential interpretation of definite descriptions which uses constant individual concepts instead of actual entities. I would like to suggest that that type of approach possibly has another advantage in being able to offer an analysis for the specific/nonspecific ambiguity of indefinites which we have been looking at. I don't believe there is any way to make indefinite descriptions referential, in the sense of having them contribute an entity which plays a role in the determination of the truth value for utterances containing them.[25] However there may be a way to have an appropriate distinction with a quantificational analysis. Recall from Chapter 4 that Montague's PTQ grammar was formulated with variables which ranged over individual concepts rather than individuals. In such a grammar, it might be possible to distinguish constant individual concepts from variable individual concepts. What we would want is two versions of the formula in (34)—one in which the variables range over variable individual concepts (for the nonspecific understanding of (28)) and one in which the variables ranged over constant individual concepts (for the specific understanding of (28)). Whether this is technically feasible is another question which remains to be determined.[26]

6.5 Concluding remarks

In this chapter we have focused on definite descriptions. We saw right away that the issue of quantification vs reference was not going to be a clear-cut one. We turned then to Strawson's objections to Russell's analysis. The indexicality that some definite descriptions possess is something that we will get to in Chapter 8. Strawson also pointed

---

[25] Below in Chapters 8–10 we will see an approach to semantics (broadly termed "dynamic semantics") on which indefinite descriptions are treated very similarly to definite descriptions, and both look sort of referential. This approach does not distinguish referential from attributive uses of definite descriptions, nor specific from nonspecific indefinites of the type we are considering here.

[26] Note that for definite descriptions, it seems, we do not need to suppose that the individual concepts are being quantified over, whereas in the case of indefinite descriptions we do need to suppose this. We will return to this issue in Chapter 11.

out that the existence and uniqueness of a denotation for a definite description are presupposed rather than asserted, and he brought up the problem of incomplete descriptions (a problem shared with (other) quantificational NPs). Both of these issues are still subjects of discussion and analysis; we return to the incompleteness problem below in Chapter 10.

A major portion of this chapter was devoted to Donnellan's referential-attributive distinction, and the question of whether the referential interpretation is something that is literally expressed in the use of a definite description or is instead, as Kripke and others have argued, merely part of a proposition which the speaker wants to convey with their use of a (quantificational) NP. We have seen some reason to believe that those arguments are not conclusive, and given some unanswered arguments in favor of a semantic analysis of the referential interpretation, we have for the moment concluded that a speaker may actually express a singular proposition using a definite description (referentially), and not simply convey it.

Given that, and the possible use of variable individual concepts to analyze the attributive use of definite descriptions, the question of whether definite descriptions are ever quantificational becomes even murkier.[27] Fortunately we are not done with definite descriptions, by any means. Not only are the issues they give rise to central to the concept of reference; as we will see in subsequent chapters other kinds of NPs—demonstrative descriptions, pronouns—share characteristics with this important category.

---

[27] But see Löbner (2000) for arguments that definite descriptions are decidedly not quantificational.

7

Plurals and generics

"Jobs BIG and small, I do them ALL!"

Joe the Plumber,
<www.joelaratheplumber.com>

In this chapter we focus on some complications which we have passed over up to now. First we take up the issue of what to do about plural NPs; there we'll see some parallels between plurals and NPs with mass head nouns. MASS (or noncount) nouns like *milk* and *spaghetti* are distinguished from count nouns (e.g. *book*, *noodle*) in a number of respects. For example, mass nouns as such cannot take the indefinite article (*a spaghetti*), or number words (*3 milks*).[1] The analysis presented below (that of Link (1983)) will help us extend Russell's analysis of definite descriptions to those with plural or mass heads. In §7.2 we look at several different ways predicates can apply to plural (and mass) NPs, and we'll also subdivide NPs depending on the way they constrain such predication. Then in §7.3 we begin to attack the problem of GENERICITY (or GENERICNESS)—the nature of general statements, and the kinds of NP interpretations that can figure in them. We'll look at several different types of generic NPs, including (in §7.4) NPs like *the average American*. As usual, the final section will try to sum up what we've seen.

7.1 Plurals and mass terms

Traditional logic was geared towards a domain of single discrete entities, as was the semantics based on it. More recently, with the application of formal methods to natural language semantics spurred

---

[1] Of course mass nouns may be turned into count nouns, via the process of "zero derivation" (no overt morphological change), typically with meanings like "type of" (*a very nice white wine*) or "serving of" (*two coffees*).

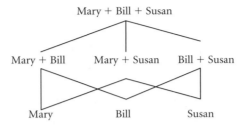

Figure 7.1. A lattice type of structure for three children.

by the work of Kripke, Kaplan, Montague, and others, various scholars have devised ways of extending these methods to deal with plurals and mass terms. What has become the standard analysis was proposed by Godehard Link (1983).

7.1.1 Link's analysis

Link proposed recognizing as part of our ontology, in addition to ordinary entities like tables and ideas, also (MEREOLOGICAL) SUMS of things. Sums are complex entities formed by combining entities (an operation for which the symbol is $+$), and defined by a particular kind of part-whole relation (for which the symbol is $\leq$). In the case of sums, the parts are the same kind of thing as the whole—a sum of pencils consists of pencils, its parts are pencils. A single pencil would not be considered the sum, in this sense, of its lead, the wood, and the eraser, even though those are parts in the ordinary sense of "part." A sum of a number of entities is similar to the set containing them, in that sums are completely defined by their members just as sets are. The main difference is that whereas sets are abstract, sums are as concrete as their constituents.

If we think about the sums that can be formed from a given number of entities, they will naturally form what is described as a lattice type of structure. An example, showing the sum structure generated by three children (Mary, Bill, and Susan) is shown in Figure 7.1.

In the structure in Figure 7.1, Mary, Bill, and Susan are the ATOMS—the elements which cannot be subdivided any more and still remain within the realm of children. These atoms can be combined into sums as indicated in the table—the sum of Mary plus Bill, the sum of Mary plus Susan, and so forth.[2] The maximal sum—the

---

[2] An alternative to viewing the plural domain in the way pictured in Figure 7.1 would be to view it in terms of sets. We could represent this by putting a pair of brackets around each

SUPREMUM—is the one consisting of all three of the children. Mary is part of the supremum (formally: Mary $\leq$ Mary + Bill + Susan), as are each of the other two children, and each of the other pairs of children (e.g. Mary + Susan $\leq$ Mary + Bill + Susan). The idea is that we add all of the elements of structures like that in Figure 7.1 to our universe of discourse, which now contains entities that are sums as well as the atomic entities. With such a structure we can define the denotation of a plural like *children* as the set of all the sums of children.

A similar type of structure can be postulated for mass nouns: if we put any amounts of milk together we get another amount of milk. The difference between the count lattice structure and the mass lattice structure is that in the latter case, we do not have atoms at the bottom. You might wonder whether or not that is really the case—for example in the case of milk, isn't there a bottom layer of "atoms" consisting of the smallest possible particles of milk? But we do not have everyday interactions with such small particles. When we are talking about milk, the portions of milk just get smaller and smaller, but never reach the level of the smallest possible particles. Looking from the bottom up, we can see that Link's analysis captures the fact that mass nouns have what Quine (1960: 91) called the property of "referring cumulatively"—putting quantities of milk together yields more milk. The same is true of count plurals: putting horses together yields more horses. (Singular count nouns, of course, do not have this property—putting a horse together with another horse gives not a horse, but horses.)

As Link points out, there is a correspondence between (singular or plural) objects and the stuff that makes the objects up, but we would still need to distinguish two structures in each case, since different properties may apply. To use Link's example, a ring may be new while the gold which makes it up is old. So corresponding to every atomic lattice structure which serves as the denotation of plural count nouns (like the one in Figure 7.1), there is a mass lattice structure for the stuff that goes to make up those entities.[3]

---

of the entities in Figure 7.1 and deleting any plus signs (giving us e.g. {Mary, Bill} instead of Mary + Bill, and {Mary} in place of Mary). If we did this, we would have to change the denotations of our predicates so that they denoted sets of sets rather than sets of ordinary entities.

[3] I have been simplifying Link's analysis substantially; see his paper for the full story.

7.1.2 Plural and mass definite descriptions

Russell's analysis of definite descriptions was confined to those with singular count noun heads. However there are definite descriptions with mass head nouns (*the broccoli in my garden*) and plural head nouns (*the marbles that she lost*). Now that we have an analysis of these kinds of nouns we should see about extending Russell's analysis. Both John Hawkins (1978: 157–67) and Richard Sharvy (1980) have pointed out that definite descriptions with plural or mass head nouns are taken to denote the **totality** of (relevant) items fitting the description expressed in the CNP. Sharvy also pointed out that, assuming a universe containing mass and plural entities (as sketched in the preceding subsection), we can extend Russell's analysis quite simply.

A schema of Russell's analysis for sentences of the form *the F is G* is given in (1):

(1) $\exists x[\forall y[F(y) \leftrightarrow y = x] \ \& \ G(x)]$

To extend this analysis to definite descriptions whose head noun is plural or mass, all we need to do is replace the identity symbol ("=") in (1) with our symbol for the part of relation ("≤"). That results in the formula in (2).

(2) $\exists x[\forall y[F(y) \leftrightarrow y \leq x] \ \& \ G(x)]$

Let us see how this formula would work for any of the examples below.

(2)   a.   The fieldmice are gratuitous.
      b.   The flatulence is gratuitous.
      c.   The fireman is gratuitous.

When we are dealing with a plural entity like fieldmice, the formula in (2) requires us to take the supremum of those in the context—everything that is a fieldmouse or fieldmice must be a part of what *the fieldmice* denotes. When instead a mass entity like flatulence is involved the same holds—every portion of flatulence in the environment of the utterance of (2b) must be a part of what *the flatulence* denotes. And since every entity is part of itself, the formula in (2) will also correctly characterize sentences with singular definite descriptions like *the fireman*.

Both Hawkins and Sharvy considered totality to capture the essence of the definite article better than uniqueness; Sharvy remarked: "... we see that the primary use of "the" is not to indicate uniqueness. Rather, it is to indicate totality; implicature of uniqueness is a side effect" (1980: 623). However one could also argue the opposite view: given that the use of *the* requires a unique denotation, the only way to achieve it with a mass or plural head is to include all of the described quantities, so that "there are no other potential referents in the shared set which are not being referred to" (Hawkins 1978: 165).[4]

7.2 Distributive, collective, and cumulative readings

What makes plural (and mass) NPs more interesting is that they can combine with predicates in several different ways. Consider the examples in (3).

(3) a. The children ate lunch.
     b. The children surrounded the teacher.
     c. The children talked with a counselor.

If the sentence in (3a) is true, then every child, or almost every child, ate lunch. The hedge ("almost every") is because it seems there is a difference between (3a) and (4):

(4) All of the children ate lunch.

While (4) does not allow for exceptions, it seems that (3a) would be judged true if only 48 out of the 50 children actually ate their lunch while the other two fed it to the squirrels on the playground. The main point about (3a) here is that eating lunch is something that individuals do on their own—it is not a **semantically** collective activity (although of course pragmatically it's more fun to eat with other people than all alone). The predicate *eat lunch* is thus characterized as a DISTRIBUTIVE predicate, because any entailments it carries concerning its subject, such as being an animate entity capable of initiating action and ingesting things like lunch, devolve onto individuals. We can express this property with the formula given in (5), where D is a variable over distributive predicates.

(5) $\forall x[D(x) \rightarrow \forall y[y \leq x \rightarrow D(y)]]$

(5) says that if something has property D, then all of its parts (in our special sense of "part") have D.

On the other hand the case of *surround* is quite different; in this case none of the individual children can be said to have surrounded anything.

---

[4] Below in Chapter 9 we will consider a number of alternatives to both uniqueness and totality as the essence of definiteness.

Rather, the predicate is collective, and applies to its subject as a group. Any entailments of the predicate concerning its subject, such as, in this case, being something that has extent, devolve onto the subject as a whole, and not to the individuals that make it up. Thus *surround* is a COLLECTIVE predicate, because it applies to its subject collectively, as a whole.

The distributive-collective distinction also seems to hold for mass terms. Compare the examples in (6).

(6) a.   The water contained mercury.
     b.   The water surrounded the castle.

Containing mercury is a property that distributes to the parts of the water; although perhaps not every speck of the water contained mercury if (6a) is true, nevertheless we expect the parts of the water referred to generally to contain mercury. On the other hand that is not true of the water which surrounds the castle. In this case it is the water collectively which does the job.

Some predicates, like *talk with*, are compatible with either a distributive or a collective interpretation. Thus example (3c)—*The children talked with a counselor*—is generally held to be ambiguous. Certainly it can be true in two different kinds of circumstances—one in which each child talked with a counselor on his or her own, and one in which the children went together to see the counselor. That is, it seems to have both distributive and collective UNDERSTANDINGS, where the term "understanding" is intended to be neutral between truly distinct semantic interpretations, on the one hand, and what are merely different ways of being true, on the other (see Zwicky and Sadock (1975)).

The possibilities for collective vs distributive interpretation interact with the scope possibilities for NPs. So an example like (7) will have many different possible understandings.

(7)   Five children talked with two counselors.

For example, when *two counselors* has wide scope, (7) can convey either that each of two counselors had five children come to talk with them (involving possibly as many as ten children altogether), or that the two counselors as a group had five children come and talk with them (again, either as a group, or individually).

There is a difference of opinion on whether the difference between distributive and collective understandings means that the NP in question is ambiguous. Link (1983) suggested that these NPs are not ambiguous—rather, it is the case that different kinds of predicates, because of their meanings, can apply to a plural subject NP (or object NP) in different ways. On the other hand Craige Roberts (1987) has argued for the opposing view that NPs like *the children*, which can occur in either distributive or collective understandings are in fact ambiguous.

We should also note, following Roberts (1987), that NPs in general can be divided into two categories based on determiner type. One large category can have both distributive and collective understandings; these are the NPs with group determiners. Examples of group determiners (in addition to *the*) are *several, many, few, some, all*. The other category of determiner imposes a distributive understanding. *Every* and *each* are obviously distributive.[5] For one thing, they result in grammatically singular NPs. *Most* is also distributive despite being plural; thus the examples in (8) are all anomalous.[6]

(8) a. #Every child surrounded the teacher.
     b. #Each child surrounded the teacher.
     c. #Most (of the) children surrounded the teacher.

Both is another example of a determiner which imposes a distributive reading. Observe that while (9a) has two interpretations, (9b) does not.

(9) a. The two children brought a cake.
     b. Both children brought a cake.

(9a) can convey either that each child brought a cake (for a total of two cakes) or that the two acted collectively in bringing a single cake. (9b), on the other hand, has only the former interpretation, for a total of two cakes. It does not have the collective reading. Thus *both* means something like *each of the two*. *Neither* is similarly necessarily distributive.

We turn now to the claim that there is a third, CUMULATIVE, understanding for plural NPs, in addition to distributive and collective interpretations—a claim which comes originally from Remko Scha (1984). Consider example (7) again.

---

[5] The difference between *every* and *each* is a delicate issue. According to the classic treatment in Vendler "... *every* stresses completeness or, rather, exhaustiveness ... ; *each*, on the other hand, directs one's attention to the individuals as they appear ... one by one" (Vendler 1962: 78). See Vendler's paper for further discussion.

[6] The judgments given here are my own. Those for whom the examples in (8) sound good may be hearing these sentences with a tacit collectivizing predicate—e.g. something like *Every child joined in surrounding the teacher*.

(7)   Five children talked with two counselors.

Beside the understandings that occur as a result of the scope interactions of the two NPs and the possibility of distributive vs collective
participation, Scha claimed that there is another reading not
accounted for by any of these options. In this case it would be a reading
where the total number of children involved in counseling was five,
and the total number of counselors involved was two, but beyond that
nothing is claimed about how many counselors each child saw, or how
many children were seen by each counselor, or whether they went
individually or collectively. This is the cumulative construal.

   Many open issues remain about whether the understandings
explained above are indeed genuinely different readings, or whether
some of them can be subsumed under other cases. Fred Landman
(1996) gives a good overview of some of these issues, with references.
(See also Schwarzschild (1996).)

7.3 Genericity

In this section we will look at some of the ways in which NPs can be
used to make general statements (saving one for the following section).
Krifka et al. (1995) distinguish two kinds of genericity, one for statements (sometimes referred to as "I-genericity") and one for NPs
(sometimes called "D-genericity"). Of the two types, statement genericity, which occurs in what they describe as "characterizing sentences,"
is somewhat broader, so let us first take a look at that.

7.3.1 Statement genericity

Essentially any statement which does not describe an occurrence at
some particular time would be classified as characterizing and thus
generic. This would include stative sentences like (10), which predicate
enduring properties of individuals.

(10)   Morgan loves to sing.

Here it is the stative verb *love* that is responsible for the generality of
the statement, but we can also find examples with nonstative verbs that
are used to indicate a habitual eventuality, as in (11):

(11)   Jalen works in the bookstore every summer.

and these would also be classed as characterizing. Thus for whole statements, the fact that a generalization is made is sufficient for it to be classified as generic.[7]

Some sentences are ambiguous, depending on whether they are taken as a description of a single event or of some continuing, and hence generic, eventuality. (12) is an example.

(12)   Sue studied hard.

(12) could describe one past event of Sue studying, perhaps for a particular exam; but it could also describe a past habit of Sue's—roughly equivalent to describing Sue as having been a diligent student. Adding *in those days* to (12) disambiguates in favor of this generic reading. One way of accounting for this kind of ambiguity would be to postulate a tacit operator—GEN (for genericity). We would then represent the two readings of (12) as in (13).

(13)   a.   PAST(study-hard)(Sue)
       b.   GEN PAST(study-hard)(Sue)

This may seem rather ad hoc, but we will see below other situations in which a somewhat modified version of our GEN operator is able to do some more serious work.[8]

Our main interest here is in NP interpretation, so let us turn now to consideration of generic NPs. For this kind of genericity, Krifka et al. impose a more stringent requirement than in the case of sentential, characterizing genericity; specifically, they reserve the term "generic NP" for NPs which denote a kind. This raises the question of which NPs denote kinds, and how that can be determined. For one answer, we turn to Greg Carlson's (1977a, b) classic analysis of bare NPs. We'll follow that with some problems for Carlson's view, and then a look at an alternative.

---

[7] There is actually some equivocation in Krifka et al. At first they describe characterizing sentences as reporting "a regularity which summarizes groups of particular episodes or facts" (2). Under this description both (10) and (11) would clearly be characterizing. However somewhat later in the presentation they give, as a test for characterizing sentences, the requirement that the properties they describe are "essential"—"not only 'descriptive' generalizations but 'normative' ones" (13), which would rule out these sentences.

[8] However Löbner (2000) argues convincingly against the use of such tacit operators, and proposes a different account of genericity.

7.3.2 Bare NPs—Carlson's analysis

We noted above that plurals and mass nouns shared the property of denoting lattice-like structures. As we saw in Chapter 1, they also share the property of being able to serve as head noun in a determinerless, or "bare," NP in English, as shown in (14) and (15).

(14) a.   God didn't make <u>little green apples</u>.
      b.   <u>Little green apples</u> lay on the ground in front of me.

(15) a.   <u>Milk from Shetler's Dairy</u> tastes better.
      b.   This time I bought <u>milk from Shetler's Dairy</u>.

One interesting problem presented by bare NPs is that <u>sometimes they seem to receive a generic interpretation</u>, as in (14a) and (15a), and <u>sometimes an existential one, as in (14b) and (15b)</u>. One of Carlson's insights was that this difference in interpretation is determined by the type of predication being expressed. The (a) examples in (14) and (15) predicate properties which an entity has on a <u>more or less permanent</u> basis; Carlson called such properties INDIVIDUAL-LEVEL properties. *[margin: generic interpretation]* Thus being tall or intelligent, being made (or not made) by God, and tasting better, are all individual-level properties—properties which something has over a long period or permanently. On the other hand the (b) examples involve predication of properties which an entity has for a <u>relatively short amount of time</u>, and Carlson called these STAGE- *[margin: existential interpretation]* LEVEL properties; so lying on the ground, being bought or sold, or smiling, are all stage-level properties which hold of something only temporarily.[9]

The term "stage" was inspired by W. V. Quine's (1960) discussion of the possibility of viewing ordinary physical entities as four-dimensional sequences of their momentary instantiations, or stages. Carlson proposed that stage-level properties are predicated, not of individuals as wholes, but only of time slices or time segments—stages—of individuals. On the other hand individual-level properties are predicated of individuals as a whole.[10] To connect individuals with their temporal stages, Carlson postulated a REALIZATION relation R. With that relation

---

[9] These facts had been observed by Milsark (1974, 1977), who called individual-level properties "properties" and stage-level properties "states." These terms are less felicitous than Carlson's, since both kinds of properties are properties, and the predicates which express **individual**-level properties are typically stative.

[10] See Kratzer (1995) for a different theory of the distinction between stage-level and individual-level predications.

Carlson was able to distinguish individual-level (characterizing) predication from stage-level predication. Thus the individual-level (16a)
would be represented as (16b), but the stage-level (17a) receives the
interpretation sketched in (17b).

(16) a. Bill is tall.
      b. tall(Bill).
(17) a. Bill is in the saloon.
      b. $\lambda y[\exists x[R(x, y) \& \text{in-the-saloon}(x)]](\text{Bill})$

Tallness is predicated of Bill as a whole, while being in the saloon is
predicated of one of the stages which realizes Bill. (Note that this view of
individuals is very much in tune with our earlier suggestions that
individuals like Bill be viewed as intensional entities—functions from
world-time points to extensions. Carlson (1989) makes this idea explicit.)

   Carlson proposed that KINDS of things, like cows and bicycles, are
also individuals—different from ordinary, non-kind individuals in
being scattered over, not only times, but also places. Both types of
individuals—ordinary entities, and kinds of things—are realized by
stages of entities. And finally, Carlson argued that bare NPs behave
semantically like proper names of kinds. Thus a generic sentence like
(18a) would receive an analysis like (18b).

(18) a. Cows are four-legged.
      b. four-legged(cows)

On the other hand an existential example like (19a) would receive the
interpretation shown in (19b).

(19) a. Cows are in the pasture.
      b. $\lambda y[\exists x[R(x, y) \& \text{in-the-pasture}(x)]](\text{cows})$

Just as with the sentences in (16) and (17) about Bill, we distinguish (18)
from (19) by whether the property in question is being predicated of
the kind cows, or only of cow stages.

   Using this analysis Carlson was able to account for some peculiar
properties of bare NPs, most notably their seeming insistence on
taking narrow scope with respect to other expressions. Thus while
indefinite NPs can usually take wide scope, bare NPs usually cannot.
Compare the two examples in (20).

(20) a. Everybody read two books.
      b. Everybody read books.

While (20a) can mean that there are two particular books that every-body read (say *Peyton Place* and the Bible), (20b) only has a reading where the books may vary with the readers.[11] Since under Carlson's analysis the existential quantification associated with *books* is intro-duced in connection with the predicate *read*, there is no way for it to take scope over *everybody*.

Although Carlson's distinction between stage-level and individual-level predications has proved to be of great utility, questions have been raised about the particulars of his analysis of bare NPs. Below we will see some problems, which will lead us to look at the main alternative which has been proposed.

7.3.3 Generic uses of singular descriptions

Traditionally, philosophers have grouped bare NP generic statements, as in (21a) below, with two other sorts of generics—those with a singular definite description, as in (21b), and those with a singular indefinite description, as in (21c).

(21)   a.   Lions like to eat zebras.
       b.   The lion likes to eat zebras.
       c.   A lion likes to eat zebras.

Thus traditionally all three sentences in (21) would have been viewed as pretty much equivalent. However Krifka et al. (1995) make a distinc-tion between the first two, on the one hand, and the third, on the other. They accord bare plurals and singular definite descriptions generic status, but not singular indefinites like *a lion* in (21c).

As noted above, Krifka et al. only consider as generic those NPs which name kinds of things. Krifka et al. cite two pieces of behavior in the course of arguing that singular indefinite descriptions do not name kinds. One is that predicates which only apply to kinds of things, like *be rare* or *be widespread*, may be predicated of both singular definites and bare plurals, but not singular indefinites, as shown in (22).[12]

---

[11] While (20b) would certainly be true if everybody happened to be reading the same books, it does not have a reading which requires this.

[12] We need to note an exception, though: indefinite singulars can, indeed, denote kinds, when they are taken to refer to a subcategory of the category labeled by the CNP with which they combine. An example is given in (i).

(i)   An American butterfly (namely, the pipevine swallowtail) feeds on Dutchman's-pipe.

Krifka et al. call this the "taxonomic" use; here *a CNP* means "a kind of CNP."

(22)   a.   Lions are plentiful in Africa.
        b.   The lion is plentiful in Africa.
        c.   #A lion is plentiful in Africa.

The infelicity of (22c) argues against the idea that singular indefinites name kinds, and thus against their being accorded the status of generic NPs.

The other piece of evidence cited by Krifka et al. invokes the idea that the kinds that are named by a true generic NP should be fairly well defined (in some ill-defined sense). They note the difference between (23a) and (23b) (their exx. 24).

(23)   a.   The Coke bottle has a narrow neck.
        b.   The green bottle has a narrow neck.

While (23a) can describe either a particular Coke bottle or the kind Coke bottles, (23b) can only be talking about a particular green bottle. However, in contrast to (23b), the singular indefinite in (24) is fine when understood generically.

(24)   A green bottle has a narrow neck.

The fact that (24) is ok indicates that singular indefinites are not limited to well-defined kinds, and thus are not behaving like proper names of kinds. Thus the judgment of Krifka et al. is that, while (24) is a characterizing, and hence generic, sentence, the subject NP *a green bottle* is not a generic NP, but is simply nonspecific.

To give an analysis of the singular indefinites in (21c) and (24), we can adapt the GEN operator mentioned above. Suppose we reinterpret our GEN operator as quantifier-like, and able to bind variables—thus as a complex operator. As we will see below in Chapter 10, indefinite NPs are often susceptible to being bound by operators external to them—in this case, we are supposing, they can be bound by the GEN operator. The result would be the kind of three-part structure which results from quantification on the restricted quantification view. Now we can represent (21c) and (24) as shown in (25), respectively.

(25)   a. GEN_x [lion(x)](like(x, to eat zebras))
        b. GEN_x [green-bottle(x)](have-narrow-neck(x))

(25a) says that it's generally true when x is a lion, that x likes to eat zebras; and similarly (25b) says that it's generally true of green bottles that they have narrow necks. The GEN operator seems to capture an important fact about generic sentences, and that is that they are most often like conditionals—stating generalizations in terms of relations between eventuality types. And in fact both of our examples could be restated in an explicit conditional format—*If something is a lion/a green bottle, it likes to eat zebras/has a narrow neck.* So we can conclude that singular indefinite descriptions achieve genericity only with the help of the GEN operator.

Returning to singular definite descriptions in their generic use, like *the lion* and *the Coke bottle* in the examples above, note that if they are regarded as proper names of kinds, then the fact that they can only be used with well-defined categories would seem to have a ready explanation based on the fact that generally only fairly well-defined sorts of things have proper names. To put it another way, if we use a proper name to refer to something, that suggests that the referent is well defined and has a certain distinguished ontological status, and the same seems to hold of singular definite descriptions used generically. Note too that the kinds we may refer to with singular definites like *the lion*, when they are naturally existing kinds, **do** often have proper names—the Latinate species names assigned to them by naturalists (*Panthera leo* in this case). Possibly also relevant here is the fact that definite descriptions may often be used as, or turn into, proper names (when they also may "grow capital letters," as Strawson put it (1950: 341))—e.g. *The Holy Roman Empire, The Monroe Doctrine.*

Unfortunately this generalization about the proper-name-like behavior of singular definites ultimately conflicts with Carlson's analysis of bare plurals as proper names of kinds. Note that bare plurals, used generically, do not have this restriction to well-defined denotations, as shown in (26).

(26)   Green bottles have narrow necks.

(26) is a perfectly natural sentence and characterizes green bottles in general, not just some indefinite group of green bottles. Despite agreeing with Carlson that bare plurals denote kinds when they occur with necessarily kind-level properties like being widespread or extinct, Krifka et al. (1995: 11) conclude that the NP *green bottles* is not being used generically in (26) (their (25b)), despite the fact that (26) is a characterizing, and hence a generic, sentence. Rather they would consider this use to be simply nonspecific, like *a green bottle* in (24) above. This brings us to the alternative to Carlson's analysis of bare plurals—one on which they are ambiguous.

7.3.4 Bare NPs—an alternative analysis

The main alternative to Carlson's analysis of bare NPs holds that they are ambiguous, and only name kinds when they occur with predicates which hold only of kinds—like *be widespread* or *be extinct*. On this analysis, bare NPs in characterizing sentences like (26), where the predicate is one that can hold of individuals, are simple indefinites. That being the case, it is necessary to distinguish (26) from something like (27).

(27)   Some green bottles have narrow necks.

Here again our adapted GEN operator will be useful in allowing us to represent the characterizing sentence (26) as in (28).

(28) GEN_x [green-bottles(x)](have-narrow-necks(x))

(28) is just like (25b) above except that now we are quantifying over plural individuals. Predicates like being a green bottle and having a narrow neck are distributive, of course, and thus (26)—*Green bottles have narrow necks* turns out to be truth-conditionally equivalent to (24)—*A green bottle has a narrow neck.*

  The GEN operator may help to resolve another problem with his analysis that Carlson (1989) has noted. He attributes the example in (29) to Milsark (1974).

(29)   Typhoons arise in this part of the Pacific.

The problem is that (29) is ambiguous, and *typhoons* can have either its generic or its existential interpretation. The reading predicted by Carlson's analysis is the false one that says that it's a characteristic of typhoons to arise in the indicated part of the Pacific. (In fact, typhoons can arise in a number of different places.) The true reading, according to which this part of the Pacific is such that typhoons can arise there, is unaccounted for. We can represent these two different readings as in (30).

(30)   a. GEN_x [typhoons(x)](arise-in-this-part-of-the-Pacific(x)]
        b. GEN_x [this-part-of-the-Pacific(x)](typhoons-arise-in(x))

(30a) represents the reading that says that it's generally true of typhoons that they arise in this part of the Pacific, while the intended interpretation of (30b) is that it's generally true of this part of the Pacific that typhoons arise here. The representation in (30b) glosses over a number of important details that a thorough analysis would have to deal with. For one thing, the GEN operator cannot be taken to imply that typhoons are constantly arising in this part of the Pacific; (29) on its (30b) reading only means that it's possible for typhoons to arise here. And for another, we must assume that there is some kind of existential binding for *typhoons* within its clause as it occurs in (30b) so that *typhoons* in this reading gets narrow scope. (29) can't mean that there are typhoons of which it is generally true that they arise in this part of the Pacific.

As is frequently noted, the difference in readings for an example like (29) is correlated with the information packaging of the sentence. The (30a) reading occurs when typhoons are taken to be the sentence TOPIC—the entity which the sentence is talking about; and arising in the Pacific is the FOCUS—what is being predicated of the topic.[13] On the other hand the (30b) reading is about this part of the Pacific, and the focus is the fact that typhoons can arise there. Generally it is the focus part of a sentence which contains new information and the main sentence stress, which would naturally occur on *this* for the (30a) reading, but on *typhoons* for the (30b) reading. Another way to influence information packaging is by altering word order and/or grammatical relations, since topics tend to occur in subject position or elsewhere early in a sentence. The pair in (31) (cf. Jackendoff (1972)) illustrates this generalization.

(31)   a.   Beavers build dams.
      b.   Dams are built by beavers.

The topic of (31a) is beavers while that of (31b) is dams. Here again the GEN operator can help us represent the difference.

(32)   a. $\text{GEN}_x \, [\text{beavers}(x)](\text{builds-dams}(x))$
      b. $\text{GEN}_x \, [\text{dams}(x)](\text{beavers-build}(x))$

(31a), which is natural, receives the interpretation in (32a), according to which it is generally true of beavers (the sentence topic) that they build dams. (31b)/(32b), on the other hand, says that it's generally true of dams that they are built by beavers, which the Army Corps of Engineers would vigorously deny.

Let us review the current situation with respect to bare NPs. They occur in three kinds of environments, illustrated in (33).

---

[13] See Gundel and Fretheim (2004), and the works cited there, on these important concepts.

(33) a. Lions are plentiful in Africa.
      b. Lions like to eat zebras.
      c. Lions roared outside my window last night.

The first two sentences are generic, while the third is about a particular episode. According to the analysis of Carlson (1977a, b), *lions*
in all three examples names a kind. The predicates in (33a) and (33b)
are predicated directly of that kind, while that in (33c) is predicated
only of lion stages which realize that kind. We have seen evidence
suggesting that the occurrence of *lions* in examples like (33b) may
instead be a generically quantified indefinite, since it can occur in
generic sentences but with an existential interpretation rather than a
generic one. We saw too that bare NPs in this type of example need
not denote well-defined kinds—recall *Green bottles have long necks*.
Krifka et al. (1995) suggest that bare plurals are ambiguous—sometimes
naming kinds ((as in (33a), when Krifka et al. would then consider
them to be true generic NPs), but other times (as in (33b, c)) merely
being indefinite NPs with or without generic binding. But it is
unfortunate that this view results in claiming an ambiguity for bare
NPs—postulation of ambiguity is to be avoided if possible. Whether
another path can be found to unifying all three kinds of occurrence
remains to be seen;[14] as with almost every bit of subject matter in this
book, research is continuing (see, e.g., Krifka (2004) and Carlson
(forthcoming) for discussion and references). However, before leaving
the topic of generic NPs completely there is a particularly troublesome subcategory that deserves some attention. We give it a section
all its own.

7.4 The average American

In this section we look at a particular type of generic-looking statement, exemplified below.

(34) a. The average American has 2.3 children.
      b. Republicans are courting Joe Sixpack this year.

---

[14] Perhaps it would be possible to defend an approach on which bare NPs are always
indefinites, and the difference between (33a) and (33b) is that in (33a) the predicate
forces a collective interpretation of the plural subject, while in (33b) the predicate is
distributive.

Such examples are particularly significant since they have contributed to an attack by Noam Chomsky and others[15] on, really, the basis of this book—the assumption that we use linguistic expressions to refer to things in the world. In an often quoted passage Chomsky remarks:

> If I say that one of the things that concerns me is the average man and his foibles, or Joe Sixpack's priorities, or the inner track that Raytheon has on the latest missile contract, does it follow that I believe that the actual world, or some mental model of mine,[16] is constituted of such entities as the average man, foibles, Joe Sixpack, priorities, and inner tracks?   (Chomsky 1995: 29)

Such remarks have spurred a number of linguists (e.g. Higginbotham (1985); Stanley (2001)) to try to give analyses of sentences like those in (34) in such a way as to blunt the effect of Chomsky's attack. Here we have space to review just two proposals—one from Greg Carlson and Jeff Pelletier (2002), and one from Chris Kennedy and Jason Stanley (2008, 2009).

We'll begin with Kennedy and Stanley's analysis, which distinguishes between "abstract" and "concrete" understandings of expressions like *the average American*. (34a) is an example of the abstract understanding; since no real person can have 2.3 children, it is assumed that *the average American* here must denote something abstract, if it denotes at all. In a sentence like (35), on the other hand

(35)   The average American does not own their home outright.

we can understand the predicate to be applying to actual individuals. Here, but not in abstract examples like (34a), *average* may be replaced by *typical* without anomaly, as shown in (36).

(36)   a.   # The typical American has 2.3 children.
        b.   The typical American does not own their home outright.

Kennedy and Stanley suggest that concrete examples may best be simply regarded as generic, and they confine their analysis to the abstract type, exemplified in (34a).

---

[15] Carlson and Pelletier quote Norbert Hornstein (1984: 58) and cite other linguists without specific references—Gilles Fauconnier, Ray Jackendoff, George Lakoff, Ronald Langacker, and Leonard Talmy; as well as philosophers Stanley Cavell, Hilary Putnam, and Richard Rorty, and literary theorists Jacques Derrida and Umberto Eco (Carlson and Pelletier 2002: 75–7).

[16] Note Chomsky's dismissal here of reference to mental entities as well as physical ones. We return to this issue briefly in Chapter 10.

The abstract examples considered by Kennedy and Stanley all involve numerical averages. The details of the analysis are rather complex, but the ultimate effect is to give special prominence to the specific number in the predicate, so that (34a) would come out equivalent to something like (37).

(37)   The average number of children had by Americans is 2.3.

The result is that the NP *the average American* does not get analyzed as a unit at all, and this creates a couple of problems.

One of the problems for the Kennedy and Stanley type of analysis results from the fact that the abstract and concrete predicates may be conjoined in an apparent single predication, as in (38).

(38)   The average American has 2.3 children, but does not own their home outright.

On their analysis the subject of (38) should have two quite different analyses. A related problem is that NPs like *the average American*, apparently in their abstract use, may serve as antecedents of pronouns, as in (39).

(39)   The average boxer receives 7.4 severe blows to the head per match, and he often suffers brain damage as a result.

This is a serious problem, since under the Kennedy and Stanley analysis abstract *average* NPs are not even constituents.

In response to these problems, Kennedy and Stanley suggest that there may be an additional tacit occurrence of *average* in such sentences, making (38), for instance, equivalent to (40).

(40)   The average American has an average of 2.3 children, but does not own their home outright.

Thus the subject in these examples may be seen as uniformly of the concrete (generic) type (allowing it also to serve as the antecedent of a pronoun), and the burden of the abstract predication is transferred to the second occurrence of *average*. However as they note, this solution gives rise to the question of why (41a) below cannot be construed as in (41b).

(41)   a.   ??The typical American has 2.3 children. [= Kennedy and Stanley 2009: ex. 101a]
        b.   The typical American has an average of 2.3 children.

If a tacit *an average of* can be heard in examples like (38), why can't it also resolve the problem of (41a)? Kennedy and Stanley do not have a confident response to this problem.

We turn now to the Carlson and Pelletier analysis of NPs like *the average American*. Carlson and Pelletier argue that such NPs are instances of a special category of NP which is neither quantitative nor referential, and which they call "encuneral" (for "not quantitative and not referential"). Still, they do assign a denotation to such NPs, and furthermore one which is a set of properties, so to that extent such NPs could be seen as parallel to generalized quantifiers. The properties in question are average values for each parameter on which averages may be constructed (e.g. number of children, height, weight, income, and so forth). Exactly which parameters these are remains something of a mystery—Carlson and Pelletier cite the contrast in (42) (their ex. 21) as one for which they have no explanation.

(42)   a.   The average couch is 2.1 meters long.
       b.   ??The average couch has 5.2 legs.

So this is one of the problems left for future research.

Carlson and Pelletier make a distinction between abstract and concrete uses of CNPs like *average American*, but in a slightly different place from where Kennedy and Stanley draw the line. While for Kennedy and Stanley the type of predicate is crucial, for Carlson and Pelletier it is not. Concrete uses, in the Carlson and Pelletier sense of "concrete," show up in examples like (43):

(43)   Average Americans cook hamburgers on the barbecue. [= Carlson and Pelletier 2002: ex. 2b]

On the Carlson and Pelletier view, examples like (43) are talking about actual people; there is no abstraction involved. On the other hand a generic example like (35) (*The average American does not own their home outright*), despite the concrete predicate, would be classified as abstract by Carlson and Pelletier, since concrete properties may be included in the postulated property sets for (abstract) *average* NPs. Thus, examples like (40), with conjoined abstract and concrete predicates, do not present a problem for them.

Carlson and Pelletier may have a problem with pronouns, as in (39) above, repeated here as (44).

(44)   The average boxer receives 7.4 severe blows to the head per
       match, and <u>he</u> often suffers brain damage as a result.

In contrast to Kennedy and Stanley, Carlson and Pelletier do interpret
average NPs as constituents, so the problem of pronouns is not as
severe for them. On the other hand, as we have seen, *average* NPs are
not normal constituents under the Carlson and Pelletier analysis. But
perhaps, correspondingly, the pronoun in (44) is a special type.[17]

   I think one problem with both of these approaches to *average* NPs
may be that they do not connect them sufficiently with singular
definite generics, with which they seem to share both form and interpretation type. Carlson and Pelletier do acknowledge some type of
relationship (2002: 75, n. 2), but do not elaborate on it. The parallel use
of proper names like *Joe Sixpack* could be taken as indicative of this
relationship—this parallel is also noted by Carlson and Pelletier (2002:
94), who suggest that, in this case at least, their analysis might be
extended to such NPs. We saw above in §7.3.3 that there is an affinity
between generic singular definite descriptions and proper names, both
being restricted to well-defined kinds. *Average* NPs in examples like
(34a) (*The average American has 2.3 children*) are also construed generically, and neither of the analyses we have looked at makes this
similarity explicit. In fact Kennedy and Stanley argue against a generic
analysis—alluding to the common assumption that generics involve
quantification over ordinary individuals, while *average* NPs, when they
occur with abstract predicates like *has 2.3 children*, cannot be so
construed (2009: 10). However, as we have noted, objections have
been raised to the idea of tacit generic quantification (cf. Löbner
(2000)), so perhaps the commonly assumed analysis of generics is
not correct. Ultimately perhaps we will be forced to recognize abstract
constructs as the referents of singular definite descriptions which are
used generically, whether those singular definites be the names of kinds
such as lions, tigers, and Coke bottles, or kinds such as the average
American; and as the data above indicate, those abstract referents
would naturally be possessed of both abstract and concrete properties.
Perhaps this is simply part of the ontology of natural language
(cf. (Emmon) Bach (1986)).

---

[17] Carlson and Pelletier suggest that perhaps pronouns like that in (44) are best viewed
as what are called "E-type" pronouns. We won't get to those until Chapter 10 below.

7.5 Concluding remarks

In this chapter we have been considering some of the most difficult issues in the area of reference and NP interpretation. We began by looking at Link's classic analysis of NPs with plural and mass head nouns, and we saw some of the ways in which such NPs can be interpreted depending on what is being predicated of their denotation. Following that we looked at NPs which can be used in generic sentences—singular indefinite and definite descriptions, and bare NPs. We concluded that when singular definite descriptions are used generically they may indeed be functioning like proper names of kinds of things. This suggests an explanation for the fact that they cannot be used in this way with kinds that are not distinctive—recall the difference between *the Coke bottle* and *the green bottle*. On the other hand singular indefinite descriptions and bare plurals seem to acquire genericity from elsewhere in the sentences they occur in, which we suggested (with reservations) might be analyzed using the quantifier-like GEN operator. Finally we looked at NPs like *the average American* which are distinctive in allowing predications of properties like having 2.3 children, which no concrete individual can possess. In the end these NPs seemed to be leading us down a primrose path toward total Platonism—let a gazillion weird entities bloom! In any case, this chapter must be considered only a basic introduction to this complex and interesting area.

8

Indexicality and pronouns

> It is the duty of pronouns to be not wild but tamed, that is, tied down;
> yet their natural tendency is toward the jungle.
>
> Jacques Barzun, *Simple & Direct*

In this chapter we take a look at two overlapping categories of NP that have in common the effect of drawing us further out of pure semantics and into the pragmatics-semantics interface. PRONOUNS, as we saw in Chapter 1, are words with only a minimal amount of descriptive content which nevertheless constitute a complete NP. Thus "proNP" might be a better label for this category of expression. Examples are personal pronouns like *it* and *our* and demonstrative pronouns like *this* and *those*.[1] On the other hand INDEXICAL or DEICTIC expressions are those which determine a referent only in conjunction with elements of the context of utterance—the text-external world (to use a happy term from Lambrecht (1994: 36f.)).[2] People often distinguish DEMONSTRA-TIVE indexicals, like *here*, *those apples*, or *that*, whose use may require help from the speaker (a physical pointing, a nod of the head, or some other indication of the intended referent) from PURE indexicals such as the first- and second-person pronouns, and adverbials like *now* and *tomorrow*, which don't require such assistance from the speaker.

There are some terminological pitfalls in this area. What philosophers call "indexicals" linguists often call "deictic" expressions. The reason for this preference of linguists may be because there is another use of "indexical" and "indexicality" in social and anthropological linguistics having to do with indicators of personal identity in a

---

[1] We will not have anything to say here about the "*wh-*" pronouns like *who* and *what*.

[2] Because their reference is determined, at least in part, by features of the utterance context, the referents of indexical expressions typically change from utterance to utterance, and sometimes the members of this category are referred to as "shifters." However, Nunberg (1993: 2, n. 2) notes that the Japanese first-person pronoun *chin* (now obsolete) could only be used by the emperor. This would be one shifter that didn't do much shifting.

social sense—such things as one's gender, age, occupation, and so forth. (Cf. Lyons (1977: §4.2).) Those kinds of issues are not in play in this book, and given that we will be citing results from both the philosophical and the linguistic literatures, I will be using the terms pretty much interchangeably in what follows.

Another potential source of confusion is the fact that all of the items we will be considering in this chapter have <u>many uses, only some of which are deictic or indexical.</u> Thus third-person pronouns (*she, they,* and so forth), for example, would be considered deictic only when they are used to refer to something in the utterance context, as in (1a) below. (1b) and (1c) illustrate possible ANAPHORIC uses, when the interpretation of a pronoun (or other NP) is linked to another linguistic expression (something in the text-internal world)—its ANTECEDENT.

(1) a. <u>He</u> [pointing] is late!
     b. Julia said that <u>she</u> would be there.
     c. No man wants to admit <u>his</u> failure.

Even pronouns which are almost always indexical, like *you,* may have other uses. One of them is illustrated in (2).

(2) Getting a bachelor of science degree doesn't make <u>you</u> a scientist.

On its most natural interpretation, *you,* in (2), is nonspecific. The utterance may have nothing particular to do with the addressee at all, and could be paraphrased with *one* replacing *you.*

Similarly, as we will see below, demonstrative NPs have nonindexical uses. There are <u>two subcategories of demonstrative NPs.</u> One consists of the <u>demonstrative pronouns</u> (*this, that, these,* and *those*), and the other is the large subcategory of DEMONSTRATIVE DESCRIPTIONS (or "complex demonstratives" as they are now frequently called—but I will use the older label). These are NPs with a demonstrative determiner, like *those apples* or *this dagger which I see before me.* Current analyses attempt to unify these two subcategories. They also attempt to unify the indexical and nonindexical uses, but retain the term "demonstrative" for all of these uses, even when no deixis is involved.

In the first four sections below we will investigate the nature of indexicality, focusing in particular on indexical NPs.[3] We will begin with some groundbreaking work by David Kaplan, which resulted in a

---

[3] For more complete treatments of indexicality/deixis from a linguistic perspective, which include other kinds of expressions in addition to NPs, see e.g. Lyons (1977), Levinson (1983), Fillmore (1997).

substantial modification of our view of semantic structure in a way which incorporates the explicit introduction of contexts of utterance. In §8.2 we'll take up a particular problem involving indexicality and propositional attitudes, and in §8.3 we take a look at some complexities in indexical interpretation pointed out by Geoffrey Nunberg (1993). §8.4 is devoted to the interpretation of demonstrative NPs. In §8.5 we shift gears and turn to (third-person) pronouns, investigating the idea that all such pronouns are like variables of logic. Here we will also be introduced to so-called "dynamic" approaches to semantics. In the penultimate section we look at some data that suggest parallels between pronouns, on the one hand, and definite and demonstrative descriptions, on the other. (We'll return to this issue, as well as other issues involving pronouns, in Chapter 10.) The final section contains a summary of our investigations.

8.1 Character and content

Recall the discussion in Chapter 3 of the development of the notion of intension, as a function from possible worlds (and times) to extensions. As noted there, an early proposal for dealing with indexicality was to expand the arguments of such functions to INDICES, which would include not only a possible world and a moment of time, but also a speaker, an addressee, a location, indicated items, and possibly other elements. (See e.g. Scott (1970); Lewis (1972).) Thus the variation in reference of indexical expressions was seen as being on a par with variations in denotation of any type of expression depending on possible world and moment of time. As mentioned in Chapter 3, the two kinds of variation are not really the same. Facts change with differences in possible worlds (or situations) and times; but facts do not change depending on who is the speaker or the addressee (except of course for those facts themselves).

In his classic paper "Demonstratives,"[4] David Kaplan gave another argument for separating out possible worlds from the referents of indexicals. Consider his example in (3).

(3)   I am here now.

---

[4] In present-day usage the title of this paper is unfortunate; as Kaplan makes clear, his intention is to discuss indexicals in general, and not just demonstrative indexicals (cf. Kaplan (1977: 489–90)).

Simplifying slightly, on a plausible view where sentence intensions are functions from indices (rather than just possible worlds) to truth values,[5] (3) would be assigned truth at every index, and would thus be treated as a necessary truth, on a par with *Bachelors are unmarried* or *2 plus 2 equals 4*. Now there is definitely something extra truthy ← about (3), since whenever it is uttered it is used to express a truth. However the truth expressed on any of those occasions, assuming it isn't God who is speaking, would be a contingent proposition. For example were I to utter (3) now, I would express a proposition concerning me and my present location—something similar to what is expressed in a nonindexical way by (4).

(4)   Barbara Abbott is in her office, at 4:15 pm on Tuesday February 12, 2008.

And it is easy to see that the proposition expressed by (4) is not a necessary truth at all—I could easily have been outside taking a walk at this time, or in Key West on vacation.

Kaplan's solution to this problem was to distinguish two different elements of meaning, which he called CHARACTER and CONTENT. Let us look first at content. The content of a typical whole utterance is the proposition expressed. (The hedging "typical" is because of utterances, like *Hi!* or *Please!*, which do not seem to express propositions.) Assuming compositionality, this content is determined by the contents of the expressions which go to make up the utterance. Since utterance contents are propositions—sentence intensions—we might have assumed that the constituents of these propositions (if indeed they have constituents) would also be intensional, the kind of thing we saw in the discussion of intensions in Chapter 3. And indeed that would be the case for most nonindexical expressions in the utterance. When it comes to indexical expressions, however, as we saw in Chapter 5, Kaplan has argued in favor of a return to Russellian singular propositions—propositions containing actual entities. While it was Russell's view that only the pronoun *this* could be used

---

[5] The plausible view being assumed is one according to which the indices are "natural," in the sense that the speaker is addressing the addressee at the time and location and indicating the indicated items. An alternative view would allow any combination of "speaker," "addressee," time, location, and items to constitute a possible index. On this view (3) would not express a necessary truth, but the fact that it is true whenever uttered would not be captured.

in the expression of propositions containing ordinary, real-world entities, Kaplan expanded this idea to include not just *this* but all indexicals; this was the origin of his theory of direct reference, which we reviewed earlier in connection with proper names and referential uses of definite descriptions.[6] Thus the proposition expressed by (3) would contain me rather than my individual concept. The predicate indexicals in (3) (*here, now*) would yield entities too, so that the complete content of my utterance in (3), according to Kaplan, would be that Russellian singular proposition containing me, my office, the present moment of time (4:15 pm on 2/12/08), plus the relation of being which holds among entities, places they are located, and times they are located there. (As before, I would urge the postulation of constant individual concepts instead of the corresponding entities for these roles.)

Turning now to Kaplan's other component, the character of an expression corresponds to the meaning conventionally encoded in it. In formal terms, the character is a function which takes the context of utterance as input and yields the content of that expression in that context as value. Indexicals have characters whose values differ from context to context. For example, the character of the English word *I* is such that it picks out of any context in which it is uttered the speaker who utters it; the character of *you* picks out the addressee(s); *today* determines the day during which the utterance takes place; and so forth. Crucially, the character of these expressions does not enter into the proposition expressed—only the content does. The character of a whole utterance, then, is a function from contexts to propositions.

It should be noted that the concepts of character and content are applicable to any type of linguistic expression—not just indexicals. It's just that the characters of nonindexical expressions are such that the content does not vary with the circumstances of utterance. Note too that, although the contents of pure indexicals are rigidly designated entities (either the actual entities, as on Kaplan's view, or their constant individual concepts, on my view), the contents of other expressions may vary from world to world. Thus a nonindexical definite description like *the inventor of bifocals* has a constant character, which

---

[6] As noted in Chapter 5, Kaplan himself was initially a bit equivocal about whether proper names were correctly regarded as directly referential, although others (e.g. Salmon (1986); Soames (2002)) have been eager to adopt this view.

TABLE 8.1. Different kinds of characters and contents of NPs

	Character is a constant function	Character is a variable function
Content is a constant function (a constant individual concept) or an actual entity	Proper names: e.g. *Barack Obama, Madonna*	Pure indexicals: e.g. *I, tomorrow*
Content is a variable function (an individual concept with variable values)	Nonindexical definite descriptions: e.g. *the inventor of bifocals*	Indexical definite descriptions: e.g. *the current president of the US*

yields the same content in every context. However that content is a variable function which picks out of each world whoever it was who invented bifocals in that world. On the other hand an indexical definite description like *the current President of the US*, has both variable character and variable content. Its character is such that the time of utterance figures in the determination of which individual concept is selected—spoken in 1965, it gets us the president in 1965. That content in turn varies from world to world—in the actual world LBJ is the value, but in an alternative world where his assassination did not take place it might pick out JFK.[7] In contrast proper names have constant character and constant content—in any context their value is the entity they rigidly designate, or that entity's constant individual concept. See Table 8.1.

By dividing up meaning into character and content, Kaplan allows us to capture the sense in which (3) (*I am here now*) seems both similar to, and different from, a necessary truth. Its character is such that the content expressed on any occasion of utterance will be true on that occasion (at that possible world and time). On the other hand, as we've seen, that propositional content will be such as to be false at other worlds and times (unless, as noted, it is God who is talking).

---

[7] We noted above in Chapter 6 that many have responded to the problem of incomplete descriptions, as in Strawson's example *The table is covered with books*, by postulating tacit indices whose values in a particular utterance serve to narrow the domain of discourse. If such analyses are correct these NPs should be added to the class of indexical expressions.

8.2 Essential indexicals?

This section takes its title from a famous paper by John Perry (1979).[8] Perry begins his discussion with a little story about a visit to the supermarket: as he is shopping, he notices a trail of sugar on the floor, and follows it around and around the aisles of the supermarket, hoping to catch up with the shopper who has a torn bag of sugar in his or her cart. We can imagine Perry having gathered quite a robust picture of this sloppy shopper without yet realizing his true identity—Perry himself. Perhaps there were mirrors at the ends of the aisles in the store, so he saw himself but still without recognizing himself. (Ernst Mach apparently once told a story about getting on a bus at the end of a long journey, seeing himself in the mirror at the other end of the bus, and wondering who that shabby creature was. This story is cited in Perry (1998: 91).) So, Perry knows that that guy is the messy shopper. What happens, then, when he eventually realizes that that guy is himself? The problem lies in specifying the proposition Perry comes to accept. Consider example (5).

(5)   [John Perry]$_i$ realized that he$_i$ was the messy shopper.

On the *de re* interpretation of (5), the proposition in the complement (*he is the messy shopper*) concerns an actual individual, Perry himself. However, no matter what version of propositional complements we assume, this interpretation is neutral on the crucial issue of whether or not Perry recognizes himself as himself—it does not distinguish Perry's knowledge before he found out that he was the messy shopper from his knowledge afterwards.

Perry gives several other examples of a similar kind of situation—in one a faculty member knows that the departmental meeting begins at noon, and has every intention of going, but does not move because he does not realize that it is noon now. In another some lost hikers know how to get home from either of two lakes, but do not know which of those lakes is the one before them.

Fodor (1975: 133ff.) had pointed out a similar problem, involving the difference between the sentences in (6).

---

[8] As Perry pointed out, the problem at issue here was first pointed out by Casteñeda (e.g. (1966, 1968)).

(6)   a.   Only Churchill remembers giving the blood, sweat and tears speech.
       b.   Only Churchill remembers Churchill giving the blood, sweat and tears speech.

(6a) is true, or at least could have been while Churchill was still alive. However (6b) is not, since lots of people remember him giving the speech. Like linguists generally at the time, Fodor assumed that the complement of *remember* in (6a) (i.e. *giving the blood, sweat and tears speech*) must be at some level a complete sentence (although in surface structure it appears to be just a VP). Fodor proposed adding a special "self" element as the complement subject in the underlying structure of such examples. However this does not tell us what the truth conditions of the complement in (6a) ought to be, since no way is given to distinguish semantically a *self* which is coreferential with *Churchill* from *Churchill*.

8.2.1 Belief states

As we saw above in Chapter 5, hidden indexical theories of propositional attitude sentences separate the propositional contents of beliefs from BELIEF STATES—the way those propositional contents are grasped. The problem with essential indexicals was one motivation for the hidden indexical approach, and the distinction between belief states and belief contents is reminiscent of Kaplan's character-content distinction, belief state corresponding to the character of a sentence. Indeed, Perry acknowledged this inspiration for his idea (1979: 21, n. 6). Thus the analysis of (5), repeated here as (7),

(7)   John Perry realized that he himself was the messy shopper.

would involve a kind of double attribution to the subject. The object of his realization would be the content of the proposition that John Perry is the messy shopper—that proposition true in any world in which John Perry is spilling sugar while shopping. But in addition, (7) attributes to Perry a particular belief state, which is a way of grasping this proposition—specifically a first-person type of way in which he grasps something like *I am the messy shopper*. (Hence the essential indexical.) As we noted above in Chapter 5, variations on this kind of approach, which distinguishes the object of a propositional attitude from a way of grasping that object (a "mode of presentation" on the current use of that phrase, or a narrow content), have been put forward by a number of others (e.g. Schiffer (1977); Richard (1990)). On the other hand, a more radical idea was proposed by David Lewis, and is reviewed in the next section.

8.2.2 Belief de se

Lewis (1979a), citing Perry's examples, introduces yet another instance calling for revision in our view of belief as a simple relation between a believer and a proposition. Here the concern is not with particular example sentences, but rather with accounting for beliefs. Lewis's example involves two gods, omniscient in all propositional matters, yet neither god knows which he is—the one on the tallest mountain who throws down manna, or the one on the coldest mountain who throws down thunderbolts. Lewis's solution is to propose that all belief is self-attribution of properties—belief *de se*, as he terms it. Ordinary beliefs which can correctly be captured propositionally would be seen, in Lewis's analysis, as self-attribution of the property of belonging to a world in which that proposition is true. Since the two gods are propositionally omniscient, and inhabit the same world, there is no way they can distinguish themselves from each other in terms of beliefs which separate only worlds—facts—from each other, i.e. in terms of propositions.[9] Instead, they seem to require further knowledge of the irreducibly *de se* type. That is, they need to be able to attribute to themselves particular properties; for example if one of them could (correctly of course—we **are** speaking of a god here) attribute to himself the property of sitting on the tallest mountain, then he would know which god he was.

Lewis makes clear that he is speaking of beliefs (and other mental attitudes) and not the semantics of sentences describing them, which he acknowledges to be "not a straightforward matter" (1979a: 154). Were we to try to adapt his account of the attitudes to semantic analysis, we would have to somehow account for the obvious mismatch between the surface syntax of such sentences and their interpretation. Coming up with the formal representation itself would not

---

[9] One might wonder whether replacing possible worlds with situations would be another way of solving this problem. It would not. Since situations basically reflect facts (or nonfacts), and the two gods agree on all knowledge of the facts, this knowledge still does not allow them to differentiate themselves from each other.

be hard. Sentences describing an ordinary propositional-looking belief such as (8a) could be assigned an interpretation as in (8b).

(8) a. John believes that sugar is cheap.
     b. Bel(j, $^\wedge\lambda$x[Cheap(sugar)])

The idea is that belief (signified by *Bel*) is now viewed as the relation that holds between an individual and a property that that individual self-ascribes—in this case the property of being such that sugar is cheap. For the irreducibly *de se* examples, like the messy shopper case, we would have something like (9b).

(9) a. John believes that he (himself) is the messy shopper.
     b. Bel(j, $^\wedge\lambda$x[Messy-shopper(x)])

In this case the belief in question is characterized as a relation between an individual (John Perry) and the property of being a messy shopper. Note that on this analysis we have done away with explicit representation of the indexical character of these examples. Instead, the indexicality has been folded into the meaning of *believe*. Whether this type of analysis (or one based on Perry's view of propositional attitudes) could be motivated syntactically is an issue which goes beyond the scope of this book.

8.3 Index vs denotation

Geoffrey Nunberg (1993) has argued that Kaplan's analysis of indexicality does not account for some interesting uses of indexicals. Consider, for example, a situation in which the speaker points at a spot on the map, or a restaurant ad in a newspaper, and utters (10).

(10) We had dinner there last week.

It is clear that what is being pointed to in the utterance of *there* is not the entity being spoken of in (10). Nunberg proposed distinguishing what he called the INDEX, which is the entity which is indicated in the utterance of an indexical expression, from what he called the "interpretation" of the indexical—the entity being talked about, or the denotation of the expression. In this example the spot on the map, or the restaurant ad, would be the index while the actual location or restaurant would constitute the interpretation—the denotation of the indexical. Interpretations correspond to indices in virtue of some relation or other. Here the relations involved would be that of places on a map to the places in the physical world they represent, or that of newspaper ads to the businesses they advertise.

Nunberg argued that similar kinds of facts hold for all kinds of indexical expressions, even the so-called "pure" indexicals. One of his examples involved the first-person plural pronoun *we* (*us, our,* etc.). The index of *we* is always the speaker, but since *we* is plural others must be involved too. In this kind of case the relation in question might be quite clear, especially if *we* serves as a determiner (as in e.g. *we residents of Leland Township*), but it also might be extremely vague. At a concert I attended recently one of the musicians introduced a portion of the program containing Mendelssohn's *Wedding March* with the comment that "this is a piece that we all use at some point in our lives." To be sure, she immediately took the comment back when she realized that many people who she might like to be addressing would in fact never use the piece, but probably even when she uttered it she did not have any clear idea of who was to be included.

Interestingly, as Nunberg pointed out, the choice of proximal or distal indexical depends on the relative location of the index rather than the interpretation, should those differ. Consider the example in (11), as uttered by a shop owner pointing at a couple of sample plates, the first of which is nearby and the second of which is across the room.

(11)   *These* are over at the warehouse, but *those* I have in stock here.
        [= Nunberg 1993: ex. 43.]

The relative locations of the items actually being talked about (the stocks of plates) is the reverse of the corresponding samples (the first group being away and the second group being nearby), but it is the relative location of the samples (the indices) that determines the choice of *these* vs *those*.

In order to account for these kinds of facts, Nunberg proposed that the logical forms of sentences containing indexical expressions need to include variables for both the index and the relation relating the index to the interpretation or denotation. The value of the index will be determined either by the character of the expression (for the pure indexicals), or by the character plus a pointing or other indication by the speaker (for demonstratives). In the unmarked case of indexical use, the interpretation (or denotation) of the NP is the index itself— the actual item being pointed at or otherwise indicated; thus the relation involved in the unmarked case is identity. As pointed out by Paul Elbourne (2008: 441), the kind of reading found in (10) and (11) above, where the interpretation of the indexical differs from the index, is only possible when the rest of the sentence is inconsistent with the unmarked denotation. Thus if, in the same situation as envisaged above for (10) (*We had dinner there last week*), the speaker had instead said (12):

(12)   Put a little x right there.

the place denoted by *there* would indeed have been what the speaker was pointing to (the spot on the map or the ad in the newspaper). As we will see in the following section, Nunberg's analysis has been incorporated and formalized in the Elbourne's (2008) analysis of demonstrative NPs.

8.4 Demonstrative NPs

We turn now to demonstrative NPs, a category which (as noted at the outset) includes demonstrative pronouns (*this*, *those*), and NPs with demonstrative determiners like *this wastebasket* and *those fine old reproductions*—demonstrative descriptions (aka "complex demonstratives"). Let us start with demonstrative descriptions. These are very similar to definite descriptions, and some of the same issues which arose in Chapter 6 to do with quantification vs referentiality arise again here. Below we will look briefly at two recent analyses of demonstratives—one quantificational (that of Jeffrey King (2001)), and one referential (that of Elbourne (2008)).[10] I want to stress "briefly"—the summaries of these analyses will, of necessity, leave out many details, and readers are hereby urged to consult the originals for those details.

Before turning to the analyses we should note at least one clear difference between demonstrative descriptions and definite descriptions: when demonstrative descriptions are used deictically, with a gesture of some kind on the part of the speaker indicating an intended denotation, that gesture plays a crucial role in determining their interpretation. The same cannot be said for definite descriptions; although they may also be accompanied with some kind of gesture on the part of the speaker, such a gesture does not play a role in determining a referent. As a consequence, as King (2001: 27) points

---

[10] Elbourne considers his analysis to be referential only in a weak sense, since on his view demonstratives denote individual concepts rather than individuals. Cf. Elbourne (2008: 430).

out, one can use multiple tokens of a given demonstrative NP in a single utterance, as shown in (13a), but not a definite description.

(13) a.   I like that house and that house, but not that house.
      b.   *I like the house and the house, but not the house.

(13a) is perfectly acceptable with different indications of different houses on the part of the speaker, but the same cannot be said for (13b).

   Both of the analyses we will review incorporate an indexical component for demonstrative descriptions which will account for the difference between the examples in (13). In addition both of the analyses are aimed at overcoming a major shortcoming with Kaplan's analysis of demonstratives. Kaplan's analysis (as he himself acknowledged in Kaplan (1977: 489f).) does not account for **non**indexical uses of demonstratives. There are in fact several kinds of nonindexical uses of demonstratives, as illustrated in (14) and (15) below. (Another kind of nonindexical use will appear later on, in §8.6.1.)

(14) a.   Kylie arrived with a lot of friends. These friends were aged 4–5 years old.
      b.   Alexander was mean to his sister. That error cost him dearly.

(15) a.   Those students who finish early should wait for the others.
      b.   Ultimately Bill selected that car which had seemed the flashiest.

The examples in (14) show anaphoric uses, where the demonstrative is intended to denote something referred to in the previous text. Those in (15) are freestanding. One might claim an ambiguity in demonstrative determiners distinguishing these examples from those in (13a), but (as I've noted several times) postulation of ambiguity without supporting evidence is not a strong move.

   Let us look first at the analysis of Jeffrey King (2001). As noted, King argues that demonstrative descriptions are quantificational NPs. Thus the determiner expresses a relation between two properties. One of these properties is, as usual, whatever property is expressed in the remainder of the sentence. The other property, on King's analysis, is a complex property with two components. The first component is the property expressed by the CNP constituent with which the demonstrative determiner combines—*house* in the examples in (13a), *friends, error, students who finish early,* and *car which had seemed the flashiest* for the examples in (14) and (15). The second, potentially indexical, component is the speaker's demonstrative intention, reflected in any

ompanies the NP in uses like those in (13a). (This
ention has a rigidifying effect on the denotation of
le to Kaplan's use of actual entities.) In nonindexical
in (14) and (15), there is no demonstrative intention
he part of the speaker; instead it is replaced with
either demand reference to something introduced
in the previous text, or simply duplicate the property expressed by the
CNP constituent.

According to the analysis of Paul Elbourne (2008) demonstrative
descriptions denote individual concepts—functions from situations to
entities. Elbourne incorporates the analysis of Nunberg, sketched
above, which includes both an index (which corresponds roughly to
the indexical component of King's analysis) and a relational component. The index, in Elbourne's analysis, must satisfy a proximal/distal
feature and this feature is what distinguishes *this/these* from *that/those*.
(King's analysis involved only the distal alternatives.) In indexical and
anaphoric uses, the index is the item pointed at or otherwise indicated
by the speaker or made salient in the context. As noted in the preceding
section, in the simple cases the relational component will specify
identity with the index (resulting in a constant individual concept).
The denotation of a demonstrative description, then, is determined by
a complex provided by the CNP constituent, the relational component,
and the index.[11]

King's analysis was not specifically extended to demonstrative pronouns, although he did discuss briefly some ideas about how to achieve
that. All of these suggestions involve regarding demonstrative pronouns
as determiners with a null CNP component (2001: 139–45). Elbourne's
analysis does include demonstrative pronouns, and (like King) proposes that they are determiners with a null CNP.[12] Interestingly, toward
the end of his article Elbourne contrasts his analysis with King's analysis, concluding that, after adjusting for inessential differences, the
difference comes down to a choice between generalized quantifiers

---

[11] As we've seen, both King and Elbourne include the descriptive content from the CNP
constituent as essential in determining the denotation of a demonstrative description. This
agrees with most other analyses (e.g. those of Roberts (2002) and Braun (2008)). One
exception is Larson and Segal (1995: 210–13), who argue otherwise (but not with a great deal
of conviction).

[12] This aspect of Elbourne's analysis is carried over from the analysis of pronouns and
definite descriptions in Elbourne (2005). The idea that pronouns are determiners (or
articles) was first proposed by Paul Postal (1966).

and individual concepts. He offers some considerations such as those reviewed above in Chapter 6 (cf. Elbourne (2008: 455f.)). However, as we noted there, such considerations do not seem conclusive.

On both King's and Elbourne's analyses, nonindexical demonstrative descriptions like those in (15) above are very similar to the corresponding definite descriptions in (16).

(16) a. <u>The students who finish early</u> should wait for the others.
      b. Ultimately Bill selected <u>the car which had seemed the flashiest.</u>

On King's analysis there is essentially no difference at all. On the other hand the index in Elbourne's analysis is retained for all uses of demonstratives. In cases where there is no gesture toward anything in the environment, the index must be something more abstract. We will return to this issue of the difference between definite and demonstrative descriptions in Chapter 10.

8.5 The interpretation of (third-person) pronouns: reference, coreference, and binding

We turn now to the interpretation of third-person pronouns. We will focus here almost entirely on singular pronouns, since they have received the most attention and seem to be the most difficult to account for. (We'll have a word to say about plural third-person pronouns at the very end of this section.) Recall from our opening remarks that such pronouns can have potentially three different kinds of use, as exemplified in (1), repeated here.

(17) a. <u>He</u> [pointing] is late!
      b. Julia$_i$ said that <u>she</u>$_i$ would be there.
      c. No man$_i$ wants to admit <u>his</u>$_i$ failure.

The pronoun in (17a) is being used deictically. On the other hand the pronouns in (17b) and (17c) are being used anaphorically, and thus are REFERENTIALLY DEPENDENT on their antecedents. We've indicated that referential dependence by matching subscript i's on the NPs. In some cases referential dependence means coreference (as in (17b)),[13] but not

---

[13] When coindexing marks coreference it is **presupposed** coreference—that is, the identity relation is assumed. Similarly, use of different indices would convey that coreference is not assumed; this can be the case even if facts should later emerge establishing coreference.

always; with the quantificational antecedent as in (17c) we can't really speak of reference. The pronoun in (17c) is particularly interesting, as it is behaving very much like a variable from logic which is bound by its quantificational antecedent. The question arises as to whether these three uses require us to assume different meanings for third-person pronouns—do they have different characters or can the uses be accounted for with a single character?

8.5.1 The "free variable" interpretation

Let us start with the working assumption that all these pronouns are like variables of logic. Intuitively that makes sense—like logical variables, they don't carry sufficient information to determine a referent, and they are susceptible of being controlled by another expression—their antecedent. Of course in a natural language pronouns often do have some minimal semantic content as part of their character. In English, gender and number are indicated for singular third-person pronouns, and number for plurals,[14] but this by itself is not enough to determine a semantic value. In a formal language, free variables are really not devoid of any interpretation; rather, they are assigned a denotation from the universe of discourse by an assignment function. In the event that they are within the scope of a coindexed quantifier, that quantifier takes over their interpretation—it binds them, which alters the interpretation accordingly; otherwise they wind up with the semantic value given them by the assignment function.[15]

We might say that a pronoun used deictically, like *he* in (17a), is like a free variable, the only difference being that while free variables have an arbitrarily assigned value, an unbound natural-language pronoun has its referent assigned by the speaker.[16] Actually this option is almost always available to any third-person (nonreflexive) pronoun (we'll get to the reflexive pronouns below). Thus versions of (17b) and (17c) without the matching subscripts, for example, would allow an interpretation where the speaker intends the pronoun to refer to some other

[14] English pronouns are also inflected for case (e.g. *she, her; they, their, them*), but this is a syntactic feature, determined by the syntactic context in which they find themselves.

[15] Technically this is not exactly right, since in a formal language ultimately "free" variables usually wind up with an interpretation according to which they are universally quantified, but we are going to ignore that here.

[16] We might want to change this conclusion and award more recognition to the comprehension side of the language equation, allowing that addressees also assign referents to unbound pronouns (ideally, and usually, the same ones as are assigned by the speaker).

person who is salient in the context. Or in a different context *his* in (17c) might refer to someone who has been mentioned in the preceding discourse, as in (18).

(18)   [Michael Jordan]$_i$ was such a fabulous athlete that no man wants to admit his$_i$ failure [as a baseball player].

In this case *his* is coreferential with *Michael Jordan*, and not bound by *no man*. These two kinds of cases would correspond to the situation in a logical formula where a variable is in the scope of a quantificational expression, but not coindexed with it and hence not bound by it.

Historically, deictic uses such as that in (17a), where reference is to some entity in the text-external world, have been distinguished from anaphoric uses like that in (17b) and (18), where the referent of the pronoun has been explicitly mentioned—i.e. where the pronoun has an antecedent NP in the surrounding discourse. However, the currently dominant view is that these should not be distinguished. (Cf. Heim and Kratzer (1998) and the works cited there; see Evans (1980) for a different opinion, and Recanati (2005) for a reply to Evans.) One argument in favor of this conclusion comes from the fact that there are intermediate cases which would be difficult to classify were we to insist on a distinction between the two. One such is (19), as uttered immediately after an openly obnoxious man has finally left the room (cf. Lasnik (1976: 2)).

(19)   Thank heavens he's gone!

In this case there is no verbal antecedent to attribute the reference of *he* to, so it could hardly count as anaphoric. Yet the individual referred to is no longer in the text-external world, and no particular nod or gesture is required for the interpretation of the pronoun, making it unlike the examples traditionally termed "deictic."

That being the case, let us simply assume that, in addition to their quantificational use, pronouns may have a free variable type of interpretation. This occurs when the speaker intends to use the pronoun to refer to some salient entity that matches the encoded characteristics of gender and number. The salience requirement arises naturally, since speakers will want their addressees to be able to interpret the pronoun correctly and with ease.[17] (Although I once knew a woman who would use *he*, *him*, and *his* seemingly (to me) completely out of the blue; it

---

[17] There is more to be said here, and we return to this issue below, in Ch. 10.

took me a while to realize that whenever she did this, she was referring to her boss.) Entities may be salient because the speaker makes them salient by pointing or nodding, or in virtue of being (or having been) saliently in the environment, or because they have been referred to in the prior discourse, or as a result of some other property. This is an option which is in general available to any third-person (nonreflexive) pronoun.

8.5.2 Dynamic semantics

At this point I want to briefly introduce a kind of approach to semantics that is relevant here because of the intuitively natural way it deals with pronouns. The approach was originally developed independently by Irene Heim (1982, 1983) and Hans Kamp (1981; Kamp and Reyle 1993). It has as one of its many benefits the ability to represent cross-sentential relationships, breaking the bonds of single sentences to treat whole discourses in a single framework. On Heim's account, a discourse consists of a number of file cards, representing entities spoken about; the sequence of utterances contributes information for those file cards as well as introducing new ones. Hence the name "File Change Semantics" for this version. Kamp's very similar approach is referred to as "Discourse Representation Theory." Here discourses are represented as collections of information associated with variables. Collectively the two come under the heading DYNAMIC SEMANTICS (reflecting the fact that this type of semantics deals with an unfolding discourse), a heading which also includes some related approaches, most notably the dynamic predicate logic of Groenendijk and Stokhof (1991).

In the Kamp/Heim approach, a discourse is true if the variables or file cards can be mapped onto entities for which the associated information holds. A simple discourse like that in (20) would be treated very similarly in the two treatments.

(20)   A woman came in. She sat down.

Indefinite NPs like *a woman* introduce new file cards, or variables, into the discourse.[18] On the other hand, pronouns like *she* must be linked

---

[18] Thus they are not treated like quantificational NPs, but instead more like referential ones; something we'll return to in the following chapter. On the other hand, we noted in the last chapter that indefinites are sometimes subject to binding by sentence operators like the GEN operator introduced there. The dynamic semantics approach was partly motivated by a desire to explain this kind of behavior, and we will see more of it below in Ch. 10.

to something else. In this case there is no other potential referent available, so it would be taken to refer to the woman mentioned in the preceding sentence. In Heim's approach the property of having sat down would be added to the file card created for the woman by the preceding sentence. In Kamp's approach this information would be associated with a variable explicitly linked to that introduced in connection with *a woman* from the preceding sentence. The bottom line is the same in both cases—(20) is true if there is a woman who came in and sat down.

There is much more to say about the Kamp/Heim dynamic semantics approach, and we will be returning to it in the following chapters.

8.5.3 Quantificationally bound pronouns

Turning now to the quantificational use of pronouns, we must consider when a quantificational NP can bind a pronoun. In a formal language, each quantifier occurring in a formula has a specific scope (the well-formed formula to which it is prefixed) which is interpreted with respect to it, and within which any (free) coindexed variable is bound by it. In natural language the situation is a bit more complex. It turns out that we must distinguish the semantic scope of a quantifier from its syntactic scope—the latter being what determines which pronouns may be bound by it. Consider the examples in (21).

(21)   a.   Somebody loves every woman.
       b.   She loves every woman.

(21a) is ambiguous; either it means that there is one person who loves all women, or it means that every woman is loved by somebody. On the latter reading *every woman* has scope over the NP *somebody* which occurs in subject position. However in (21b) the pronoun *she*, which is also in subject position, nevertheless cannot be bound by *every woman*—(21b) cannot mean what *Every woman loves herself* means.

Specifying exactly what the syntactic conditions are for a quantificational NP to be able to bind a pronoun turns out to be an extremely difficult task—one which has not been completely successfully accomplished up to now.[19] The following sketch is definitely incomplete, and

---

[19] See Reinhart (1983) for a classic theory within Chomskyan linguistics, including some unsolved problems. See also Heim and Kratzer (1998), and the works cited there, for this and other approaches.

there are exceptions to many of the statements, but hopefully it will give us enough to be going on with.

First we want to get reflexive pronouns sorted out—those are pronouns which (in English) end in *self* or *selves*, plus reciprocals like *each other*. Getting these sorted out requires a minimal bit of syntax—the notion of a syntactic ARGUMENT position.[20] Roughly speaking, the argument positions in a clause are those containing an NP whose referent plays a role in the relation denoted by the predicate. This includes the subject, direct object, and indirect object, but may also include other NPs related by the predication. The non-argument positions are all the others—NPs in adverbial phrases or serving as determiners, for example. In the examples below, the underlined NPs are all in argument positions while the italicized NPs are not.

(22)   a.   <u>Mary</u> loves/worries about/takes good care of <u>Bill</u>.
       b.   <u>Mary</u> loves *Bill's* <u>mother</u>.
       c.   <u>Mary</u> put <u>the equipment</u> next to *Bill*.

We need this notion because it turns out that any pronoun which is in an argument position (other than subject position), and is interpreted as coreferential with an NP which occurs within the same clause, must be reflexive. (The converse is also true—i.e. any reflexive in an argument position must have an antecedent within its own clause.) This means that ordinary pronouns in an argument position cannot have an antecedent in their own clause. The examples in (23a) below show a reflexive in argument positions. The nonreflexive pronouns in (24) and (25) are in non-argument positions.

(23)   a. Mary_i loves/worries about/takes good care of herself_i.
       b.   *Mary_i loves/worries about/takes good care of her_i.

(24) Mary_i loves her_i mother.

(25) Mary_i put the equipment next to her_i.

The same facts hold for quantificational binders.

Turning now to quantificational NPs, we find that quantificational NPs in subject position are able to bind pronouns anywhere else in the

---

[20] There is some degree of overlap between syntactic arguments and semantic arguments—arguments of functions. However that overlap is by no means complete. Negation, for example, is an operator that takes the truth value of the sentence it combines with as its semantic argument. However, syntactically, that sentence is not a subject or object of the negation.

sentence, while quantificational NPs in a VP cannot bind pronouns outside of that VP. The following examples ((26)–(29)) are a partial illustration of these constraints; a starred index means that that interpretation is not possible.

(26)   a.   Every man$_i$ was proud of him$_{*i, \, j}$.
       b.   Every man$_i$ was proud of himself$_{i, \, *j}$.

In these sentences *every man* is in the same clause with *him* and *himself*; therefore it cannot bind *him* (because *him* is not reflexive), and it must bind *himself* (because there is no other possible antecedent for *himself*).

(27)   a.   When [he or she]$_i$ is injured, no cat$_i$ likes to be touched.
       b.   When [he or she]$_{*i}$ is injured, owners should touch no cat$_i$.

Here, *he or she* can be bound by *no cat* in (27a), because *no cat* is the subject of the sentence. (Note too that (27a) shows that a pronoun can precede its "antecedent.") However in (27b) *no cat* is the direct object and thus within the VP, and so it cannot bind *he or she*.

(28)   Deanna [$_{VP}$ put each paper$_i$ in its$_i$ own folder].

Its is in the same VP with *each paper*, and thus susceptible to being bound by it. (The word *own* probably makes this binding the only option for this sentence.)

(29)   a.   Every woman$_i$ [$_{VP}$ thought that she$_{i, \, j}$ would be invited].
       b.   John [$_{VP}$ asked every woman$_i$ whether she$_{i, \, j}$ was going to be invited].

In these sentences *she* is in an embedded clause which is part of the main clause VP; thus it is susceptible to binding by either the subject or the object of the main verb.

There are some other kinds of situations in which a quantificational NP can bind a pronoun, but we will put off consideration of one of them for a bit because we need to note one surprising aspect of binding—namely, that the binder apparently does not have to be a quantificational NP.

8.5.4 Non-quantificational binding

Consider the pronoun (*she*) in example (30).

(30)   Mary said that she would be here.

Since there is only one other NP in the sentence (*Mary*), and it is not quantificational, we might suppose that the pronoun must be the free variable kind. That still leaves two possibilities—either the speaker intends *she* to refer to some salient female entity not explicitly mentioned in the sentence, or the speaker intends the pronoun to refer to Mary. These two interpretations are quite easy to get, and there does not seem to be any other reading for the sentence. However, there is some evidence that we need to recognize a third possibility.

The evidence for the third possibility comes from a construction referred to as "VP ellipsis." This construction occurs with conjoined sentences where the second sentence is superficially missing a fully spelled-out VP but is nevertheless interpreted with full VP content. A simple example is given in (31).

(31)   Jalen left in a hurry and so did Morgan.

We interpret (31) as expressing the thought that both Morgan and Jalen left in a hurry; the *so did* in (31) is a kind of pro-VP which receives its interpretational content from the preceding full VP, the latter serving as antecedent.

In cases of VP ellipsis when the antecedent contains a pronoun, we can often have three readings, instead of the two we would have expected. See what happens when we conjoin (30) above with another sentence, as in (32).

(32)   Mary said that she would be here, and so did Bill.

(32) is three ways ambiguous. On one interpretation, where the speaker has chosen some outside referent for *she*, the sentence means that both Bill and Mary said that that person would be here. On a second interpretation, where *she* has been assigned Mary as a referent, the sentence says that both Mary and Bill said that Mary would be here. The problem is that (32) has a third reading according to which it conveys that Bill said that Bill would be here. This (following Ross (1967)) is called the "sloppy identity" reading, and the problem is how to account for it.

One solution (proposed initially by Keenan (1971); see also Sag (1976)) is to allow ordinary NPs to bind pronouns like quantificational NPs do. If we allow that, then we can assign an additional logical form to (30), one which looks something like this:

(33) $(Mary_x)[x$ said that x would be here$]$

We can read (33) as saying something like this: "Mary is an x such that x said that x would be here." When the first sentence in (32) has this analysis, the *so did* would stand for the predicate *[x said that x would be here]*. Then *Bill* as the subject binds the *x*'s, and we get the sloppy reading according to which Mary said that Mary would be here and Bill said that Bill would be here.

The result is that (30) (*Mary said that she would be here*) has a funny kind of ambiguity. It has two readings which have the same truth conditions, namely, that Mary said that she herself would be here. That is, we would have one interpretation in which *she* is a free pronoun to which the speaker assigns Mary as the referent, but then also an interpretation on which *she* is a variable bound by *Mary*. (Of course it has the other reading too, where *she* is used to refer to a different female entity.)

This analysis predicts that in the case of VP ellipsis where the antecedent contains a pronoun bound by a quantificational NP, there will only be a two-way ambiguity. Consider an example like (34).

(34)   Every woman said that she would be there.

Here there is only one way to link *she* to *every woman* and that is by the binding relation. On its free variable interpretation, *she* cannot be coreferential with a quantificational antecedent; its only option is to be assigned some outside person. An example like (35) confirms that this prediction of a simple two-way ambiguity is indeed correct.

(35)   Every woman said that she would be there, and so did Bill.

One possibility is that *she* refers to some outside person. When *she* is linked to *every woman*, (35) only means that Bill said that he would be there—it has only the sloppy reading. (35) cannot mean that Bill said that every woman would be there.

On the other hand an example like (36), with definite descriptions, **does** have the same kind of three-way ambiguity that (32) had, with proper names.

(36)   The author of the book said that she would be there, and so did the bookstore owner.

When *she* means the author of the book, we have both sloppy and tidy readings for the ellipsed VP—it can mean either that the bookstore owner said that he himself would be there (the sloppy reading), or that the bookstore owner said that the author would be there (the tidy reading). This provides some support for our conclusion in Chapter 6, that definite descriptions have a referential interpretation.

To sum up the results of this section so far: we have tentatively concluded that it makes sense to view third-person pronouns as similar to variables of a formal logic language. Like logical variables, there are two possible interpretations for pronouns: they may be assigned a referent by the speaker (this corresponds to free variables in a formal language), or they may be bound by another NP. One difference from formal languages is that apparently in natural language nonquantificational NPs such as proper names can bind variables; the evidence for this was the existence of sloppy identity readings when VP ellipsis includes a pronoun.

Thus far we have what I hope is a fairly straightforward and intuitive view of pronouns. However there remain some difficult cases which we need to try to account for. We will put these off until Chapter 10, however, when we turn explicitly to issues of reference in discourse.[21]

8.5.5 Plural pronouns

All of our examples up to now have involved only singular pronouns, so we need to say something about third-person plural pronouns. Unfortunately there does not seem to be a very extensive literature on this subject (although see Reinhart (1987), Roberts (2004), and especially Kamp and Reyle (1993)), so a few meager comments will have to suffice for now. One striking fact is that plural pronouns seem to be freer in their referential capabilities than singular pronouns. This may be simply because there are more plural things around to be talked about (Kamp and Reyle 1993: ch. 4). So, for instance, it is possible for a pronoun to pick up its reference from the CNP of another NP, rather than the whole NP. When the head noun is a count noun, however, the pronoun in question must be plural. Since count nouns occur more frequently than mass nouns in English, this means that plural pronouns will enjoy this opportunity more frequently. Compare the examples in (37).

---

[21] One other consideration is worth mentioning here. For the cases above involving "long-distance" binding, there is potential for a compositionality problem. That is, we have tacitly postulated a semantic structure where a binder at the sentence level binds a pronoun buried within the sentence, and thus changes the interpretation of that pronoun. Pauline Jacobson has argued in favor of VARIABLE-FREE semantics, which does not include such long-distance binding. See, e.g., Jacobson (1996, 2000); Barker and Jacobson (2007).

(37) a. Some children failed—the problems <u>they</u> had been given
           were very hard.
      b. One child failed—the problems <u>she</u> had been given were
           very hard.
      c. Some rice was moldy—<u>it</u> hadn't been kept in an airtight
           container.

The pronoun *they*, in (37a), may naturally be construed as referring to
all of the children involved, not just those who failed. However the
singular pronoun *she* in (37b) cannot be so construed. To take an
earlier CNP as antecedent, a singular pronoun requires a mass head,
as shown in (37c), where *it* can mean either the moldy rice, or all of
the rice.

   For another example illustrating the greater flexibility of plural
pronouns, compare the sentences in (38).

(38) [Every woman]$_i$ went to the ceremony.
      a.   #She$_i$ had a good time.
      b.   They$_i$ had a good time.

In (38a) *every woman* is not able to bind the singular pronoun *she*
across a sentence boundary. Indeed this is just what we would expect of
the variable binding relationship, and it is what we have assumed in the
previous section. However, in (38b) the plural pronoun *they* **can** be
understood as referring to the women who went to the ceremony. In
this case the existence of the women in the discourse context is
sufficient to provide a referent for *they*—no binding is required. (I
should note, though, that while the contrast in (38) seems quite clear-
cut, we will see some puzzling exceptions below in Chapter 10.)

8.6 Pronouns and descriptions

We turn now to some unexpected parallels between pronouns, on the
one hand, and definite and demonstrative descriptions, on the other.
These are of two kinds: first, we have instances in which definite and
demonstrative descriptions seem to behave like pronouns in being
able to be bound by quantificational NPs; and second, we have
instances in which pronouns appear to have descriptive uses. (We
will see a third parallel in Chapter 10, when we return to pronouns in
discourse.)

8.6.1 Bound descriptions

Many people have observed that definite and demonstrative descriptions can have bound uses (e.g. Evans (1980); King (2001)). One of the earliest was George Wilson (1984, 1991), who pointed out examples like (39).

(39)   Every scientist who was fired from the observatory at Sofia was consoled by someone who knew [him] *the fired scientist* as a youth. [= Wilson 1991: ex. 1]

Here *the fired scientist* clearly has an interpretation on which it functions as a bound variable, just as *him* would if it had been used instead. And (40), with a demonstrative description, is, if anything, more felicitous.

(40)   Every scientist who was fired from the observatory at Sofia was consoled by someone who knew *that scientist* as a youth.

Paul Elbourne contributes the example in (41):

(41)   Mary talked to no senator before that senator was lobbied. [= Elbourne 2008: ex. 2]

The analyses of both King and Elbourne which were reviewed above in §8.4 were designed to handle data of this type.

It should be noted that in response to Wilson, Simons (1996) argued that there was no true parallel between pronouns and definite descriptions which serve as bound variables, since the privileges of occurrence are different. However the only examples she gave to illustrate this difference are repeated below in (42)–(45) (= Simons 1996: exx. (3)–(6); Simons used italics rather than subscripts to indicate referential dependence).

(42)   a. *Every soprano* admires *her* accompanist.
        b. *Kathleen* admires *her* accompanist.

(43)   a. ?*Every soprano* admires *the soprano's* accompanist.
        b. **Kathleen* admires *the soprano's* accompanist.

(44)   a. *Every scientist's* mother loves *him*.
        b. *Hugo's* mother loves *him*.

(45)   a. ?*Every scientist's* mother loves *the scientist*.
        b. **Hugo's* mother loves *the scientist*.

An important thing to note here is that the main contrast in behavior is not between pronouns and definite descriptions as bound by a quantificational NP, but rather between the two in their ability to be bound by a preceding proper name. Furthermore no explanation for this particular difference in behavior was offered.[22]

Any such explanation should take note of the fact that, with a little fiddling around, some of these examples can be made markedly better. (45b), for instance, uttered with heavy stress on *loves* and anaphoric destressing on *the scientist* is really not that bad. Furthermore if we replace *the scientist* with *her son*, as in (46) below, the example is further improved.

(46)   Hugo's mother loves her son.

More tinkering can result in further improvements; (46), understood with coreference between *Mickey Mantle* and *the speedy center-fielder*, would not raise a sports-page reader's eyebrow.

(47)   Mickey Mantle's mother loved the speedy center-fielder.

It is also worth noting that we would expect pronouns to be more felicitous in general than definite or demonstrative descriptions, where both are possible with the same interpretation. This is because pronouns are easier to say; Gricean considerations lead us to expect that if a speaker uses a more complex NP than is necessary, there must be some reason for it. It begins to seem that the perception of ungrammaticality for examples (43b) and (45b) above may have more to do with pragmatic factors than with any syntactic or semantic difference between pronouns and definite descriptions in their bound variable use.

8.6.2 Descriptive pronouns

In addition to distinguishing the index from the interpretation of indexical expressions, Nunberg (1993) pointed out another interesting feature, and that is the ability of pronominal indexicals to function quite similarly to definite descriptions. One example involving *we* is (48) (Nunberg's (18)), as spoken by a Supreme Court Justice.

(48)   We might have been liberals.

---

[22] Simons may have been assuming that quantificational NPs, but not other NPs, are raised from their surface-structure location when they bind other positions. However according to Heim and Kratzer (1998), all kinds of NPs are raised in order to bind other positions. The pattern of facts we observed above in 8.5.4 seemed to require it.

(48) might be used to convey that the speaker plus the other Justices might themselves have been liberals. But (48) might also be used to convey that in other circumstances, with appointments made by different presidents, it might have been the case that the Supremes were liberals. Thus the interpretation of *we* seems to be able to vary scope with respect to the modal *might*, just as the definite description in (49) does.

(49)   The Supreme Court Justices might have been liberals.

Another of Nunberg's examples, cited by Recanati (2005: 297), is given in (50) below. Here we are to imagine that the speaker gestures towards Pope John Paul II, shortly after his election, as he delivers a speech with a Polish accent.

(50)   He is usually an Italian, but this time they thought it wise to elect a Pole.

In this example the pronoun *he* can convey the description *the pope*. Note that the only sensible construal is with that content taking narrow scope with respect to *usually*.

It appears too as though pronouns can participate in a referential-attributive distinction, just like definite descriptions. Of course we expect pronouns to have referential uses; what is remarkable is that they can apparently have attributive ones as well. Recall Donnellan's example, given in (51) below.

(51)   The murderer of Smith is insane.

A suitable context for the attributive construal might be when the police first arrive on the scene, and base their judgment on the brutality of the murder and the fact that Smith was a nice guy. But in this context an officer might just as easily have uttered (52),

(52)   He's insane.

intending to convey the same proposition—that whoever it is that murdered Smith is insane.[23] And Schiffer has given the following example:

(53)   He must be a giant!

in a context in which the speaker and addressee have just observed a huge footprint. Interestingly, Schiffer also suggests that the explanation

---

[23] I'm grateful to Dick Oehrle for pointing this fact out to me roughly 35 years ago.

for the relative rarity of such examples lies in the fact that typically a context of utterance will not supply sufficient descriptive content (Schiffer 1995: 123f.).[24]

8.7 Concluding remarks

In this chapter we began with Kaplan's analysis of indexicality, which resulted in a separation of Fregean sense into two parts. Kaplan's concept of character corresponds to the sense of "sense" in which the sense of an expression is a part of the language, and is grasped by speakers, while content corresponds to that which we express in an utterance, and that to which we are related by our propositional attitudes. We also took note of the problem that indexicality can cause for our theory of propositional attitudes, and looked at proposals from Perry and from Lewis for solving it. We looked next at arguments from Nunberg that Kaplan's analysis needs to be supplemented by separating the index of an indexical (the indicated item) from its denotation. Although these will often coincide, they need not. We also spent a bit of time with the various interpretations of demonstratives, reviewing two proposals which attempt to unify these various interpretations.

The remainder of the chapter considered the various uses of third-person pronouns—referential, where the speaker (and addressee) assign a referent, which is similar to a free variable of logic; and bound, where the interpretation of the pronoun is governed by an antecedent NP which may or may not be quantificational. In the midst of this we had a brief look at the dynamic semantics approach. And finally we looked at some data showing some parallels between definite descriptions and pronouns. As noted, we will have more to say about pronouns in Chapter 10 below, when we look at reference from a discoursal point of view. There we will see that we apparently need to recognize a third type of pronoun use, which is not variable-like but rather definite description-like. But before doing that we need to investigate some cross-classifying NP properties which seem especially relevant to the issue of reference.

---

[24] Bezuidenhout (1997), citing examples like these, offers an analysis of the referential-attributive distinction within the framework of Sperber and Wilson's (1986, 1995) Relevance Theory.

9

Definiteness, strength, partitives, and referentiality

It is the nature of thought to be indefinite;—definiteness belongs to external imagery alone.

Samuel Taylor Coleridge, *Lectures and Notes on Shakespeare*

In Chapter 5 we examined proper names, in Chapter 6 we investigated definite descriptions, and in Chapter 8 we took a look at pronouns and demonstrative descriptions. These four categories would generally be considered to belong to a super-category of, DEFINITE NPs. Intuitively and pre-theoretically, all of these NP types can be used by a speaker to direct an addressee's attention to some particular entity (including a plural sum entity—occasionally hereafter I may neglect to mention this possibility explicitly) that the speaker wishes to talk about. Thus definiteness seems to be closely related to referentiality, and indeed definiteness and referentiality are often taken to be essentially the same thing. In this chapter we will look closely at definiteness, as well as some related concepts. First we'll look at a traditional linguistic diagnostic for definite NPs—failure to occur felicitously in an existential sentence. Following that we will look at four characterizations of "definite NP," no two of which agree completely on exactly which NPs should be so characterized. In §9.3 we will look at another, related, cross-classification of NPs—the strong-weak distinction. And lastly in §9.4 we take up partitive NPs—NPs of the form *Det of NP* (e.g. *some of the apples*). The Partitive Constraint on the embedded NP (e.g. *the apples* in *some of the apples*) has been traditionally thought of in terms of definiteness, and so it will be of particular interest.

9.1 Existential sentences

Existential sentences, sometimes called "*there-be* sentences," have the dummy expletive *there* in subject position, followed by a form of the verb *be* and then an NP which I'll call the "focus NP."[1] They also typically include a constituent following the focus NP—often this is a prepositional phrase which gives a location, although other kinds of phrase are possible—e.g. gerundive or infinitival VPs. Some examples are given below in (1).

(1) a.   There is some pizza in the fridge.
     b.   There are several sycophants waiting to see you.
     c.   There was no reason to act that way.

In what follows I will use "XP" as a cover term for the constituent following the focus NP (*in the fridge, waiting to see you*, etc.).[2] In the early days of transformational grammar, existentials were derived by a rule called "*there* insertion." This rule would operate on sentences like (2a) below, and turn them into sentences like (2b).[3]

(2) a.   A dog is in the yard.
     b.   There is a dog in the yard.

As you can see, the rule takes the underlying NP subject, moves it after the verb *be*, and plugs *there* into subject position.

It was soon noticed that this rule needed to be constrained, since not every NP type could occur felicitously in the focus position (i.e. following *be*) in an existential sentence. Thus definite descriptions have a problem in this position—we would not want to derive (3b) from (3a).

(3) a.   The dog is in the yard.
     b.   *There is the dog in the yard.

---

[1] This use of "focus" is related to the technical term which was introduced in Chapter 7; these NPs convey the main new information in the utterance.

[2] In some cases there may be a question about whether the sequence following the focus N is a separate constituent, as I assume here, or instead a part of the NP. A phrase like *several sycophants waiting to see you*, for instance, can occur by itself in subject position, as in (i), where we must assume it is a single NP.

(i)   Several sycophants waiting to see you did not have the proper authorization.

See Keenan (1987: 301ff.) for arguments that in existentials, the XP phrases following the focus N do indeed form a separate constituent.

[3] Technically, transformational rules did not operate on sentences but rather on underlying structures of sentences, where underlying structures were stages in the development of the ultimate surface structure form.

This sensitivity came to be called "the definiteness effect."[4] Note that all four of the subcategories of NP noted at the beginning of the chapter as being intuitively definite—definite descriptions, proper names, pronouns, and demonstrative descriptions—do not appear as the focus NP in a felicitous existential sentence. (4) gives some additional illustrative ill-formed examples.

(4) a. *There is Mary in the yard.
     b. *There is it in the yard.
     c. *There are those clothespins in the yard.

This confirms our intuitive grouping.

On the other hand NPs which are intuitively indefinite are quite felicitous in existentials, as shown in (5).

(5) There are some/several/15/many/too few/no apples in that basket.

All of the determiners underlined in (5) would readily be classified as indefinite.

In Chapter 7 we saw that bare NPs have two distinct interpretations—they can be understood either generically, or as nonspecific indefinites, depending on the rest of the sentence. When bare NPs occur in focus position in an existential, they are disambiguated in favor of their nonspecific indefinite reading, as shown in (6).

(6) There are fleas on my dog.

In (6) we are not talking about the flea species as a whole (something intuitively fairly well-defined and definite), but only locating some indefinite number of fleas. Also, we noted in Chapter 6 that there is a

---

[4] (3b) is only bad on a parsing where *in the yard* is a separate constituent giving the location of the independently identifiable dog in question. There is another way of parsing it, so that *in the yard* is a restrictive modifier within the NP which serves to identify the dog being spoken about. Parsed in this way, (3b) could occur naturally in the dialog in (i).

(i) A: Is there anything we have to watch out for at this next house?
     B: Well, there's the dog in the yard...

This type of existential sentence is different from those in the text. For one thing, existentials of this type do not occur felicitously at the beginning of a discourse. Instead, they typically serve to provide suggestions or reminders to the addressee, relevant to some issue which has already been raised. The intonation pattern is that of a suggestion, rather than an ordinary declarative statement. This type of existential has variously been called "list" (Rando and Napoli 1978), "enumerative" (Lumsden 1988), or "contextualized" (Abbott 1993), and given that it accepts both definites and indefinites in focus position, it is not relevant as a test for definiteness vs indefiniteness, and thus should be ignored.

kind of NP which looks like a demonstrative description with determiner *this*, but which is actually a kind of indefinite description.
Example (7) below (from Chapter 6),

(7)   There was (this) dishy logician at Mary's party.

is a natural existential, confirming that this type of NP is indeed
different from genuine demonstrative descriptions.

Some other kinds of NPs add complexity to the picture. First,
consider possessive NPs—those NPs with a genitive determiner.
Some are OK in existentials while some are not, as shown in (8).

(8)   a.   *There was Smith's murderer on trial.
       b.   *There was the student's book on the table.
       c.   There was a student's book on the table
       d.   There were several dogs' leashes hanging in the closet.

As indicated by the pattern in (8), it appears that the definiteness or
indefiniteness of a possessive NP is determined by the definiteness
or indefiniteness of the determiner NP: *Smith* and *the student*
confer their definiteness on the focus NPs in (8a) and (8b), while
a student and *several dogs* confer indefiniteness in (8c) and (8d).[5]
Compare too the related example in (9) (from Woisetschlaeger
1983: 142):

(9)   There was the wedding photo of a young black couple among his
       papers.

The focus NP here (which is underlined) is intuitively in the same class
with possessives, but with the possessor phrase (*a young black couple*)
postposed.

Up to now the diagnostic powers of the existential construction have
seemed to do a fairly good job of sorting intuitively indefinite NPs
from intuitively definite NPs. The intuitive indefinites (bare nongene-
ric NPs; NPs with determiners like *a/an*, *several*, *many*, or indefinite
this; and possessives with intuitively indefinite NP determiners) are
felicitous in existentials while intuitive definites (proper names, pronouns, definite and demonstrative descriptions, and possessives with
intuitively definite NP determiners) are not. However now we run into
some problems. First, the infelicity of the examples in (10) below

---

[5] This pattern was pointed out in Barker (2000). See also Peters and Westerståhl (2006: 276f.).

would prompt us to add universally quantified NPs to the definite group.

(10) a. *There were all (of the) students at the train station.
      b. *There was each/every student at the train station.

Should we then conclude that universally quantified NPs are definite? One problem with this conclusion is that, as noted above, definiteness is often associated with referentiality, and referentiality has tradition- ally been seen as inconsistent with quantification. (We saw this in Chapter 6, when we were worrying about definite descriptions.) Below we'll have more to say about whether universally quantified NPs should be characterized as definite. Another fly in the existential ointment is presented by NPs with determiner *most*; these are not intuitively definite and yet they also do not occur felicitously in existentials, as shown in (11).[6]

most vs. some ??

(11) *There were most (of the) apples in the basket.

As a result of these problems with using existentials as a test for definiteness, Gary Milsark (1977) proposed a new pair of terms— STRONG, for those NPs which do not occur naturally in existentials, and WEAK, for those NPs which do. At this point we will plunge on in pursuit of the essence of definiteness, putting off consideration of the essence of strength (in Milsark's sense) until §9.3.

---

[6] Although I've described NPs with *most* as intuitively indefinite, the fact remains that *most* is morphologically a superlative form (cf. *much, many; more*), and superlatives are invariably definite. This is reflected in the requirement of the definite article in adjectival uses, as shown in (i).

(i)   Who has the/*a/*some most ribbons?

It is possibly also significant that NPs of the form *most CNP* seem to be most naturally used in generic (characterizing) sentences, as in (ii).

(ii)   a.   Most bananas peel easily.
       b.   #Most bananas were sitting on the counter.

It may be this generic sense that is interfering with *most*'s ability to occur naturally in an existential. On the other hand the problem with the partitive (*most of the apples*) in (11) could be due to the definiteness of the embedded NP (*the apples*). Note that (iii), with an embedded indefinite, is ok.

(iii) There was most of a birthday cake sitting on the buffet.

We will come to partitives below in §9.4.

9.2 Characterizations of "definite NP"

We turn now to various approaches to characterizing the notion "definite NP." This enterprise may seem a little strange, given that we have no independent means to delimit this category for which we seek the essence, but hopefully it will at least bring out some interesting semantic and pragmatic characteristics of NPs. We'll start with a theory that is inspired by Russell's theory of descriptions, and follow that with three other proposals.[7]

9.2.1 Uniqueness

The term "uniqueness" is often used in connection with definite NPs, but we need to be careful to distinguish two distinct ways in which an NP can be described as "uniquely referring." In Chapter 2 we were introduced to Russell's theory of definite descriptions, and in Chapter 7 we saw how it could be modified, as suggested by Sharvy (1980) and Hawkins (1978, 1991), to include definite descriptions with plural and mass heads. (We've also seen how the existence and uniqueness elements of Russell's analysis can be included in a nonquantificational analysis of definite descriptions.) If this theory of definite descriptions correctly captures their contribution to truth conditions, then the essence of definite descriptions is uniqueness of applicability (in context) of the descriptive content of the NP—i.e. there is **at most one thing** (which may be an atomic entity or a group or mass individual) in the relevant context or situation which matches that descriptive content. The definite article conveys uniqueness in that sense—that there will be only one possible referent matching the description used. Let us call this SEMANTIC UNIQUENESS.[8] So that is one way in which NPs could be said to be uniquely referring. But another way, which also holds of definite descriptions, is that the speaker intends to use them to refer to some particular entity or group of entities, and expects the addressee to be able to identify that very intended referent. (Recall Strawson's comment, quoted above in Chapter 6, that use of a definite

---

[7] I regret not being able to consider here the interesting proposal in Löbner (2000). The reader is directed to Löbner's paper for details of his theory.

[8] This conception of semantic uniqueness corresponds fairly closely to what Craige Roberts calls "informational uniqueness" (2003: 307), although the latter is defined to mean uniqueness with respect to the common ground. Roberts reserves the term "semantic uniqueness" for Russell's theory, without the relativization to situations which seems to be required by incomplete definite descriptions.

description conveys that there is only one thing "being referred to by the speaker" (Strawson 1950: 332). Cf. also the concepts of "unique identifiability" and "individuation" discussed by Birner and Ward (1998: 121f.)) This is a pragmatic property which we might call REFERENTIAL UNIQUENESS. According to Russell's analysis and its descendents, definite descriptions achieve this pragmatic goal because of uniqueness of the semantic type—unique applicability of the descriptive content within the relevant situation.[9]

Proper names are similar to definite descriptions in these respects. Proper names present themselves as being associated with a single referent; the term "proper" indicates this property—everyone and everything that has one is expected to have their own.[10] This property is further reflected in the fact that proper names, used as such, constitute a complete NP and do not accept restrictive modifiers or determiners. (If I describe someone as "a real Einstein," I'm not using the name *Einstein* as a proper name of the person Albert Einstein.) Thus proper names incorporate semantic uniqueness. On the pragmatic side, as with definite descriptions, speakers expect addressees to be able to determine, from the use of a proper name, who or what is being spoken about. Technically, it should be the case just from the fact that a proper name is used, that the referent is determined. However in practice people do not use proper names that they believe may be new to their addressees without some kind of additional indication of the intended referent (see Prince (1992: 301); we return to this fact below in Chapter 10).

Our third and fourth types of intuitively definite NPs—pronouns and demonstrative descriptions—are referentially unique, but may not be semantically unique. This is probably clearest in the case of third-person pronouns, which incorporate only minimal descriptive content; in English, only number and (for singulars) gender. As a consequence,

[9] It must be acknowledged that there are many instances of definite descriptions which do not seem to meet the requirement of either semantic uniqueness or referential uniqueness. Some examples are given in (i):

(i) a.   I'm planning to take the train to Boston tomorrow.
     b.   My uncle took the message and he wrote it on the wall.

For discussion of these and other examples, see Abbott (2004: 131f.) and Carlson et al. (2006).

[10] Of course these days there are just too many people for there to be enough reasonably sized names to go around, but the linguistic behavior of proper names was established when that was not the case.

use of a third-person pronoun requires that the addressee be able to determine the intended referent from other information supplied in the context, since pronouns share with definite descriptions an indication that the addressee is expected to be able to determine that referent uniquely—they are referentially unique. As we have seen, demonstrative NPs, like pronouns, can be used deictically, and in that case they often call for some kind of indication—a gesture, nod, pointed glance, etc.—on the part of the speaker, unless the speaker can be sure that their addressee already has their attention focused on the intended referent. Of course a demonstrative may be used when there is only one entity in the environment which meets their descriptive content. I can make the request in (12) when there is only one hammer in the room.

(12)   Please pass me that hammer.

However, crucially, I may also use (12) in a room chock-full of salient hammers, as long as I indicate to my addressee which hammer it is that I want.[11]

So on the uniqueness theory, what definite descriptions, proper names, pronouns, and demonstrative descriptions all seem to share is referential uniqueness—an intention on the part of the speaker using them to speak about a particular entity which they assume that the addressee should be able to identify. Note that if this property turns out to be correct as a criterion for definiteness, then we might wonder whether universally quantified NPs (those with *all*, *every*, or *each* as determiner) should also be included in this category, since their denotation should similarly be identifiable to an addressee. Many linguists would indeed include them (e.g. Prince 1992), but many philosophers would not, simply because (as we have already noted) quantificational NPs are seen as by definition not referential.[12] And, as

---

[11] The same does not hold of definite descriptions, and as a result, as we saw in the last chapter, a single demonstrative description can be used repeatedly in a given utterance with different referents, while definite descriptions may not be so used. We return in the next chapter to other differences between these kinds of definites, and some more elaborated schemes for classifying NPs from a discourse perspective.

[12] It is probably important to distinguish universally quantified NPs which are used to talk about specific groups of entities, as in (i) below, from those which are used to make generic statements, as in (ii).

(i)   a.   All of the children sat down.
       b.   Every child was quiet.
       c.   Each child worked on a project.

we see below, others have other reasons for excluding universally quantified NPs from the class of definites.

If the essence of definiteness is uniqueness of intended reference, does that mean that the essence of indefiniteness is **non**uniqueness? No. Let us look first at indefinite descriptions—those with the indefinite article *a/an* as determiner. It is true that use of an indefinite typically does convey both semantic and referential nonuniqueness. However Hawkins (1991) has argued convincingly that this can be explained as a Gricean conversational implicature. (See also Hawkins (2004); Horn (2007).) It is relevant that *the* and *a/an* in English are paradigmatic alternatives in singular NPs. This is illustrated in the following bit of text (for which I am grateful to Larry Horn).

(13)   The Google phone is real, and it's finally here. Stand clear of popping corks.

     Actually, to be completely accurate, there isn't anything called "the Google phone." You can't buy "the Google phone," any more than you can buy "the Windows PC." Google makes the software (called Android), and it's up to the phone manufacturers to build cellphones around it.

     What has its debut on Oct. 22, therefore, is *a* Google phone . . . (New York Times 10/16/08; italics in original, underlining added.)

The contrast here is, of course, one of uniqueness. If we assume that *the* is, as Russell proposed, semantically encoded for uniqueness while *a/an* is unmarked, then use of one of the weaker expressions will naturally convey that the stronger meaning was not intended. This would be just another example of a Gricean conversational implicature—specifically of the scalar type. We will return to this issue in the next chapter.

A nice consequence of this analysis, which Hawkins pointed out, is that in circumstances where the uniqueness factor is not relevant, as in (14) below, the nonuniqueness implicature is neutralized.

(14)   A movie that Mary was watching last night was really interesting. [= Hawkins 1991: ex. 16]

The fact that (14) does not imply that Mary watched more than one movie last night, and is thus perfectly consistent with her having only

(ii)   a.   All children like applesauce.
      b.   Every child wants to play as much as possible.
      c.   Each child should have the love of a caregiver.

seen one, shows that nonuniqueness cannot be semantically encoded in the indefinite article.

When we include other indefinite determiners, such as *several* or *many*, the picture is a bit more complex, since these determiners convey something about the relative quantity of denoted entities. However there is evidence that these determiners too do not encode nonuniqueness of denotation in the fact that they can co-occur adjectivally with a definite determiner, as in *the many parties we went to*, *those several obscure books*. If the meaning of words like *several* and *many* contained a semantic component of nonuniqueness we might expect such NPs to sound contradictory, so the fact that they don't indicates that nonuniqueness is not an element of their meaning.

9.2.2 Familiarity

We look now at a major competitor to Russell's uniqueness theory. In Chapter 8 we were briefly introduced to Heim's (1982, 1983) File Change approach to semantics. One of the most interesting features of this approach was not mentioned there, however, and that is the fact that definite and indefinite descriptions were treated as quite parallel: both were held to introduce a variable with information concerning some entity. The difference, in Heim's view at that time, was to be found in the differing conditions on these associated variables: indefinite descriptions were required to introduce novel entities while definite descriptions were required to denote familiar ones, ones for which a card was already on file in the discourse.[13]

Heim's familiarity theory of definiteness goes back at least to Paul Christophersen, who made the following comment in an often-cited passage: "Now the speaker must always be supposed to know which individual he is thinking of; the interesting thing is that the *the*-form supposes that the hearer knows it, too" (Christophersen 1939: 28).[14] We

[13] As we noted in Chapter 8, Kamp independently introduced his own version of dynamic semantics at about the same time as Heim. However Kamp (1981) did not treat definite descriptions. Kamp (2001) cites unique identifiability as criterial for definiteness.

[14] Though Christophersen is usually cited as having put forward the familiarity theory of definiteness, it is possible to overstate his adherence to this theory. Elsewhere in his book he makes comments quite sympathetic to Russell's uniqueness view, e.g., that in using the *the* form "the centre of attention must necessarily be so narrow as to comprise only one individual" (Christophersen (1939: 30); I'm grateful to Larry Horn for passing along this observation of his student Elitzur Bar-Asher). And indeed, as we will see below, there is no reason for these two elements (uniqueness and familiarity) to be seen as inconsistent with each other.

noted above that both Frege and Strawson stressed the idea that definite descriptions presuppose the existence of a referent (rather than asserting it, as Russell's theory seems to imply). The familiarity theory of definiteness is very much in tune with an approach to presuppositions which views them as part of the common ground in a conversation—beliefs which the speaker believes to be shared between speaker and addressee (see, e.g., Stalnaker (1974, 2002)).

The main problem with the familiarity theory of definiteness (as well as more generally with the common ground theory of presuppositions) is that there are many counterexamples. Three are given in (15) below.

(15)   a.   The New York City Board of Health voted yesterday to adopt <u>the nation's first major municipal ban on the use of all but tiny amounts of artificial trans fats in restaurant cooking</u>.... [*The New York Times* online, 12/6/06; underlining added]

        b.   If you're going into the bedroom, would you mind bringing back *the big bag of potato chips that I left on the bed*? [= Birner and Ward 1994: ex. 1b, italics in original]

        c.   <u>The case of a Nazi sympathizer who entered a famed Swedish medical school in 2007, seven years after being convicted of a hate murder</u>, throws a rarely discussed question into sharp focus.... [*The New York Times* online, 1/28/08; underlining added.]

In each of these examples, the entities in question are being mentioned for the first time. We saw above in Chapter 3 that Löbner (1985) and Rothschild (2007) have distinguished semantic or role-type definite descriptions, where the CNP content determines a unique referent, from pragmatic or particularized definite descriptions, where the uniqueness in context is signaled by the definite article itself. As Löbner pointed out, the familiarity theory of definiteness neglects the first kind, which can naturally be used to introduce new entities into the discourse (1985: 320). (15a) above would be one example of use of a role-type definite description to introduce a new entity. However, as shown by (15b, c), particularized definite descriptions may also be used to introduce new entities into the discourse.

The usual response to such examples, by those who favor a familiarity theory of definiteness, is to invoke the concept of accommodation proposed by David Lewis (1979b). Briefly, Lewis suggested that when an expression is used which requires some background to be present (in these cases, that the addressee be familiar with the referent of the description used), and that background is not in fact present, it will be automatically added—the utterance will be accommodated. However, as has been frequently observed (e.g. by Gazdar (1979: 107); Soames (1982: 461, n. 5); Abbott (2000: 1419)), appeals to accommodation in this case make the claim of familiarity virtually vacuous. Furthermore such appeals do not explain the fact that it is possible to explicitly deny any assumption that the referent of a definite description is familiar to the addressee, as shown in (16).

(16)   The new curling center at MSU, which you probably haven't heard of, is the first of its kind. [= Abbott 2008a: ex. 6]

If it were correct that familiarity were conventionally encoded in definite descriptions, then (16) should be anomalous. However it is not.[15]

On the other hand there is evidence that uniqueness is conventionally encoded in definite descriptions. For one thing, when *the* and *a/an* are explicitly contrasted it is uniqueness that is at issue, not familiarity. This was shown in the Google phone example above ((13)). For another, denying uniqueness for an associated definite description does result in anomaly, as shown in (17).

(17)   # Russell was the author of *Principia Mathematica*; in fact, there were two. [= Abbott 2008a: ex. 11]

This indicates that uniqueness is part of the meaning of the definite article while familiarity is not. In fact, thinking pre-theoretically, we would expect something like familiarity, a pragmatic element, to be derived pragmatically.[16] Given that in using a definite description, the speaker signals their assumption that the addressee can identify a unique referent, it must often be the case that the addressee is already familiar with that referent.

[15] Roberts (2002, 2003, 2004) has put forward a theory on which definite NPs (definite descriptions, demonstrative descriptions, and pronouns) presuppose both uniqueness in context, and "weak familiarity," where weak familiarity means that the existence of the discourse referent is entailed by the common ground—information presumed by the speaker to be shared by speaker and addressee. (Cf. Roberts (2004: 507ff.)) This approach also runs afoul of examples like those in (15) and (16).

[16] See Ludlow and Segal (2004) for an example of the reverse approach—trying to derive uniqueness pragmatically from semantically encoded familiarity; and see Abbott (2008a) for a reply. Abbott (1999) and Gundel et al. (2001) contain other arguments against the familiarity view.

9.2.3 Non-null intersection

We turn now to another attempt to characterize definiteness—one which will be of particular interest when we come to partitive NPs in §9.4 below. Working within their generalized quantificational framework (which we reviewed above in Chapter 4), Barwise and Cooper (1981) gave a definition of what it takes to be a definite determiner—a definition which explicitly excluded the universal determiners. To understand their definition we need to think about the kind of generalized quantifier that is associated with, say, a proper name. The interpretation of *Madonna*, for example, would be (ignoring intensionality) the set of all and only those sets that Madonna belongs to. We can represent this using the lambda notation introduced in Chapter 4, letting m stand for Madonna and S serve as a variable over sets.

(18) $\lambda S[S(m)]$

Now by definition, Madonna is a member of each of these sets. It is also true that Madonna also is the **only** entity that belongs to all these sets, since one of the sets in question is Madonna's unit set—the singleton containing just Madonna. Now consider the intersection ($\cap$) of this set of sets: the intersection of a set of sets is that set which contains all and only those entities that belong to all the sets. In this case that is going to be the set containing just Madonna herself. (19) gives this equivalence formally (recall the curly bracket notation for sets which was introduced in Chapter 4).

(19) $\cap\lambda S[S(m)] = \{m\}$

The singleton $\{m\}$ is called the GENERATOR of the set in (18).[17] Similarly for a definite description like *the present queen of England*: the generalized quantifier in this case would contain all and only the sets that Elizabeth II belongs to. And again, this set of sets would have the singleton set of Elizabeth herself as their intersection or generator.

Let us now contrast a typical indefinite NP, like *a spotted dog*. On the generalized quantifier analysis, this NP denotes the set of all (and only) those sets that contain at least one spotted dog. (20) shows this set of sets.

(20) $\lambda S[\exists x[\text{spotted-dog}(x) \,\&\, S(x)]]$

[17] Barwise and Cooper (1981: 184) refer to this set as the generator. Other treatments refer to the membership of that set, in this case the individual m (Madonna), as the generator.

One of those sets would be the set of dogs with long tails (since at least one spotted dog has a long tail), and another of those sets would be the set of dogs with short tails (since at least one spotted dog has a short tail). Similarly two other sets in this generalized quantifier would be the set of friendly dogs and the set of vicious dogs, since there are spotted dogs in both of those categories. I think you can see that the intersection of this set of sets is going to be empty—that is, there is not going to be anything that belongs to all of the sets in **this** generalized quantifier. Using Ø to stand for the null set (the set with no members, also known as "the empty set"), we can state this fact as in (21).

(21) $\cap\lambda S[\exists x[\text{spotted-dog}(x) \, \& \, S(x)]] = \emptyset$

And a similar fact will hold for other quantified NPs like *many dogs* and *most dogs*. So Barwise and Cooper proposed having a non-null intersection as the defining property of definite NPs.[18] That would include proper names and definite descriptions, but exclude indefinite descriptions and most other quantificational NPs.

Now we come to one small sticky detail. As noted above, Barwise and Cooper wished to exclude universally quantified NPs from the class of definites. But it seems as though a universally quantified NP, interpreted as a generalized quantifier, would have a non-null intersection. Let's look at the generalized quantifier representation of something like *every spotted dog*.

(22) $\lambda S[\forall x[\text{spotted-dog}(x) \rightarrow S(x)]]$

This is going to contain all and only those sets that have every spotted dog in them (e.g. sets like the set of spotted things, the set of dogs, the set of mammals, etc.). To put this in other terms, (22) is going to include all of the supersets of the spotted dog set. It seems clear that this generalized quantifier is going to have a non-null intersection—in fact, that this intersection is going to be the set of spotted dogs. That fact is stated formally in (23).

(23) $\cap\lambda S[\forall x[\text{spotted-dog}(x) \rightarrow S(x)]] = \{x: \text{spotted-dog}(x)\}$

So it looks like universally quantified NPs would be included under Barwise and Cooper's definition of definiteness.

However Barwise and Cooper postulated a difference between definite descriptions, on the one hand, and universally quantified

---

[18] This is a simplified version of their proposal; cf. Barwise and Cooper (1981: 183f.).

NPs, on the other. As we saw above in Chapter 4, according to Barwise and Cooper definite descriptions semantically presuppose the existence of something meeting the descriptive content of the NP in question, so that they are undefined when there is none, as for current utterances of *The present king of France is bald*. (This is like the position of Frege and Strawson.) On the other hand, Barwise and Cooper did not believe that universally quantified NPs carry a semantic existence presupposition,[19] so an NP like *every unicorn* is defined, even though there are no unicorns. As a result, its generalized quantifier (the set of all supersets of the null set) has a null intersection, as shown below.

(24) $\cap\lambda S[\forall x[\text{unicorn}(x) \rightarrow S(x)]] = \{x: \text{unicorn}(x)\} = \varnothing$

So in their definition of definiteness Barwise and Cooper required that the generalized quantifier in question **always** have a non-null intersection. As we have just seen, on their view it is possible for universally quantified NPs to fail this condition (when the CNP does not apply to anything); hence universally quantified NPs are excluded from the class of definites.

In summary, the definition of "definite" according to Barwise and Cooper (1981) includes definite descriptions and proper names, and presumably would also include pronouns and demonstrative descriptions (which they did not analyze in their paper), but not any overtly quantified NPs.

9.2.4 Type *e*

We saw above in Chapter 4 that Partee (1986) proposed a number of type-shifting principles, whereby NPs occurring naturally in one type could be shifted, or coerced, into a different type for the purposes of some construction. Recall that the three possible types for NPs are *e* (the type of NPs which denote entities), $<e,t>$ (the type of NPs which denote sets of entities), and $\ll e,t>,t>$ (the type denoting generalized quantifiers—sets of sets). Of particular interest in our present investigation of the notion of definiteness would be those NPs which can

---

[19] In this Barwise and Cooper differed from Strawson, who suggested towards the end of his famous 1950 attack on Russell's theory of descriptions that universally quantified statements were also presuppositional:

A literal-minded and childless man asked whether all his children are asleep will certainly not answer "Yes" on the ground that he has none; but nor will he answer "No" on this ground. Since he has no children, the question does not arise.   (Strawson 1950: 344)

appear in type *e*—the type of NPs which denote entities. Intuitively those seem to be the ones most likely to be definite.

Partee's type-shifting principle which applies to NPs of type $\ll e,t>$, *t*> and yields NPs of type *e* is called "*lower.*" *Lower* only applies to generalized quantifiers which are generated by single entities (including, however, the plural entities proposed by Link's analysis of plurals), and maps them on to those entities. Thus, for instance, Mary's property set would be mapped onto Mary. Overtly quantificational NPs (e.g. *no rabbits, most people, few sausages*), which are not property sets of single entities, are not subject to this principle. Partee notes that the traditional division between referential expressions and quantificational expressions seems to correlate well with the division between NPs which may be of type *e* and those which may not be. Note the following comment toward the end of the paper:

> ... there remain NP's for which none of our operations provide *e*-type readings: these, not surprisingly, are the ones traditionally thought of as the most clearly "quantificational": *no man, no men, at most one man, few men, not every man, most men.* ... Such NP's can occur in *e*-type positions only by "quantifying in", which would account for the traditional distinction between them and "referring expressions".
>
> (Partee 1986: 132, footnote omitted)

Thus we might recast the traditional referential-quantificational distinction as one of type, specifically type *e* vs type $\ll e,t>,t>$. For the most part this would give us the same distinction as Barwise and Cooper's distinction between definite and indefinite. However there is one difference in Partee's treatment—indefinite descriptions.

As we have seen, the Kamp-Heim dynamic semantics approach treats indefinite descriptions as being quite similar to definite descriptions.[20] Both introduce a variable (accompanied by the information contained in the CNP). The only difference, in the File Change semantics version, is that definite descriptions must be associated with an existing file card—representing an entity assumed to be familiar to the addressee, while indefinites introduce a novel one. One parallel between the two kinds of NP which served a crucial role in Partee's findings is that both definite and indefinite descriptions (as well as proper names and demonstratives) are able to serve as the antecedent of a singular discourse pronoun. Overtly quantificational NPs are not able to do this. The examples below are from Partee (1986: exx. 7, 8).

---

[20] Recall from §6.4 that others (e.g. Chastain (1975); Fodor and Sag (1982)) have also argued that indefinite descriptions may have a referential interpretation.

(25) a. John/the man/a man walked in. He looked tired.
   b. Every man/no man/more than one man walked in. *He looked tired.

The ability to serve as the antecedent of a singular discourse pronoun was Partee's criterion for being of type e.

In order to achieve a type e interpretation for indefinite descriptions, Partee suggested that they might receive a generalized quantifier interpretation of the form in (26).[21]

(26) $\lambda S[S(x_n) \,\&\, CNP(x_n)]$

The x_n here is intended to stand for some particular variable to which a discourse referent would be assigned. So an indefinite like *a man* in a particular utterance might be assigned the generalized quantifier in (27).

(27) $\lambda S[S(x_{23}) \,\&\, man(x_{23})]$

If *lower* applies to (27) it would assign to *a man* the e-type reading x_{23} together with the condition that x_{23} be a man. This would presumably be the interpretation for (25a) above with *a man*, i.e. (28).

(28)   A man walked in. He looked tired.

Any implementation of this proposal would have to avoid the problem with specific indefinites noted above toward the end of Chapter 6— namely, that no particular person can be assigned as the denotation of *a man*, since the existence (in the context) of any man satisfying the requirements of (28) (i.e. walking in and looking tired) makes (28) true.[22]

If Partee is right, then we would have to conclude either that being of type e does not correspond to being definite, or that indefinite descriptions can be definite (this would be when they introduce a discourse referent). The more important question for the purposes of this book is whether or not being of type e is an appropriate characterization of referentiality. If it is, then referentiality will probably have to be distinguished from definiteness.

Before leaving this section I do want to mention one potential conflict within the criteria for type classification. As just noted, the criterion for being of type e is ability to serve as the antecedent for a

---

[21] Here Partee was following an idea of Henk Zeevat, eventually published in Zeevat (1989).

[22] Most likely this would be handled with discourse-level existential binding. My proposal in Chapter 6 involving constant individual concepts would be an alternative to the Zeevat/Partee proposal.

singular discourse pronoun. On the other hand proper names (and definite descriptions), which might otherwise seem to be most naturally of type *e*, were assumed to be able to occur as generalized quantifiers in order to explain their ability to conjoin with overtly quantificational NPs, as in, for example, *Sally and most of the boys*, the assumption being that only expressions of the same type are able to be conjoined with each other (Partee 1986: 117; cf. also 140, n. 7). However it is possible for a single occurrence of a proper name (or a definite description) to do both at once, as in (29).

(29)   Sally and most of the boys met after class. She was planning to share her class notes with them.

One might question any of the assumptions that led to this conflict, including the assumption that quantificational NPs cannot be of type *e*, the assumption that only NPs of type *e* can serve as antecedents for singular pronouns, and the assumption that only expressions of like type may be conjoined. In §9.4 below we will see some more reasons to question the assumption that quantificational NPs cannot be of type *e*, and in Chapter 10 we will see some evidence suggesting that being of type *e* is not essential for the antecedents of singular pronouns. As for the assumption that only expressions of like type may be conjoined, examples like those in (30) below seem to cause a problem for it.

parallelism

(30)   a.   We waited <u>impatiently</u> but <u>with hope in our hearts</u>.
       b.   Tom wanted to be both <u>handsome</u> and <u>from a prominent family</u>.
       c.   <u>Paris</u> or <u>near the Seine</u> is where I want to spend my final days.

It may be that conjoinability is more an issue of the context in which an expression may occur than the details of its syntactic structure. That is, if two expressions may occur in a given context, and be related to the rest of the context in the same way, that fact may override differences in syntactic category and allow them to be conjoined. So possibly conjoinability of two NPs does not have to mean they are both of the same type.

9.3 Strong and weak

We saw above in §9.1 that existential (*there-be*) sentences played an early role in Chomskyan linguistics in seeming to provide a criterion for definiteness. Gary Milsark's (1974, 1977) classic work on this topic revealed many of the complications surrounding this criterion, and it is to his credit that he created the new terms "weak" and "strong": weak NPs can occur naturally in an existential, while strong NPs are the ones which cannot. Examples of these categories are given in (31), below, and illustrative existential examples in (32) and (33).

(31)   Weak: *an apple, some/several/many/too few/no apples*
       Strong: *Mary, it, the/every/each/neither apple, all/most/both apples*

(32)   a.   There was an apple in the basket.
       b.   There were some/several/many/too few/no apples in the basket.

(33)   a.   *There was Mary/it in the basket.
       b.   *There was the/every/each/neither apple in the basket.
       c.   *There were all/most/both apples in the basket.

Milsark attempted to account for this difference in behavior by assuming, first, that the weak quantificational determiners (e.g. *a/an, several, many, too few, no*) are not genuinely quantificational—he called them "cardinality words," reflecting the fact that they give amounts rather than proportions. On the other hand Milsark hoped that all of the strong determiners could ultimately be given a quantificational analysis. The ungrammaticalities in (33), then, could be explained as a result of the conflict between the existential quantification expressed by *there be* and the additional quantification expressed by the strong determiner.[23] The main problem with this explanation is that it requires proper names and pronouns to be seen as quantificational. Of course Montague analyzed **all** NPs as generalized quantifiers, but that would include all the weak ones as well as the strong ones.

Barwise and Cooper (1981) proposed a different characterization of the weak/strong distinction, one which they also hoped would provide an explanation for the pattern of facts in (32) and (33). The formal definition is rather strange and difficult to get a grip on, but the net effect is to classify those NPs as strong when sentences of the form *NP exists* are either necessarily true (for "positive strong" NPs) or necessarily false (for "negative strong" NPs). The weak NPs are those for which neither condition holds, and thus for which *NP exists* is

---

[23] If Milsark's analysis were correct, the problem with the examples in (33) would seem to be semantic rather than syntactic, calling for a # designation rather than *. This is one kind of case, alluded to in the opening chapter, where the choice between these two is difficult because a fully satisfactory explanation for what the problem is has not yet been found.

contingent on the facts.[24] The examples in (34) below should strike you as necessarily true no matter what *glarph* means. The example in (35) should seem necessarily false, and the ones in (36) should seem possibly true and possibly false, depending on whether there are any, or several, or many glarphs.

(34)   a.   Every/each glarph exists.
       b.   All/most glarphs exist.

(35)   Neither glarph exists.

(36)   a.   A/no glarph exists.
       b.   Some/several/many glarphs exist.

Then the explanation for the pattern of facts in (32) and (33) would be that, with a strong NP as focus, the existential is asserting something that is necessarily true or false, and hence silly (and thus anomalous), while with a weak NP the existential is asserting something sensible.

Ed Keenan (1987) offers a number of problems for the Barwise and Cooper analysis. One is that their analysis assumes that the syntactic form of existentials is *There is NP*—thus what we have been calling "the XP" constituent is, on their account, part of the focus NP. There are examples for which this assumption cannot be maintained, for example (37) (= Keenan's (28a)):

(37)   There are <u>two students who object to that</u> enrolled in the course.

The underlined sequence in (37) is not a well-formed NP. Keenan also points out some problems presented by compound determiners like *either zero or else more than zero* and *fewer than zero*. These would be classified as strong under the Barwise and Cooper analysis, but they can appear in existentials, as shown in (38) (Keenan's (48b)).

(38)   Your argument is ingenious, Mr. Jones. It proves among other things that there are fewer than zero perfect numbers.

Keenan presents his own analysis of the strong-weak distinction, which actually agrees in results with that proposed by Barwise and Cooper, to a great extent, while avoiding the problems presented by examples like

---

[24] By using "exists" here I am modifying Barwise and Cooper's proposal in a way they would not approve of. The actual property is belonging to the model (in the semantic sense), not any absolute kind of existence. As Barwise and Cooper note, what actually exists might be only a subset of what is in the model (1981: 216, n. 7). However it's hard to get good example sentences using that property.

(37) and (38).[25] Thus Keenan's analysis is an improvement, but as Keenan himself points out, it has a problem with possessive NPs (1987: 296f.). As we saw above, some possessive NPs (those with indefinite NP determiners) are acceptable in existentials. Examples (8c, d) from §9.1 above are repeated here.

(39) a. There was a student's book on the table
      b. There were several dogs' leashes hanging in the closet.

Keenan did modify his analysis so as to include such examples, but in a rather ad hoc way (Keenan 1987: 297). Another problem, which he did not address, was the possibility of partitive NPs in existentials—we'll see some examples in the next section. And finally, there is a further complication with Milsark's weak-strong distinction which we have been ignoring up to now, and which is not addressed by Keenan.

Milsark noted that what look like weak NPs—those with *some, several, many* etc. as determiners—sometimes show strong behavior. To see this most easily it is helpful to acknowledge another difference between weak and strong NPs, and that is their ability to occur with individual-level predications. We've already seen (above in Chapter 7) that bare plurals are disambiguated in favor of their generic readings with individual-level predicates. (40) has only the generic reading for *dolphins*.

(40) Dolphins are intelligent.

Note now that (41), with the indefinite article, also has only the generic reading.

(41) A dolphin is intelligent.

Paul Postal (1966) had already pointed out a difference between two *some* determiners. One of them, which he spelled *sm*, is always unstressed and occurs only with plurals. The other, spelled *some*, may be stressed and typically receives a partitive interpretation, indicating a portion of some established group. Milsark observed that individual-level predications occur only with the latter. Compare (42a) and (42b).

(42) a. #Sm dolphins were intelligent.
      b. We examined a pod of dolphins: some ((of the) dolphins) were intelligent (while others were not).

adjectival use vs. noun

---

[25] Keenan's calls the weak determiners "existential." Note too that the title of his paper is "A semantic definition of 'indefinite' NP," indicating that he views Milsark's category of weak (or existential) NPs as coterminous with indefinites. We have seen reason to question this view, and will see more reason below.

(I've used a # rather than a * for (42a), since the problem seems to be semantic and/or pragmatic.) The weak determiners *many* and *several* similarly have both weak and strong uses.

It also appears to be the case, as Milsark pointed out, that the strong versions of weak NPs do not occur felicitously in existentials. Making them explicitly partitive brings out this infelicity, as shown in (43).

(43)   #There were some/many/several of the dolphins swimming behind us.

It is to Keenan's credit that his analysis of Milsark's weak–strong distinction correctly classifies the partitive NPs in (43) as strong (or nonexistential, to use Keenan's term). On the other hand examples like those in (43) are definitely not as bad as the examples above in (33)—presumably a reflection of the fact that although the embedded NP (*the dolphins*) is definite, the NP as a whole is not. And as we will soon see, there are examples of partitives with embedded indefinites that are good in existentials.

As we can see, there is a long line of attempts to characterize exactly which NPs can go naturally in an existential and which cannot. At the moment it cannot be said that we have a good clear analysis which is also explanatory. My own view is that the constraint on NPs in existentials is a pragmatic one—the result of a conflict between the assertion of existence in an existential sentences and a presupposition of existence associated with the NP in question. I believe the gradations in ill-formedness that we have seen in, for example, the difference between (43) and (31), are indicative of this pragmatic aspect. But to fully account for all the data we have seen and are about to see, more would have to be said than we have space for here. (Plus I'd have to have figured it all out.)

9.4 Partitive NPs[26]

As noted above, partitive NPs seem to have the form *Det of NP*—some examples are given in (44).[27]

(44)   *some of the apples, few of those options, all of Mary's dogs*

---

[26] Many of the points in this section were made in Abbott (1996), and some of the examples below are adapted from examples given in that paper.

[27] Not everybody assumes that partitives have this structure: Keenan and Stavi (1986: 287) and Peters and Westerståhl (2006: 269) are four who argue that partitives have the structure *[[Det of Det] CNP]*.

Partitive NPs present an interesting problem: ordinarily determiners combine with CNPs, which denote sets of entities. But as we have seen above, NPs themselves for the most part seem to denote either generalized quantifiers (sets of sets), or entities, and as such do not provide a suitable kind of set for another determiner to combine with. We will spend a bit of time reviewing the semantics (and pragmatics) of partitives, since this topic has broader implications than one might at first have thought.

In the earlier days of Chomskyan linguistics it was assumed that the NP embedded in a partitive had to be definite; this was termed "the Partitive Constraint" (Jackendoff 1977). Making this assumption, Barwise and Cooper (1981) proposed the analysis of "definite NP" (within their generalized quantifier approach) which we looked at above in §9.2.3. As we saw, this definition requires a definite NP to always have a non-empty intersection—thus including definite descriptions (and proper names), but excluding universally quantified NPs as well as all other overtly quantified NPs.[28]

The beauty of the Barwise and Cooper analysis was that it suggested an explanation for the Partitive Constraint, since (it seems) it is only possible for a generalized quantifier with a nonempty intersection to yield a set for the initial determiner to combine with. Consider the partitive *some of the apples*, for instance. *The apples* denotes the set of all supersets of the set of (contextually relevant) apples. The intersection of this generalized quantifier will be that set of apples—and there we have a set for *some* to combine with. (The word *of*, in a partitive, could then be viewed as an instruction to take the intersection of its object NP.) On the other hand an NP like *many apples* will have an empty intersection (since it's true that many apples are wormy, but also true that many apples are not wormy—and nothing is both wormy and not wormy). Thus we account for the assumed ungrammaticality of *some of many apples*.

Seen in this light, it may seem arbitrary to have ruled out universally quantified NPs from the category of definites, since they will always have a nonempty intersection unless the CNP fails to denote (as, e.g., in the case of *every unicorn*). The reason Barwise and Cooper took

---

[28] Keenan and Stavi assume that the second Det in their *Det of Det* partitive structure must be definite (1986: 297). Peters and Westerståhl conclude that it must be either definite or possessive, where some possessives (as we have seen) are not definite, at least according to the existential test (cf. Peters and Westerståhl (2006: 278)).

pains to exclude universally quantified NPs is because, contrary to what we would expect given the explanation in the preceding paragraph, they believed that universally quantified NPs do not occur embedded in partitives. This was a standard assumption at the time, based on examples like (45).

(45)   Most of every candidate appeared on TV.

It is true that (45) cannot have what should be the plausible interpretation, according to which most of the candidates appeared on TV. However the reason for that is that *every* (as we observed above in Chapter 7) is a necessarily distributive quantifier—hence its denotation cannot be taken as a group. Below we will see that the universal quantifier *all* does allow a group interpretation, and does appear embedded in partitives.

We should note (45) does have an interpretation with a MASS partitive, where the initial determiner (*most* in this case) applies to the individual candidates rather than the candidates as a group. Thus (45) might describe a situation where the camera operator for the TV station was not very competent and did not get the whole of the candidates into the picture. The necessary distributivity of *every* forces the initial determiner to apply to the individuals in the denotation of its NP. We saw in Chapter 8 that *each, most, both,* and *neither* are also necessarily distributive. The failure of NPs with these determiners to occur embedded in a group partitive is a result of this property. They may readily occur in mass partitives however, as shown in (46).

(46)   a.   The Smithsonian donated most of both rare book exhibits.
        b.   One third of each book Chomsky writes is footnotes.
        c.   At least some of most fruits consists of rind and seeds.

Since in mass partitives like these the initial quantifier is applying to individuals within the denotation of the embedded NP, and not that NP as a whole, the definiteness or lack thereof of that NP is not relevant for the Partitive Constraint.

Leaving aside the case of the necessarily distributive NPs, there remain many counterexamples to the Partitive Constraint, viewed as a requirement of definiteness. This is true whether we take Barwise and Cooper's analysis of "definite NP," or almost anybody else's. Thus consider the examples in (47)–(51) (the sources are given following the examples).

(47) a. <u>One of some boys who were playing in the alley</u> got arrested.
b. He ate <u>three of some apples he found on the ground</u>.
(Stockwell, Schachter, and Partee 1973: 144)

(48) a. That book could belong to <u>one of three people</u>.
b. This is <u>one of a number of counterexamples to the PC</u>.
c. John was <u>one of several students who arrived late</u>.
(Ladusaw 1982: 240)

(49) They called the police because <u>seven of some professor's manuscripts</u> were missing.
(Keenan and Stavi 1986: 297)

(50) a. Only <u>one of many people who saw the accident</u> would testify.
b. Only <u>one of many applicants</u> passed the test.
(Reed 1989: 421)

(51) a. Not being <u>one of six children</u>, I have nothing to say on the matter.
b. What about the interaction between <u>any two of three intelligent species?</u>
c. I would hate for my boyfriend and me to be <u>two of seventeen housemates</u>—we would never be able to kiss in private.
(Ionin et al. 2006: 364)

Each of the underlined partitives in these examples has an embedded NP which would not be classified as definite by Barwise and Cooper (or indeed by almost anybody else's definition of "definite"). And once you put your mind to it, it isn't hard to come up with more such examples.[29]

(52) a. Ants had gotten into <u>most of some jars of jam Bill had stored in the basement</u>.
b. <u>Three quarters of half the population</u> will be mothers at some point in their lives.

---

[29] There are also many examples of mass partitives with embedded indefinites. (i) below is from Selkirk (1977: 315, n. 7).

(i) I heard <u>too much of one speech</u> and not enough of the other.

(ii) a. I could follow <u>a little of some of those arguments</u>.
b. They quoted <u>about half of several ancient texts</u>.

(Cf. also (53d) below in the text.) In fact mass partitives accept embedded indefinites more readily than group partitives do. The reason for this is explored in my 1996 paper.

c.   Any of several options are open to us at this point.
d.   Each student only answered a few of many questions that they could have.
e.   Half of all dentists who chew gum prefer Trident.

The last example—(52e)—is one of the type promised above, with a universally quantified NP embedded in a (group) partitive. *All dentists who chew gum* here has a group interpretation, and the initial determiner (*half*) applies to that group.

In fact the only NPs which seem to be absolutely excluded from partitives are bare NPs. Examples like those in (53) seem to be totally bad—ungrammatical and not merely awkward or infelicitous.

(53)   a.   *Many of French people like wine.
        b.   *We had a few of reheated sausages for breakfast.
        c.   *Some of lard may be used instead of butter.

This is true whether the embedded bare NP is interpreted generically or nonspecifically, so definiteness does not appear to be playing a role here either. Note that this behavior is another way in which bare NPs are different from proper names, since the latter are allowed in (mass) partitives, as shown in (54).

(54)   If global warming continues, most of Kiribati will soon be under water.

(Back in Chapter 7 we observed that bare NPs were different from proper names and definite descriptions in their generic uses, in not requiring a well-defined kind to denote.)

As promised above, we see that partitives with embedded indefinites may occur naturally in existential sentences.

(55)   a.   There were three of some student's books on the table.
        b.   There was some of a half-eaten roll scattered on the floor.
        c.   There are any of several options open to us at this point.
        d.   There was most of a birthday cake and all of a large vegetarian pizza sitting on the buffet.

We saw above with the examples in (43) that partitives with an indefinite initial determiner but an embedded definite were not very good in existentials, although not as bad as total definites. The examples in (55) indicate that it is the embedded NP that has the stronger influence on acceptability in an existential.

We noted above that the exclusion of universally quantified NPs from Barwise and Cooper's definition of "definite NP" seemed arbitrary, since usually the generalized quantifier corresponding to a universally quantified NP would have a nonempty intersection. Now we see that indeed a universally quantified NP can appear embedded in a partitive, as long as it can have a group interpretation. But that's of little comfort since it seems that **any** quantificational NP that can have a group interpretation (with the exception of bare NPs) can also be embedded in a (group) partitive—including those with determiners like *some, three, several,* and *many.* These would have been assumed by Barwise and Cooper never to have a nonempty intersection.

What to do? Barker (1998), following Ladusaw (1982) and Reed (1989), takes an NP's occurrence in a partitive as an indication that that NP denotes an entity. He remarks that "whenever an NP occurs in a partitive, it must denote an individual in the context in which that partitive is used" (Barker 1998: 692). He assumes further that Partee's type-shifting principles can work to give us a type *e* interpretation for any such NP. The result is that any NP that can occur embedded in a partitive must be assumed to be of type *e*. (See also Ionin et al. (2006) for a similar conclusion.) But this would present a problem for Partee's suggestion that being of type *e* is an indicator of referentiality, at least as that term has been traditionally understood. Notice that speakers can use partitives with embedded indefinites when they have no particular group in mind as the denotation of the embedded NP. Indeed, such partitives can occur with narrow scope with respect to quantifiers, propositional attitude verbs, sentence adverbs, and conditionals. The examples below in (56) illustrate these facts; in each case the embedded group NP is underlined.

(56) a. John was apparently one of <u>several students who arrived late</u>—I have no idea how many, or who the others were.

 b. Mary thinks that this is only one of <u>a number of counter-examples to the PC</u>.

 c. Each speaker will tell only two of <u>all the possible jokes related to their topic</u>.

 d. Every year only a few of <u>many applicants</u> is admitted to the program.

 e. If three or more of <u>some professor's manuscripts</u> get published, the University benefits.

TABLE 9.1. Definiteness criteria and NP types

	Proper names	Definite & demonstrative descriptions	Pronouns	Bare NPs (generic)	all, each, every, most	Indefinite descriptions	Several, many, few,…	Bare NPs(indefinite)
Existentials	+	+	+	+	+	−	−	−
Referential uniqueness	+/−	+	+	+	+/−	−	−	−
Familiarity	+/−	+/−	+	+/−	+/−	−	−	−
Nonnull ∩	+	+	+	+	+/−	−	−	−
Type e (Partee)	+	+	+	?	−	+	−	−
Strong (B&C; Keenan)	+	+	+	?	+	−	−	−
Partitives	+	+	+	−	+	+	+	−

If we do admit these NPs as referential, then the traditional opposition between referentiality and quantification will have broken down pretty completely. But we had already seen this hoary distinction start to crumble back in Chapter 6.

9.5 Concluding remarks

In this chapter we have looked at a number of different properties which cross-cut categories of NP. We found that the NPs excluded from existential sentences, while often intuitively definite, were not necessarily so. We then looked at several characterizations of what it means to be definite. Referential uniqueness is a quality held by those four types of NP typically cited as being definite: namely, definite and demonstrative descriptions, pronouns, and proper names. However, universally quantified NPs would also seem to be referentially unique, and while they are excluded from existential sentences they are often not viewed as definite—possibly because definites are supposed to be referential and referentially has traditionally been opposed to quantification. The characteristic of familiarity does apply to many intuitive definites but by no means all. The nonempty intersection criterion of Barwise and Cooper again selects most intuitive definites, but seems to rule out universally quantified NPs in an ad hoc way. The final proposal—being of type e—is very insecure in virtue of its analysis relativity. That is, it may be possible to analyze all sorts of NPs as being of type e, with the result that nothing about definiteness or referentiality can be concluded. Table 9.1 summarizes our findings. We turn next to consider NPs in discourse.

10

NPs in discourse

Alas, poor Yorick! I knew him, Horatio, a fellow of infinite jest, of most excellent fancy.

William Shakespeare, *Hamlet*

We closed the last chapter with the thoughts that there seemed to be no independent characterization of definiteness or referentiality, and that even the traditional opposition between referentiality and quantification might not be tenable. Let us then take a different look at the situation, from the point of view of a speaker/writer in a DISCOURSE (a sequence of utterances, or a text) who is intent on conveying information to their addressee. We will start by focusing on pronouns, and a particular problem—the problem of so-called DONKEY PRONOUNS. This problem occurs within sentence boundaries, but also across them, and will lead us to recognize another kind of pronoun (as promised above in Chapter 8)—one which does not behave like a variable of logic. Following that, we broaden our attention to consider the use of NPs in discourse more generally. In the previous chapters of this book we have looked at the many kinds of NP that exist in English, giving somewhat greater attention to those more likely to be classified as referential—proper names, definite and demonstrative descriptions, and pronouns; but also attending to quantificational NPs of various types. In §10.2 of this chapter we look at NPs as they are used by speakers, reviewing a number of proposals for ordering or classifying NPs in terms of, roughly speaking, their information value, given assumptions about the assumed knowledge state of the addressee. The result is a suggestion that referentiality may be an issue of degrees. Finally, in §10.3 we take a brief look at discourse referents; what they are and how they relate to the things that make our utterances true, and what to do about nonexistent entities. And that will probably be enough to tackle.

10.1 Pronouns in discourse

10.1.1 Donkey pronouns

The title of this subsection comes from some examples given by Peter Geach (1962).[1] The standard examples are given in (1).

(1)   a.   Every farmer <u>who owns [a donkey]</u>$_i$ beats it$_i$.
      b.   If a farmer owns a donkey, he beats it.

Let us focus on (1a):[2] the problem here is the interpretation of the pronoun *it* when (as indicated by the subscripts) its antecedent is *a donkey*. It would <u>seem that</u> it cannot be a referential pronoun—there is no particular <u>donkey being spoken of</u>. The only other possibility we have, given what we have seen so far, is to regard the *it* as a bound variable, bound by *a donkey*. But the problem with that is that structurally, *a donkey* lies within a relative clause (underlined), and is thus not in a syntactic position which should allow it to bind the pronoun. (Recall from Chapter 3 that relative clauses often behave like islands.) Note, for example, that binding is not possible in an example like (2).

(2)   *The vet <u>who checked [every donkey]</u>$_i$ vaccinated it$_i$.

The same thing holds if we were try to translate (1a) into its traditional logical form and assume, following Russell, that indefinite descriptions are translated using the existential quantifier. What we would come up with would be the logical form in (3).

(3) $\forall x[[\text{farmer}(x) \;\&\; \exists y[\text{donkey}(y) \;\&\; \text{own}(x, y)]] \rightarrow \text{beat}(x, y)]$

The final occurrence of *y* in this formula is not within the scope of the existential quantifier. It is thus free, and not related to any donkeys owned by anybody. Translated back into English, (3) would read: "Every farmer who owns a donkey beats something or other."[3]

---

[1]   As noted by Geach, this type of example, including the mention of donkeys, goes back to medieval texts. In view of this hallowed tradition I use them, despite their potential for upsetting sensitive animal lovers.

[2]   The problem presented by the conditional in (1b) is very much the same as that presented by (1a), although perhaps not identical (see the comment about (8) below). We will stick to the nonconditional versions of these sentences since we have not really talked much about the semantics of conditionals in this book.

[3]   The same would hold true if we used our restricted quantification notation, as shown below in (i).

(i) $\text{Every}_x[\text{farmer}(x) \;\&\; a_y[\text{donkey}(y)](\text{own}(x, y))](\text{beat}(x, y))$

Since the interpretation of *a donkey* is introduced within the restrictor clause of *every farmer*, it cannot bind a variable in the scope portion of that NP.

On the other hand, it would not help to move the existential quantifier to the front of the formula, so that it would bind the final y. That would result in (4).

(4) $\forall x \exists y[[farmer(x) \ \& \ [donkey(y) \ \& \ own(x, y)]] \rightarrow beat(x, y)]$

Translated back into English, (4) says "For every farmer there is something such that, if it is a donkey and he owns it, he beats it." This is made true by the mere existence of something that is not a donkey or not owned by any farmer.

Below we look at several attempts to solve the problem of donkey pronouns. We'll start with the solution proposed within dynamic semantics. Following that, we'll look at a different approach—one which capitalizes on a parallel between pronouns and definite (and demonstrative) descriptions similar to what we already observed in Chapter 8.

10.1.2 Dynamic semantics and unselective binding

In Chapter 8 above we were introduced to the dynamic semantics approach of Irene Heim (1982, 1983) and Hans Kamp (1981; Kamp and Reyle 1993). Recall that indefinite descriptions introduce new variables, or file cards, into a discourse while pronouns must be associated with variables or file cards representing entities whose existence has already been established. Another aspect of this kind of approach, and the one which is especially relevant to the donkey sentence problem, is that the new variables introduced by indefinite NPs may become bound by other operators.[4] Such "unselective" binding had already been observed by David Lewis (1975), citing examples such as those in (5).

(5)   a.   A quadratic equation never has more than two solutions. [=Lewis 1975: ex. 11]
      b.   A farmer who owns a donkey always feeds it now and then.

---

[4] We exploited this feature of indefinite descriptions above in Chapter 7, when we suggested that generic indefinites might be bound by a tacit GEN operator. We should note that an indefinite description not in the scope of any binder, as in (i) below, would be assumed to be bound by some kind of discourse-level existential quantifier.

(i)   Yesterday I saw a donkey.

Intuitively, (5a) means the same as *No quadratic equation has more than two solutions*. The quantification here is coming from the adverb *never* rather than the indefinite description. (5b) also makes clear that such adverbs are quantifying over cases rather than times in the literal sense—there is no conflict between the unselective binder *always*, and the genuine temporal adverb *now and then*. According to Lewis, *always* in this example quantifies over farmer-donkey pairs.

Returning to (1a) (*Every farmer who owns a donkey beats it*), on the dynamic semantics approach, the universal quantifier of the subject NP, *every farmer who owns a donkey*, is able to bind the variable introduced by the indefinite *a donkey*. The result is similar to Lewis's account of (5b)—universal quantification over farmer-donkey pairs. The logical form would look like (6).

(6) $\forall x,y[[\text{farmer}(x) \ \& \ \text{donkey}(y) \ \& \ \text{own}(x, y)] \rightarrow \text{beat}(x, y)]$

Now there is no problem with the *it*, which corresponds to the final occurrence of the variable y in (6), since it is bound by the universal quantifier at the beginning of the formula.

One problem with this solution to the donkey sentence problem is that it does not make correct predictions when we replace *every* with other quantifiers. Compare (7).

(7)   Most farmers who own a donkey beat it.

This problem, pointed out by Partee (1984), has been dubbed "the proportion problem." (See also Kadmon (1990) and Barker (1996), among others.) If we were to follow the type of analysis suggested by the dynamic semantics approach, we would predict that (7) says that for most pairs of a farmer and a donkey that he owns, the farmer beats the donkey. Yet in a situation with nine loving farmers who own one donkey each and don't beat them, and just one mean farmer who owns fifty donkeys and beats them all, (7) would not be true, despite the fact that in the situation described the vast majority of the farmer-donkey pairs are such that the farmer beats the donkey (fifty to nine). In other words the quantifier in (7) (and thus presumably also in (1a)) seems to be quantifying over the farmers, and not farmer-donkey pairs. (Whether this also holds for an example like (8) below, with an unselective adverb, is another question—one which I am not sure of the answer to.

(8)   Usually, if a farmer owns a donkey, he beats it.

We turn now to a different proposal for solving the donkey sentence problem.

10.1.3 E-Type pronouns

A rather different solution to the donkey sentence problem was proposed by Gareth Evans (1977, 1980). In Evans's view donkey pronouns are indeed referential, but referential in a special way. He called them E-TYPE pronouns (the "E" apparently standing for "Evans"—no other source is given (Evans 1977: 104)), and asserted that they obtain their reference via a definite description which can be gleaned from the sentence in which their antecedents are introduced. This is the new, nonvariable-like, pronoun usage that we promised above in Chapter 8; as advertised, it shows another parallel between pronouns and definite descriptions.

Evans gave several characteristics distinguishing E-type pronouns from the variable-like kind. Consider his example in (9) (= Evans 1980: ex. 7).

(9)   Few congressmen admire Kennedy, and they are very junior.

Evans pointed out that the pronoun *they* in (9) could not be considered to be bound by *few*, since that would give the wrong meaning—it would say that there are few congressmen who both admire Kennedy and are very junior, which (unlike (9)) could still be true if lots of congressmen admired Kennedy, as long as most of them were not very junior. Furthermore pronouns that are bound by quantificational antecedents, like *they* in (10) below (Evans 1980: ex. 6)

(10)   Few congressmen admire only the people they know.

are not referential—it would not make sense to ask who *they* in (10) refers to. However the occurrence of *they* in (9) does seem to be referential—it refers to the congressmen who admire Kennedy. The difference can be brought out sharply, as Evans noted, by replacing *few congressmen* with *no congressmen*, since in the latter case there will be nothing for an E-type pronoun to refer to.[5]

---

[5] We noted above in Chapter 8 that pronouns can pick up their reference from the CNP of an antecedent NP, and with a slight adjustment to (11b) we can make *they* refer to congressmen in general, as in (i) below.

(i)   No congressmen admire Kennedy, since they are all too competitive.

(11)   a.   No congressmen admire only the people they know.
       b.   #No congressmen admire Kennedy, and they are very junior.

Thus E-type pronouns, according to Evans, refer to the objects which satisfy the clause containing their antecedent—they are equivalent to definite descriptions. In the case of (9), *they* means 'the congressmen who admire Kennedy.'

We can now see how Evans's idea can be applied to our troublesome donkey pronouns. Example (1a) above is repeated here as (12).

(12)   Every farmer who owns a donkey beats it.

If we regard *it* here as an E-type pronoun, (12) comes out as equivalent to (13).

(13)   Every farmer who owns a donkey beats the donkey that he owns.

It is easy to see that this type of solution to the donkey sentence problem does not run into the proportion problem. An Evans type of paraphrase for (14a) below is given in (14b).

(14)   a.   Most farmers who own a donkey beat it.
       b.   Most farmers who own a donkey beat the donkey that they
             own.

Here it is clear that the *most* is quantifying only over farmers who own a donkey, not farmer-donkey pairs.

Evans's approach has a lot of appeal, but we must now consider how to realize it in an explicit grammar of English. Should E-type pronouns be derived from underlying definite descriptions? If so how are they generated, and what should their exact form be? Robin Cooper (1979) sidestepped such problems by developing a similar approach, but one which postulates free variables for the semantic content of the definite description in question. As developed by Heim (1990; cf. also Heim and Kratzer (1998)), Cooper's representation for (12) would be something like (15).

(15) $\text{every}_x[\text{farmer }(x) \,\&\, a_y[\text{donkey }(y)](\text{own }(x, y))]\,(\text{beat}(x, \underline{\text{the}_z[R}$
       $\underline{(z, x)]}))$

Presumably this kind of interpretation is not readily available for (11b) itself because of the implausibility of congressmen in general being very junior and/or the incoherence of conjoining this statement about their being junior with a statement that none of them admire Kennedy.

The part of this formula that represents the donkey pronoun *it* is underlined. Translated back into English, (15) says that every farmer who owns a donkey beats the entity which bears relation R to him or her. The interpretation of *R* is left to pragmatics, the idea being that in the context of (15), the most natural interpretation for *R* would be "is a donkey owned by." Heim and Kratzer (1998: 291) suggest a rule turning a definite article with no associated CNP content into a pronoun (an idea which had been put forward somewhat earlier by Paul Postal (1966)).

Cooper pointed out some other circumstances in which E-type pronouns may occur.[6] Most significant are the infamous PAYCHECK sentences, originally pointed out by Lauri Karttunen (1969b).

(16) a. The man who gave his paycheck to his wife was wiser than the man who gave it to his mistress. [= Karttunen 1969b: ex. 18]
      b. This year the president is a Republican. Next year he will be a Democrat. [= Cooper 1979: ex. 35a]

Such pronouns are often called "pronouns of laziness," the idea being that the pronoun saves the speaker from having to repeat an NP,[7] but as Elbourne (2005) points out, this term does not capture a crucial feature of these pronouns, which is that they introduce new entities into the discourse. Elbourne refers to them as NEONTOLOGICAL pronouns (2005: 22).

Note that (16b) is simpler than (16a) (as well as the donkey sentences we have been considering) in that the tacit descriptive content for the pronoun does not relate its referent to anything. That is, while the pronoun in (16a) means something like "his paycheck," the pronoun in (16b) simply means "the president." So instead of a variable over relations, for (16b) we only need a property variable. Cooper's analyses of these examples, as updated by Heim and Kratzer (1998), would look something like (17).

---

[6] Cooper did not use the term "E-type" for these pronouns. Indeed, although he considered deriving these pronouns from fully spelled out definite descriptions, as suggested by Evans's work, he nevertheless was apparently not familiar with this work at the time he wrote his 1979 article, and did not cite it. It should also be noted that the pronouns which we are about to look at, and to which Cooper (and following him Heim and Kratzer) have applied this analysis, were not considered E-type by Evans himself.

[7] The term itself was introduced by Geach (1962: 125) for a different kind of example. Partee (1972: 435) applied it to examples like those in (16).

(17) a. the$_x$[man(x) & gave(x, the$_y$[x's paycheck(y)], x's wife)] was wiser than the$_z$[man(z) & gave(z, <u>the$_w$[R(w, z)]</u>, z's mistress]

b. Now the$_x$[president(x)] (Republican(x)). Next year <u>the$_x$[P (x)]</u> (Democrat(x))

(17a) says, roughly, that the man who gave his paycheck to his wife was wiser than the man who gave the entity bearing relation R to him to his mistress. Here R is most naturally construed as "is the paycheck of." (17b) says that while the president now is a Republican, next year the entity with property P (presumably the property of being the president) will be a Democrat.[8]

Another potential application for this type of analysis suggested by Heim and Kratzer (1998: 296f.) are cases which Craige Roberts (1987, 1989) has termed "modal subordination." These are examples like those in (18) (Roberts 1989: ex. 13, (credited to Fred Landman)).

(18) a. A thief might break into the house.
b. He would steal the silver.

Note that the modality for (18a) differs from that for (18b)—(18a) says that it's possible that some thief will break into the house, while (18b) says that such a thief would definitely steal the silver. Robert's analysis of this example (carried out within the framework of Kamp's Discourse Representation Theory) involves postulating a tacit *if* clause for (18b), to capture the idea of "such a thief"; (18) comes out as equivalent to (19).

(19) a. It's possible that a thief will break into the house.
b. If a thief does break into the house, then he will (certainly) steal the silver.

The *if* clause here is "accommodated," according to Roberts—i.e. addressees see the need for this clause, and add it automatically.[9]

It seems that with a small modification, the E-type approach would make the accommodation of an *if* clause for this type of example unnecessary. At several points we have seen the suggestion that situation variables can be used to constrain descriptive content, and possibly we could use them again here. Consider the E-type representation

---

[8] See Jacobson (2000) for an alternative analysis within her variable-free approach.

[9] We were introduced this sense of "accommodation" (from Lewis 1979b) above in §9.2.2.

for (18) given below in (20). (Recall from Chapter 3 that the diamond (◇), as in (20a), stands for "it is possible that.")

(20) a. $◇a_x[thief(x)]$ (break-into-the-house(x))
      b. $the_x[R(x, s)]$ (steal the silver(x))

In (20b) I have inserted the variable *s* which is intended to be a variable over situations. The idea is that (20b) should express the thought that the x which is related to situation s will steal the silver. In the context following the assertion of (18a), the situation in question would naturally be that under which a thief breaks into the house, and then the logical choice for the x related to that situation would be the thief.

10.1.4 Some remaining issues

On balance the E-type approach seems to do better than the un-selective quantification approach: it does not have the proportion problem for donkey sentences, it does not require the accommodation of tacit *if* clauses, and it is applicable in a wider range of cases, including the "paycheck" examples.[10] However, there remain some problem areas.

(i) *Uniqueness.* The E-type analysis seems to have a potentially troublesome entailment. Consider again a donkey sentence like (21).

(21) Every farmer who owns a donkey beats it.

If *it* is semantically equivalent to 'the donkey that he or she owns,' that would seem to entail that the farmers under discussion own only one donkey each. In her dissertation, Heim (1982) was arguing against the Evans analysis of donkey pronouns, and in favor of the unselective binding approach, and she gave several examples which were problem-atic for Evans. Two of these are given in (22) (= Heim 1982: 89, exx. 12, 13).

(22) a. Everybody who bought a sage plant here bought eight others along with it.
      b. Every man who owns a donkey owns a second one to keep it company.

---

[10] But see Chierchia (1992, 1995) for arguments that both types of analysis are necessary for dealing with pronouns in discourse.

The E-type analysis seems to predict that these sentences will sound contradictory, but they don't.[11]

Somewhat later, Heim (1990) came to realize that her own un-selective quantification approach was problematic, and argued in favor of the E-type approach. To solve the problem presented by examples like those in (22), Heim proposed bringing situations into the picture much as we did above for example (18).[12] The idea is that we interpret donkey pronouns with respect to the minimal situations described in the sentences containing their antecedents; the truth conditions of their containing sentence then may be interpreted with respect to larger situations containing those minimal situations. For example in (22a) the minimal situation in question is one where a person has bought a sage plant; with respect to that situation there is a unique sage plant, and then that situation can be enlarged to include the eight others.

Unfortunately there are examples which seem to tax this solution: the examples in (23) come from oral contributions by Jan van Eijck and Hans Kamp, respectively.

(23) a. If [a man]$_i$ shares an apartment with [another man]$_j$, he$_i$ shares the housework with him$_j$ too.
      b. If [a bishop]$_i$ meets [a bishop]$_j$, he$_i$ blesses him$_j$.

Although these are conditional sentences, unlike most of the others we have considered up to now, the pronoun problem is essentially the same as in those cases. And the particular problem here is that we cannot have minimal situations for the first clauses of these sentences without both men and both bishops. (See Elbourne (2005: ch. 4) for further discussion of this problem and one possible solution.)

---

[11] See Neale (1990) for a modification of Evans's analysis. Neale's D-type pronouns express ("go proxy for" (187)) a kind of number-neutral definite description. Cooper argued that his version of the E-type analysis would not suffer from this uniqueness problem, because the variable standing for the descriptive content of the definite descrip-tion need not stand for the property of being a donkey owned by x—"it could well be some other property which uniquely picks out one of [x]'s donkeys" (Cooper 1979: 84). But this response to the problem is not convincing, given that no other property has been suggested. Abbott (2002) argues that a demonstrative paraphrase (*that donkey*), which does not imply uniqueness, better captures the sense of donkey pronouns; see also Kanazawa (1994) for discussion of variation in donkey pronoun interpretations.

[12] Heim credits Berman (1987) with the idea of using situations to solve this problem.

(ii) *Presence (or absence) of a formal link.* Cooper's analysis, as adapted by Heim and Kratzer, leaves the interpretation of the R relation in E-type pronouns completely open to context. As pointed out by Heim (1990), this analysis has a problem with distinguishing the pair in (24) (similar to examples pointed out by Evans (1977: 147)).

(24) a.   Every man who has a wife sits next to her.
      b.   #Every married man sits next to her.

It is plausible that *man who has a wife* and *married man* equally bring to mind the relation of marriage, and yet the pronoun in (24a) is natural while the one in (24b) is not. As we noted above in Chapter 8, Elbourne (2005, 2008) has proposed an analysis of definite and demonstrative descriptions which incorporates a variable similar to that proposed by Cooper. In Elbourne (2005) this kind of analysis is extended also to E-type pronouns. One difference between Cooper's analysis and Elbourne's is that Elbourne's relation variable is of the type of a CNP constituent. Thus, while (24a) provides a natural antecedent for such a variable (the word *wife*), (24b) does not.[13] This also presumably provides an explanation for the acceptability of examples like (25) below (from Jacobson 2000: n. 11): we are to imagine that the speaker is a new faculty member who has just gotten her first paycheck out of her mailbox, and is waving it in the air.

(25) Do most faculty members deposit it in the Credit Union?

Although the relevant CNP has not been uttered, the waved paycheck makes this content available.

(iii) *Singular vs plural.* The final issue I would like to mention here concerns the difference between singular and plural pronouns which have universally quantified antecedents. We have been assuming all along that binding by a quantificational determiner is strictly a sentence-level phenomenon, and cannot occur across sentence boundaries—including sentential conjunctions. This assumption is typically illustrated with singular pronouns, as in the examples below in (26) (with assumed coreference between the quantified NPs in the first sentence and the pronouns in the second, respectively).

---

[13] See Roberts (2002, 2003) for a different approach within the dynamic semantics framework. Elbourne (2008: 459–62) presents some problems for Roberts's approach.

(26) a. Every man walks in the park. *He whistles. [= Elbourne
          2005: 25, ex. 57]
      b. Every woman was invited. *She was pleased. [≈ Heim and
          Kratzer 1998: 285, ex. 11[14]]

And indeed, it seems crucial to the assumed illformedness here that the
pronouns (*he* and *she*) are singular; as we noted above in Chapter 7,
plural pronouns occur more freely than singular ones, having more
variable reference possibilities. Thus the examples in (27) are fine.

(27) a. Every man walks in the park. They whistle.
      b. Every woman was invited. They were pleased.

Presumably the occurrences of *they* here would be classified as E-type
pronouns, denoting, respectively, the men and the women mentioned
in the preceding sentence.

   The puzzling thing is that there are a number of examples floating
around in the literature of singular pronouns with universally quantified antecedents in a preceding sentence. Roberts (1989: 717) attributes
(28a) below to Barbara Partee; (28b) is from Fodor and Sag (1982: 393,
n. 6).

(28) a. Each degree candidate walked to the stage. He took his
          diploma from the Dean and returned to his seat.
      b. Each student in the syntax class cheated on the exam, and
          he was reprimanded by the Dean.

Roberts refers to this phenomenon as TELESCOPING: "from a discussion of the general case, we zoom in to examine a particular instance"
(Roberts 1989: 717). Undoubtedly the determiner *each*, which is the
most intensely distributive of the universal determiners, helps to get
this effect. However we can also find examples with *every*, e.g. (29).[15]

(29) [Every woman]ᵢ had a hat. Sheᵢ wore it rakishly.

---

[14] I've taken the liberty of adding the asterisk to this example. Heim and Kratzer note
that this example "does not allow any anaphoric reading" (285).
[15] Possibly we can even have examples like (i) below:

(i) No woman wore a hat to the reception. If she had, she would have felt very out of
     place.

Implicitly (i) is about a fixed group of women—those who were at the reception. Thus
perhaps *no woman* is equivalent (in some sense) to *none of the women*. However a full
explanation of why the singular pronouns are ok here remains to be given.

And with a little work, examples very like those in (26) can be made quite acceptable, as shown in (30).

(30)   a.   [Every man who has a dog]$_i$ walks it in the park. He$_i$ whistles to call his dog, or just for the pure joy of it.
       b.   [Every woman]$_i$ was invited, and she$_i$ showed her pleasure by bringing a gift.

Of course we have to be careful of the "Zimmer Effect"—so called from the observation by Karl Zimmer that, other things being equal, the longer the sentence, the better it sounds. However (29) is pretty simple and basic, and it sounds impeccable to me.

In each of these cases, the pronoun in question could be replaced with a singular definite description, as shown in (31).

(31)   a.   Each degree candidate walked to the stage. The candidate took his diploma from the Dean and returned to his seat.
       b.   Each student in the syntax class cheated on the exam, and the student was reprimanded by the Dean.
       c.   Every woman had a hat. The woman wore it rakishly.
       d.   Every man who has a dog walks it in the park. The man whistles to call his dog, or just for the pure joy of it.
       e.   Every woman was invited, and the woman showed her pleasure by bringing a gift.

This would suggest that we once again have E-type pronouns, but why singular pronouns are permitted here and not in other cases is a mystery to me.[16]

I'm afraid we must leave these problems in an unresolved state. Donkey sentences as well as the other problematic sorts of sentences considered here continue to be a subject of research, and I think it is fair to say that there is no widespread agreement as yet on the correct analysis. To that extent, then, it cannot be said that we have a full understanding of how pronouns work, but see, for example, Roberts

---

[16] For what it's worth, Fodor and Sag noted the difference between their example (28b) and the much less acceptable (i) below.

(i)   Each student in the syntax class was accused of cheating on the exam, and he has a Ph.D. in astrophysics.

However they did not offer an explanation for this difference in behavior. Roberts suggests that the problem with (i) has to do with "narrative continuity"—there is not enough of it in (i) for the telescoping effect (Roberts 1989: 717f.).

(2004), Barker and Jacobson (2007), Elbourne (2008), and the works cited there for continuing discussion.

10.2 Choosing NPs in discourse

We turn now to the more general problem of how speakers choose NPs to refer to things in the course of a discourse. There are, of course, myriad ways to talk about anything—*a cat, the cat, our black cat, Louise, she*. In this section we will look at some ideas about what determines which NP a speaker should use. We'll start by reviewing Ellen Prince's work on this topic, and then turn to the approaches of Mira Ariel and Jeanette Gundel, Nancy Hedberg, and Ron Zacharski.

10.2.1 Prince (1981b, 1992)

Prince (1981b) was concerned with how information is organized in a text, and specifically how the speaker's assumptions about the addressee's knowledge state affects this organization. Prince distinguished several different categories of addressees' assumed familiarity with denoted entities—including Brand-new, for entities that are being introduced to the addressee for the first time; Unused, for entities that the speaker assumes the addressee is familiar with, but which haven't been alluded to in the current conversation; Inferable,[17] for entities which haven't been specifically mentioned but whose existence can be inferred; and Evoked, for those entities which have either been mentioned in the discourse, or which are denizens of the text-external world. These categories are illustrated in the monolog in (32).

(32)   Guess what—I [Evoked-external] just ran into <u>Jeanne</u> [Unused]. <u>She</u> [Evoked-text] bought <u>a dog</u> [Brand-new] yesterday. It's a Pekinese puppy—looks just like <u>that dog over there</u> [Evoked-external]. <u>The guy she bought it from</u> [Inferable] said it had been abandoned, poor thing—<u>one of its ears</u> [Inferable] was missing.

As would be expected, Brand-new entities are typically introduced with indefinite or (other) weak quantificational NPs, while Unused or Evoked entities are usually referred to with definites—pronouns,

---

[17] Prince consistently spells "inferable" with two r's (as have many others following her). However none of my dictionaries allow that spelling.

proper names, definite or demonstrative descriptions, or strong quantifiers. Pronouns, as we would expect, are reserved for Evoked entities of one kind or another. A definite description would be the most common type of form used for an Inferable entity that is unique (like the guy Jeanne bought her dog from, in (32)), while an indefinite would be used in the case of more than one (the dog's missing ear).[18]

Eleven years later, Prince (1992) revised her approach, distinguishing two cross-cutting parameters. Discourse-new and Discourse-old, as the names suggest, distinguish entities which have not been explicitly introduced into the conversation from those which have. Hearer-new and Hearer-old, on the other hand, distinguish entities assumed to be completely new to the addressee from those which the speaker assumes the addressee is familiar with. Anything Discourse-old is assumed automatically to be Hearer-old (although that assumption has been challenged—see Birner (2006)), but the other three cells are all live possibilities. Discourse-new, Hearer-new NPs correspond pretty directly to Prince's earlier category of Brand-new; Discourse-new, Hearer-old is the category for Unused entities (and presumably also for situationally Evoked entities—Prince did not discuss those entities in this paper); and Discourse-old (and thus also Hearer-old) corresponds to the earlier category of textually Evoked entities. It was not immediately obvious where the earlier category of Inferables fits in the new scheme, but in fact they seemed to pattern with non-pronominal Discourse-old NPs.

As noted above in n. 18, Prince's main concern in this work was to examine what factors determine the grammatical placement of NPs—especially what determines whether or not a particular NP occurs in subject position. Nevertheless, her categories raise the question of whether looking at NPs from the point of view of assumptions about the cognitive status of the addressee can lead to any insights. This has been the goal of several other researchers, to whom we now turn.

---

[18] In addition to categorizing the informational content of NPs, Prince was interested in determining any patterns of grammatical placement for these various categories. She examined one oral and one written text, and determined that there did indeed seem to be patterns, and furthermore some systematic differences between the oral and written texts. Interestingly, while the oral text had almost exclusively NPs denoting Evoked entities in subject position (93%), the written text had almost as great a proportion of NPs denoting Inferable entities as those for Evoked (42% to 50%).

10.2.2 Ariel (1988, 1990)

As we have just seen, Prince's work focused on NP referents—entities out in the world. Mira Ariel has instead concentrated on the forms of NPs used to denote those entities. Her theory is that choice of NP form is determined by how ACCESSIBLE its referent is. Accessibility, in Ariel's theory, is determined by a number of factors. One important one is whether an entity is being referred to for the first time, or whether the NP in question is anaphoric. For anaphoric NPs an important factor is distance—how far back in the discourse its antecedent is. However, though distance is important it is not the only factor determining the accessibility of an anaphoric NP's denotation. Other factors are the following: salience, which is related to, but not identical with, topic-hood; how many competitors this entity has (i.e. how many other things have been referred to in the preceding text); and facts about the structure of the intervening discourse. To these factors Ariel (2001) adds "expectedness"—the degree to which that referent would be typical.

In her earlier work (Ariel 1988, 1990), Ariel had grouped NPs into three main large categories—those associated with Low Accessibility, Intermediate Accessibility, and High Accessibility. In the first group are proper names and definite descriptions, the second group contains first- and second-person pronouns and demonstratives, and the third, High Accessibility, group contains third-person pronouns as well as Ø NPs, as illustrated in (33) (which might be found, e.g., on the lint filter of a clothes dryer).

(33)   Clean Ø before loading Ø.

However this gives a much too simplified picture; as Ariel notes, full proper names have a different distribution from either last names used alone or first names. Similarly long, more informative definite descriptions require less accessibility than short, less informative ones. Consequently Ariel (2001) abandons the three-way distinction in favor of a more articulated picture, in which accessibility is a scale with many degrees.

Another aspect of this approach, and an important one, is the claim that degrees of accessibility are actually encoded in the different NP forms. Thus Ariel says: "I suggest that natural languages code the *degree of Accessibility* of an antecedent...." (Ariel 1990: 10, italics in original); and "each referring expression codes a specific (and different) degree of mental accessibility" (Ariel 2001: 30). Kent Bach (1998) suggests that this assumption is problematic, and that the facts about accessibility may instead follow from the informativeness of the NPs themselves:

> The obvious alternative [to the assumption that degrees of accessibility are encoded] is that the different degrees of accessibility associated with different types of referring expressions are not encoded at all and that the correlation is instead a byproduct of the interaction between semantic information that *is* encoded by these expressions and general facts about rational communication.
>
> (Bach 1998: 336, italics in original)

Thus, for example, proper names have, in principle, a unique referent; definite descriptions also have a unique intended referent, and in addition may encode any amount of descriptive content whatsoever, from a detailed description (e.g. *woman wearing a blue suit and sitting to the right of the priest*) to what is conveyed by a single very general common noun like *thing*; third-person pronouns encode only number and (for singulars) gender; while Ø anaphors contain no information at all (although their syntactic location marks an NP slot). Although Ariel acknowledges that the information content of an NP correlates with its place in the accessibility hierarchy, nevertheless she apparently does not believe it is sufficient to determine that place. Instead, as we just saw, she believes that the NPs themselves encode the degree of accessibility enjoyed by their denotations.[19] I agree with Bach that our aim should be to try to derive facts about language use from what is obviously encoded in various expression types. Of course it is one thing to note the desirability of deriving use from form and content, and another to actually do this. Before we try, we should take a look at a different approach along similar lines.

10.2.3 Gundel, Hedberg, and Zacharski (1993, 2001)

In their classic 1993 paper, Gundel et al. proposed a "givenness" hierarchy—a ranking of NP types based on what speakers can be expected to assume about the cognitive status for the addressee of the NP's denotation. That hierarchy is given below in (34) (=Gundel et al. 1993: ex. 1).

---

[19] One practical difficulty, not noted by Bach, is the locus of this encoding. As Ariel points out, different kinds of definite descriptions are used with different levels of accessibility, so we cannot suppose that it is the definite article itself that is encoded with a particular degree.

(34) THE GIVENNESS HIERARCHY:

in focus >	activated >	familiar >	uniquely identifiable >	referential >	type identifiable
it	that this this N	that N	the N	indefinite this N	a N

The hierarchy in (34) is intended to be a linear one—each category imposes all the constraints of all the categories to its right, plus something else. The least restrictive category, the one on the far right, requires only "type identifiability"—that the addressee is presumed to be familiar with the kind in question. Thus a speaker's use of the NP *a morphophonological process* indicates that that speaker assumes that their addressee knows what morphophonological processes are. The next place on the hierarchy—referentiality—requires in addition to type identifiability that the addressee be able to construct a mental representation of such an entity. The indefinite *this* NPs, which we have run across several times before, indicate that the speaker has a particular entity in mind as denoted by the NP, one that he or she intends to speak further about.

The definite article in English, according to Gundel et al., imposes a further requirement—that the addressee be able to identify the entity which the speaker is speaking about, based on the descriptive content of the NP. Use of NPs of the form *that* CNP conveys, in addition, that the speaker believes the addressee to be familiar with the referent in question. Demonstrative pronouns, and demonstrative NPs of the form *this* CNP, require their referents to be not only familiar to the addressee, but also present in their consciousness, while third-person pronouns require a referent to be not only activated but in focus—at the center of attention.[20]

These usages may be illustrated in the series of examples in (35) and (36) (adapted from Gundel et al. 1993).

(35) I couldn't sleep last night...
   a. ...a dog kept me awake.
   b. ...this dog kept me awake.
   c. ...the dog next door kept me awake.
   d. ...that dog next door kept me awake.

[20] This sense of "focus" must be distinguished from the sense we have seen before, where "focus" meant (roughly) the new information in an utterance. The two senses are almost diametrically opposed.

(36)   <u>That</u>, in turn, kept my husband awake. <u>He</u> was furious.

As we can see from these examples, the successively higher places in the referential hierarchy indicate an assumed correspondingly higher place in the awareness of the addressee.

Note in particular the feature that distinguishes definite descriptions from distal demonstratives on this account—assumed familiarity to the addressee. Interestingly, this feature was not included in the accounts of demonstrative descriptions reviewed above in Chapter 8.[21] The reader may also recall that we were unable to account, in that chapter, for any difference between pairs (37) and (38).

(37)   a.   <u>Those students who finish early</u> should wait for the others.
        b.   <u>The students who finish early</u> should wait for the others.

(38)   a.   Ultimately Bill selected <u>that car which had seemed the flashiest</u>.
        b.   Ultimately Bill selected <u>the car which had seemed the flashiest</u>.

The feature noted by Gundel et al. may be helpful here; it predicts that in a context where an intended referent is uniquely identifiable but not familiar to the addressee, a definite description should sound better than a demonstrative description. So for (38), for example, consider a situation in which Bill has been car-hunting, but nothing has been mentioned about which features he is likely to consider in his search. In such a context, (38a) is somewhat strained while (38b) is completely natural.

An additional feature of the Gundel et al. analysis which sets it apart from that proposed by Ariel is that these various categories are not mutually exclusive.[22] Any NP which satisfies the requirements on assumed cognition of a place in the hierarchy may, in principle, be used in situations where more stringent requirements would also be satisfied. Thus, again in principle, an indefinite description could be used any time, as long as the minimal requirement of type identifiability were satisfied. And indeed, we can construct contexts in which

[21] Elbourne (2008: 445) notes this feature, but only for some examples involving generic situations.

[22] There are other differences between the two. Ariel considers more different types of NP, including proper names and Ø NPs, while Gundel et al. include a cross-linguistic study of four languages in addition to English: Japanese, Mandarin Chinese, Russian, and Spanish.

that might be the case. Suppose, for example, that you and I are observing a small child who is having a tantrum. You might assert (39)

(39)   Someone is ready for their nap.

using an indefinite to speak of an entity who would be considered to be at least activated and probably also in focus.[23] According to Gundel et al., the reason we do not usually use an NP above its station, so to speak, is Gricean. Use of an indefinite description typically conversationally implicates that the speaker does not expect the addressee to be able to identify a unique referent, much less one that they would be assumed to be familiar with. This in turn means that in special circumstances, as in the case of (39) above where indirectness is motivated by a desire to appear polite, the relevant implicature will not be either intended or drawn. (This is a generalization of the kind of reasoning proposed by Hawkins (1991), which we looked at above in §9.2.1.)

Although the analysis of Gundel et al. differs importantly from that proposed by Ariel, they do share the claim that information about accessibility/assumed cognitive status of denotations is encoded in the NPs that denote them. Thus the abstract of Gundel et al. (1993) begins: "In this paper we propose six implicationally related cognitive statuses relevant for explicating the use of referring expressions in natural language discourse. These statuses are the conventional meanings signaled by determiners and pronouns..." (Gundel et al. 1993: 274). Thus this work too potentially runs afoul of Bach's criticism, cited above, that cognitive statuses resulting in these patterns of use should not be regarded as semantically encoded but should rather be derivable via pragmatic considerations. It is time to look more closely at this assumption of semantic encoding.

10.2.4 What is encoded?

As we noted above, certain elements of meaning are unquestionably encoded in NPs, or their determiners, and it is Bach's idea that the place of a given NP type in a correct cognitive hierarchy, and thus facts about its use that would be predicted from that place, ought to be derivable from those patently encoded elements of meaning. Another

---

[23] Such examples seem to present a problem for Roberts's (2004: 514) claim that indefinites presuppose that their denotation is new with respect to the common ground. It may be discourse novelty that is relevant here.

potential troubling feature of the approach of Ariel and Gundel et al. is the lack of intuitive contact with some of the proposed degrees of accessibility or cognitive statuses; usually we can be made consciously aware of aspects of the meaning of expressions of our language, but in these cases that is not so.[24] So let us see how far we can get using information that is obviously encoded.

In some cases the derivation of usage patterns from unquestionably encoded meanings seems quite smooth. Third-person pronouns in English encode only minimal information—number in the case of plurals, number and gender in the case of singulars. Thus it stands to reason that these will not be used unless the intended referent is extremely clear, which would typically only be the case if that entity were currently under discussion (though above in Chapter 8 I mentioned the department secretary who often referred to her boss with a pronoun on first mention—apparently the boss was such a dominant figure in her workday life that she assumed that he would always be in focus). Of course information from the rest of the sentence can also serve as a clue; examples like the pair in (40) (originally pointed out by Terry Winograd (1972)) are well known.

(40)   The university administrators had the demonstrators arrested...
         a.   ...because <u>they</u> were worried about damage to the campus.
         b.   ...because <u>they</u> were threatening damage to the campus.

Although the university administrators and the demonstrators are pretty much equally in focus in these examples, the property ascribed to the referent of *they* makes clear that in (40a) it is the administrators that are being referred to while in (40b) it is the demonstrators.[25]

The usage conventions for proper names seem similarly to follow from their content. As we have noted several times, although proper

[24] One must be careful here of course. It is a truism these days that correct semantic analyses need not be intuitively accessible. However when we are talking about word meanings the situation may be a bit different.

[25] These examples seem to present a problem for the theory presented in Roberts (2004), which does not take into account the sentential context in which the pronoun occurs (cf. the conditions she gives on p. 517). There is, of course, much more that could be said about how pronouns are used in discourse, and what determines which referents are suitable for pronouns. Centering Theory is one prominent approach—see Walker et al. (1998), and the works cited there. See also Kehler et al. (2008), Garnham and Cowles (2008) for alternatives.

names (in English anyway) do not encode uniqueness of referent morphemically (e.g. in a special determiner or affix), nevertheless this aspect of their meaning emerges in their grammatical peculiarities—the fact that they constitute a complete NP and do not take determiners or restrictive modifiers.[26] On the other hand, proper names do not include descriptive content which might enable an addressee to figure out the referent, so typically a speaker will not use one unless they assume that their addressee already knows the referent by that name. (In written contexts such as newspapers, initial use of a proper name is often accompanied by an appositive description to help in identifying the referent—see example (41) below.)

   Similarly definite descriptions may encode a lot or only a little information. In general we would expect that when a definite description encodes a lot of information it is because the speaker feels that the addressee needs that much information in order to be able to uniquely identify the referent. Of course there are circumstances in which this would not be the case; newspapers are known for bundling substantial amounts of information into NPs, simply as a way of conveying that information efficiently. Thus examples like the one in (41) below are not unusual in this context.

(41)   Police said Thursday that they have caught the Baseline Killer, the gunman responsible for nine slayings that spread terror across the Phoenix area for nearly a year and a half. [Traverse City Record Eagle, 12/08/06, p. 5A; underlining added.]

In this example an entity, the Baseline Killer, has already been identified and can be assumed to be at the forefront of the reader's consciousness. The definite description here is not being used for referential purposes but rather to supply information about an entity that has already been identified. The definite description in (41) is used appositively, but it is relatively easy to find examples where definite descriptions are used referentially for entities in focus, where a pronoun could easily have been used but without the benefit of providing additional facts about that entity. (42) is from today's paper.

---

[26] Following Whorf (1945) we might refer to this as a "covert" categorization.

(42)   Super Bowl hero Plaxico Burress accidentally shot himself in the
        right thigh and spent the night in the hospital, another dramatic
        turn in a tumultuous season in which <u>the star New York Giants
        receiver</u> has been fined and suspended. [Traverse City Record
        Eagle, 11/30/08, p. 4C; underlining added]

This item is all about Plaxico Burress, who is thus in focus at the point
at which the underlined definite description occurs. A pronoun, or the
last name (*Burress*) by itself, could easily have been used instead, but
would not have provided the additional information.[27]

When we come to demonstrative pronouns and determiners, things
become more complicated. In the unmarked case *this* contrasts with
that, like *here* vs *there*, in being proximal as opposed to distal. It is clear
that no absolute sense of distance is involved however, since we readily
speak of how things are here in this galaxy, for instance. Rather what is
crucial is the **contrast** between proximal and distal elements—we
contrast this galaxy, the one containing us, with others that do not
contain us and hence are more distant. But given these facts there
remain patterns of use which do not seem easily explainable, even with
a lot of hand-waving. One is the necessarily specific but nevertheless
indefinite *this* that keeps cropping up (as in *There was <u>this strange dog
at the pound today</u>*). It would be very interesting to know how this
determiner arose (assuming it to be a separate lexical item from the
demonstrative *this*). Presumably it evolved out of the standard proximal use of the deictic determiner of the same form, but exactly how is
a mystery to me. And another interesting contrast is the one noted
above between NPs with the definite article and those with *that*, as
illustrated in the difference between (35c) and (35d) from above,
repeated here.

(35)   c.   ...<u>the dog next door</u> kept me awake.
        d.   ...<u>that dog next door</u> kept me awake.

I agree with Gundel et al. that the use of *that* signals an assumption that
the addressee is familiar with the referent in question, and that this is
the crucial difference between *that* and *the* in such NPs, but how this
came about (again, presumably from the original distal deictic use) is
another mystery. Thus there is still quite a way to go in making good

---

[27] This type of example is especially difficult for Ariel's theory to account for; if definite
descriptions really encoded Low Accessibility, then examples like (42) should be puzzling
to readers. But obviously they aren't, or sports pages wouldn't be filled with them.

on Bach's claim that information about cognitive status should be derivable from obviously encoded semantic features.

We turn now to the issue of discourse referents, and how they are related to ordinary referents.

10.3 Referents

Almost the whole of this book has been concerned with NPs and how they achieve their work of relating to extralinguistic stuff. We turn in this section to that stuff—the referents themselves. We'll take on two issues: What are discourse referents and how do they relate to "real" referents? And what do we do about reference to fictional and other nonexistent entities? Each of these topics deserves much more consideration than we can give it here.

10.3.1 Discourse referents

Earlier in this chapter we were introduced to the various dynamic semantics approaches which in one way or another make discourse referents central to the interpretation of texts and conversations. The concept of a discourse referent goes back earlier than these approaches, however, most notably to Lauri Karttunen's classic paper "Discourse Referents" (1976; cf. also Karttunen (1969a, b)). In that paper Karttunen was primarily concerned with indefinite descriptions and whether or not they could serve as antecedents for referential expressions. He noted, e.g., the difference between (43a) and (43b) (Karttunen's (3) and (4) respectively).

(43)   a.   Bill has a car. It/the car/Bill's car is black.
        b.   Bill doesn't have a car. *It/the car/Bill's car is black.

The definite NPs in (43a) are E-type anaphors, and we have already seen that they are only suitable if the prior discourse has established something for them to denote.

It might be thought that discourse referents associated with true discourses would correspond one-to-one to actual entities (and thus to referents *tout court*), but we have already seen that things are more complicated than that. The variety of intensional constructions, as well as other phenomena included under the heading of modal subordination, shows that a true discourse can introduce discourse entities which are not actual. This happens when they are introduced within the scope of a quantifier or in an intensional context, as in the examples below (reproduced from above).

(44) a. Mary hopes to hire some tax consultants, and thinks that they'll help her get a big refund.
      b. Every farmer who owns a donkey feeds it. He takes it to the vet when it isn't feeling well.
      c. A thief might break into the house. He would steal the silver.

Similarly generic indefinites introduce the GEN operator, which allows anaphoric reference within its scope.

(45) A panda bear likes to eat bamboo. She'll pull the leaves off and chew them up.

Examples like (45) should probably also be included under the heading of "modal subordination."

The examples in the preceding paragraph are cases where there is no actual entity corresponding to the indefinite description. Heim (1983) points out the converse kind of case, where there may be more than one actual entity corresponding to a discourse referent, as in (46).

(46) John came, and so did Mary. *One of them* brought a cake. [= Heim 1983: ex. 4; italics in original]

In this case the indefinite *one of them* introduces a new discourse entity, although one which must be identified with either John or Mary for (46) to be true.

So it is clear that discourse referents do not match up cleanly with referents out there in the world. In the dynamic semantics approaches mentioned above, these differences are handled with semantic rules which specify the ultimate truth conditions for texts, so that discourse referents which are introduced within the scope of operators or which must be identified with another undetermined discourse referent (as in (46)), do not end up being required to correspond to independently existing entities in the actual world. I refer the reader to the works cited above by Kamp, Heim, and Groenendijk and Stokhof for the details of how this works.

Suppose now that we have sorted out all of these special kinds of cases, where discourse referents are within the scope of some operator or must be identified with another undetermined discourse referent, and put them off to one side. What about a simple example such as (47)?

(47)   A man is downstairs in the kitchen. He is cooking dinner.

I have just uttered (47) as a description of the current situation in my home. A man, my partner Larry Hauser, is downstairs in the kitchen and he is cooking dinner. In this case the discourse referent established in my utterance of the NP *a man* matches up nicely with Larry, whose behavior in turn makes my utterance of the whole of (47) true. Then we may still raise at least two questions: (a) Do *a man* and *he* in (47) refer to Larry? (b) By *Larry* in the preceding question, do we mean an actual flesh-and-blood person, or some mental construct?

Let us take the first question first. Above in Chapter 6 we noted a strong argument against considering Larry to be the semantic referent of the NP *a man* in (47), an argument for which there is no refutation that I know of. The problem is that if we suppose *a man* in (47) refers to Larry, then if it turns out that Larry is not downstairs in the kitchen, but another man does happen to be there, then the first sentence of (47) would have to be considered false as uttered. But it is just not possible to see that sentence as expressing a false proposition under those circumstances. (Cf. also the arguments in Russell (1919); these are discussed in Ludlow and Neale (1991).) We may admit that in uttering (47) I intended to speak of Larry in using the NP *a man*, but that is a different matter from supposing that Larry is the referent of the NP itself. Thus this would be another case in which a discourse referent did not match up with a semantic referent—more subtle than the others because in this case we do have an actual individual who the speaker means to speak about in using the NP *a man*.

What about the pronoun *he* in the second sentence of (47), as uttered by me now in the situation described above? Does that pronoun have Larry as its semantic referent? If this pronoun was uttered with the intention of having *a man* as its antecedent, then no—it is not referential and does not have Larry as its referent. This follows by the same reasoning as was used in the preceding paragraph—the discourse in (47) is made true if and only if there is a man downstairs in the kitchen who is cooking dinner, regardless of whether or not that person is who I think it is. Of course it would be possible for the sequence in (47) to be uttered by someone who intends to use *he* deictically, or anaphorically but with a different antecedent than *a man*—that would be a different situation. But in the situation as described, neither *a man* nor *he* is referential.

The second question is a rather more complex and difficult one—the question of what it is that we are talking about, whether by "what we are talking about" we mean speaker's referents or semantic referents or both. The commonsense view, sometimes called SEMANTIC REALISM, is that in ordinary situations like the one described above we are in fact talking about ordinary people and things that exist out in the world independent of our perceptions—like Larry and the kitchen and the dinner which he is cooking there. Semantic realism is opposed to a number of views, one of which, called SEMANTIC IDEALISM (or ANTI-REALISM), is that we are not actually talking about mind-independent things in the world, but only about entities constructed with our thoughts and dependent in various ways on how we think about them. There is not time here (or maybe even in the life of the universe) to resolve this issue, but fortunately it does not seem to make much difference in our semantics, so we may set it to one side.[28]

10.3.2 Nonexistent entities

In the preceding subsection we saw that the introduction of discourse entities within the scope of expressions can result in their not being required to correspond to anything in the actual world in order for that discourse to be true. However, we need to take note of the possibility of using expressions which look like perfectly good referring expressions, and which are not in any kind of intensional context, to talk about things which do not exist. The most obvious case is that of the names of fictional characters, like *Sherlock Holmes* and *Santa Claus*, so let us start there. As we saw in Chapter 5, empty names like these seemed to pose a serious problem for the nondescriptional theory of proper names. I suggested there that the Russellian Singular Proposition, or RSP, view was in worse shape in this regard than the Constant Individual Concept, or CIC, view. Let us look a little more closely at the situation.

One thing that makes fictional names tricky is that we want to make seemingly contradictory pairs of sentences like those in (48) both true.

(48) a. Sherlock Holmes played the violin.
       b. Sherlock Holmes never really existed.

---

[28] Readers who are interested in pursuing this topic might look at my 1997 article "Models, truth and semantics" and the works cited there as one possible place to start.

David Lewis (1978) argues that examples like (48a) are true only when heard with a tacit prefix—something like *according to such-and-such fiction*. Such propositions are then evaluated against alternative possible worlds where the fiction in question is told as truth rather than fiction. (Cf. also Brock (2002).) On the other hand, (48b) is true without such a prefix, when we are speaking simply of the actual world.

This seems like an approach which the CIC supporter could adopt fairly straightforwardly. If the name *Sherlock Holmes* expresses a constant individual concept, then in worlds that comport with Conan Doyle's fictions, (48a) will be correctly evaluated as true. On the other hand the absence of Sherlock Holmes in the actual world (at any time) makes (48b) true as well. However there is a potential complication which must be acknowledged. Recall that Kripke's nondescriptional theory of proper names (which we are implicitly adopting) was associated with a metaphysical claim about the source of those names. This was the causal/historical chain theory, which requires an initial dubbing of an entity with the name in question before the name is passed down through the speech community. That dubbing, in turn, is typically held to require a causal (i.e. perceptual) relation between the namer and the namee. If that is a requisite part of the story then we have a problem, since fictional characters can't have been dubbed. However I tried to suggest in Chapter 5 that this part of the theory is questionable on independent grounds.

Let us see what supporters of the RSP view have had to say about these kinds of examples. Salmon (1998), following van Inwagen (1977, 1983), argues that fictional characters like Santa Claus and Sherlock Holmes **do** exist, as abstract objects within stories. (See also Soames (2002: 89–95).) Thus sentences like (48a) are not literally true; however, understood as a description within the fiction, with a tacit prefix like *According to the Conan Doyle stories*, (48a) does express a truth. "The object-fictional sentence is not true with respect to the real world, since abstract entities make terrible musicians. But it is true with respect to the fiction or true 'in the world of the fiction'" (Salmon 1998: 303). This is not so different from the Lewis account.

The problem, then, is how to account for the apparent truth of (48b) as well. Given that Sherlock Holmes does exist, on this view, (48b) should be considered false, contrary to our intuitions. Salmon argues that it is indeed false, and that its seeming truth is a result of a reinterpretation of the name *Sherlock Holmes* as a disguised description, to mean something like "Holmes as he is depicted in the Conan

Doyle stories." But such a true proposition, he suggests, is not one actually expressed by (48b). "Since this interpretation requires a reinterpretation of the name, it might be more correct to say that the speaker expresses this proposition than to say that [*Sherlock Holmes does not exist*] itself does" (Salmon 1998: 304). In response, it could be objected that Salmon seems to be assuming an ambiguity in the name *Holmes* for which there is insufficient support.

The problem of names for fictional entities might not seem that pressing. However Salmon's discussion of the issue brings to light another class of entities we like to talk about which are a bit more important to us. Consider the sentences in (50):

(50) a.   Socrates exists.
      b.   Socrates does not exist.

About these Salmon asserts the following:

> ... [50a] is true with respect to the year 400 BC, and [50b] false. With respect to the present day, these truth values are reversed. Socrates is long gone. **Consequently, singular propositions about him, which once existed, also no longer exist.**
>
> (Salmon 1998: 286; boldface added)

On Salmon's RSP view the propositions expressed by sentences with the proper name *Socrates* contain Socrates himself as a constituent. Since Socrates is no longer with us, neither are the propositions expressed by such sentences.[29]

Notice how far-reaching this conclusion is. It would hold not only for assertions about Socrates, but for assertions about any no longer existing thing—Bertrand Russell, W.V. Quine, my parents (Horace and Bobbie Abbott), the World Trade Center. And not only for assertions about them using proper names but also for those expressed using referential definite descriptions, pronouns, or demonstratives (the latter perhaps with the aid of an index such as a photo), which together must surely constitute the bulk of all of our assertions about them.

Salmon argues that this is nothing to worry about. It is clear from the quote above that he thinks nonexistence of a proposition is no bar to its having a truth value. Similarly he believes that nonexistent propositions can serve as the objects of propositional attitudes—just

---

[29] It should be noted that Kent Bach apparently holds a different view on this issue. He says: "A singular proposition is not only object-involving but also object-dependent, in that it would not exist if its object-constituent did not exist (**at some time or other**)" (Bach 2006: 530, n. 13; boldface added).

as Socrates' current nonexistence does not prevent our admiring him, so the nonexistence of propositions about him does not prevent our grasping them. (Cf. Salmon (1998: 290f.)) But I'm not sure this analogy goes through. For one thing, note that although Socrates himself is completely nonexistent at this time, parts of the propositions about him do exist—properties like not existing, having been curious or snub-nosed, and so forth. More importantly, while Socrates' nonexistence prevents him from having many properties and relations that living people have (e.g. being located somewhere, loving someone or something, needing a shave), it seems that there is no property or relation that the nonexistence of a proposition, or one or more of its parts, prevents it from indulging in. Given that propositions with missing parts are able to function completely normally, one wonders whether those missing parts really play any role at all—whether they are really missing, or were never there to begin with. Although the CIC theory is not without its own problems, it does have the advantage of providing us with all the constituents for propositions that we need.

10.4 Concluding remarks

In this chapter we have broadened our view to include issues of reference in discourse. We looked at the problem of donkey pronouns, and the dynamic semantics theories that were designed, in part, to solve that problem. Ultimately, however, it seemed that the E-type solution—viewing donkey pronouns as similar to anaphoric definite descriptions—held more promise. Following that we looked at some more general theories about the use of different kinds of NPs in discourse to talk about things. One of the remaining challenges in this area is to try to derive the patterns of language use from meanings which can plausibly be assigned to the different kinds of NP, plus plausible pragmatic principles. And finally we considered, all too briefly, the nature of discourse referents, how they correspond (or fail to correspond) to stuff out there in the world we talk about, and what the consequences of that might be for theories of reference.

11

Taking stock

The word is half his that speaks and half his that hears it.
Michel de Montaigne, *Essays*

We noted in the introductory chapter that there is some tension between the semantic conception of reference and the pragmatic conception of reference. Now that we have a somewhat fuller idea of the semantics and pragmatics of NPs, perhaps we can resolve some of this tension. But before commencing with that we need to clear something up: a thread which has run through several of the preceding chapters has been an attempt to argue for the utility of individual concepts. As we will see, this issue is relevant to the question of which NPs can be involved in referential relations, and in §11.1 an attempt will be made to draw the thread together into a nice tidy knot. With that settled, we'll attack the pragmatic conception of reference in §11.2, and try to determine which kinds of NPs can appropriately be described as being used to refer. Following that we will take on the semantic conception, and again see which NPs (if any) have the right stuff. We'll be limiting ourselves here to **singular** reference, as is customary in discussions of this type.[1] Of course, as we saw in Chapter 2, Frege assumed compositionality at the level of reference—that the reference (truth value) of a whole sentence is determined by the references of its parts (plus the way they are put together syntactically). This suggests that each of the constituents in a sentence would need to contribute some kind of reference in order that the truth value of the whole can be determined, but in many cases that contribution won't be an ordinary single entity but rather a set, or a function, or some other sort of thing. We'll be ignoring those other cases for the most part here. In the course

---

[1] Ever since Chapter 7 we've known that it is possible for groups of entities to behave like single individuals. So when we speak of individuals, entities, or singular referents, it should be understood that this can include plural entities of one kind or another.

of the discussion we'll be looking in particular at the views of Kent Bach—one of the most prolific writers on the subject of reference. The final section has some concluding thoughts.

11.1 Individual concepts

It will be recalled that individual concepts are functions from possible world-time points (or possible situations) to individuals. As we saw in Chapter 3, constant individual concepts, which pick out the same individual no matter what the circumstances, correspond one-to-one to individuals. There are several ways in which it seems to me that individual concepts, and in particular constant individual concepts, can be useful. One is as the interpretation of nondescriptional singular terms (proper names and deictically used pronouns); another is as the interpretation of referentially used definite and demonstrative descriptions. As we've seen, many philosophers (e.g. Kaplan, Salmon, Soames) currently adopt the view that such expressions contribute actual entities to the propositions expressed by sentences containing them, in effect taking the denotation/reference of such an NP as its connotation/sense. (This results in the kind of propositions we've been calling "RSPs," for "Russellian Singular Propositions.") In the preceding chapter we looked at one serious problem for this view—that presented by NPs with no (currently existing) denotation. We reviewed a prominent response to that problem, but found it less than completely satisfying. If instead of the actual individuals we take constant individual concepts as the expressed content of these NPs, we skirt the problem of nonexistent entities.[2]

The other use I suggested for constant individual concepts was as the interpretation for specifically used indefinite descriptions—e.g. *a man* in an example like (1), understood as being uttered about a particular person.

(1)   A man is downstairs in the kitchen cooking dinner.

As we've seen, we cannot view the truth conditions of an utterance of (1) as involving any particular man—say, the one the speaker has in mind. The argument was that, if that man is not actually doing what (1) says, but there is another man who is, then (1) must still be counted

---

[2] Of course the interpretation of predicative expressions would have to be adjusted accordingly. Our look at Montague's PTQ grammar in Chapter 4 gave some indication of what might be involved.

true. (This is different from the case with proper names, pronouns, and demonstrative and definite descriptions—all of which have uses which could in principle be assumed to involve particular entities.) Thus (1) seems to be irreducibly quantificational. In this case an analysis involving constant individual concepts would involve rather more complications than in the case of referential NPs, since it would require us to quantify over individual concepts, and distinguish the constant ones from the variable ones.[3] I am not a logician, and not in a position to attempt the formalization of this idea, so I do not know whether ultimately it would be workable. I toss it out here in the hope that someone who is more knowledgeable than I am can evaluate it.[4] And I am encouraged by the fact that recently several others have found uses for individual concepts in their formal approaches: Elbourne (2008), as we saw in Chapter 8 above, and also Aloni (2005a, b).

We turn now to consider reference: who gets to participate and who doesn't?

11.2 Which NPs can be used to refer?

The pragmatic conception of reference, as I'm sure we all remember from Chapter 1, is the one that stems from our ordinary everyday uses of words like "refer" in utterances like that in (2).

(2)   When you said "that jerk from the Dean's office", who were you referring to?

It is (at least) a three-place relation—speakers use expressions to refer to entities. For Kent Bach (e.g. (1987, 2006)) this sort of reference is in

---

[3] We know that Montague's PTQ grammar involved quantification over individual concepts. However he did not distinguish constant from variable individual concepts.

[4] I proposed this idea at a workshop in Ann Arbor (November 2007), and Rich Thomason was kind enough to give me a couple of comments. On the one hand he pointed out that quantifying over individual concepts would result in the truth of (i):

(i) $\Box \exists x Px \rightarrow \exists x \Box Px$

which he said would be pretty awful (or words to that effect). But sometime later, in an email, he pointed out that the existence of functional answers to universal *wh* questions, as in (ii) below,

(ii)   A: Who does every boy love most?
       B: His mother.

might be some evidence in favor of what I'm proposing.

fact a four-place relation—speakers use expressions to refer their addressees to entities. The extra place is important for Bach because of his interest in thought, and in what a speaker can convey to an addressee. Here we may bring in a Gricean distinction between the proposition actually expressed in an utterance, and a proposition which the speaker wishes to convey to their addressee but which is not actually expressed in the utterance. This distinction is also stressed by Peter Ludlow and Stephen Neale (1991), whose views are similar to those of Bach. Let us look at what is required on Bach's conception, and what the bottom line is as regards kinds of NPs that can be used to refer.

We must note, to begin with, that Bach is one of those who believe that singular propositions are RSPs. However he's not as restrictive as Russell on the question of what it takes to be able to grasp such propositions; perception of the entity in question is sufficient, but not necessary. Memory of such a perception is also sufficient, as is having been informed about the object via a causal/historical chain of communication "originating with a perception of the object" (Bach 2006: 522). Thus for Bach, singular reference requires some kind of causal-historical relation between the agent and the object referred to.[5] This is because Bach believes that this kind of relation is necessary for *de re* thought. Then, in order to convey such a proposition one must use a singular term denoting that object (a proper name, a definite or demonstrative description, a pronoun) in a referential way. (This leaves out attributive uses of definite descriptions.) When all of these conditions are satisfied, one can be said to have used the NP in question to refer.

The borderline cases are those involving indefinite descriptions. Bach, as well as Ludlow and Neale, assume that referential use of an indefinite description is possible, but only where the utterance is "about an individual that is already the focus of mutual attention" (Bach 2006: 532). Ludlow and Neale (1991: 177) give (3) as an example, as uttered in a situation where the speaker is at someone else's house looking out the window into the garden.

(3)   Look! A man is uprooting your turnips.

---

[5] Although Bach is more lenient than Russell in his requirements for comprehension of RSPs, he is less lenient than others. Kaplan, for example, believes that one can express RSPs about entities which do not yet exist, like the first child born in the 22nd century. Cf. Kaplan (1978: 241); Bach (2006: 530f.) has a response to Kaplan on this point.

Let us assume that the speaker can see that their addressee is looking at the same man, and intends them to recognize that he is the one being spoken about. In this case Bach holds that the speaker may succeed in referring. Bach, and Ludlow and Neale, agree that the proposition actually expressed in this case would be a quantificational one; however the proposition meant by the speaker—one which the speaker wishes to convey to the addressee—is the RSP containing the man the speaker of (3) sees.

Bach follows Ludlow and Neale in distinguishing referential uses of indefinites from specific uses. For the latter, Bach believes that the speaker does not refer—indeed, there is no attempt at reference in those cases. So consider an utterance of (3) without the *Look!*, i.e. (4),

(4)   A man is uprooting your turnips.

when the speaker is in the same situation as for (3) except that they are talking on the phone to the homeowner. In this case, according to Bach, the speaker does not refer but rather merely ALLUDES to the man in the garden. This is because it is not possible for the speaker to convey an RSP to their addressee with such an utterance.

Bach (533) gives an argument which was also given by Ludlow and Neale (e.g. 178f.) and which (as they acknowledge) goes back to Russell (1919: 168). If the speaker had succeeded in referring to the man in the garden, and had meant the resulting RSP, then the addressee would not have been able to understand what was meant since they were not in appropriate cognitive contact with the man in the garden. Since the addressee at the other end of the phone line **is** presumably perfectly capable of understanding the utterance in question, that utterance cannot have meant the corresponding RSP.

I find much to disagree with here. We have already seen problems with the idea that propositions contain actual entities—with the assumption that singular propositions are RSPs. Bach's view contains an additional constraint which seems to preclude referring to abstract entities, and others with which one cannot be in perceptual contact. As we've seen, Bach believes that reference requires a causal-historical relation between the agent and the object referred to, and (as he notes in earlier work) "Abstract entities simply cannot enter into causal relations" (Bach 1987: 12). To be fair, Bach does also indicate at times that he is simply leaving abstract entities out of consideration (e.g. Bach (2006: n. 8)), but the fact remains that the account of reference he gives seems to make it impossible to refer to them. This seems arbitrary to me. I don't know why one can't have singular thoughts about numbers, for example. A number like 647 is a unique thing with its own special properties; it's maybe not one that I personally think about a lot, but other people may. There have been reports recently of people who associate particular colors and other qualities with numbers,) Synesthesia? which enables them to perform arithmetic calculations of amazing complexity in their heads, and with remarkable speed (cf., e.g., Tammet (2007)). For such people numbers may be more like acquaintances or even old friends. So while I would agree with Bach that one can refer using definite and demonstrative descriptions, proper names, and so forth, I would want to go further and allow reference to have been made even to abstract entities—in short, in any case in which referential uniqueness has been attained.

On the other hand turning to indefinite descriptions, I have to confess that I have not been able to establish intuitive contact with the distinction that Bach, and Ludlow and Neale suppose exists between referential uses of indefinite descriptions, and those uses which are merely specific. For one thing, there seems to be a whole range of possibilities spanning this supposed distinction, without a clear way to draw a line. Consider the case of the man uprooting turnips. For the referential use we imagined speaker and addressee standing together, looking out the same window at the same individual. But what should we say if the addressee is not looking out the window, but only comes to look out the window on hearing the utterance of (3)? It would be strange to say that the speaker's utterance of (3) was referential in the first case but not the second. But then suppose that the homeowner being addressed over the phone in the utterance of (4) was listening on her cell phone, and arrived in her driveway moments later in time to see the man in the garden, and that the speaker knew that this would be the case. Is this then so different from the other two situations? It does not seem so to me.

The kind of argument given by Russell (and repeated by Ludlow and Neale, and by Bach) concerning an addressee's ability to comprehend referential utterances depends crucially on a view of reference which involves RSPs.[6] If we take away that assumption, as I would like to, then the argument simply does not go through. What we are left with is

---

[6] Thus I find it misleading (to say the least) when Ludlow and Neale remark toward the beginning of their paper:

On Russell's account, a referring expression "*b*" may be combined with a (monadic) predicate expression to express a proposition which simply could not be entertained or expressed if the

a difference between nonspecific uses and specific uses. In the latter case, someone can perfectly well understand a proposition involving a constant individual concept of a man without having any kind of acquaintance with the man the speaker was speaking about. One just needs to know what men are, and what an individual is. That being the case, we can eliminate the divide between examples (3) and (4) above, about the man in the garden. If the speaker of (3) has used *a man* to refer to someone, then so has the speaker of (4). Beyond that it seems difficult to say whether we should conclude that the speaker has referred in both cases or in neither.

11.3 Which NPs (if any) have a (singular) referent?

As we noted in back in Chapter 1, the semantic conception of reference arises via several routes. One is that which is derived from the pragmatic sense of the word via "instrument promotion."[7] That is, just as we can go from speaking of someone using a knife to cut, to speaking of the knife itself doing the cutting, so talk of people using expressions to refer can lead us to speak of the expressions themselves doing the referring. Once we leave the user out of the picture we suggest a semantic relation—one holding between words and the world. If the only source for the semantic conception of reference were via instrument promotion, that conception would almost certainly be regarded as invalid. However there are at least a couple of other sources which must be taken more seriously.

The most important of these other sources is Frege's seminal paper "Über Sinn und Bedeutung," or "On sense and reference." It must be acknowledged that "reference" is not the only possible translation for *Bedeutung*; others that have been used include 'denotation,' 'nominatum,' and 'meaning.'[8] Nevertheless, the relation Frege was apparently talking about—that which holds between a linguistic expression

entity referred to by "*b*" did not exist. Russell often puts this by saying that the referent of "*b*" is a constituent of such a proposition; it will be convenient to follow him in this, but **nothing in the present paper turns on this conception of a so-called *SINGULAR* proposition.**

(Ludlow and Neale 1991: 172; italics in original, boldface added, and reference footnote omitted.)

[7] This source for the semantic conception of reference was noted in a 2004 talk by Richard Larson. Cf. also Bach (2006: 516).

[8] See Beaney (1997: 36–46) for an interesting discussion of the problem of finding an appropriate translation for *Bedeutung*, as Frege used it in this paper.

and something extralinguistic with which that expression is associated and which plays a role in determining the truth value of sentences containing that expression—is quite parallel to the pragmatic conception of "reference" reviewed above, at least until we get to supposed referential uses of indefinites. That is, when a speaker is using a singular term to refer their addressee to some entity, then it is natural to see the singular term and the entity as standing in Frege's relation. It is true that this very parallel might lead to some unhealthy commingling of the two (as I will suggest below), and for that reason choice of a different term for the semantic relation might have been a good idea. However it wouldn't have changed the facts.

Before getting down to work I'd like to suggest another route which brings us to the idea that expressions bear relations to extralinguistic entities, and that route comes from the fact that people are as much consumers of language as they are producers. When focusing on the speaking/writing role it is natural to think of the agent as using expressions to refer. But as a group, language users engage in the comprehension role much more frequently, since a typical written text has one author but many readers, and even when speaking, occasions of speaking to oneself must be heavily outnumbered by those on which we speak to more than one other person. And for the language consumer, the significance comes from the words themselves. Now Reddy (1979) has forcefully reminded us that language comprehenders must do a serious amount of work in constructing a message from the words that are presented to them. On the other hand, comprehenders are able to do this because the conventions established by the previous generations of language users have not only invested those words with their standard meanings, but have also established systematic rules for combining those meanings to make the meanings of phrases and whole utterances. As Wittgenstein has observed, we can't say *bububu* and mean 'If it doesn't rain I shall go for a walk' (1953: 18). Neither can we interpret *bububu* to mean 'If it doesn't rain I shall go for a walk.'

Turning now to the NPs, we saw in Chapter 2 that Russell had a very constrained idea of which ones could correctly be said to pick out an entity that plays a role in the proposition expressed in an utterance. That was because any such expression, properly used, should guarantee the existence of the denoted entity. This is very difficult for a poor little expression to do, and hence almost all NPs were, for Russell, quantificational—that is, they could only be used to express general propositions not involving any particular individuals. Ultimately he decided that the sole exception was the word *this*, used demonstratively (Russell 1917: 216 and n. 5). (On the other hand, we saw in Chapter 8 that on at least one plausible analysis, that of King (2001) as it might be extended to proximal demonstratives, *this* itself should be regarded as a quantificational expression. If King is right, then Russell shouldn't even have allowed that one exception. And below I will argue that it would be strange to have just one, or a very few, NPs singled out for this special property.)

When it comes to semantic reference Bach takes a position which approaches Russell's in restrictiveness. He arrives at this position via what he describes as "an embarrassingly simple argument," which is repeated below in (5) (Bach (2006: 542); I've replaced his Arabic numerals with Roman numerals).

(5)   (i)   Virtually any expression that can be used to refer can also be used literally but not referentially.
      (ii)   No variation in meaning (semantic ambiguity of under-specification, indexicality, or vagueness) explains this fact.
      (iii)   So the meaning of such an expression is compatible with its being used non-referentially.
      (iv)   So virtually any expression that can be used to refer is not inherently referential.

A footnote indicates that the exceptions to the generalization in premise (5i) (signaled by Bach's "virtually") are *I*, *today*, "and a few others ('pure' indexicals)," possibly including *you* (Bach 2006: 542, n. 31). These are the only NPs that could possibly be taken to have a (singular) referent.

We have seen in the preceding chapters that NPs can typically be used in a number of different ways, not all of which would be considered (by anyone) to be referential. We have attributive, generic, and bound variable uses of definite and demonstrative descriptions, in addition to their referential use; both indefinite and generic uses of bare NPs; pronouns that function as bound variables as well as deictically, anaphorically, and descriptively. Bach discusses many of these kinds of uses, as well as some others, to show that all of these kinds of NP have uses which would not be considered referential (in the "singular reference" sense).

Bach also gives a number of examples to argue that proper names also have nonreferential uses, and I want to pause briefly to consider one of them. Example (6) below illustrates the apparent variable binding use of proper names which we saw above in Chapter 8.

(6)   Bob hates his boss, and so does every other employee. [= Bach 2006: ex. 17]

Of interest here is the sloppy identity reading, where everybody hates their own boss. It is generally assumed that this reading requires that both *Bob* and *every other employee* bind a variable corresponding to the pronoun *his* in order to obtain this reading. Note that if this piece of evidence constitutes a valid argument for nonreferentiality, then *I*, *you*, and *today*, as well as Russell's demonstrative *this*, would also be excluded from the class of referential NPs, given examples like those in (7).

(7)   a.   I hate my boss, and so does every other employee.
      b.   You should take your vitamins, and so should everybody else.
      c.   Today has its own troubles, as does every other day.
      d.   This [pointing at a jar] is missing its top, and so are all of those.

All of these can have the sloppy reading, and in the case of (7b, c, d) this is much the preferred interpretation (if not the only one). Thus we would have to conclude that no NPs can be said to have referents.[9]

  In a way this result—that no NPs can be said to have referents—would be a natural one. As I remarked above, with respect to Russell's views, it would be very strange if just one NP in all of English were able to have a semantic referent. The same holds for Bach's position, which is only slightly more liberal than Russell's. So suppose I say something like (8) to my cousin Lyn, with our friend Kathy standing by:

(8)   I play tennis and you bike, but she [nodding at Kathy] hikes.

Is it really reasonable that my first clause, and possibly the second, express one kind of proposition while the third clause expresses a different one? And isn't it also suspicious that there is some question

---

[9] On the other hand it is not so clear that the proper name in (6), or the indexicals in (7), need actually be seen as binding any variables. A plausible logical form for the first sentence of (6), on the sloppy identity reading of that sentence, is (i).

(i) $\lambda x[x$ hates x's boss$](Bob)$

Here it is the lambda operator that is binding the variables, not *Bob*. And as we've noted, on a variable-free approach there would not be any long-distance binding at all.

as to where the middle case falls?[10] In short, I cannot see that there is any great divide between NPs like *I, you, this,* and *today,* on the one hand, and all of the other NPs in the language, on the other. Similarly the propositions expressed using these expressions do not seem any different from those expressed with other NPs when they are used to talk about specific individuals.

Returning to the main issue of which NPs can have semantic referents, I think there is a more fundamental problem with Bach's argument, and that is the idea that an NP's having a (semantic) referent is a consequence of some semantic feature that it expresses each time it is being used (literally) to refer to something. I think it is a mistake to think of semantic reference in that way. For one thing, it confounds semantic reference with the pragmatic conception that arises from our everyday talk of referring. That is, the criterion for semantic reference which is implicit in Bach's "embarrassingly simple" argument is consistency in pragmatic reference. But instead of trying to derive a semantic conception of reference from the pragmatic one, perhaps we should take to heart the Fregean roots that already exist for the semantic conception of reference. If we are interested in particular in singular reference, then we should look for NPs whose contribution to the truth value of an utterance in which it occurs can sometimes involve a particular entity. On those occasions when an NP actually has such a contribution to make, it is referential in the semantic sense. On this view the old standards would be included as potentially contributing such a referent: proper names, definite and demonstrative descriptions and pronouns, in at least some of their uses. Indefinite descriptions and other quantificational NPs would not.

It is through no fault of its own that a given NP sometimes makes such a contribution and sometimes does not. It is rather a consequence of its surroundings; we need not suppose any ambiguity. Consider the underlined NP in examples such as the following.

(9) a. The tallest student in the class (I forget her name) is waiting outside.
     b. The tallest student in the class (which varies from class to class) is always asked to close the blinds.

[10] Thus Bach's footnote quoted above indicates an inclination to include *you* among the referential NPs but John Perry's (2006) distinction between automatic and discretionary indexicals would put *I* in a class by itself. And we know that Russell had *this* as the sole member of this elite category.

Suppose we agree that *the tallest student in the class* denotes, with respect to any situation, the unique entity who is the tallest student in the class. Then for an utterance of (9a) to be true there must be, in the situation spoken of, such an entity who is waiting outside. That person plays a role in determining whether (9a) is true or false; thus she (or her constant individual concept) is the semantic referent of the NP *the tallest student in the class* as it occurs in the utterance of (9a), on this Fregean conception of semantic reference. On the other hand (9b), on the intended reading where the NP is within the scope of *always*, is generic, having truth conditions involving a variety of different situations with potentially different individuals involved. For an utterance of (9b) on this reading to be true it must be the case that in all of those situations, the entity who is the tallest student is asked to close the blinds. In this case there is no one entity whose properties determine the truth or falsity of (9b). Thus we do not have a singular referent. We have not supposed any change in the meaning of the NP *the tallest student in the class*, yet in one case it has a semantic referent of the singular type and in the other case it does not.

Note that on this conception attributively used definite descriptions will have a semantic referent, since whether (10) below is true or false depends on whether or not the person who murdered Smith is insane.[11]

(10) The murderer of Smith is insane.

That is the case regardless of whether (10) is asserted attributively or referentially. The difference between the two assertions can be seen as lying in the proposition expressed (one containing a variable individual concept or a constant one). On the other hand when definite descriptions are in the scope of other operators there may be no (singular) semantic referent. This is true of (9b) above, when the adverb *always* takes scope over a definite description. Another example, with a definite description within the scope of a quantificational NP, is (11) (from Chapter 6).

---

[11] If we agree with Bach that in using a definite description attributively the speaker does not refer to anyone or anything, but also agree with me that attributively used definite descriptions have a semantic referent, then we will have arrived at a position which Salmon (2004: 239, n. 13) describes as "curious." But perhaps it is only curious for the holder of what Salmon calls the "speech-act centered conception of semantics." In this paper Salmon himself argues for an expression-centered conception, and I agree with him on that.

(11)   Every child read <u>the book that had been assigned to them</u>.

We saw in Chapter 8 that definite descriptions can even be bound by other operators, as in (12) below.

(12)   Every scientist who was fired from the observatory at Sofia was consoled by someone who knew <u>the fired scientist</u> as a youth.

But this kind of variability in use does not require us to propose different semantic interpretations for the NPs themselves.

So, is this picture the correct one? Bach admits that he doesn't have a knock-down argument for his position (2006: 518), and I don't have one for mine. However it seems to me difficult to argue that this conception of semantic reference is not at least one plausible one.

11.4 Concluding remarks

One of my main aims in writing this book was to present as clear as possible a picture of what people are talking about when they talk about reference, and what kinds of contributions NPs can make to the meanings of sentences in which they occur. It may be the case that this picture has revealed the blurriness of many traditional boundaries. We have seen at least two different ways in which people speak of reference—the pragmatic way, when it is speakers who refer, using expressions provided by the language; and the semantic way, when the expressions themselves can be said to refer. Getting clear on when either of these applies is a difficult task. And there are other fuzzy boundaries that have emerged in the course of the preceding chapters—between reference and quantification, between definiteness and indefiniteness, between indexicality and nonindexicality, and probably others as well. And beyond that we have come across many many other kinds of unsolved problems in the course of this book. It is my sense that current work in the area of reference and noun phrase interpretation is in a stage of ferment, with new facts and ideas bubbling to the surface while others rotate underneath. I would like to close by encouraging readers to go out and solve those problems.

References

Abbott, Barbara (1989). Nondescriptionality and natural kind terms. *Linguistics and Philosophy* 12: 269–91.
—— (1993). A pragmatic account of the definiteness effect in existential sentences. *Journal of Pragmatics* 19: 39–55.
—— (1996). Doing without a partitive constraint. In Jacob Hoeksema (ed.), *Partitives: Studies on the Syntax and Semantics of Partitive and Related Constructions*. Berlin: Mouton de Gruyter, 25–56.
—— (1997). Models, truth and semantics. *Linguistics and Philosophy* 20: 117–38.
—— (1999). Support for a unique theory of definiteness. In Tanya Matthews and Devon Strolovitch (eds), *Semantics and Linguistic Theory (SALT) 9*. Ithaca, NY: CLC Publications, 1–15.
—— (2000). Presuppositions as nonassertions. *Journal of Pragmatics* 32: 1419–37.
—— (2001). Definiteness and proper names: Some bad news for the description theory. *Journal of Semantics* 19: 191–201.
—— (2002). Donkey demonstratives. *Natural Language Semantics* 10: 285–98.
—— (2004). Definiteness and indefiniteness. In Laurence R. Horn and Gregory Ward (eds), *The Handbook of Pragmatics*. Oxford: Blackwell, 122–49.
—— (2005). Proper names and language. In Gregory N. Carlson and Francis Jeffry Pelletier (eds), *Reference and Quantification: The Partee Effect*. Stanford, CA: CSLI Publications, 63–81.
—— (2008a). Issues in the semantics and pragmatics of definite descriptions in English. In Jeanette K. Gundel and Nancy Hedberg (eds), *Reference: Interdisciplinary Perspectives*. Oxford: Oxford University Press, 61–72.
—— (2008b). Presuppositions and common ground. *Linguistics and Philosophy* 31: 523–38.
Abusch, Dorit (1994). The scope of indefinites. *Natural Language Semantics* 2: 83–135.
Aloni, Maria (2005a). A formal treatment of the pragmatics of questions and attitudes. *Linguistics and Philosophy* 28: 505–39.
—— (2005b). Individual concepts in modal predicate logic. *Journal of Philosophical Logic* 34: 1–64.
Ariel, Mira (1988). Referring and accessibility. *Journal of Linguistics* 24: 65–87.
—— (1990). *Accessing Noun-phrase Antecedents*. London: Routledge.

Ariel, Mira (2001). Accessibility theory: An overview. In Ted Sanders, Joost Schilperoord, and Wilbert Spooren (eds), *Text Representation: Linguistic and Psycholinguistic Aspects*. Amsterdam: John Benjamins, 29–87.

Bach, Emmon (1986). Natural language metaphysics. In Ruth Barcan Marcus, Georg J. W. Dorn, and Paul Weingartner (eds), *Logic, Methodology and Philosophy of Science* VII. Amsterdam: Elsevier, 573–95.

Bach, Kent (1987). *Thought and Reference*. Oxford: Oxford University Press.

—— (1998). Review of *Reference and Referent Accessibility*, edited by Thorstein Fretheim and Jeanette K. Gundel. *Pragmatics and Cognition* 8: 335–8.

—— (2000). Quantification, qualification and context: A reply to Stanley and Szabó. *Mind and Language* 15: 262–83.

—— (2002). Giorgione was so-called because of his name. *Philosophical Perspectives* 16: 73–103.

—— (2004). Descriptions: Points of reference. In Marga Reimer and Anne Bezuidenhout (eds), *Descriptions and Beyond*. Oxford: Clarendon Press, 189–229.

—— (2006). What does it take to refer? In Ernest Lepore and Barry C. Smith (eds), *The Oxford Handbook of Philosophy of Language*. Oxford: Clarendon Press, 516–54.

Barker, Chris (1996). Presuppositions for proportional quantifiers. *Natural Language Semantics* 4: 237–59.

—— (1998). Partitives, double genitives and anti-uniqueness. *Natural Language and Linguistic Theory* 16: 679–717.

—— (2000). Definite possessives and discourse novelty. *Theoretical Linguistics* 26: 211–27.

—— and Jacobson, Pauline (eds.) (2007). *Direct Compositionality*. Oxford: Oxford University Press.

Barwise, Jon (1989). *The Situation in Logic*. Stanford, CA: CSLI.

—— and Cooper, Robin (1981). Generalized quantifiers and natural language. *Linguistics and Philosophy* 4: 159–220.

—— and Perry, John (1981). Situations and attitudes. *Journal of Philosophy* 78: 369–97.

—— —— (1983). *Situations and Attitudes*. Cambridge, MA: MIT Press.

Barzun, Jacques (1985). *Simple and Direct: A Rhetoric for Writers*. New York: Harper & Row.

Bäuerle, Rainer (1983). Pragmatisch-semantische Aspekte der NP-Interpretation. In Manfred Faust, Roland Harweb, Werner Lehfeldt, and Götz Wienold (eds), *Allgemeine Sprachwissenschaft, Sprachtypologie und Textlinguistik. Festschrift für Peter Hartmann*. Tübingen: Gunter Narr Verlag, 121–31. Cited in Elbourne (2005).

Beaney, Michael (1997). Introduction. In Michael Beaney (ed.), *The Frege Reader*. Oxford: Blackwell, 1–46.

Bennett, Michael (1974). Some extensions of a Montague fragment. Doctoral dissertation, Los Angeles, CA: UCLA. Reproduced by the Indiana University Linguistics Club, 1975.

Berger, Alan (2002). *Terms and Truth: Reference Direct and Anaphoric.* Cambridge, MA: MIT Press.

Berman, Stephen R. (1987). Situation-based semantics for adverbs of quantification. In Juliette Blevins and Anne Vainikka (eds), *University of Massachusetts Occasional Papers* 12. Amherst, MA: University of Massachusetts. Cited in Heim (1990).

Bezuidenhout, Anne (1997). Pragmatics, semantic underdetermination and the referential/attributive distinction. *Mind* 106: 375–409.

Birner, Betty J. (2006). Inferential relations and noncanonical word order. In Betty J. Birner and Gregory Ward (eds), *Drawing the Boundaries of Meaning: Neo-Gricean Studies in Pragmatics and Semantics in Honor of Laurence R. Horn.* Philadelphia, PA: John Benjamins, 31–51.

——and Ward, Gregory (1994). Uniqueness, familiarity, and the definite article in English. *Berkeley Linguistic Society (BLS)* 20: 93–102.

————(1998). *Information Status and Noncanonical Word Order in English.* Philadelphia, PA: John Benjamins.

Braun, David (2008). Complex demonstratives and their singular contents. *Linguistics and Philosophy* 31: 57–99.

Brock, Stuart (2002). Fictionalism about fictional characters. *Noûs* 36: 1–21.

——(2004). The ubiquitous problem of empty names. *Journal of Philosophy* 101: 277–98.

Butler, Joseph (1729). *Fifteen Sermons Preached at the Rolls Chapel upon the Following Subjects. Upon Humane Nature. . . . Upon the Ignorance of Man.* The second edition, corrected, to which is added a preface. London: James and John Knapton.

Carlson, Gregory N. (1977a). Reference to kinds in English. Doctoral dissertation, Amherst, MA: University of Massachusetts. Reissued 1980, *Outstanding Dissertations in Linguistics* series. New York: Garland Press.

——(1977b). A unified analysis of the English bare plural. *Linguistics and Philosophy* 1: 413–56.

——(1989). On the semantic composition of English generic sentences. In Gennaro Chierchia, Barbara H. Partee, and Raymond Turner (eds), *Properties, Types and Meaning* II. Dordrecht: Kluwer, 167–92.

——(forthcoming). Genericity. In Klaus von Heusinger, Claudia Maienborn, and Paul Portner (eds), *Semantics: An International Handbook of Natural Language Meaning.* Berlin: Mouton de Gruyter.

——and Pelletier, Francis Jeffry (2002). The average American has 2.3 children. *Journal of Semantics* 19: 73–104.

Carlson, Gregory N., Sussman, Rachel, Klein, Natalie, and Tanenhaus, Michael (2006). Weak definite noun phrases. In Chris Davis, Amy Rose Deal, and Youri Zabbal (eds), *Proceedings of the North Eastern Linguistic Society (NELS) 36*. Amherst, MA: GLSA, 179–96.

Carnap, Rudolf (1947). *Meaning and Necessity: A Study in Semantics and Modal Logic*. Chicago: University of Chicago Press.

Casteñeda, Hector-Neri (1966). "He": A study in the logic of self-consciousness. *Ratio* 8: 130–57.

—— (1968). On the logic of attributions of self knowledge to others. *Journal of Philosophy* 65: 439–56.

Chastain, Charles (1975). Reference and context. In Keith Gunderson (ed.), *Minnesota Studies in the Philosophy of Science, Volume 7: Language Mind and Knowledge*. Minneapolis: University of Minnesota Press, 194–269.

Chierchia, Gennaro (1992). Anaphora and dynamic binding. *Linguistics and Philosophy* 15: 111–84.

—— (1995). *Dynamics of Meaning: Anaphora, Presupposition, and the Theory of Grammar*. Chicago: University of Chicago Press.

Chisholm, Roderick M. (1967). Franz Brentano. In *The Encyclopedia of Philosophy, Volume 1*, 365–8.

Chomsky, Noam (1957). *Syntactic Structures*. The Hague: Mouton.

—— (1995). Language and nature. *Mind* 104: 1–61.

Christophersen, Paul (1939). *The Articles: A Study of Their Theory and Use in English*. Copenhagen: Munksgaard.

Cooper, Robin (1979). The interpretation of pronouns. In Frank Heny and Helmut S. Schnelle (eds), *Syntax and Semantics, Volume 10: Selections from the Third Groningen Round Table*. New York: Academic Press, 61–92.

Copi, Irving M. (1953). *Introduction to Logic*. New York: Macmillan.

Crimmins, Mark and Perry, John (1989). The prince and the phone booth. *Journal of Philosophy* 86: 685–711.

Davidson, Donald (1969). On saying that. In Donald Davidson and Jaakko Hintikka (eds), *Words and Objections: Essays on the Work of W. V. Quine*. Dordrecht: Reidel, 158–74. References are to the 1984 reprint, in Donald Davidson, *Inquiries into Truth and Interpretation*. Oxford: Clarendon Press, 93–108.

Davidson, Matthew (2000). Direct reference and singular propositions. *American Philosophical Quarterly* 37: 285–300.

Devitt, Michael (1981). *Designation*. New York: Columbia University Press.

—— (2004). The case for referential descriptions. In Marga Reimer and Anne Bezuidenhout (eds), *Descriptions and Beyond*. Oxford: Clarendon Press, 280–305.

—— and Sterelny, Kim (1999). *Language and Reality*. Second edition. Cambridge, MA: MIT Press.

Donnellan, Keith S. (1966). Reference and definite descriptions. *Philosophical Review* 77: 281–304.

—— (1970). Proper names and identifying descriptions. *Synthese* 21: 335–58. References are to the 1972 reprint, in Donald Davidson and Gilbert Harman (eds), *Semantics of Natural Language*. Dordrecht: D. Reidel, 356–79.

Dowty, David R., Wall, Robert E., and Peters, Stanley (1981). *Introduction to Montague Semantics*. Dordrecht: D. Reidel.

Elbourne, Paul D. (2005). *Situations and Individuals*. Cambridge, MA: MIT Press.

—— (2008). Demonstratives as individual concepts. *Linguistics and Philosophy* 31: 409–66.

Evans, Gareth (1977). Pronouns, quantifiers, and relative clauses (I). *Canadian Journal of Philosophy* 7: 467–536. References are to the 1985 reprint in Gareth Evans, *Collected Papers*. Oxford: Clarendon Press, 76–152.

—— (1980). Pronouns. *Linguistic Inquiry* 11: 337–62.

—— (1982). *The Varieties of Reference*, ed. John McDowell. Oxford: Clarendon Press.

Fillmore, Charles J. (1997). *Lectures on Deixis*. Stanford, CA: CSLI Publications.

von Fintel, Kai (2004). Would you believe it? The king of France is back! (Presuppositions and truth-value intuitions). In Marga Reimer and Anne Bezuidenhout (eds), *Descriptions and Beyond*. Oxford: Clarendon Press, 315–60.

Fodor, Janet Dean and Sag, Ivan A. (1982). Referential and quantificational indefinites. *Linguistics and Philosophy* 5: 355–98.

Fodor, Jerry A. (1975). *The Language of Thought*. Cambridge, MA: Harvard University Press.

—— (1980). Methodological solipsism considered as a research strategy in cognitive psychology. *The Behavioral and Brain Sciences* 3: 63–109.

—— and Lepore, Ernest (1992). *Holism: A Shopper's Guide*. Oxford: Blackwell.

Forbes, Graeme (1990). The indispensability of *Sinn*. *Philosophical Review* 99: 535–63.

—— (2006). *Attitude Problems*. Oxford: Clarendon Press.

Frege, Gottlob (1884). *Die Grundlagen der Arithmetik*. Breslau: W. Koebner. Trans. 1950 by J. L. Austin as *The Foundations of Arithmetic*. Oxford: Blackwell.

—— (1892a). Über Begriff und Gegenstand. *Vierteljahrsschrift für Wissenschaftliche Philosophie* 16: 192–205. Trans. as On concept and object, in Peter Geach and Max Black (eds), *Translations from the Philosophical Writings of Gottlob Frege*. Oxford: Blackwell, 42–55.

—— (1892b). Über Sinn und Bedeutung. *Zeitschrift für Philosophie und Philosophische Kritik*, 25–50. Trans. as On sense and reference, in Peter Geach and Max Black (eds), *Translations from the Philosophical Writings of Gottlob Frege*. Oxford: Blackwell, 56–78.

Gabriel, Gottfried, Hermes, Hans, Kambartel, Friedrich, Thiel, Christian, and Veraart, Albert (eds) (1980). *Gottlob Frege: Philosophical and Mathematical Correspondence*. Chicago: University of Chicago Press.

Garnham, Alan and Cowles, H. Wind (2008). Looking both ways: The JANUS model of noun phrase anaphor processing. In Jeanette K. Gundel and Nancy Hedberg (eds), *Reference: Interdisciplinary Perspectives*. Oxford: Oxford University Press, 246–72.

Gazdar, Gerald (1979). *Pragmatics: Implicature, Presupposition, and Logical Form*. New York: Academic Press.

Geach, Peter Thomas (1962). *Reference and Generality: An Examination of Some Medieval and Modern Theories*. Ithaca, NY: Cornell University Press.

Geurts, Bart (1997). Good news about the description theory of names. *Journal of Semantics* 14: 319–48.

Graff, Delia (2001). Descriptions as predicates. *Philosophical Studies* 102: 1–42.

Grice, H. Paul (1975). Logic and conversation. In Peter Cole and Jerry L. Morgan (eds), *Syntax and Semantics, Volume 3: Speech Acts*. New York: Academic Press, 41–58. Reprinted 1989 in H. Paul Grice, *Studies in the Way of Words*. Cambridge, MA: Harvard University Press, 22–40.

—— (1989). *Studies in the Way of Words*. Cambridge, MA: Harvard University Press.

Groenendijk, Jeroen and Stokhof, Martin (1991). Dynamic predicate logic. *Linguistics and Philosophy* 14: 39–100.

Gundel, Jeanette K., Hedberg, Nancy, and Zacharski, Ron (1993). Cognitive status and the form of referring expressions in discourse. *Language* 69: 274–307.

—— —— —— (2001). Definite descriptions and cognitive status in English: Why accommodation is unnecessary. *English Language and Linguistics* 5: 273–95.

—— and Fretheim, Thorstein (2004). Topic and focus. In Laurence R. Horn and Gregory Ward (eds), *The Handbook of Pragmatics*. Oxford: Blackwell, 175–96.

Hawkins, John A. (1978). *Definiteness and Indefiniteness*. Atlantic Highland, NJ: Humanities Press.

—— (1991). On (in)definite articles: implicatures and (un)grammaticality prediction. *Journal of Linguistics* 27: 405–42.

—— (2004). *Efficiency and Complexity in Grammars*. Oxford: Oxford University Press.

Heim, Irene (1982). The semantics of definite and indefinite noun phrases. Doctoral dissertation, Amherst, MA: University of Massachusetts.

—— (1983). File change semantics and the familiarity theory of definiteness. In Rainer Bäuerle, Christoph Schwarze, and Arnim von Stechow (eds), *Meaning, Use and the Interpretation of Language*. Berlin: Walter de Gruyter, 164–89.

—— (1990). E-type pronouns and donkey anaphora. *Linguistics and Philosophy* 13: 137–78.

—— and Kratzer, Angelika (1998). *Semantics in Generative Grammar*. Oxford: Blackwell.

Higginbotham, James (1985). On semantics. *Linguistic Inquiry* 16: 547–93.

Hintikka, Jaakko (1967). Individuals, possible worlds, and epistemic logic. *Noûs* 1: 33–62.

Horn, Laurence R. (1972). On the semantic properties of logical operators in English. Doctoral dissertation, Los Angeles, CA: UCLA.

—— (2004). Implicature. In Laurence R. Horn and Gregory Ward (eds), *The Handbook of Pragmatics*. Oxford: Blackwell, 3–28.

—— (2007). Toward a Fregean pragmatics: *Voraussetzung, Nebengedanke, Andeutung*. In Istvan Kecskes and Laurence R. Horn (eds), *Explorations in Pragmatics: Linguistic, Cognitive and Intercultural Aspects*. New York: Mouton de Gruyter, 39–69.

Hornstein, Norbert (1984). *Logic as Grammar*. Cambridge, MA: MIT Press.

Hurford, James R. (2007). *The Origins of Meaning*. Oxford: Oxford University Press.

Ionin, Tania, Matushansky, Ora, and Ruys, E. G. (2006). Parts of speech: toward a unified semantics for partitives. In Chris Davis, Amy Rose Deal, and Youri Zabbal (eds), *Proceedings of NELS* 36. Amherst, MA: University of Massachusetts GLSA, 357–70.

Jackendoff, Ray (1972). *Semantic Interpretation in Generative Grammar*. Cambridge, MA: MIT Press.

—— (1977). *X-bar Syntax: A Study of Phrase Structure*. Cambridge, MA: MIT Press.

—— (1979). How to keep ninety from rising. *Linguistic Inquiry* 10: 172–6.

Jacobson, Pauline (1996). The locality of interpretation: The case of binding and coordination. In Teresa Galloway and Justin Spence (eds), *Semantics and Linguistic Theory (SALT)* 6. Ithaca, NY: Cornell Working Papers in Linguistics, 111–35.

—— (2000). Paycheck pronouns, Bach-Peters sentences, and variable-free semantics. *Natural Language Semantics* 8: 77–155.

Justice, John (2001). On sense and reflexivity. *Journal of Philosophy* 98: 351–64.

Kadmon, Nirit (1990). Uniqueness. *Linguistics and Philosophy* 13: 273–324.

Kamp, Hans (1981). A theory of truth and semantic representation. In Jeroen Groenendijk, Theo M.V. Janssen, and Martin Stokhof (eds), *Formal Methods in the Study of Language*. Amsterdam: Amsterdam Center,

277–322. References are to the 1984 reprint in Jeroen Groenendijk, Theo M.V. Janssen, and Martin Stokhof (eds), *Truth, Interpretation and Information: Selected Papers from the Third Amsterdam Colloquium*. Dordrecht: Foris, 1–41.

—— (2001). Presupposition computation and presupposition justification: One aspect of the interpretation of multi-sentence discourse. In Myriam Bras and Laure Vieu (eds), *Semantic and Pragmatic Issues in Discourse and Dialogue: Experimenting with Current Dynamic Theories*. Oxford: Elsevier, 57–84.

Kamp, Hans and Reyle, Uwe (1993). *From Discourse to Logic: Introduction to Modeltheoretic Semantics of Natural Language, Formal Logic and Discourse Representation Theory*. Dordrecht: Kluwer.

Kanazawa, Makoto (1994). Weak vs. strong readings of donkey sentences and monotonicity inference in a dynamic setting. *Linguistics and Philosophy* 17: 109–58.

—— Kaufmann, Stefan and Peters, Stanley (2005). On the lumping semantics of counterfactuals. *Journal of Semantics* 22: 129–51.

Kaplan, David (1969). Quantifying in. In Donald Davidson and Jaakko Hintikka (eds), *Words and Objections: Essays on the Work of W. V. Quine*. Dordrecht: Reidel, 178–214. References are to the 1971 reprint in Leonard Linsky (ed.), *Reference and Modality*. Oxford: Oxford University Press, 112–44.

—— (1972). What is Russell's theory of descriptions? In David F. Pears (ed.), *Bertrand Russell: A Collection of Critical Essays*. Garden City, NJ: Doubleday Anchor, 227–44.

—— (1977). Demonstratives: An essay on the semantics, logic, metaphysics, and epistemology of demonstratives and other indexicals. Paper read (in part) at the March 1977 meeting of the Pacific Division of the American Philosophical Association. Published in full in Joseph Almog, John Perry, and Howard Wettstein (eds) (1989), *Themes From Kaplan*. Oxford: Oxford University Press, 481–563.

—— (1978). Dthat. In Peter Cole (ed.), *Syntax and Semantics, Volume 9: Pragmatics*. New York: Academic Press, 221–43.

—— (1989). Afterthoughts. In Joseph Almog, John Perry, and Howard Wettstein (eds), *Themes from Kaplan*. Oxford: Oxford University Press, 565–614.

Karttunen, Lauri (1969a). Problems of reference in syntax. Doctoral dissertation, Bloomington, IN: Indiana University.

—— (1969b). Pronouns and variables. In Robert I. Binnick, Alice Davison, Georgia M. Green, and Jerry L. Morgan (eds), *Papers from the Fifth Regional Meeting of the Chicago Linguistic Society (CLS)*. Chicago: Department of Linguistics, University of Chicago, 108–16.

—— (1976). Discourse referents. In James D. McCawley (ed.), *Syntax and Semantics, Volume 7: Notes from the Linguistic Underground*. New York: Academic Press, 363–85.

Katz, Jerrold J. (1977). A proper theory of names. *Philosophical Studies* 31: 1–80.

—— (1994). Names without bearers. *Philosophical Review* 103: 1–39.

—— (2001). The end of Millianism: Multiple bearers, improper names, and compositional meaning. *Journal of Philosophy* 98: 137–66.

Keenan, Edward L. (1971). Names, quantifiers, and a solution to the sloppy identity problem. *Papers in Linguistics* 4/2.

—— (1987). A semantic definition of "indefinite NP." In Eric J. Reuland and Alice G. B. ter Meulen (eds), *The Representation of (In)definiteness*. Cambridge, MA: MIT Press, 286–318.

—— and Stavi, Jonathan (1986). A semantic characterization of natural language determiners. *Linguistics and Philosophy* 9: 253–326.

Kehler, Andrew, Kertz, Laura, Rohde, Hannah, and Elman, Jeffrey L. (2008). Coherence and coreference revisited. *Journal of Semantics* 25: 1–44.

Kennedy, Christopher and Stanley, Jason (2008). What an *average* semantics needs. Forthcoming in *Semantics and Linguistic Theory (SALT) 18*.

—— —— (2009). On *average*. *Mind* 118: 583–646.

King, Jeffrey C. (2001). *Complex Demonstratives: A Quantificational Account*. Cambridge, MA: MIT Press.

Kneale, William (1962). Modality *de dicto* and *de re*. In Ernest Nagel, Patrick Suppes, and Alfred Tarski (eds), *Logic, Methodology and the Philosophy of Science: Proceedings of the 1960 International Congress*. Stanford, CA: Stanford University Press: 622–33.

Kratzer, Angelika (1977). What "must" and "can" must and can mean. *Linguistics and Philosophy* 1: 337–55.

—— (1989). An investigation of the lumps of thought. *Linguistics and Philosophy* 12: 607–53.

—— (1995). Stage-level and individual-level predicates. In Gregory N. Carlson and Francis Jeffry Pelletier (eds), *The Generic Book*. Chicago: Chicago University Press, 125–75.

Krifka, Manfred (2004). Bare NPs: Kind-referring, indefinites, both, or neither. In Robert B. Young and Y. Zhou (eds), *Semantics and Linguistic Theory (SALT) 13*. Ithaca, NY: CLC Publications.

—— Pelletier, Francis Jeffry, Carlson, Gregory N., ter Meulen, Alice, Chierchia, Gennaro, and Link, Godehard (1995). Genericity: An introduction. In Gregory N. Carlson and Francis Jeffry Pelletier (eds), *The Generic Book*. Chicago: University of Chicago Press, 1–124.

Kripke, Saul (1972). Naming and necessity. In Donald Davidson and Gilbert Harman (eds), *Semantics of Natural Language*. Dordrecht: Reidel, 253–355 and 763–9. Page references are to the monograph reissue, 1980, Cambridge, MA: Harvard University Press.

—— (1977). Speaker's reference and semantic reference. In Peter A. French, Theodore E. Uehling, Jr., and Howard Wettstein (eds), *Midwest Studies in Philosophy Volume II: Studies in the Philosophy of Language*. Morris, MN: University of Minnesota, 255–76.

—— (1979). A puzzle about belief. In Avishai Margalit (ed.), *Meaning and Use*. Dordrecht: D. Reidel, 139–83.

Ladusaw, William A. (1982). Semantic constraints on the English partitive construction. *Proceedings of the West Coast Conference on Formal Linguistics (WCCFL)* 1, 231–42.

Lambrecht, Knud (1994). *Information Structure and Sentence Form*. Cambridge: Cambridge University Press.

Landman, Fred (1996). Plurality. In Shalom Lappin (ed.), *The Handbook of Contemporary Semantic Theory*. Oxford: Blackwell, 425–57.

Larson, Richard and Segal, Gabriel (1995). *Knowledge of Meaning: An Introduction to Semantic Theory*. Cambridge, MA: MIT Press.

Lasnik, Howard (1976). Remarks on coreference. *Linguistic Analysis* 2: 1–22.

Levinson, Stephen C. (1983). *Pragmatics*. Cambridge: Cambridge University Press.

—— (2000). *Presumptive Meanings: The Theory of Generalized Conversational Implicature*. Cambridge, MA: MIT Press.

Lewis, David (1972). General semantics. In Donald Davidson and Gilbert Harman (eds), *Semantics of Natural Language*. Dordrecht: Reidel, 169–218.

—— (1973). *Counterfactuals*. Cambridge, MA: Harvard University Press.

—— (1975). Adverbs of quantification. In Edward L. Keenan (ed.), *Formal Semantics of Natural Language*. Cambridge: Cambridge University Press, 3–15.

—— (1978). Truth in fiction. *American Philosophical Quarterly* 15: 37–46. Reprinted with Postscripts in 1983, David Lewis, *Philosophical Papers, Volume I*. Oxford: Oxford University Press, 261–80.

—— (1979a). Attitudes *de dicto* and *de se*. *Philosophical Review* 88: 513–43. References are to the 1983 reprint in David Lewis, *Philosophical Papers, Volume 1*. New York: Oxford University Press, 133–59.

—— (1979b). Scorekeeping in a language game. *Journal of Philosophical Logic* 8: 339–59.

—— (1997). Naming the colours. *Australasian Journal of Philosophy* 75: 325–42. References are to the 1999 reprint (with Postscript) in David Lewis, *Papers in Metaphysics and Epistemology*. Cambridge: Cambridge University Press, 332–58.

Link, Godehard (1983). The logical analysis of plurals and mass terms: A lattice-theoretical approach. In Rainer Bäuerle, Christoph Schwarze, and

Arnim von Stechow (eds), *Meaning, Use, and Interpretation of Language*. Berlin: Walter de Gruyter, 302–23.

Linsky, Leonard (1967). *Referring*. New York: Humanities Press.

Löbner, Sebastian (1985). Definites. *Journal of Semantics* 4: 279–326.

—— (2000). Polarity in natural language: Predication, quantification and negation in particular and characterizing sentences. *Linguistics and Philosophy* 23: 213–308.

Ludlow, Peter and Neale Stephen (1991). Indefinite descriptions: In defense of Russell. *Linguistics and Philosophy* 14: 171–202.

—— and Segal, Gabriel (2004). On a unitary semantical analysis for definite and indefinite descriptions. In Marga Reimer and Anne Bezuidenhout (eds), *Descriptions and Beyond*. Oxford: Oxford University Press, 420–36.

Lumsden, Michael (1988). *Existential Sentences: Their Structure and Meaning*. London: Croom Helm.

Lyons, Christopher (1999). *Definiteness*. Cambridge: Cambridge University Press.

Lyons, John (1977). *Semantics*. Cambridge: Cambridge University Press.

Marcus, Ruth Barcan (1961). Modalities and intensional languages. *Synthese* 13: 303–22.

Mates, Benson (1950). Synonymity. In *Meaning and Interpretation: University of California Publications in Philosophy Volume 25*: 201–26.

McCawley, James D. (1979). Presupposition and discourse structure. In Choon-Kyu Oh and David A. Dinneen (eds), *Syntax and Semantics, Volume 11: Presupposition*. New York: Academic Press, 371–88.

Mill, John Stuart (1843). *A System of Logic, Ratiocinative and Inductive, Being a Connected View of the Principles of Evidence, and the Methods of Scientific Investigation*. London: John W. Parker.

Milsark, Gary (1974). Existential sentences in English. Doctoral dissertation, Cambridge, MA: MIT.

—— (1977). Toward an explanation of certain peculiarities of the existential construction in English. *Linguistic Analysis* 3: 1–29. [The author of this article is mistakenly given as Gary Milwark.]

Montague, Richard (1970). Universal grammar. *Theoria* 36: 373–98. References are to the 1974 reprint in Richmond Thomason (ed.), *Formal Philosophy: Selected Papers of Richard Montague*. New Haven: Yale University Press, 222–46.

—— (1973). The proper treatment of quantification in ordinary English. In Jaakko Hintikka, Julius Moravcsik, and Patrick Suppes (eds), *Approaches to Natural Language: Proceedings of the 1970 Stanford Workshop on Grammar and Semantics*. Dordrecht: Reidel, 221–42. References are to the 1974 reprint in Richmond Thomason (ed.), *Formal Philosophy: Selected Papers of Richard Montague*. New Haven: Yale University Press, 247–70.

Musan, Renate (1999). Temporal interpretation and information-status of noun phrases. *Linguistics and Philosophy* 22: 621–61.

Neale, Stephen (1990). *Descriptions.* Cambridge, MA: MIT Press.

Nunberg, Geoffrey (1993). Indexicality and deixis. *Linguistics and Philosophy* 16: 1–43.

Partee, Barbara H. (1972). Opacity, coreference, and pronouns. In Donald Davidson and Gilbert Harman (eds), *Semantics of Natural Language.* Dordrecht: Reidel, 415–41.

—— (1974). Opacity and scope. In Milton Munitz and Peter Unger (eds), *Semantics and Philosophy.* New York: New York University Press, 81–101.

—— (1975). Montague grammar and transformational grammar. *Linguistic Inquiry* 6: 203–300.

—— (1984). Nominal and temporal anaphora. *Linguistics and Philosophy* 7: 243–86.

—— (1986). Noun phrase interpretation and type-shifting principles. In Jeroen Groenendijk, Dick de Jongh, and Martin Stokhof (eds), *Studies in Discourse Representation Theory and the Theory of Generalized Quantifiers.* Dordrecht: Foris, 115–43.

Peacocke, Christopher (1975). Proper names, reference, and rigid designation. In Simon Blackburn (ed.), *Meaning, Reference, Necessity.* Cambridge: Cambridge University Press, 109–32. References are to the 1998 reprint in Gary Ostertag (ed.), *Definite Descriptions: A Reader.* Cambridge, MA: MIT Press, 201–24.

Percus, Orin (2000). Constraints on some other variables in syntax. *Natural Language Semantics* 8: 173–229.

Perry, John (1979). The problem of the essential indexical. *Noûs* 13: 3–21.

—— (1998). Myself and I. In Marcelo Stamm (ed.), *Philosophie in Synthetisher Absicht (A Festschrift for Dieter Heinrich).* Stuttgart: Klett-Cotta, 83–103.

—— (2006). Using indexicals. In Michael Devitt and Richard Hanley (eds), *The Blackwell Guide to the Philosophy of Language.* Malden, MA: Blackwell, 314–34.

Peters, Stanley and Westerståhl, Dag (2006). *Quantifiers in Language and Logic.* Oxford: Clarendon Press.

Postal, Paul M. (1966). On so-called "pronouns" in English. In Finbar Dinneen (ed.), *The 19th Monograph on Languages and Linguistics.* Washington, DC: Georgetown University Press. Reprinted 1969 in David A. Reibel and Sanford A. Schane (eds), *Modern Studies in English: Readings in Transformational Grammar.* Englewood Cliffs, NJ: Prentice-Hall, 201–24.

Prince, Ellen F. (1981a). On the inferencing of indefinite *this* NPs. In Aravind K. Joshi, Bonnie L. Webber, and Ivan A. Sag (eds), *Elements of Discourse Understanding.* Cambridge: Cambridge University Press, 231–50.

—— (1981b). Toward a taxonomy of given-new information. In Peter Cole (ed.), *Radical Pragmatics*. New York: Academic Press, 223–55.

—— (1992). The ZPG letter: Subjects, definiteness, and information status. In William C. Mann and Sandra A. Thompson (eds), *Discourse Description: Diverse Linguistic Analyses of a Fund-raising Text*. Philadelphia, PA: John Benjamins, 295–326.

Putnam, Hilary (1975). The meaning of "meaning." In Keith Gunderson (ed.), *Language, Mind and Knowledge, Minnesota Studies in the Philosophy of Science VII*. Minneapolis, MN: University of Minnesota Press. Reprinted 1975 in Hilary Putnam, *Philosophical Papers, Volume 2: Mind, Language and Reality*. Cambridge: Cambridge University Press, 215–71.

Quine, W. V. (1953a). Reference and modality. In W. V. Quine, *From a Logical Point of View*. Cambridge, MA: Harvard University Press. References are to the 1961 reprint. New York: Harper and Row, 139–59.

—— (1953b). Two dogmas of empiricism. In W. V. Quine, *From a Logical Point of View*. Cambridge: Harvard University Press. References are to the 1961 reprint. New York: Harper and Row, 20–46.

—— (1956). Quantifiers and propositional attitudes. *Journal of Philosophy* 53: 177–87. References are to the 1971 reprint in Leonard Linsky (ed.), *Reference and Modality*. Oxford: Oxford University Press, 101–11.

—— (1960). *Word and Object*. Cambridge, MA: MIT Press.

Rando, Emily and Napoli, Donna Jo (1978). Definites in *there*-sentences. *Language* 54: 300–13.

Recanati, François (1993). *Direct Reference: From Language to Thought*. Oxford: Blackwell.

—— (2005). Deixis and anaphora. In Zoltán Gendler Szabó (ed.), *Semantics vs. Pragmatics*. Oxford: Clarendon Press, 286–316.

Reddy, Michael (1979). The conduit metaphor—a case of frame conflict in our language about language. In Andrew Ortony (ed.), *Metaphor and Thought*. Cambridge: Cambridge University Press, 284–324.

Reed, Ann M. (1989). Discourse groups and semantic groups. In Joyce Powers and Kenneth de Jong (eds), *Proceedings of the Fifth Eastern States Conference on Linguistics (ESCOL)*. Columbus, OH: The Ohio State University, 416–27.

Reimer, Marga (1998). Donnellan's distinction/Kripke's test. *Analysis* 58: 89–100.

—— and Bezuidenhout, Anne (eds) (2004). *Descriptions and Beyond*. Oxford: Oxford University Press.

Reinhart, Tanya (1983). *Anaphora and Semantic Interpretation*. Chicago: University of Chicago Press.

—— (1987). Specifier and operator binding. In Eric J. Reuland and Alice G. B. ter Meulen (eds), *The Representation of (In)definiteness*. Cambridge, MA: MIT Press, 130–67.

Richard, Mark (1990). *Propositional Attitudes*. Cambridge: Cambridge University Press.

Roberts, Craige (1987). Modal subordination, anaphora, and distributivity. Doctoral dissertation, Amherst, MA: University of Massachusetts. Reissued 1991, *Outstanding Dissertations in Linguistics* series. New York: Garland Press.

—— (1989). Modal subordination and pronominal anaphora in discourse. *Linguistics and Philosophy* 12: 683–721.

—— (2002). Demonstratives as definites. In Kees von Deemter and Roger Kibble (eds), *Information Sharing: Reference and Presupposition in Language Generation and Interpretation*. Stanford, CA: CSLI, 89–136.

—— (2003). Uniqueness in definite noun phrases. *Linguistics and Philosophy* 26: 287–350.

—— (2004). Pronouns as definites. In Marga Reimer and Anne Bezuidenhout (eds), *Descriptions and Beyond*. Oxford: Clarendon Press, 503–43.

Rodman, Robert (1976). Scope phenomena, "Movement transformations," and relative clauses. In Barbara Hall Partee (ed.), *Montague Grammar*. New York: Academic Press, 165–76.

Ross, John Robert (1967). Constraints on variables in syntax. Doctoral dissertation, Cambridge, MA: MIT.

Rothschild, Daniel (2007). Presuppositions and scope. *Journal of Philosophy* 104: 71–106.

Russell, Bertrand (1905). On denoting. *Mind* 14: 479–93.

—— (1912). *The Problems of Philosophy*. Indianapolis, IN: Hackett.

—— (1917). Knowledge by acquaintance and knowledge by description. Revised version in *Mysticism and Logic*. London: Longmans Green & Co. References are to the 2004 republication. Mineola, NY: Dover Publications, 165–83.

—— (1919). Descriptions. In *Introduction to Mathematical Philosophy*, London: Allen and Unwin, 167–80.

—— (1957). Mr. Strawson on referring. *Mind* 66: 385–9.

Sag, Ivan (1976). Deletion and logical form. Doctoral dissertation, Cambridge, MA: MIT. Reissued 1980, *Outstanding Dissertations in Linguistics* series, New York: Garland Press.

Salmon, Nathan (1981). *Reference and Essence*. Princeton, NJ: Princeton University Press.

—— (1986). *Frege's Puzzle*. Cambridge, MA: MIT Press.

—— (1989). How to become a Millian heir. *Noûs* 23: 211–20.

—— (1990). A Millian heir rejects the wages of Sinn. In C. Anthony Anderson and Joseph Owens (eds), *Propositional Attitudes: The Role of Content in Logic, Language, and Mind*. Stanford, CA: CSLI, 215–47.

—— (1998). Nonexistence. *Noûs* 32: 102–85.

—— (2004). The Good, the Bad, and the Ugly. In Marga Reimer and Anne Bezuidenhout (eds), *Descriptions and Beyond*. Oxford: Clarendon Press, 230–60.

Saul, Jennifer M. (1997). Substitution and simple sentences. *Analysis* 57: 102–8.

—— (1998). The pragmatics of attitude ascription. *Philosophical Studies* 92: 363–89.

Scha, Remko (1984). Distributive, collective and cumulative quantification. In Jeroen Groenendijk, Theo M.V. Janssen, and Martin Stokhof (eds), *Truth, Interpretation and Information: Selected Papers from the Third Amsterdam Colloquium*. Dordrecht: Foris, 131–58.

Schiffer, Stephen (1977). Naming and knowing. *Midwest Studies in Philosophy* 2: 28–41.

—— (1992). Belief ascription. *Journal of Philosophy* 89: 499–521.

—— (1995). Descriptions, indexicals and belief reports: Some dilemmas (but not the ones you expect). *Mind* 104: 107–31.

Schwarzschild, Roger (1996). *Pluralities*. Dordrecht: Kluwer.

—— (2002). Singleton indefinites. *Journal of Semantics* 19: 289–314.

Scott, Dana (1970). Advice on modal logic. In Karel Lambert (ed.), *Philosophical Problems in Logic*. Dordrecht: Reidel, 143–73.

Searle, John R. (1958a). Proper names. *Mind* 67: 166–73.

—— (1958b). Russell's objections to Frege's theory of sense and reference. *Analysis* 18: 137–43.

—— (1983). Proper names and intentionality. In *Intentionality: An Essay in the Philosophy of Mind*. Cambridge: Cambridge University Press, 231–61.

Segal, Gabriel M. A. (2000). *A Slim Book about Narrow Content*. Cambridge, MA: MIT Press.

Selkirk, Elisabeth O. (1977). Some remarks on noun phrase structure. In Peter W. Culicover, Thomas Wasow, and Adrian Akmajian (eds), *Formal Syntax*. New York: Academic Press, 285–316.

Sharvy, Richard (1980). A more general theory of definite descriptions. *Philosophical Review* 89: 607–24.

Simons, Mandy (1996). Pronouns and definite descriptions: A critique of Wilson. *Journal of Philosophy* 93: 408–20.

Soames, Scott (1982). How presuppositions are inherited: A solution to the projection problem. *Linguistic Inquiry* 13: 483–545. References are to the 1991 reprint in Steven Davis (ed.), *Pragmatics: A Reader*. Oxford: Oxford University Press, 428–70.

—— (2002). *Beyond Rigidity: The Unfinished Semantic Agenda of* Naming and Necessity. Oxford: Oxford University Press.

Sperber, Dan and Wilson, Deirdre (1986). *Relevance: Communication and Cognition*. Cambridge, MA: Harvard University Press. Second edition, 1995, Oxford: Blackwell.

Stalnaker, Robert C. (1968). A theory of conditionals. In Nicholas Rescher (ed.), *Studies in Logical Theory*. Oxford: Blackwell, 98–112.

—— (1972). Pragmatics. In Donald Davidson and Gilbert Harman (eds), *Semantics of Natural Language*. Dordrecht: Reidel, 380–97.

—— (1973). Presuppositions. *Journal of Philosophical Logic* 2, 447–57.

—— (1974). Pragmatic presuppositions. In Milton K. Munitz and Peter K. Unger (eds), *Semantics and Philosophy*. New York: New York University Press, 197–214. References are to the 1991 reprint in Steven Davis (ed.), *Pragmatics: A Reader*. Oxford: Oxford University Press, 471–82.

—— (1976). Propositions. In Alfred F. MacKay and Daniel D. Merrill (eds), *Issues in the Philosophy of Language: Proceedings of the 1972 Oberlin Colloquium in Philosophy*. New Haven: Yale University Press, 79–92.

—— (1978). Assertion. In Peter Cole (ed.), *Syntax and Semantics, Volume 9: Pragmatics*. New York, Academic Press: 315–22.

—— (1984). *Inquiry*. Cambridge, MA: MIT Press.

—— (1999). *Context and Content: Essays on Intentionality in Speech and Thought*. Oxford: Oxford University Press.

—— (2002). Common ground. *Linguistics and Philosophy* 25: 701–21.

Stanley, Jason (2001). Hermeneutic fictionalism. *Midwest Studies in Philosophy* 25: 36–71.

—— and Szabó, Zoltán Gendler (2000a). On quantifier domain restriction. *Mind and Language* 15: 219–61.

—— —— (2000b). Reply to Bach and Neale. *Mind and Language* 15: 295–8.

Stockwell, Robert P., Schachter, Paul, and Partee, Barbara Hall (1973). *The Major Syntactic Structures of English*. New York: Holt, Rinehart and Winston.

Strawson, P. F. (1950). On referring. *Mind* 59: 320–44.

—— (1952). *Introduction to Logical Theory*. London: Methuen. References are to the 1967 University Paperback edition.

Tammet, Daniel (2007). *Born on a Blue Day: Inside the Extraordinary Mind of an Autistic Savant*. New York: Free Press.

Thomason, Richmond (1974). Home is where the heart is. Ms. Pittsburgh: University of Pittsburgh.

Van Fraassen, Bas C. (1966). Singular terms, truth-value gaps, and free logic. *Journal of Philosophy* 63: 481–94.

—— (1971). *Formal Semantics and Logic*. New York: Macmillan.

Van Inwagen, Peter (1977). Creatures of fiction. *American Philosophical Quarterly* 14: 299–308.

—— (1983). Fiction and metaphysics. *Philosophy and Literature* 7: 67–77.

Vendler, Zeno (1962). Each and every, any and all. In *Mind* 71: 145–60. References are to the 1967 reprint in Zeno Vendler, *Linguistics in Philosophy*. Ithaca, NY: Cornell University Press, 70–96.

Walker, Marilyn A., Joshi, Aravind K., and Prince, Ellen F. (eds) (1998). *Centering Theory in Discourse*. Oxford: Oxford University Press.

Wettstein, Howard (1981). Demonstrative reference and definite descriptions. *Philosophical Studies* 40: 241–57.

—— (1983). The semantic significance of the referential-attributive distinction. *Philosophical Studies* 44: 187–94.

Whorf, Benjamin Lee (1941). The relation of habitual thought and behavior to language. In Leslie Spier (ed.), *Language, Culture, and Personality: Essays in Memory of Edward Sapir*. Menasha, WI: Sapir Memorial Publication Fund, 75–93. References are to the 1956 reprint in John B. Carroll (ed.), *Language, Thought, and Reality: Selected Writings of Benjamin Lee Whorf*. Cambridge, MA: MIT Press, 134–59.

—— (1945). Grammatical categories. *Language* 21: 1–11.

Wilson, George M. (1984). Pronouns and pronominal descriptions: A new semantical category. *Philosophical Studies* 45: 1–30.

—— (1991). Reference and pronominal descriptions. *Journal of Philosophy* 88: 359–87.

Winograd, Terry (1972). *Understanding Natural Language*. New York: Academic Press.

Wittgenstein, Ludwig (1922). *Tractatus Logico-philosophicus*. London: Routledge & Kegan Paul.

—— (1953). *Philosophical Investigations*, trans. G. E. M. Anscombe. Oxford: Basil Blackwell. References are to the 1968 edition.

Woisetschlaeger, Erich (1983). On the question of definiteness in "an old man's book." *Linguistic Inquiry* 14: 137–54.

Zeevat, Henk (1989). A compositional approach to Discourse Representation Theory. *Linguistics and Philosophy* 12: 95–131.

Zwicky, Arnold M., and Sadock, Jerrold M. (1975). Ambiguity tests and how to fail them. In John P. Kimball (ed.), *Syntax and Semantics, Volume 4*. New York: Academic Press, 1–36.

Index

a priori knowledge 16, 24–5, 101

Abbott, Barbara 99, 107, 120 n., 137 n., 211 n., 215 n. 9, 220, 230 n. 26, 247 n. 11

Abusch, Dorit 51

accessibility 253–4, 257–8, 260 n.

accommodation 219–20, 245, 246

acquaintance (knowledge by) 26, 27, 29, 34–6, 128, 274

all 164, 213, 216–17, 227–8, 234, 236

Aloni, Maria 91 n., 270

analytic sentence/statement 16, 24–5, 101, 102, 106

angle brackets (< >) 33 n.

antecedent(s) 181, 194–6, 199–202, 204–8, 224–6, 239, 242–3, 247–9, 253, 261, 263

Ariel, Mira 253–4, 256–61

arrow, see *if-then*

asterisk (*) 7, 11

atom(s) 159–60, 214

Bach, Emmon 178

Bach, Kent 118, 120, 122–3, 139 n. 13, 151 n. 20, 253–4, 257, 261, 266 n., 270–3, 276–80

Bar-Asher, Elitzur 218 n. 14

bare NP, *see* noun phrase(s) (NP(s)), bare

Barker, Chris 84, 203 n., 212 n., 235, 241, 251

Barwise, Jon 63–4, 83, 93–6, 132 n. 3, 221–3, 224, 227–8, 231–3, 235, 237

Barzun, Jacques 180

Bäuerle, Rainer 51

Beaney, Michael 274 n. 8

belief *de se* 188–9

belief state(s) 187–8

Bennett, Michael 91

Berger, Alan 112

Berman, Stephen R. 247 n. 12

Bezuidenhout, Anne 138 n. 12, 208 n.

binding 204, 239
   existential 173, 225 n. 22
   generic 174, 197 n.
   long-distance 203
   nonquantificational 200–3, 277
   quantificational 199–200, 248–50
   unselective 240–1, 246, 247

Birner, Betty J. 215, 219, 252

bite-the-bullet theory (of proper names) 114, 123–4, 125–7, 128

both 164

Braun, David 193 n. 11

Brentano, Franz 68

broad content 124

Brock, Stuart 113 n. 10, 265

Butler, Joseph 16

cardinality (| |) 95

cardinality word(s) 227

caret, *see* raised caret; raised inverted caret

Carlson, Gregory N. 166–9, 171–2, 174, 175, 177–8, 215 n. 9

Carnap, Rudolf 2, 41, 52, 63, 64–5, 66, 69, 75, 76, 106, 109

Carroll, Lewis 69

Casteñeda, Hector-Neri 186 n.

categorial grammar 84–5

causal chain 108, 117–18, 122, 265, 271, 272–3

Cavell, Stanley 175 n. 15

character (Kaplan) 183, 184–5, 187, 191, 195, 208
characteristic function(s) 53, 81–2, 133
characterizing sentence(s) 165–6, 170, 171, 172, 213 n.
Chastain, Charles 154, 224 n.
Chierchia, Gennaro 246 n.
Chisholm, Roderick M. 68
Chomsky, Noam 22 n., 44, 175, 198 n., 226, 231
Christophersen, Paul 218
cluster theory (of proper names) 102–3, 104, 106, 117, 128
CNP, see common noun phrase
Coleridge, Samuel Taylor 209
collective interpretation (of plural NPs) 162–4, 165, 174 n.
common ground 214 n. 8, 219, 220 n. 15, 257 n.
common noun phrase (CNP) 5–6, 85 n. 9, 131–2, 161, 203–4, 231, 244, 248
complex demonstratives, see demonstrative descriptions
compositionality 18–19, 60, 93, 117, 203 n.
    Frege's principles of 19–20, 24–5, 37, 57, 136, 268
    in Montague Grammar 78–80, 84, 87
conditional(s) 44, 171, 235, 247
    generic 44, 239
    indicative 44
    subjunctive 44, 60, 64
conjunction (&) 3 n. 4, 43–4, 132 n. 3, 248
connective (logical), see logical connective
connotation (Mill) 12–14, 17, 18, 24, 128
constant individual concept (CIC), see individual concept, constant

content (Kaplan) 183–5, 187
context(s) of utterance 8, 56–7, 124, 136, 180–1, 184, 208
contingent property/ proposition 102, 103, 105–6, 109, 183
contraction approach (to incomplete descriptions) 138–9, 140, 151 n. 20
Cooper, Robin 83, 93–6, 132 n. 3, 221–3, 224, 227–8, 231–3, 235, 243–5, 247 n. 11, 248
Copi, Irving M. 128
Cowles, H. Wind 258 n. 25
Crimmins, Mark 90 n., 124
crosshatch (#) 11, 227 n., 230
cumulative interpretation (of plural NPs) 164–5
curly brackets ({ }) 94, 221

Davidson, Donald 64 n. 14, 116–17
Davidson, Matthew 128
de dicto 32, 38, 46–8, 60, 66–7, 78 n., 88–9, 91, 93, 121, 143–5, 153
de re 32, 46–8, 67, 78 n., 88–9, 91, 121, 143–5, 153, 186, 271
definite descriptions 6, 36–7, 130–57, 214–23
    attributive 140–52, 157, 207, 271, 279
    bound 205–6, 280
    in existential sentences 210–11
    E-type pronouns and 242–6
    generic 169, 171, 178, 179
    incomplete 137–40, 150–1, 185 n.
    indefinite, see incomplete
    indexical 135–6, 185
    informational 259–60
    nonindexical 184–5
    particularized (pragmatic) 50, 120 n., 141 n., 219
    referential 184, 202–3

role-type (semantic) 50–1, 120 n.,
       141 n., 219
   Russell's analysis of 28–9, 95, 161–2
definiteness effect 211–13
deictic expression/use 180–1, 191,
       194–6, 216, 269
deixis; *see also* indexicality 181 n.
demonstrative description(s) 6, 181,
       191–4, 236
   bound 205–6
   in existential sentences 211–12
   uniqueness and 216
   vs definite descriptions 255–6
denotation (Mill) 12–14, 17, 36
deontic modal 48 n.
Derrida, Jacques 175 n. 15
descriptional theories (of proper
       names) 24–5, 33–5, 39, 100–7,
       117–20
determiner phrase (DP) 4 n. 5, 6 n. 7
determiner(s) 3 n. 4, 4–7, 139, 164,
       211, 212–13, 231–5, 257
   compound 228
   definite 221–3
   demonstrative 191–4
   genitive 5, 212
   indefinite 154, 218
   strong, *see* noun phrase(s) (NP
       (s)), strong
   quantificational 27–8, 42–3, 83, 94,
       131–2 n. 3, 138, 227
   weak, *see* noun phrase(s) (NP(s)),
       weak
Devitt, Michael 118, 122, 147, 151
direct reference 36, 110–12, 125, 184
discourse-level binding 225 n. 22,
       240 n.
discourse referent(s) 220 n. 15, 225,
       261–4
Discourse Representation
       Theory 197–8, 245
Discourse-new, -old entity
       (Prince) 252

disjunction (∨) 43–4, 103
distributive interpretation (of plural
       NPs) 134 n. 5, 162–5, 172, 174 n.,
       232, 249
Donnellan, Keith 104–5, 107, 108, 117,
       140–52, 207
downstar (⁎) 90
Dowty, David R. 91, 98, 106 n. 6
dynamic semantics 156 n. 25, 197–8,
       218 n. 13, 224, 240–1, 248 n.,
       261–2

each 164, 213, 216–7, 227–8, 232, 236
Eco, Umberto 175 n. 15
Elbourne, Paul D. 51, 64, 91 n., 134 n.
       6, 139 n. 13, 190, 191–4, 205, 243,
       247, 248, 251, 256 n. 21
empiricism, philosophical 26, 30, 115
empty name(s), *see* noun phrase(s)
       (NP(s)), empty
empty set, *see* null set
entailment 71, 72
epistemic modal 48 n., 50 n.
Evans, Gareth 196, 205, 242–4, 246,
       247 n. 11, 248
every 26–7, 164, 213, 216–7, 227–8,
       232, 236
excluded middle, law of 29, 37–8
existence independence 66–8, 77,
       78 n.
existential quantifier (∃) 27
existential sentence(s) 210–13,
       226–30, 234, 236
   contextualized (enumerative,
       list) 211 n.
expansion approach (to incomplete
       descriptions) 138–9, 151 n. 20
extension(s) 3 n. 4, 52–3, 55
extensionality 57–8

factive predicate 67–8
familiarity 218–20, 236
Fauconnier, Gilles 175 n. 15

fictional entities 264–6

Fido-Fido theory 15; *see also* nondescriptional theories (of proper names)

File Change Semantics 197–8, 218, 224, 240–1

Fillmore, Charles J. 181 n.

von Fintel, Kai 137

first order logic 81, 94

focus (vs topic) 173, 210–12, 228, 255 n.

Fodor, Janet Dean 154, 224 n., 249, 250 n.

Fodor, Jerry A. 16 n. 1, 124, 186–7

Forbes, Graeme 67, 78 n., 89 n., 110, 124 n.

formal language 2 n. 2, 69–70, 76–7, 78, 84, 93–4, 198, 203

Frege, Gottlob 2, 15–25, 32, 34, 36–40, 52–5, 57, 60, 64 n. 14, 85, 88, 92, 95–6, 99, 100–2, 116–17, 124, 131, 134 n. 6, 136–7, 208, 219, 268, 274–5, 278–9

Fretheim, Thorstein 173 n.

Gabriel, Gottfried 34

Garnham, Alan 258 n. 25

Gazdar, Gerald 220

Geach, Peter Thomas 53 n., 239, 244 n. 7

general term(s) 7, 13–14, 52, 85 n. 9, 97

generalized quantifier(s) 83, 87, 89, 93–98, 132–3, 221–6

generator (of a set) 221

genericity 165–74

   D-genericity 165

   I-genericity 165

Geurts, Bart 119

Givenness Hierarchy 254–7

Graff, Delia 130 n. 2

Grice, H. Paul 9, 70–5, 126, 147, 206, 217, 257, 271

Groenendijk, Jeroen 197, 262

Gundel, Jeanette K. 173 n., 220 n. 16, 254–7, 258, 260

Hamilton, Sir William 53 n.

Hawkins, John A. 161–2, 214, 217, 257

head (of an NP) 4–5, 6 n. 7, 37, 158, 161–2, 167, 203–4

Hearer-new, -old entity (Prince) 252

Hedberg, Nancy 254–7

Heim, Irene 42, 196, 197–8, 206 n., 218, 224, 240, 243–5, 246–7, 248–9, 262

hidden indexical theory (of proper names) 114, 123–5, 127–8, 187

Higginbotham, James 175

higher order logic 81

Hintikka, Jaakko 75, 143

historical chain, *see* causal chain

Horn, Laurence R. 73 n., 75, 217, 218 n. 14

Hornstein, Norbert 175, n. 15

Hurford, James R. 1

hyperintensionality 63

identity of indiscernibles 20 n.

if and only if ($\leftrightarrow$) 29

if-then ($\rightarrow$) 26, 132 n. 3

IL 84, 85–8, 90–1

implicature(s) 70–75

   conversational 71–5, 95, 126–7, 161, 217, 257

   conventional 71

   informativeness 74, 95

   scalar 73–4, 217

indefinite descriptions 6, 97–8, 153–6, 236

   generic 169–71

   in discourse 255–7, 261–2

nonspecific 47, 77, 89, 153–6,
    170–1, 274
nonuniqueness and 217–18
novelty and 218
referential 271–4
specific 47, 152, 153–6, 225, 269,
    272–4
taxonomic 169 n. 12
type *e* 224–5
unselective binding of 240–1
indefinite *this*, see *this*, indefinite
index (Nunberg) 189–91, 193–4, 266
indexical(s) 57, 135–6, 180–1, 182–5,
    189–91, 206–8, 278 n.
    demonstrative 180–1, 191–4
    essential 186–9
    pure 180, 184, 185, 190, 276–7
indexicality 8, 56–7, 136, 180–94
indiscernibility of identicals 20 n.;
    see also substitutivity
individual concept(s) 54–5, 193–4
    constant (CIC) 54, 92, 106, 145–6,
        274, 269–70
    and Donnellan's
        distinction 145–7, 150, 279
    and indefinite descriptions 156
    in Montague Grammar 87–91,
        270 n. 3
    variable 54, 105, 185
    vs. RSPs 66, 109–14, 128–9, 264–7
individual-level property 167–9,
    229–30
individual variable 79
infinitival VP complements 22 n.,
    77 n., 210
intension(s) 52–6, 61, 109, 146, 182–3
    in Montague Grammar 85–8
intensional construction(s) 44,
    76–8, 83–91, 261; *see also*
    operator(s), modal;
    propositional attitude(s);
    subjunctive conditional(s)

intensional isomorphism 63 n., 65
intensional structure 64–5
intensionality 58–60, 67–8, 76–8,
    86–88
intentional, intentionality 58–9 n. 10,
    68
intersection (of sets) (∩) 95, 221–3,
    231, 235
Ionin, Tania 233, 235
island (syntactic) 49–50, 239

Jackendoff, Ray 91, 173, 175 n. 15,
    231
Jacobson, Pauline 84, 203 n., 245 n. 8,
    248, 251
Justice, John 119

Kadmon, Nirit 241
Kamp, Hans 197–8, 203, 218 n. 13,
    224, 240–1, 245, 247, 262
Kanazawa, Makoto 64 n. 16, 247 n. 11
Kaplan, David 11, 40, 75, 99–100, 107,
    109, 110–12, 127–8, 143–7, 155–6,
    182–5, 192–3, 271 n.
Karttunen, Lauri 153–4, 244, 261
Katz, Jerrold J. 118
Keenan, Edward L. 201–2, 210 n. 2,
    228–30, 231 n., 233, 236
Kehler, Andrew 258 n. 25
Kennedy, Christopher 175–8
King, Jeffrey C. 191–4, 205, 276
Kneale, William 32, 48, 119
Kratzer, Angelika 48 n., 64, 167 n. 10,
    196, 198 n., 206 n., 243–5, 248,
    249
Krifka, Manfred 165–6, 169–71, 174
Kripke, Saul 47, 75, 104–8, 110–11,
    119–22, 125, 127–8, 147–52, 265

Ladusaw, William A. 233, 235
Lakoff, George 175 n. 15
lambda conversion 82

lambda operator (λ), *see* operator, lambda (λ)

Lambrecht, Knud 180

Landman, Fred 165, 245

Langacker, Ronald 175 n. 15

Larson, Richard 193 n. 11, 274 n. 7

Lasnik, Howard 196

law of substitutivity, *see* substitutivity

Leibniz, Gottfried 20 n., 52

Leibniz' Law 20 n.; *see also* substitutivity

Lepore, Ernest 16 n. 1

Levinson, Stephen C. 74, 181 n.

Lewis, David 57 n., 60, 65, 106 n. 6, 118, 140, 182, 188–9, 219–20, 240–1, 265

Link, Godehard 159–60, 164, 224

Linsky, Leonard 31–2, 38

Löbner, Sebastian 50, 157 n., 166 n. 8, 178, 214 n. 7, 219

logical connective 43, 44, 58, 94n., 132 n. 3; *see also* conjunction; disjunction; *if and only if*; *if-then*; negation

Ludlow, Peter 220 n. 16, 263, 271–4

Lumsden, Michael 212 n.

Lyons, Christopher 130 n. 1

Lyons, John 181

Mach, Ernst 186

Marcus, Ruth Barcan 104

Mates, Benson 63–4 n. 13

McCawley, James D. 140

member (of a set) (∈) 97

mention (vs use) 20 n., 21

mereological sum(s), *see* sum(s), mereological

metalanguage 10, 94–5

metalinguistic theories (of proper names) 114–20, 122–3

Mill, John Stuart 2, 12–15, 17, 18, 24, 36–9, 54 n., 92, 100, 104, 107, 119, 128, 131

Milsark, Gary 167 n. 9, 172, 213, 227, 229–30

misdescription characteristic 142, 147, 148–50

modal operator(s) *see* operator(s), modal

modal subordination 245–6, 261, 262

mode of presentation 17, 55, 124–7, 187–8

Montague Grammar 3 n. 4, 40, 66, 83–92

Montague, Richard 3 n. 4, 6 n. 7, 9, 11, 22 n., 68, 69–70, 75–93, 95–97, 104, 106, 109, 128, 132–3, 146, 156, 269 n., 270 n. 3

Montaigne, Michel de 268

most 94, 95, 164, 213, 222, 224, 227, 228, 232, 236

Musan, Renate 56 n.

name(s), *see* proper name(s)

Napoli, Donna Jo 211 n.

narrow content 124, 188

narrow scope, *see* scope, narrow

natural kind term(s) 107, 108, 112

Neale, Stephen 138, 247 n. 11, 263, 271–4

necessity (□) 48, 92

negation (∼) 27, 37–8, 42–3, 45, 58, 199 n.

neither 164, 227, 228, 232

Nominal Description Theory (NDT) 122–3

nondescriptional theories (of proper names) 24, 39, 92, 100, 104–14, 123–8, 264

noun phrase(s) (NP(s)) 4–7
  average 174–8
  bare 4, 167–74, 211, 234
  definite 209–236
  demonstrative 180–1, 191–4
  empty 20, 29, 37–8, 66–8, 101–2, 112–3, 264–7

encuneral 177
focus 210–12, 228
generic 167–173
group partitive 230–4
indefinite 212–13, 217–8, 221–2,
    240–1
mass partitive 232, 233 n.
null (∅) 5 n., 253
partitive 230–7
plural 134 n. 5, 158–65, 203–4
possessive 6, 32, 212, 229
quantificational 6–7, 42–3, 78–83,
    131–4, 198–200, 224–6
strong vs weak 213, 226–30
NP, *see* noun phrase(s)
null set (∅) 222, 223
number word(s) 5, 49, 87 n., 91; *see
    also* proper name(s)
Nunberg, Geoffrey 180 n. 2, 189–91,
    193, 206–7

object dependent proposition 112,
    266 n.
object language 10, 11
Oehrle, Dick 207 n.
opaque context 23, 101, 132, 153
operator(s):
    complex 42
    GEN 166, 170–1, 172–3, 240 n., 262
    lambda (λ) 81–2, 221, 277 n.
    logical 71
    modal 47–9, 50, 59–60, 63, 76–7,
        105–7, 119–20, 207; *see also*
        deontic modal; epistemic modal
    sentence 37, 41, 42–4, 197 n.
    truth functional 58

part of (≤) 64, 159–61
Partee, Barbara H. 64 n. 15, 75, 78,
    96–8, 133, 154, 223–6, 233, 235,
    236, 241, 244 n. 7, 249
Partitive Constraint 210, 231–5, 236

Peacocke, Christopher 151
Pelletier, Francis Jeffry 175, 177–8
Percus, Orin 51
Perry, John 63–4, 90 n., 124, 186–8,
    189, 278 n.
Peters, Stanley 10 n., 91, 98, 106 n. 6,
    134, 212 n., 230 n. 27, 231 n. 28
possibility (◇) 48, 50 n.
possible world(s) 52–7, 105–7, 182–5
    and fictional entities 265
    propositions as sets of 61–3
Postal, Paul M. 193 n. 12, 229, 244
pragmatic conception of
    reference 2–3, 4, 135, 270–4
predicate logic 26–8, 69, 197
presupposition(s) 37, 136–7, 194 n.,
    219–20, 223, 257 n.
primary occurrence 31, 33, 35, 40, 77
Prince, Ellen F. 106 n. 6, 154, 215, 216,
    251–2
PRO 22 n., 77 n.
pronoun(s) 4, 180
    anaphoric 181, 194–5, 196, 263
    bound 198–203
    deictic 180–1, 194–6, 263, 269
    demonstrative 180–1
    descriptive 206–8
    donkey 239–44, 246–8; *see also*
        E-type
    E-type 178 n., 242–8, 250, 261
    laziness 244
    neontological 244
    paycheck 244–4
    plural 203–4
    reflexive/reciprocal 199–200
proper name(s) 4, 14–15, 24–5, 33–6,
    91–2, 99–129
    and propositional attitudes, *see*
        propositional attitudes, proper
        names and empty 101–2, 112–13,
        264–7
    in discourse 234, 236, 258–9

proper name(s) (*cont.*)
  partially descriptive 126 n.
  uniqueness and 215
  see also nondescriptional theories
    (of proper names)
property 7, 27, 36, 42, 55
  contingent, *see* contingent
    property/proposition of
    properties 87, 91
  sets of 81, 92, 96
proportion problem 241–2, 243
proposition(s) 7–8, 55, 60–6
  Frege's view 19
  Mill's view 15
  possible worlds analysis 55, 61–3
  Russellian Singular (RSP) 33–34,
    65–6, 110–14, 123–7, 264–7
  Russell's view of 33–6
  situations and 63–4
  structured 64–6
propositional attitude(s) 22, 38–9,
  45–6
  Donnellan's referential-attributive
    distinction and 143–6
  essential indexicals in 186–9
  existence independence and 66–8
  Frege's view 22–4
  intensionality of 60
  objects of 63–5
  proper names and 114–27
  Russell's view 30–3
  verbs 22, 49
Putnam, Hilary 107, 124, 175 n. 15

Quine, W.V. 16 n. 1, 23 n., 32, 77,
  78 n., 115–16, 160, 167
quotational context(s) 20–1

raised caret ($^\wedge$) 86
raised inverted caret ($^\vee$) 86
Rando, Emily 211 n.
Recanati, François 119, 120, 196, 207

Reddy, Michael 275
Reed, Ann M. 233, 235
referential dependence 194–5, 205;
  see also pronoun(s), anaphoric;
  bound
referential opacity 23–4, 32–3, 38–9,
  47, 88–9, 115; *see also* intensional
  construction(s), intensionality
Reimer, Marga 138 n. 12, 147, 151–2
Reinhart, Tanya 198 n., 203
relative clause(s) 4, 49–50, 239
Relevance Theory 208 n.
restricted quantifier 43, 45, 80, 131,
  170, 239 n. 3
restriction (quantificational) 42–3,
  48 n., 94, 132 n. 3
Reyle, Uwe 197, 203, 240
Richard, Mark 110, 124 n., 188
rigid designator(s) 105–7, 109,
  110–12, 145–6, 150, 184–5
Roberts, Craige 164, 193 n. 11, 203,
  214 n. 8, 220 n. 15, 245, 248 n.,
  249, 250, 257 n., 258 n. 25
Rodman, Robert 49–50
Rorty, Richard 175 n. 15
Ross, John Robert 201
Rothschild, Daniel 50–1, 120 n., 219
rule-to-rule correspondence 78, 84,
  87
Russell, Bertrand 2, 12, 26–39, 52,
  65–6, 69, 77, 92, 100–2, 104,
  110–11, 128, 130, 131–2, 135–40,
  148–9, 161, 214, 272–3, 275–7
Russellian singular proposition
  (RSP), *see* proposition(s)
  Russellian Singular

Sadock, Jerrold M. 163
Sag, Ivan 154, 201, 224 n., 249, 250 n.
Salmon, Nathan 17 n., 24 n., 104 n. 4,
  110, 111–12, 113 n. 11, 126–7, 152 n.
  22, 265–7, 279 n.

salva veritate 20 n., 21, 66
samesaying 116
Saul, Jennifer M. 126–7, 129
scalar implicatures 73–3, 217
Scha, Remko 164–5
Schachter, Paul 233
Schiffer, Stephen 124–5, 188, 207–8
Schwarzschild, Roger 51, 165
scope 42, 164–5, 195–6, 207, 262, 280
    ambiguity 44–51, 133–4
    narrow 31–2, 37–8, 60, 66–8, 77–8, 88–9, 120 n., 168–9, 235
    semantic 41–51, 198
    syntactic 198
    wide 31–3, 37–8, 77–8, 88–9
    see also *de dicto, de re,* primary occurrence, secondary occurrence
Scott, Dana 182
Searle, John R. 30 n., 103, 104, 105, 106–7, 117
secondary occurrence 31, 35
seek 77–8, 89, 90–1
Segal, Gabriel M.A. 124, 193 n. 11, 220 n. 16
Selkirk, Elisabeth O. 233 n.
semantic conception of reference 3, 274–80
semantic types, *see* types, semantic
semantic value ($\| \; \|$) 94
sentence(s):
    characterizing 165–6, 168, 179, 171, 172, 213 n.
    existential 210–3, 226–30, 231 n., 234, 236
    intension of 56, 61–2, 65, 183
    open 27, 42–3
sentential complement 22–3, 45, 46, 59, 78, 89
set theory notation 94–5, 97
Shakespeare, William 209, 238

Sharvy, Richard 161–2, 214
shifter(s) 180 n. 2
Simons, Mandy 205–6
singleton (set) 97, 132 n. 3, 221
singular proposition 35 n. 14, 212, 152, 157, 271, 272, 274 n. 6; *see also* Russellian singular proposition (RSP)
singular reference 25, 268, 270–80
singular term(s) 4, 18, 52–3, 54, 99, 269, 271, 275; *see also* definite descriptions; demonstrative descriptions; pronouns; proper names
situation(s) 63–4, 65, 139–40, 188 n., 193, 247
    variable(s) over 139, 245–6
sloppy identity 201–2, 203, 277
Soames, Scott 64 n. 15, 110, 126, 184 n., 220, 265
Sperber, Dan 208 n.
stage-level property 167–9
Stalnaker, Robert C. 60, 62 n., 137, 145 n. 18, 219
Stanley, Jason 139 n. 13, 175–7, 178
statement(s):
    existence 38, 113, 118, 264–7
    identity 16–18, 101, 113–14, 117
Stavi, Jonathan 230 n. 27, 231 n. 28, 233
Sterelny, Kim 118
Stockwell, Robert P. 233
Stokhof, Martin 197, 262
Strawson, P.F. 69, 135–40, 271, 214–15, 219, 223
subset ($\subseteq$) 94
substitutivity (law of) 20, 21, 22–4, 33, 49, 60, 77–8, 116, 120
sum(s) (mereological) ($+$) 159–60, 209
supremum 160, 161
Swift, Jonathan 1

symbols: *see* angle brackets ($<$, $>$); asterisk (*); cardinality($|$, $|$); conjunction (&); crosshatch (#); curly brackets ({, }); disjunction ($\vee$); downstar ($_*$); existential quantifier ($\exists$); *if and only if* ($\leftrightarrow$); *if-then* ($\rightarrow$); intersection (of sets) ($\cap$); lambda operator (λ); member (of a set) ($\in$); necessity ($\Box$); negation ($\sim$); null NP ($\varnothing$); null set ($\varnothing$); part of ($\leq$); possibility ($\Diamond$); raised caret ($^\wedge$); raised inverted caret ($^\vee$); semantic value ($\|$, $\|$); subset ($\subseteq$); sum(s) (mereological) ($+$); universal quantifier ($\forall$)
synthetic sentence/statement 101
Szabó, Zoltán Gendler 139 n. 13

Talmy, Leonard 175 n. 15
Tammet, Daniel 273
Tarski, Alfred 69, 75
telescoping 249–50
text-external world 180, 196, 251
text-internal world 181
this:
    indefinite 154, 212, 255, 260
    Russell's view on 35, 275–6
Thomason, Richmond 91, 270 n. 4
time in NP(s) 56 n.
topic 173, 253
truth functional operator, *see* operator(s), truth functional
type shifting 96–98, 223–5, 235
type(s), semantic 85–6, 93, 96, 133

uniqueness:
    in definite descriptions 28–9, 137–40, 161–2, 214–18, 220
    in E-type pronouns 246–7
    informational 214 n. 8

referential 215, 216–17, 236
    semantic 214–15
universal quantifier ($\forall$) 26
universe of discourse 94, 139, 160, 195
use (vs mention), *see* mention (vs use)

van Eijck, Jan 247
van Fraassen, Bas C. 137
van Inwagen, Peter 265
variable-free semantics 203 n., 245 n. 8
Vendler, Zeno 164 n. 5
verb phrase (VP) 4, 7, 55–6, 79, 131, 200; *see also* infinitival VP complement(s); VP ellipsis
VP, *see* verb phrase
VP ellipsis 201–3

Walker, Marilyn A. 258 n. 25
Wall, Robert E. 91, 98, 106 n. 6
Ward, Gregory 215, 219
Westerståhl, Dag 10 n., 134, 212 n., 230 n. 27, 231 n.
Wettstein, Howard 147
what is said (Grice) 71
Whorf, Benjamin Lee 34 n. 15, 259 n.
wide scope, *see* scope, wide
Wilson, Deirdre 208 n.
Wilson, George M. 151 n. 21, 152 n. 22, 205
Winograd, Terry 258
Wittgenstein, Ludwig 2, 68, 103, 105, 106, 128, 275
Woisetschlaeger, Erich 212

Zacharski, Ron 254–7
Zeevat, Henk 225, n. 21
zero derivation 158
Zimmer Effect 250
Zimmer, Karl 250
Zwicky, Arnold M. 163